P9-DTN-367

DLE	Data link escape (character)
DNA	Distributed network architecture (DEC)
DPLL	Digital phase-locked loop
DS	Directory services
DTE	Data terminal equipment
EBCDIC	Extended Binary Coded Decimal Interchange Code
ECMA	European Computer Manufacturers Association
EIA	Electrical Industries Association
FCS	Frame check sequence
FDDI	Fibre distributed data interface
FDM	Frequency-division multiplexing
FEP	Front-end processor
FM	Frequency modulation
FSK	Frequency-shift keying
FTAM	File transfer access and management
HDLC	High-level data link control
IA5	International Alphabet Number Five
IEEE	Institute of Electrical and Electronics Engineers
IP	Internet protocol
ISDN	Integrated services digital network
ISO	International Standards Organization
ITU	International Telecommunications Union

DATA COMMUNICATIONS,
COMPUTER NETWORKS
AND OSI

ELECTRONIC SYSTEMS ENGINEERING SERIES

Consulting Editor   **E L Dagless**
University of Bristol

OTHER TITLES IN THE SERIES

Advanced Microprocessor Architectures   *L Ciminiera and A Valenzano*

Optical Pattern Recognition Using Holographic Techniques   *N Collings*

Modern Logic Design   *D Green*

Microwave Components and Systems   *K F Sander*

SECOND EDITION

DATA COMMUNICATIONS, COMPUTER NETWORKS AND OSI

FRED HALSALL
University of Sussex

 ADDISON-WESLEY PUBLISHING COMPANY

Wokingham, England · Reading, Massachusetts · Menlo Park, California
New York · Don Mills, Ontario · Amsterdam · Bonn
Sydney · Singapore · Tokyo · Madrid · San Juan

© 1988 Addison-Wesley Publishers Limited
© 1988 Addison-Wesley Publishing Company, Inc.

All rights reserved. No part of this publication may be reproduced, stored in a retrieval system, or transmitted in any form or by any means, electronic, mechanical, photocopying, recording, or otherwise, without prior written permission of the publisher.

The programs presented in this book have been included for their instructional value. They have been tested with care but are not guaranteed for any particular purpose. The publisher does not offer any warranties or representations, nor does it accept any liabilities with respect to the programs.

Cover design by Marshall Henrichs.
Illustrations by Chartwell Illustrators.
Typeset by CRB Typesetting Services, Ely.
Printed in Great Britain by The Bath Press, Avon.

First printed 1988. Reprinted 1988, 1989 (twice) and 1990

British Library Cataloguing in Publication Data
Halsall, Fred
  Data communications, computer networks
  and OSI.—2nd ed.
  1. Computer networks
  I. Title
  004.6   TK5105.5

  ISBN 0-201-18244-0

Library of Congress Cataloguing in Publication Data
Halsall, Fred
  Data communications, computer networks, and OSI.

  Rev. ed. of: Introduction to data communications
and computer networks. c1985.
  Bibliography: p.
  Includes index.
  1. Data transmission systems.   2. Computer networks.
3. Local area networks (Computer networks)   4. Computer network
protocols.   I. Halsall, Fred. Introduction to data communications
and computer networks.
[I. Title.
TK5105.H35   1988   004.6   87-27087
ISBN 0-201-18244-0

67060

To my wife Rhiannon

CAMROSE LUTHERAN COLLEGE
LIBRARY

PREFACE

Aims and objectives

The subject of data communications was, until recently, a relatively specialized area of electronic engineering. The dramatic advances in computer technology over the past decade, however, have resulted in an increasing number of information processing systems now being implemented as a linked set of computer-based equipment. The latter includes not only computers *per se* but also a wide range of other types of equipment that incorporate some local intelligence; for example, computer-based visual display terminals, advanced workstations as used in an automated office, intelligent instrumentation equipment as used in industrial process plants, point-of-sale terminals as used in large department stores, and so on. This means that an essential consideration in the design of most forms of computing equipment installed today is the type of data communication facility that is to be used to allow the equipment to communicate with other similar devices. In many instances, this necessitates a knowledge not only of the alternative types of data transmission circuits that may be used but also an understanding of the interface requirements to the many different types of computer communication networks available for this purpose. Data communications and the allied subject of computer networks have thus become essential topics in all modern courses on computer systems design.

In many applications of computer networks, providing a means for two systems to exchange information solves only part of the problem. In an application that involves a distributed community of heterogeneous computers exchanging files of information over a computer network, for example, such issues as the use of different operating (and hence file) systems and possibly different formats (syntaxes), used for representing programs and data in the various systems, must also be addressed if the systems are to communicate in an unconstrained (open) way. This is the goal of the various application-oriented protocols associated with the International Standards Organization (ISO) Reference Model for Open Systems Interconnection (OSI). It is essential when considering the applications of computer networks, therefore, to gain an understanding of these protocols. This book has been written as an introductory text to each of these topics.

New in this edition

Since the first edition of this book was published, a number of important developments have taken place both in the field of computer networks and also in the area of protocol standards relating to open systems interconnection. The primary aim of the second edition, therefore, has been to incorporate these changes and, in general, to bring the material covered more up to date.

In the field of computer networks, the rapid adoption of integrated services digital networks (ISDNs) by most national network providers, together with the publication of international standards for interfacing to them, means that such networks will very quickly become the preferred choice of communication facility in most wide area network applications. Thus, the material relating to wide area networks has been expanded to include a description of the different forms of user interface associated with ISDNs (page 295) and the international standards that have now been produced for use with them (page 299).

In the field of OSI, a range of protocol standards pertaining to the higher, application-oriented, layers of the ISO Reference Model have now been formulated. Thus, the coverage of these protocols has been expanded considerably and includes:

- a tutorial overview of the ISO Reference Model and the method used by ISO for specifying a protocol (pages 205–232);

- a methodology for the implementation of a protocol entity in structured program code (pages 249–256);

- a description of the function and specification of most of the application-oriented protocols that have now been produced (Chapter 9: pages 383–443);

- a description of how the various protocol layers interact to implement a particular user application service (pages 451–465);

- a methodology for the implementation of a complete communication subsystem based on the ISO Reference Model (pages 465–475);

- an introduction to the topics of network management and open distributed processing (pages 475–494).

Also, a number of smaller additions and changes have been made:

- the structure and contents of the first chapter have been refined to set the material covered in the book in a better context with respect to distributed computing systems;

- to meet a common criticism of the first edition, the chapter concerned with the electrical interface (Chapter 2) has been moved forward and has been expanded to include the underlying theory associated with data communications;

- the chapter relating to local area networks (Chapter 8) has been expanded and more figures have been added;

- Appendix A has been expanded to include convolutional codes – the latter are used extensively in satellite communications and have been included to complement the material in Chapter 3 on data transmission;

- the list of references has been expanded considerably and now includes suggestions for further reading;

- a new appendix has been added that presents an overview of the different national and international standards organizations and their relationship to one another.

Structure and contents

As a result of the changes listed, the book has now been divided into three parts to reflect the three major topics considered:

Part One – Data Communications: This is concerned with the fundamentals of data communication and, in particular, the techniques that are used to achieve the reliable transfer of data between two devices connected by means of a direct transmission path.

- **Chapter 1   Distributed System Architectures**: This outlines the historical development of distributed computing systems and identifies the different types of data communication network that have evolved for use with them. [pages 3–19]

- **Chapter 2   The Electrical Interface**: This provides an overview of the electrical characteristics and international standards that have been defined for interfacing a device to the different types of physical transmission media. [pages 21–64]

- **Chapter 3   Data Transmission**: This is concerned with the different ways data are structured prior to transmission across a data link in addition to the different clock synchronization and error-detection methods that may be employed. [pages 65–106]

- **Chapter 4   Data Link Protocols**: This is concerned with the different techniques that are used, firstly, to overcome the effect of transmission errors (bit corruptions) and, secondly, to control the rate of flow of data across a data link. [pages 107–156]

- **Chapter 5   Terminal Networks**: This builds on the general principles introduced in the previous chapters to describe two standard data link protocols that are in widespread use with terminal-based networks. [pages 157–199]

Part Two – Computer Networks: This is concerned with the mode of operation and the various interface standards and protocols associated with the different types of data network that are used for computer-to-computer communication.

- **Chapter 6 Computer Communication**: This presents an overview of the function of the various protocol layers associated with the ISO Reference Model for open systems interconnection and identifies those standards relating to the operation of the different types of computer networks. An example protocol specification and implementation methodology is also presented. [pages 203–259]

- **Chapter 7 Public Data Networks**: This describes the various modes of operation and interface protocols associated with the different types of public data networks that have now been installed by the telecommunications authorities in most countries. [pages 261–308]

- **Chapter 8 Local Area Data Networks**: This presents an overview of the operation and interface protocols associated with the different types of private (local area) data networks that are now in widespread use and also how they may be linked to the various public data networks. [pages 309–379]

Part Three – OSI: This is concerned with the range of international standard protocols that have been defined to achieve open systems interconnection in various application environments.

- **Chapter 9 Application-Oriented Protocols**: This describes the function and specification of the various protocols associated with the application-oriented layers: session, presentation and application. [pages 383–443]

- **Chapter 10 System Aspects**: This describes how the various application-oriented layers discussed in the previous chapter act together to implement a specific (open) distributed information processing task. [pages 445–497]

The book also contains five appendices. Appendix A is concerned with forward error correction and is intended to complement the material covered in Chapters 3 and 4. Appendix B is concerned with data encryption and, although of more general interest, is related to the material in Chapter 9. Appendix C describes the structure of three existing proprietary protocol architectures and compares them with the ISO Reference Model. Appendix D describes the different national and international standards organizations and their relationship to one another. Finally, Appendix E contains an extensive glossary of terms relating to the subjects of data communications, computer networks and OSI.

Intended usage

To the lecturer   The book is based on a course of lectures given by the author both to teams of computer professionals involved in the implementation of computer communication subsystems and also as an undergraduate textbook to both electronic engineering and computer science students. Care has been taken, therefore, to avoid any significant prerequisite knowledge in either subject.

The amount of material covered in the book is sufficient for a single course of lectures running over a full academic year. Because of its structure, however, it may also be used as a text for three shorter courses. The first, fundamentals of data communications, would use just Part One and Appendix A; the second, computer networks and their protocols, Part Two; and the third, open systems interconnection, Chapter 6 and Part Three.

To the student   The book is suitable for self-study: examples are included in most chapters and, to help understanding, a list of problems is included at the end of each chapter. Because the topics covered in different parts of a chapter are often interrelated, all the summaries are presented in a diagrammatic, flowchart-like style. The latter include not only the interrelationships of the topics covered within that chapter, but also how they relate to the material covered in other chapters.

Related material

As an aid to teaching the above courses, a selection of the more important figures from each chapter of the book is available on request to lecturers adopting the book. These are in their original A4 form and may be readily used, therefore, to produce either overhead transparencies or slides.

Acknowledgements

Finally, I would like to take this opportunity to express my sincere thanks, firstly, to Christine Thornton-Clough for typing the manuscript and making numerous corrections, additions and alterations without a word of criticism; secondly, to Debra Myson-Etherington of Addison-Wesley for her valued help in the final preparation of the book; and, thirdly, to my wife Rhiannon for her patience and understanding while I was writing the book.

Fred Halsall
January 1988

CONTENTS

PART ONE
DATA COMMUNICATIONS

The need for data communications has evolved almost from the earliest days of computing. However, although the reader of this book is likely to be aware of the basic terminology and devices associated with computers themselves – bits and bytes, gates and highways, BASIC and Pascal, etc. – equally, there is a fundamental set of techniques and terminology associated with data communications and these are often less well understood. Before describing the different types of distributed systems and network types, therefore, the first part of this book is devoted to a review of the fundamentals and terminology associated with data communications on which all forms of distributed system are based. In particular, it is concerned with the different techniques that are utilized to achieve the reliable transfer of data between two devices connected by means of a direct data transmission path. The physical separation of two devices may vary from a few tens of metres – for example, between a computer and a locally connected terminal – to several hundreds of kilometres, if the two devices are connected by a transmission path through a national telephone network, for example.

Chapter 1 describes the historical development of distributed computing systems that has taken place as a result of advancing technology and identifies the different types of data communication networks that have evolved for use in such systems. Also, it identifies the intended application domain of each network type and lays the foundation for the following chapters.

Chapter 2 is concerned with the electrical characteristics of the different types of physical transmission medium used. It also outlines the various international standards that have been defined both for encoding data and for interfacing a device to the different media.

As will be seen, data are normally transmitted between two devices bit serially in blocks comprising varying numbers of binary digits (bits). Chapter 3, therefore, describes the various techniques that enable the receiving device to determine, firstly, the start and end of each block being transmitted and, secondly, if any errors (bit corruptions) have occurred during transmission.

Chapter 4 presents the different techniques that are used, firstly, to overcome the effect of transmission errors and, secondly, to control the rate of flow of data across a data link. Both these functions form part of the protocol associated with the data link.

Chapter 5 builds on the general principles introduced in the foregoing chapters to describe two standard data link protocols that are in widespread use for controlling the exchange of data between a distributed community of terminals and a central computer.

DISTRIBUTED SYSTEM ARCHITECTURES

1

CHAPTER CONTENTS

CHAPTER OBJECTIVES

When you have completed studying the material in this chapter you should be able to:

- describe the historical development of the different types of distributed computing system;

- draw schematic diagrams to illustrate the architecture of the different types of distributed system;

- appreciate that, irrespective of the application of the system, there is only a limited number of different types of data network that may be used to provide the underlying data communication services;

- understand that there is a degree of commonality to the structure and function of the communication software used within the various interconnected equipments making up the system, which is independent of both the application of the system and the type of data communication network used.

- describe the various international bodies that are concerned with establishing standards for use in the computer and telecommunications industries.

1.1 INTRODUCTION

Distributed computing systems are concerned with the processing and communication of information between distributed communities of computer-based equipment. In general, the various types of equipment are referred to as **data terminal equipment**, or simply **DTE**. These include not only distributed communities of computers but also a wide range of other devices; for example, intelligent visual display terminals, computer-based workstations and associated equipment as used in an automated office, intelligent instrumentation equipment for the control of large industrial process plants, point-of-sale terminals as used in large department stores, microprocessor-based domestic electricity meters designed for remote reading, and many others. This wide range of devices means that there are many different types of distributed systems. For example, a system may be made up of a large community of visual display terminals physically distributed over a wide geographical area and communicating with a large centralized computing complex. Alternatively, a system may comprise a number of computer-based office workstations physically distributed around a single block of offices providing, for example, word processing functions and access to various shared resources, such as printers, copiers, file systems, etc.

Although the overall processing functions performed in the different types of distributed system may vary considerably from one application to another, there is only a limited number of types of data network that may be used to provide the underlying data communication services. Moreover, the advent of international standards for both the structure and function of much of the communication software means that there is a degree of commonality which is independent of the system's application. When designing the data communication facilities to be used with any form of distributed system, therefore, it is essential to have:

(1)   a working knowledge of the different types of data communication networks available and their corresponding modes of operation and application areas; and

(2)   an understanding of the various international standards that have now been established to aid the use of these networks.

This book is concerned specifically with these aspects of distributed computing systems.

1.2 COMMUNICATION NETWORK CLASSIFICATION

Before discussing the various types of distributed computing systems, it is perhaps helpful to outline the classification of the different types of communication networks and thus identify those networks to which the material in this book relates.

Communication networks can be classified into four categories according to the physical separation of the communicating devices:

(1)   Miniature (<5 cm):   Such networks are concerned with the interconnection of multiple computational elements which are implemented on the same integrated circuit.

(2)   Small (<50 cm):   Such networks are concerned with the interconnection of multiple computational units which are located within a single rack or piece of equipment.

(3)   Mean (<1 km):   Such networks are concerned with the interconnection of items of computing equipment (office workstations, intelligent instrumentation, etc.) which are distributed over a localized area, such as a university campus or process plant. They are referred to, therefore, as **local area networks** or **LANs**.

(4)   Large (>10 km):   Such networks are concerned with the interconnection of items of computing equipment (mainframe and minicomputers, computer-based terminals, etc.) which are distributed over a wide geographical area, be it countrywide or worldwide. These networks are referred to, therefore, as **wide area networks** or **WANs**.

Due to the short physical separations of the computational elements in the first two types of networks, all message (data) transfers are accomplished in a world-parallel mode using multiple – one line per bit – sets of physical conductors. Hence, these networks are referred to as **closely coupled systems**. In the second two types of networks, however, because of the wider physical separations between the computational elements, all message transfers are carried out in a bit-serial mode over a single pair of conductors. Such networks are referred to, therefore, as **loosely coupled systems**.

In general, closely coupled systems are concerned with the exchange of data (messages) between a homogeneous set of computational elements. The primary aim in such systems is to achieve minimum time overheads associated with each data transfer. Normally, this is accomplished by having an area of memory – **global** or **shared memory** – that is directly addressable by all the processing elements within the system. In this way, all message transfers between elements are accomplished by passing the address pointers of messages between elements, rather than by physically transferring the complete messages.

In contrast, loosely coupled systems are concerned with the exchange of messages – or, more generally, information – between heterogeneous computers and other items of computer-based equipment. Moreover, because of their wider physical separations, messages are physically transferred (or transmitted) from one system to another. Hence, the probability of transmission errors – bit corruptions – occurring during data transfers is much higher. The primary aims in loosely coupled systems are:

(1) to achieve reliable message transfers; that is, the data comprising the messages should not have any residual bit errors and should be delivered in the same order that it was presented; and

(2) to ensure that the transferred messages have the same meaning in all systems; that is, they are interpreted in the same way.

To achieve these aims, loosely coupled systems use various forms of data communication networks, in addition to internationally agreed communication protocols, and it is this type of system that is the subject of this book.

1.3 HISTORICAL EVOLUTION

The evolution of loosely coupled distributed computing systems can perhaps best be traced by following the development of the computing resources used within any large organization. The earliest commercially available computers used were characterized by expensive hardware and relatively primitive software. Typically, an organization would purchase a single computer system which would then be centrally located in a large, air-conditioned room. It would consist of a central processing unit (CPU) with a limited quantity of primary (RAM) memory, some secondary (tape or drum) storage, a printer, a punched-card reader and an operator console. Users normally prepared their programs and data **off-line** on a card punch located in a different room, and the operator would then load and run the prepared programs sequentially. This type of early computer system is shown in diagrammatic form in Figure 1.1.

As computer technology and its operating software advanced, fast secondary storage – large magnetic drums and later disks – and multi-programming operating systems were developed. This made it possible to **time share** the central processing unit between a number of active

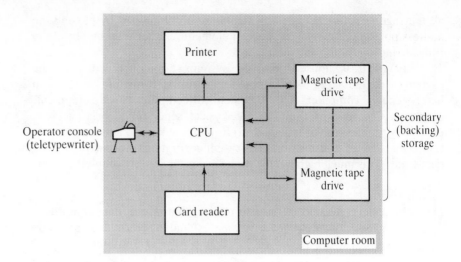

FIGURE 1.1

Typical early computer system.

programs (or processes), thereby allowing multiple users to run their programs **interactively** and to access stored data simultaneously via their own separate terminal. The terminals were normally electromechanical teletypewriters (TTYs) similar to those already in use in international telex networks. They were designed, therefore, to transmit and receive data over long distances and operated in a **serial mode**.

To exploit these developments, the computers used within organizations were upgraded to support, say, five or more such terminals. The computers then became known as **multi-access systems** providing **on-line** access to stored data. Initially, the terminals were all located in close proximity to the main computer complex but, because of their basic mode of operation, it soon became common practice to distribute the terminals: at first locally in different offices and later, with the aid of the ubiquitous switched telephone network and modems, nationally over wide geographical areas. An operational computer system typical at that time is shown in Figure 1.2(a).

The use of the switched telephone network as the basic data communication medium meant that communication line costs could no longer be regarded as insignificant and, indeed, soon constituted a substantial proportion of the system operating costs. To minimize these costs, therefore, devices such as statistical multiplexers and cluster controllers were introduced. Essentially, these allowed a single communication line – often permanently leased from the public telecommunications authorities – to be shared between a number of simultaneous users all located, for example, at the same remote site. In addition, the increasing

(a)

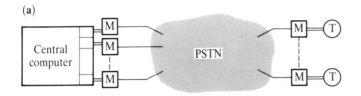

(b)

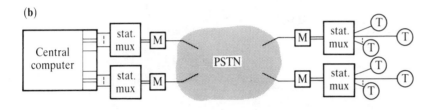

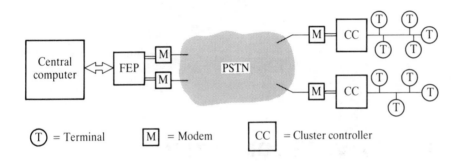

$\widehat{T}$ = Terminal $\boxed{M}$ = Modem $\boxed{CC}$ = Cluster controller

FIGURE 1.2

Terminal-oriented networks: some examples.

level of usage of computers within organizations soon gave rise to systems containing many hundreds of terminals. The effect of this was that the central computer could no longer cope with the processing overheads associated with servicing the various communication lines in addition to its normal processing functions. This predicament gave rise to the front-end processor (FEP), which essentially offloaded the processing overheads associated with the various communication lines from the central machine. The FEP thus effectively signalled the beginning of distributed computing systems, two examples of which are shown in Figure 1.2(b). This type of distributed system is still in widespread use today and the method of operation of the various items of equipment shown in the figure can be found in Chapter 5.

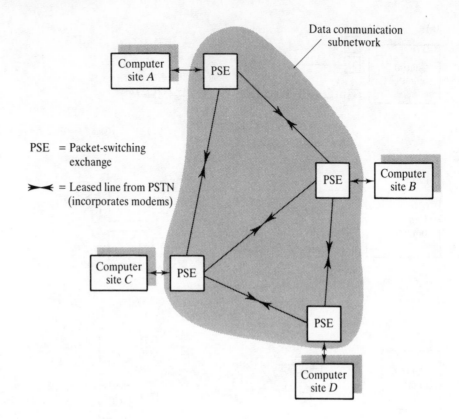

PSE   = Packet-switching
         exchange

⟩—⟨ = Leased line from PSTN
         (incorporates modems)

FIGURE 1.3

Early private computer
communication network.

1.4 PRIVATE COMPUTER COMMUNICATION NETWORKS

The structures shown in Figure 1.2 are particularly prevalent in organizations normally holding large quantities of information at a single central
site, such as the major clearing banks and airlines. In such organizations,
the distributed community of users access and update the information
using the communication facilities outlined. However, in many organizations, it is not necessary to hold all the information centrally, and hence
it soon became common place for organizations to have a number of
autonomous computer systems located at different sites around the country. Typically, these systems provided a local computing function, but
there was often a requirement for them to communicate with each other,
both to share resources – hardware and software – and to exchange
information. To meet this type of interconnection, however, a more
flexible, effectively switched communication facility was required. This
development also meant that a conceptually different approach to pro-

viding the necessary data communication services had to be found as the communications link established using the switched telephone network and modems had a limited data capacity. It was at this point that it became economically more attractive to provide a separate autonomous **data communication network**. The requirements for such a network were in many ways similar to those provided by the normal telex network, which operates in a **message store-and-forward mode**. This mode, as will be expanded upon in later chapters, is ideally suited to the sporadic nature of communications between computers and other computer-related equipment.

With the telex network, the internal message units used may be long with the effect that the response time of such networks – that is, the time delay between a message entering and subsequently leaving the network – can be degraded whilst a number of long messages are in transit. To overcome this limitation, communication networks that carry computer data normally operate using a smaller maximum message unit known as a packet. The resulting communication network is then said to operate using packet switching or in a packet store-and-forward mode. Furthermore, since the interconnected computers are normally physically distributed over a wide geographical area, such a system is also referred to as a wide area computer communication network, or WAN. This type of distributed system is shown in diagrammatic form in Figure 1.3.

1.5 PUBLIC-SWITCHED DATA NETWORKS

Initially, organizations implemented their own private nationwide data communication networks using communication lines leased from the public telecommunications authorities and their own proprietary switching equipment. Consequently, the larger computer manufacturers produced suitable communication software packages to enable their computers to communicate and exchange data using these networks. With time, however, as the impact of computer technology on the operation of organizations grew, the need arose for a computer in one organization – and hence from one manufacturer – to communicate with a (possibly different) computer in another organization; for example, to transfer funds from one bank computer to another. It was at this point that the **public telecommunications authorities** (or **PTTs**, standing for Post, Telephone and Telecommunications) in a number of countries accepted that a **public-switched data network (PSDN)** analogous to the normal **public-switched telephone network (PSTN)** was justified. Moreover, since it was intended that this network should be used to provide a communication facility for the interconnection of a possibly large number of different types of equipment from a range of manufacturers, the definition of agreed interface standards became all important.

After much discussion in various standards committees, firstly at national and later at international level, a set of internationally agreed standards were defined for interfacing and controlling the flow of information between a data terminal equipment and the various types of PSDN. An increasing number of public data networks that support these standards have now been implemented. A schematic of this type of distributed system is shown in diagrammatic form in Figure 1.4.

More recently, the continuing advances in integrated circuit technology have resulted in the PTTs in many countries changing the mode of operation of the conventional switched telephone network to an all digital mode of working. This means that, instead of requiring a modem to transmit data over a PSTN, it is possible to transmit data directly, and at much higher data rates than are currently used. Also, the call set-up times associated with this new generation of networks is significantly reduced. Because of their all digital mode of working and the ability of such networks to be used for both voice and data directly, they are referred to as **integrated services digital networks** or **ISDNs**. The operation of the different types of public data network and their interface standards are discussed in Chapter 7.

1.6   LOCAL AREA NETWORKS

Although the computing resources in an organization steadily increased with developing technology, the advent of the microprocessor and the associated advances in integrated circuit technology meant that, in addition to the systems just outlined, it soon became common to find a multiplicity of different computer-based devices physically located within the same building or block of offices; for example, a community of intelligent computer-based workstations performing word processing and other related functions. Although the availability of processing power within each of these systems means that many computing tasks can be carried out locally, in many cases there is often a requirement for these systems to communicate with each other; for example, to exchange (electronic) mail or to access an expensive shared resource, such as a supercomputer for performing a specialized computing task. Since the linked computing devices in this type of network are physically located close to one another within the same organization, the communication facility provided is referred to as a private local area data network, or simply an LAN. It is perhaps not surprising that there are a number of different types of LAN,

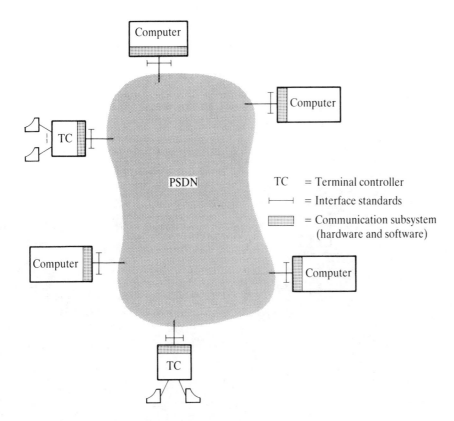

FIGURE 1.4

PSDN-based distributed system.

both in terms of their topology and their mode of operation, since each has been designed for use in a different application domain. Thus, there are LANs that have been designed for use in technical and office environments, LANs for use in manufacturing industry, and so on. Two examples of typical LAN-based distributed systems are shown in Figure 1.5. The first (Figure 1.5(a)) is intended for use in a technical and office environment, such as a university campus, whereas the second (Figure 1.5(b)) is typical of the topology used in manufacturing industry.

Although the architectures shown in Figure 1.5 are typical of those used within a single organization, an increasing number of large organizations are establishing countrywide and indeed worldwide communication networks. In this way, a system such as an advanced workstation connected to an LAN in one part of a country can communicate in a transparent way – that is, without any regard to its physical location – with a system connected to an LAN in a different part of the country or indeed a different country. Typically, the intermediate link between the two LANs may be through one or more public data networks with, possibly, a satellite link between them. This is shown in diagrammatic form in Figure 1.6. The devices that form the link between the various networks are known as

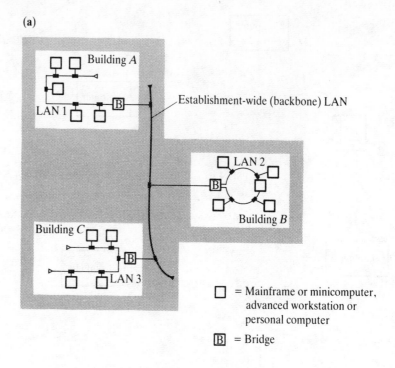

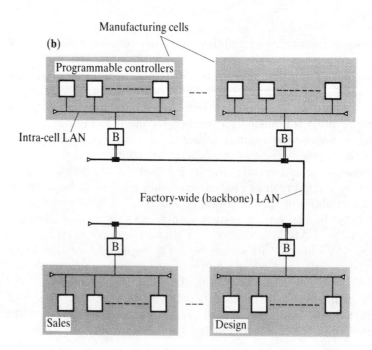

FIGURE 1.5

LAN-based distributed systems:
(a) technical and office
automation; (b) manufacturing
automation.

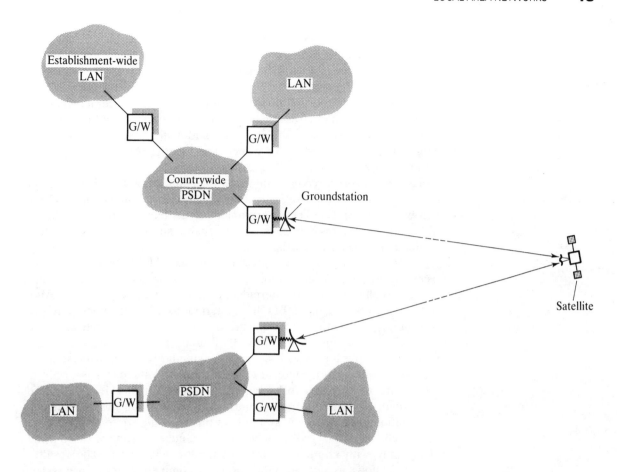

FIGURE 1.6

World-wide distributed system.

internetwork bridges (to link together two LANs) and internetwork gateways (to link together an LAN and a PSDN), respectively. Their operation is described in Chapter 8, which also discusses the different types of LAN and their associated communication protocols.

1.7 STANDARDS ACTIVITIES

Until recently, the standards established for use in the computer industry by the various international bodies have been concerned primarily with either the internal operation of a computer or the connection of a local peripheral device to it. The effect of this has been that all of the early communication networks offered by manufacturers, in terms of both hardware and software, have enabled only their own computers, and so-called plug-compatible systems, to exchange information. Because of this, these distributed systems are known as **closed systems**, since equipment from other manufacturers cannot be connected to such networks nor information exchanged without adhering to the (proprietary) standards of a particular manufacturer.

In contrast, the various international bodies concerned with the establishment of standards for use with (PTT-supplied) public networks have for many years formulated internationally agreed standards for connecting a device to these networks. The V-series recommendations, for example, are concerned with the connection of a DTE to an existing PSTN; the X-series recommendations for connecting a DTE to a public data network; and the I-series recommendations for connecting a DTE to the emerging ISDNs. These recommendations have, in turn, resulted in multi-vendor systems being available to enable purchasers to connect their equipment to such networks.

Initially, the services provided by most PTTs were concerned primarily with data transmission, and hence the associated standards only related to the method of interfacing a device to these networks. More recently, however, the PTTs have started to provide more extensive distributed information services, such as the exchange of electronic messages (Teletex) and access to PTT-supported customer databases (Videotex). To cater for such services, the standards bodies associated with the telecommunications industry have formulated standards not only for interfacing to such networks but also so-called higher level standards concerned with the format (syntax) and control of the exchange of information (data) between systems. In this way, the equipment from one manufacturer, which adheres to these standards, can be used interchangeably with equipment from another manufacturer. The resulting system is known as an **open system** or, more completely, as an **open systems interconnection environment**.

In the mid 1970s, as the different types of distributed systems (based on both public and private data networks) started to proliferate, the potential advantages of open systems were acknowledged by the computer industry. As a result, a range of standards started to be introduced. The first was concerned with the overall structure of the complete communication system within each computer. This was produced by the **International Standards Organization (ISO)** and was known as the ISO Reference Model for Open Systems Interconnection (OSI). Since then, a range of standards have been defined concerned with both the lower level network-dependent functions associated with LANs and the various types of PSDN, and, more recently, the higher level network-independent (or application-oriented) functions. The structure and components of the ISO/OSI Reference Model are introduced in Chapter 6 and a number of the higher level standards are discussed in Chapter 9. A brief summary of the development of standards is shown in diagrammatic form in Figure 1.7.

(a)

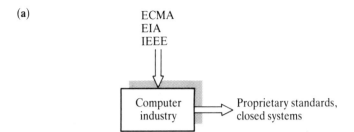

(b)

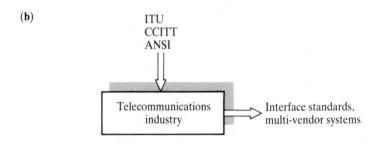

(c)

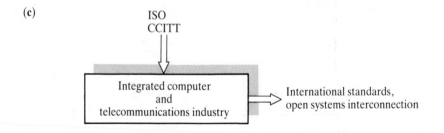

Standards bodies

ECMA = European Computer Manufacturers Association
EIA   = Electrical Industries Association
IEEE = Institution of Electrical and Electronics Engineers
ISO   = International Standards Organization
ITU   = International Telecommunications Union
CCITT = Consultative Committee of International Telegraph and Telephone
ANSI = American National Standards Institute

FIGURE 1.7

Standards evolution.

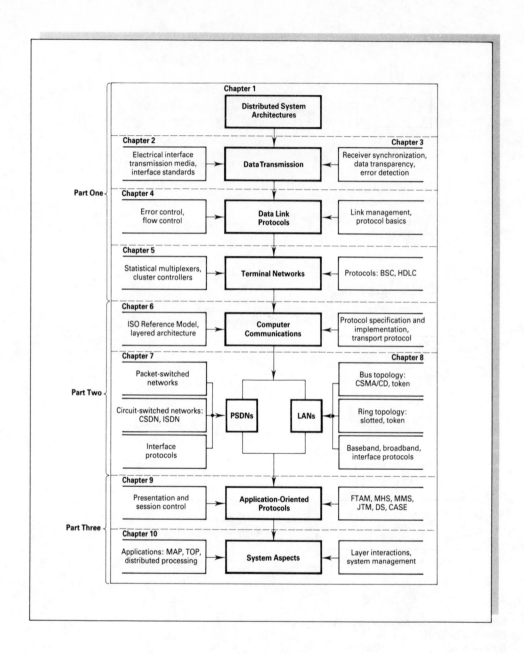

Chapter 1

Distributed System Architectures

Chapter 2

Electrical interface transmission media, interface standards

Chapter 3

Receiver synchronization, data transparency, error detection

Data Transmission

Chapter 4

Error control, flow control

Data Link Protocols

Link management, protocol basics

Chapter 5

Statistical multiplexers, cluster controllers

Terminal Networks

Protocols: BSC, HDLC

Chapter 6

ISO Reference Model, layered architecture

Computer Communications

Protocol specification and implementation, transport protocol

Chapter 7

Packet-switched networks

Circuit-switched networks: CSDN, ISDN

Interface protocols

PSDNs   LANs

Chapter 8

Bus topology: CSMA/CD, token

Ring topology: slotted, token

Baseband, broadband, interface protocols

Chapter 9

Presentation and session control

Application-Oriented Protocols

FTAM, MHS, MMS, JTM, DS, CASE

Chapter 10

Applications: MAP, TOP, distributed processing

System Aspects

Layer interactions, system management

Part One

Part Two

Part Three

CHAPTER SUMMARY

This chapter has shown that there is a wide range of distributed systems in operation today, each of which has been designed to meet the requirements of a specific application domain. Indeed, when designing any form of distributed system, it is important to analyze the particular set of application requirements before deciding on the most suitable form of data communication system to be used. It is for this reason that the book has been organized into a number of distinct sections, each devoted to a particular type of distributed system. It is felt that in this way the reader can more readily appreciate the reasons for the use of the specific types of network and communication protocols adopted. The contents and structure of the various chapters in this book are outlined in the flowchart diagram shown opposite.

THE ELECTRICAL INTERFACE

2

CHAPTER CONTENTS

CHAPTER OBJECTIVES

When you have completed studying the material in this chapter you should be able to:

- describe the different types of physical transmission media that are used to transmit data;

- appreciate the characteristics and limitations of each type of medium;

- explain the different forms of electrical signal that are used with some of the alternative transmission media;

- appreciate that standards have been defined for connecting a DTE to a piece of data communication-terminating equipment, which include the type of transmission medium, the form of the electrical signals to be used and the use of additional control lines to regulate the flow of data across the interface;

- understand the function of a number of additional control lines that are used with some of the more common standards, and be aware that the same standards are often used for defining the interface between a computer and a peripheral device that operates in a serial mode;

- appreciate that when data are transmitted using a PSTN, a modem must be used;

- describe some of the alternative designs for the modulator and demodulator sections of a modem.

2.1   INTRODUCTION

To transmit binary data over a transmission line, the binary digits making up each element to be transmitted must be converted into physical electrical signals. For example, a binary 1 may be transmitted by applying a voltage signal (or level) of amplitude $+V$ volts to the sending end of a transmission line and a binary 0 by applying $-V$ volts. On receipt of such signals, the receiving device would then interpret the $+V$ volts as a binary 1 and the $-V$ volts as a binary 0. In practice, however, the transmitted electrical signals can become **attenuated** (smaller) and **distorted** (misshapen) due to the imperfect nature of the physical transmission medium. This has the effect that in the limit the receiver is unable to discriminate between the binary 1 and 0 signals. Some of the effects of attenuation and distortion are shown in Figure 2.1. The degree of each effect is strongly influenced by such factors as:

- the type of transmission medium;
- the bit rate of the data being transmitted; and
- the distance between the two communicating devices.

The various sources of impairment will be expanded upon later in the chapter.

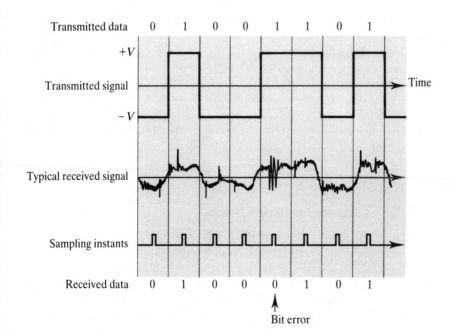

FIGURE 2.1

Effect of imperfect transmission medium.

As the effects caused by attenuation and distortion can be quantified for different types of transmission media and physical separations, there are now sets of well-defined, internationally agreed standards laid down for the electrical interface between a DTE and a piece of data communication-terminating equipment. These standards include not only a definition of the electrical signal levels to be used but also the use and meaning of any additional control signals and conventions that are used at the physical level. The two bodies that formulate standards for interconnecting pieces of equipment are the **Consultative Committee of the International Telegraph and Telephone (CCITT)** in Europe and the **Electrical Industries Association (EIA)** in the United States. Although the standards defined by both bodies use slightly different terminology, the basic signals and their meaning are the same.

This chapter is divided into three sections: the first describes some of the alternative transmission media that are currently in widespread use; the second, the different forms of electrical signals in use; and the third, some of the additional aspects of a number of the more common physical layer standards.

2.2 TRANSMISSION MEDIA

The transmission of an electrical signal between two pieces of equipment requires the use of a transmission medium which normally takes the form of a **transmission line**. In most cases, this consists of a pair of conductors or wires; however, transmission is sometimes achieved by passing a beam of light through a piece of glass fibre or an electromagnetic wave through free space. The type of transmission medium used is important, since it determines the maximum rate, in terms of **binary digits** (bits) per second or **bps**, that data can be transmitted. Some of the more common types of transmission media are discussed in the following sections.

2.2.1 Two-wire open lines

A **two-wire open line** is the simplest type of transmission medium. In such a line, each wire is insulated from the other and both are open to free space. This type of line is perfectly adequate for connecting two pieces of equipment that have a short physical separation (less than, say, 50 m) and a modest bit rate (less than, say, 19.2 kbps). The signal, which is typically a voltage or current level relative to some ground reference, is applied to one wire while the ground reference is applied to the other.

Although a two-wire open line may be used to connect two devices (DTEs) together directly, it is used mainly for connecting a DTE to a local piece of **data communication-terminating equipment (DCE)** – a modem, for example. As will be seen, such connections usually utilize multiple lines, the most common arrangement using a separate insulated wire for each signal and a single wire for the common ground reference. The complete set of wires is then either enclosed in a single protected cable called a **multicore cable** or moulded into the form of a **flat ribbon cable** as shown in Figure 2.2(a).

With this type of line, care is needed to avoid cross coupling of electrical signals between adjacent wires in the same cable. This is known as **crosstalk** and is caused by **capacitive coupling** between the two wires. In addition, the open structure of this type of line makes it susceptible to the pick-up of spurious **noise signals** from other electrical signal sources caused by **electromagnetic radiation**. The main problem with interference signals of this type is that they may be picked up in just one wire – the signal wire, for example – and not the ground wire. As a result, an additional difference signal can be created between the two wires and, since the receiver normally operates using the difference signal between the two wires, this can give rise to an erroneous interpretation of the combined (signal plus noise) received signal. These factors all contribute to the limited lengths of line and bit rates that can be used reliably.

2.2.2 Twisted pair lines

Much better immunity to spurious noise signals, referred to as **noise immunity**, can be obtained by employing a pair of wires that are twisted together. This is then known as a **twisted pair line**. The resulting close proximity of both the signal and ground reference wires means that any interference caused by extraneous signal sources is picked up by both wires and hence its effect on the difference signal is reduced. Furthermore, if multiple twisted pairs are enclosed within the same cable, the twisting of each pair within the cable further reduces interference effects caused by crosstalk. A schematic of a twisted pair line is shown in Figure 2.2(b).

Twisted pair lines are suitable, with appropriate line driver and receiver circuits that exploit the potential advantages gained by using such a geometry, for bit rates in the order of 1 Mbps over short distances (less than 100 m) and lower bit rates for longer distances. With some twisted pair cables, an additional protective screen or shield is used to reduce further the effects of extraneous interference signals. This is then referred to as a **shielded twisted pair**.

2.2.3   Coaxial cable

The main limiting factor of a twisted pair line is caused by a phenomenon known as the **skin effect**: as the bit rate (and hence frequency) of the transmitted signal increases, the current flowing in the wires tends to flow only on the outside surface of the wire, thus using less of the available cross-section. This has the effect of increasing the electrical resistance of the wires for higher frequency signals which in turn causes more attenuation of the transmitted signal. In addition, at higher frequencies, an increasing amount of signal power is lost due to radiation effects. Hence, for those applications that demand a bit rate higher than 1 Mbps, it is normal to use another type of transmission media. One type of transmission line that minimizes both of these effects is the **coaxial cable**.

In a coaxial cable, the signal and ground reference wires take the form of a solid centre conductor running concentrically (coaxially) inside a solid (or braided) outer circular conductor as shown in Figure 2.2(c). The space between the two conductors should ideally be filled with air, but in practice it is normally filled with a dielectric insulating material with either a solid or honeycomb structure.

Due to its geometry, the centre conductor is effectively shielded from external interference signals and also only minimal losses occur due to electromagnetic radiation and the skin effect. Coaxial cable can be used with a number of different signal types, but typically 10 or even 20 Mbps over several hundred metres is perfectly feasible. Also, as will be expanded upon later, coaxial cable is applicable to both point-to-point and multipoint topologies.

2.2.4   Optical fibre

Although the geometry of the coaxial cable significantly reduces the various limiting effects, the maximum signal frequency, and hence the information rate, that can be transmitted using a solid (normally copper) conductor, although very high, is limited; this is also the case for twisted pair lines. **Optical fibre cable** differs from these types of transmission media in that it carries the transmitted information in the form of a fluctuating beam of light in a glass fibre, rather than an electrical signal in a piece of wire. Light waves have a much wider bandwidth than electrical waves and hence optical fibre cable can be used for transmitting very high bit rates, in the order of hundreds of megabits per second. Furthermore, the use of a light beam makes optical fibre cable immune to the effects caused by spurious electromagnetic interference signals and crosstalk effects. Optical fibre cable, therefore, is also extremely useful for the transmission of lower bit rate signals through extremely noisy electrical environments – in steel plants, for example, which employ much high-voltage and current-

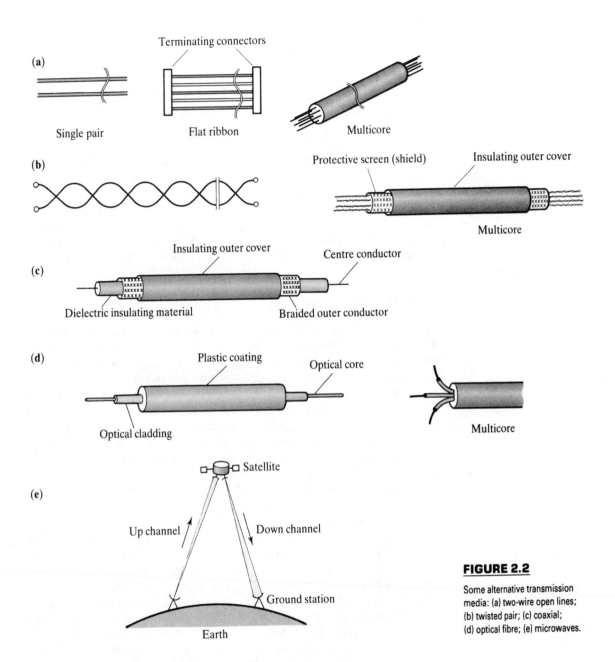

(a)

Terminating connectors

Single pair

Flat ribbon

Multicore

(b)

Protective screen (shield)

Insulating outer cover

Multicore

(c)

Insulating outer cover

Centre conductor

Dielectric insulating material

Braided outer conductor

(d)

Plastic coating

Optical core

Optical cladding

Multicore

(e)

Satellite

Up channel

Down channel

Ground station

Earth

FIGURE 2.2

Some alternative transmission media: (a) two-wire open lines; (b) twisted pair; (c) coaxial; (d) optical fibre; (e) microwaves.

switching equipments. It is also being used increasingly in environments that demand a high level of security, since it is difficult to physically tap an optical fibre cable.

An optical fibre cable consists of just a single glass fibre, for each signal to be transmitted, contained within a protective cover, which also shields the fibre from any external light sources. A schematic diagram of such a cable is shown in Figure 2.2(d). The light signal is generated by a special optical transmitter unit, which performs the conversion from normal electrical signals as used in a DTE. Similarly, at the other end of the line, a special optical receiver module is used to perform the reverse function. Typically, the transmitter uses a **light-emitting diode (LED)** to perform the conversion operation and the receiver a light-sensitive **photodiode** or **photo transistor**. As the fibre is coated with a reflective film, the majority of the light produced by the LED remains inside the fibre and hence the attenuation effect is low. In general, optical fibre cable systems are more expensive than coaxial cable and, because of their construction, they are mechanically weaker, which makes them more difficult to install. It is also more difficult to join (or split) fibre cable due to the high coupling losses that occur, and hence they are only considered when either very high bit rates are required or enhanced levels of noise immunity are needed.

2.2.5 Microwaves

All the transmission media mentioned so far have used a physical line to carry the transmitted information. However, data can also be transmitted using electromagnetic (radio) waves through free space. One example of such a media is **satellites**: a collimated **microwave beam**, on to which the data are modulated, is transmitted to the satellite from the ground and this is then received and retransmitted (relayed) to the predetermined destination(s). A typical satellite channel has an extremely high bandwidth and can provide many hundreds of high bit rate data links using a technique known as multiplexing. This will be described in more detail later but, essentially, the total available capacity of the channel is divided into a number of subchannels, each of which can support a high bit rate link.

Satellites used for communication purposes are normally **geostationary**, which means that the satellite orbits the earth in synchronism once every 24 hours and hence appears stationary from the ground. The orbit of the satellite is chosen so that it provides a line-of-sight communication path to both the transmitting station(s) and the receiving station(s). The degree of the collimation of the microwave beam retransmitted by the satellite can be either coarse, so that the signal may be picked up over a wide geographical area, or finely focussed, so that it may only be picked up over a limited area. With the latter, the signal power is higher and hence smaller diameter receivers, such as **antennas** or **dishes**, can be used. Satellites are in widespread use as a data transmission medium and the applications range from interconnecting different national computer communication networks to providing high bit rate interconnecting paths to link communication networks located in different parts of the same country. A schematic of a typical satellite system is shown in Figure 2.2(e).

Microwave links are also widely used to provide communication links when it is impractical or too expensive to install physical transmission media; for example, across a river or perhaps a busy motorway or highway. Such links are referred to as **terrestrial microwave links**. As the collimated microwave beam travels through the earth's atmosphere with this type of application, it can be disturbed by such things as man-made structures and adverse weather conditions. With a satellite link, on the other hand, the beam travels most of its path through free space and hence it is less affected by such effects. Nevertheless, line-of-sight microwave communication through the earth's atmosphere can be used reliably over distances up to 50 km.

2.3 SIGNAL TYPES

When two pieces of communicating equipment (DTEs) are situated relatively close to one another and only modest bit rates are used, the data can be transmitted by using just two-wire open lines and simple interface circuits, which change the signal levels used within the equipment to a suitable level for use on the interconnecting cable. However, as the physical separation between the two pieces of equipment and the bit rate increase, more sophisticated circuits and techniques must be employed. Moreover, if the two pieces of equipment are situated in, say, different parts of the country (or world) and there are no public data communication facilities available, then the only cost-effective approach is to use lines provided by the various PTT authorities for telephone purposes. When using this type of communication medium, currently, it is necessary to convert the electrical signals output by the source DTE into a form analogous to the signals used to convey spoken messages. Similarly, on receipt of these signals, it is necessary to convert them back into a form suitable for use by the destination DTE. The equipment used to perform these functions is known as a modem. Some of the different signal types used by modems and also other forms of transmission lines are discussed in the following sections.

2.3.1 RS-232C/V.24

The RS-232C interface (defined by the EIA) and the V.24 interface (defined by the CCITT) were originally defined as the standard interface for connecting a DTE to a PTT-supplied (or approved) modem, thereby allowing the manufacturers of different equipment to use the transmission facilities available in the switched telephone network. The physical separation between the DTE and the modem is therefore relatively short and the maximum possible bit rate relatively low (9600 bps). Since their original introduction, however, these interfaces have been adopted as the standard for connecting any character-oriented peripheral device (VDU, printer, etc.) to a computer, thus allowing peripherals from a number of different manufacturers to be connected to the same computer.

Due to the very short distances (less than a few centimetres) between neighbouring subunits within a DTE, the signal levels used to represent the binary data are often quite small. For example, a common logic family used in digital equipment is **transistor transistor logic**, or **TTL**. This uses a voltage signal of between 2.0 V and 5.0 V to represent a binary 1 and a voltage of between 0.2 V and 0.8 V to represent a binary 0. Voltages between these two levels can yield an indeterminate state: in the worst case, if the voltage level is near one of the limits, the effect of even modest levels of signal attenuation or electrical interference can be very disruptive. Consequently, the voltage levels used when connecting two pieces of equipment together are normally greater than those used to connect subunits together within the equipment.

The signal levels defined for use with the RS-232C (V.24) interface are shown in Figure 2.3 together with the appropriate interface circuits. As can be seen, the voltage signals used on the lines are symmetric with respect to the ground reference signal and are at least 3 V: +3 V for a binary 0 and −3 V for a binary 1. In practice, the actual voltage levels used are determined by the supply voltages applied to the interface circuits, ±12 V or even ±15 V not being uncommon. The transmit circuits convert the low-level signal voltages used within the pieces of equipment to the higher voltage levels used on the transmission lines. Similarly, the receive circuits perform the reverse function. The interface circuits, known as **line drivers** and **line receivers**, respectively, also perform the necessary voltage inversion functions.

The relatively large voltage levels used with this interface means that the effect of signal attenuation and noise interference are much improved over normal, say, TTL logic levels. The RS-232C (V.24) interface normally uses a flat ribbon cable or multicore cable with a single ground reference wire for connecting the pieces of equipment together, and hence the effect of noise picked up in a signal wire can be troublesome. To reduce the effect of crosstalk, it is not uncommon to connect a **capacitor** across the output of the transmitter circuit. This has the effect of rounding off the transition edges of the transmitted signals, which in turn removes some of the troublesome higher frequency components in the signal. As the length of the lines or the bit rate of the signal increases, the attenuation effect of the line reduces the received signal levels to the point that any external noise signals of even low amplitude produce erroneous operation.

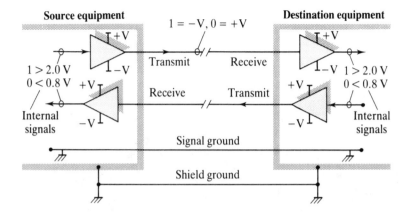

FIGURE 2.3

RS-232C/V.24 signal levels.

The RS-232C and V.24 standards specify maximum physical separations of less than 15 m and bit rates lower than 9.6 kbps, although larger values than these are often used when connecting a peripheral to a computer.

2.3.2 20 mA current loop

An alternative type of electrical signal that is sometimes used instead of that defined in the RS-232C standard is the 20 mA current loop. This, as the name implies, utilizes a current signal, rather than a voltage, and, although not extending the available bit rate, substantially increases the potential physical separation of the two communicating devices. The basic approach is shown in Figure 2.4.

Essentially, the state of a switch (relay or other similar device) is controlled by the bit stream to be transmitted: the switch is *closed* for a binary 1, thus passing a current (pulse) of 20 mA, and *opened* for a binary 0, thus stopping the current flow. At the receiver, the flow of the current is detected by a matching current-sensitive circuit and the transmitted binary signal reproduced.

The noise immunity of a current loop interface is much better than a basic voltage-driven interface since, as can be seen from Figure 2.4, it uses a pair of wires for each signal. This means that any external noise signals are normally picked up in both wires – often referred to as **common-mode noise** or **pick-up** – which has a minimal effect on the basic current-sensitive receiver circuit. Consequently, 20 mA current loop interfaces are particularly suitable for driving long lines (up to 1 km), but at modest bit rates, due to the limited operational rate of the switches and current-sensitive circuits. It is for this reason that some manufacturers very often provide two separate RS-232C output interfaces with a piece of equipment: one

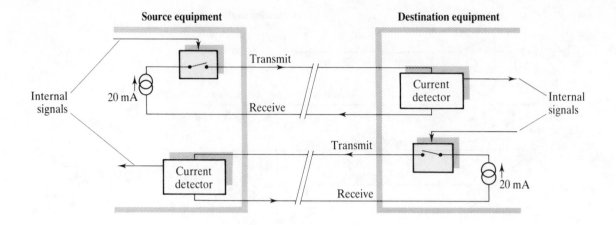

FIGURE 2.4

20 mA current loop.

produces voltage output signals and the other 20 mA current signals. The user can then decide which interface to use depending on the physical separation of the two pieces of equipment.

2.3.3 RS-422/V.11

If the physical separation and the bit rate are both to be increased, then the alternative RS-422/V.11 signal definitions should be used. These are based on the use of a twisted pair cable and a pair of **differential** (also referred to as **double-ended**) **transmitter and receiver circuits**. A typical circuit arrangement is shown in Figure 2.5.

A differential transmitter circuit produces two signals of equal and opposite polarity for every binary 1 or 0 signal to be transmitted. As the differential receiver is sensitive only to the difference between the two signals on its two inputs, any noise picked up in both wires will not affect the operation of the receiver. Differential receivers, therefore, are said to have good **common-mode rejection** properties. A derivative of the RS-422, the RS-423, can be used to accept the single-ended voltages output by an RS-232C interface with a differential receiver. The RS-422 is suitable for use with twisted pair cable for physical separations of, say, 100 m at 1 Mbps or greater distances at lower bit rates.

An important parameter of any transmission line is its **characteristic impedance** (Z_0); that is, a receiver only absorbs *all* of the received signal if the line is terminated by a resistor equal to Z_0. If this is not the case, then **signal reflections** will occur, which in turn cause further distortion of the received signal. It is for this reason that lines are normally terminated by a resistor equal to Z_0, values from 50 to 200 ohms being common.

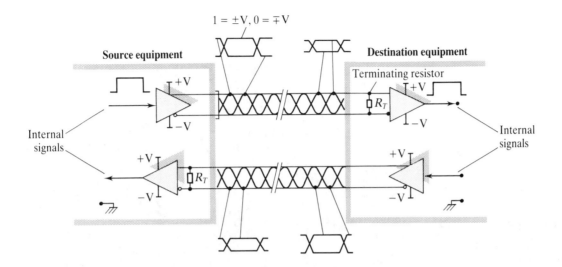

$1 = \pm V, 0 = \mp V$

Source equipment

Destination equipment

Terminating resistor

$+V$

$+V$

R_T

$-V$

$-V$

Internal
signals

Internal
signals

$+V$

$+V$

R_T

$-V$

$-V$

FIGURE 2.5

RS-422/V.11 signal levels.

2.3.4 Modem signals

When data are transmitted using the transmission lines from an existing PSTN, it is first necessary to convert the electrical signals output by the source DTE into a form that is acceptable to the PSTN. The latter was of course designed for speech communications which are assumed to be made up of a mix of (audio) frequencies in the range 400 to 3400 Hz. This is shown in diagrammatic form in Figure 2.6.

The range of signal frequencies that a circuit passes is known as the **bandwidth**. Thus, the PSTN is said to have a bandwidth of from 400 to 3400 Hz or simply 3000 Hz. This means that a telephone line will not pass very low frequency signals which may arise, for example, if the data stream to be transmitted is made up of a continuous string of binary 1s or 0s. For this reason, it is not possible to simply apply two voltage levels to the telephone line, since zero output would be obtained for both levels if the binary data stream was all 1s or all 0s. Instead, it is necessary to first convert the binary data into a form compatible with a speech signal at the sending end of the line and to reconvert this signal back into its binary form at the receiver. The circuit that performs the first operation is known as a **modulator** and the circuit performing the reverse function a **demodulator**. Since each side of a data link must normally both send and receive data, the combined device is known as a **modem**.

Using modems, data can be transmitted through the PSTN either by first dialling and thereby setting up a switched path through the network, as with a normal telephone call, or by leasing a **dedicated** (or **leased**) **line** from the PTT authorities. Since the latter bypass the normal switching

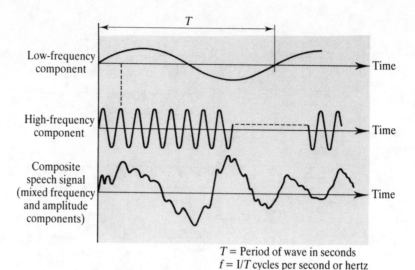

Low-frequency component

Time

High-frequency component

Time

Composite speech signal (mixed frequency and amplitude components)

Time

T = Period of wave in seconds
f = $1/T$ cycles per second or hertz

FIGURE 2.6

Speech waveform frequency components.

equipment (exchange) in the network, and are set up on a permanent or long-term basis, they are only economically justifiable for those applications having a high utilization factor. An added advantage of a leased line is that its operating characteristics can be more accurately quantified than for a short-term switched circuit and hence higher signalling (bit) rates are possible. For clarity, the modulation and demodulation functions will be considered separately.

Modulation

There are three basic types of modulation that may be employed for the conversion of a binary signal into a form suitable for transmission on a PSTN. These are amplitude modulation, frequency modulation and phase modulation. The general principle of each is illustrated in Figure 2.7.

With **amplitude modulation (AM)**, the level or amplitude of a single frequency audio tone is is switched or **keyed** between two levels at a rate determined by the transmitted binary data signal. The single frequency audio tone is known as the **carrier frequency** and is selected to be within the acceptable range of frequencies for use in the PSTN. This type of modulation, although the simplest, is prone to the effect of varying signal attenuation caused, for example, by varying propagation conditions as different routes through the PSTN are selected. In its basic form, therefore, this type of modulation is not often used, although it is utilized in conjunction with phase modulation in more sophisticated modem designs primarily used on leased lines.

With **frequency modulation (FM)**, the frequency of a fixed ampli-

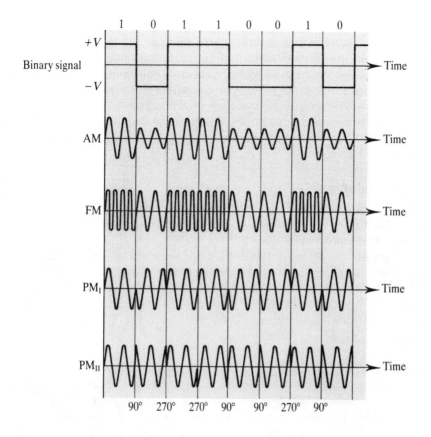

FIGURE 2.7

Modulation methods.

tude carrier signal is changed according to the binary stream to be transmitted. Since there are only two frequencies (audio tones) required for binary data, this type of modulation is also known as **digital FM** or **frequency-shift keying** (**FSK**). This type of modulation is the method most frequently used with lower bit rate modems (300 to 1200 baud) designed to operate with switched connections across the PSTN, and the demodulation circuitry needed is relatively simple and the bandwidth requirements are low.

With **phase modulation** (**PM**), the frequency and amplitude of the carrier signal are kept constant while the carrier is shifted in phase as each bit in the data stream is transmitted. One form of PM uses two fixed carrier signals, for binary 1 and binary 0, with a 180° phase difference (equivalent to a signal reversal) between them. This is known as **phase-shift keying** (**PSK**). As this type of PM must maintain a reference carrier signal at the receiver against which the phase of the received signal is compared, it is also known as **phase-coherent PSK**. In practice, such an arrangement can involve complex demodulation circuitry and also this type of modulation is very susceptible to random phase changes in the transmitted waveform. It is for these reasons that an alternative form of PM is often used. This alternative form employs shifts in phase at each bit transition determined by the state of the next bit to be transmitted relative to the current bit. Thus, a phase shift of 90° relative to the current signal indicates a binary 0 is being transmitted and a phase shift of 270° a binary 1. In this way, the demodulation circuitry need only determine the magnitude of each phase shift rather than the absolute value. This type of PM is therefore known as **differential PSK**.

Demodulation

To understand how the various modulated signals shown in Figure 2.7 are demodulated at the receiver to reproduce the transmitted data stream, it is necessary to understand some basic properties of these types of signal. As it is outside the scope of this book to derive the complex mathematical expressions for the waveforms produced by the different modulation methods, the aim here is to outline in a qualitative way the various effects that must be considered during the demodulation process. Some of these effects are shown in diagrammatic form in Figure 2.8. The following points should be noted when interpreting the figure:

(1) When a carrier signal of fixed frequency, f_c, is modulated by a second fixed frequency signal, f_m, a number of additional frequency components known as **sidebands** are produced (Figure 2.8(a)). With AM, just two sidebands are produced, at $f_c + f_m$ and $f_c - f_m$, each containing a fraction of the power contained within the carrier; note, however, it is the sidebands that contain the information required, f_m. With both FM and PM, many sidebands are produced at multiples of f_m from the carrier ($f_c + f_m$, $f_c + 2f_m$, etc.) whose amplitude is derived using **Bessel functions**.

(2) Using a mathematical technique known as **Fourier analysis**, it can be shown that a **square wave** – equivalent to a repetitive binary data string of 0, 1, 0, 1, 0, 1, etc. – is made up of an infinite number of sinusoidal frequency components. These comprise a **fundamental frequency**, f_n, equal to one-half the bit rate in **cycles per second** or **hertz**, and multiples of this frequency ($3f_n$, $5f_n$, $7f_n$, etc.), known as **harmonics**, the amplitude of which decrease with increasing frequency.

(3) When a binary data stream is transmitted, the bit pattern changes continuously; hence, the fundamental frequency (and the associated harmonics) will also continuously change. At one extreme, the data stream may be a square wave (equivalent to a string of 0, 1 transitions) while at the other it may be a zero frequency (dc) signal (equivalent to a continuous string of 0s or 1s).

(a)

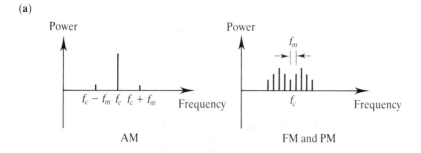

(b)

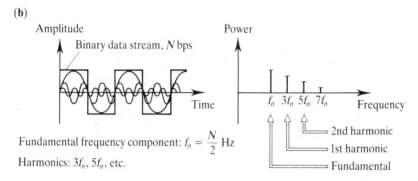

Fundamental frequency component: $f_n = \dfrac{N}{2}$ Hz

Harmonics: $3f_n, 5f_n$, etc.

(c)

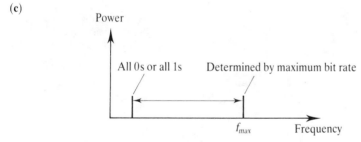

FIGURE 2.8

Modulation: (a) power–frequency spectrum; (b) square wave frequency components; (c) fundamental frequency of binary data stream.

It can be concluded therefore that the signal produced after modulating a sinusoidal carrier signal with a binary data stream is made up of the carrier plus a possibly infinite number of additional frequency components which contain the required information. Because most power is contained in the fundamental frequency of the modulating bit stream and the primary sidebands of the resulting modulated signal, it is possible in practice to determine the transmitted information by detecting just a limited band of frequencies either side of the carrier and ensuring that this band embraces the primary sidebands produced by the maximum modulation frequency. This, in turn, is determined by the maximum bit rate being used, since the sidebands produced by any lower bit rate signals in the transmitted data stream will automatically be nearer to the carrier and hence within this band.

(a)

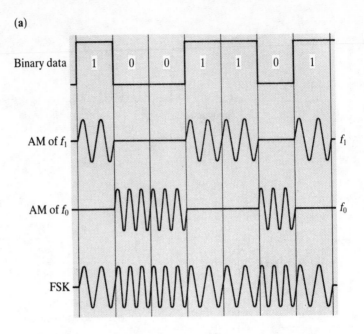

(b)

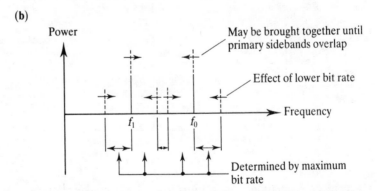

FIGURE 2.9

FSK frequency components:
(a) FSK modulation components;
(b) power–frequency spectrum.

For example, an FSK modulated signal can be considered as being made up of two separate carrier frequencies – one for binary 0 and the other for binary 1 – each of which is keyed on and off at the maximum bit rate frequency as shown in Figure 2.9(a). The **frequency spectrum** of this type of signal is shown in Figure 2.9(b). Now, if the maximum bit rate is, say, 300 bps, this has a maximum fundamental frequency component of 150 Hz. The frequency spectrum, therefore, will contain primary sidebands spaced at 150 Hz on each side of the carriers. Hence, if a frequency separation between the two carriers of, say, 200 Hz is selected, this would embrace the primary sidebands of each carrier. Similarly, if the maximum bit rate is 1200 bps, this has a maximum fundamental frequency component

(a)

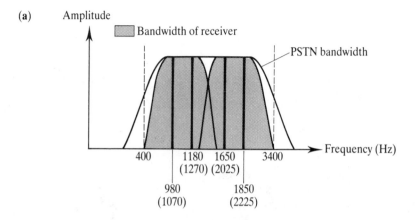

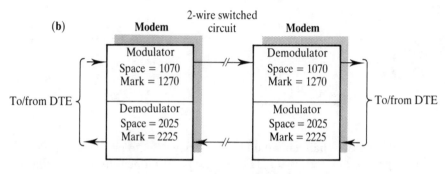

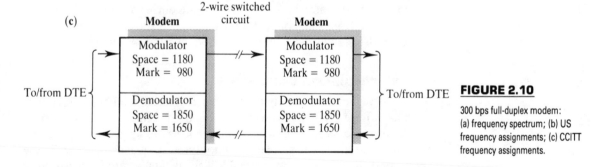

FIGURE 2.10

300 bps full-duplex modem:
(a) frequency spectrum; (b) US
frequency assignments; (c) CCITT
frequency assignments.

of 600 Hz, and hence a frequency separation in the order of 1000 Hz is normally selected. It should be noted, however, that a bit rate of 9600 bps has a maximum fundamental frequency component of 4800 Hz, which exceeds the bandwidth of a line through the PSTN. Thus, this rate of operation cannot be accomplished with the basic modulation techniques outlined.

Figure 2.10(a) illustrates how a pair of channels is obtained in practice from a single pair of wires derived from a connection through a

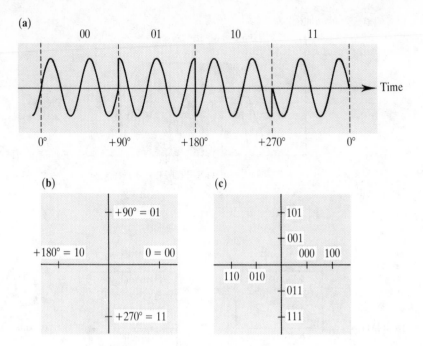

(a)

00   01   10   11

Time

0°   +90°   +180°   +270°   0°

(b)

+90° = 01

+180° = 10   0 = 00

+270° = 11

(c)

101

001

000   100

110   010

011

111

FIGURE 2.11

Alternative modulation
techniques: (a) phase–time;
(b) phase diagram; (c) AM–PSK.

PSTN. The two channels would be used, typically, to provide a full-duplex 300 bps link between two DTEs. This type of modem uses FSK with the lower pair of frequencies carrying data in one direction and the higher pair data in the reverse direction. The actual frequencies used for this type of modem differ from one country (and hence PTT) to another but Figure 2.10(b) and (c) show two alternative frequency assignments.

Hybrid modulation techniques

To derive higher bit rate channels from a normal telephone line, it is necessary to use more sophisticated modulation techniques. In the examples discussed so far, the bit rate was the same as the **signalling rate**; that is, the number of times per second the amplitude, frequency or phase of the transmitted signal changes per second. The signalling rate is measured in **baud** and hence in the examples the bit rate has been equal to the baud rate. It is possible, however, when transmitting a signal across a PSTN line to utilize more than two different values, four or eight not being uncommon. This means that each signal element may contain two (four values) or three (eight values) bits of encoded information. The resulting bit rate is then two or three times the baud rate.

An example is provided by PM where four different phase changes (0, 90, 180 and 270) may be employed instead of just two. Hence, the phase change of each signal can convey two bits. This is shown in two different forms in Figure 2.11(a) and (b). Also, the different modulation techniques may be combined to produce, for example, **amplitude modulated–phase shift keying (AM–PSK)**, as shown in schematic form in Figure 2.11(c). It should be noted, however, that although it is possible to increase the information content of the signal by increasing the number of signal changes per transmitted element, the bandwidth of the line always imposes a maximum limit on the information (bit) rate. This will be expanded upon in the next section.

2.3.5   Attenuation and distortion sources

The various attenuation and distortion effects that can occur to a signal during transmission are shown in diagrammatic form in Figure 2.12. As can be seen, a signal transmitted across any form of transmission medium will be affected by attenuation, limited bandwidth, delay distortion and noise. Although each will be present and produce a combined effect, the source of each impairment will be considered separately.

Attenuation

As a signal propagates along a transmission medium line its amplitude decreases. This is known as **signal attenuation**. Normally, to allow for attenuation, a defined limit is set on the length of a particular cable that can be used to ensure that the electronic circuitry at the receiver will reliably detect and interpret the received attenuated signal. If the length of cable required exceeds this limit, one or more **amplifiers** – also known as **repeaters** – must be inserted at these set limits along the cable to restore the received signal to its original level.

   The amount of attenuation a signal experiences also increases as a function of frequency. Hence, since a transmitted signal comprises a range of different frequency components, this has the additional effect of distorting the received signal. To overcome this problem, either the amplifiers are designed to amplify different frequency signals by varying amounts or additional devices, known as **equalizers**, are used to equalize the amount of attenuation across a defined band of frequencies.

Limited bandwidth

Since a typical digital signal is comprised of a large number of different frequency components, then only those frequency components that are within the bandwidth of the transmission medium are received. It may be recalled that the amplitude of each frequency component making up a digital signal diminishes with increasing frequency. It can be concluded, therefore, that the larger the bandwidth of the medium, the more higher

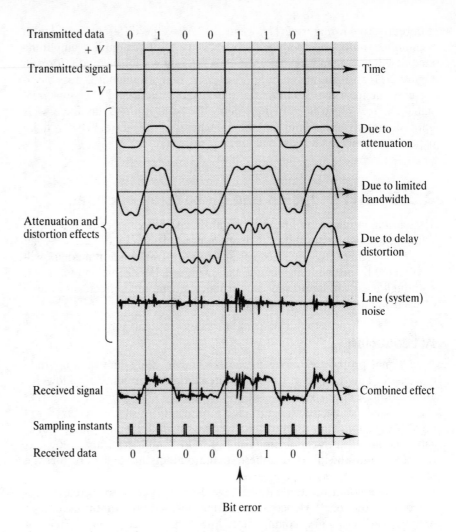

FIGURE 2.12

Sources of attenuation and distortion.

frequency components are passed and hence a more faithful reproduction of the original (transmitted) signal is received.

A formula derived by Nyquist can be used to determine the maximum information (data) rate of a transmission medium as a function of its bandwidth. If a system or transmission line has a bandwidth of B hertz, Nyquist showed that the maximum data rate, assuming just two levels per signalling element, is $2B$. More generally, the Nyquist formula to determine the maximum data transfer rate of a line or system, C, assuming M levels per signalling element, is given by:

$$C = 2B \log_2 M \text{ bps}$$

EXAMPLE

A modem to be used with a PSTN uses an AM–PSK modulation scheme with eight levels per signalling element. If the bandwidth of the PSTN is 3100 Hz, deduce the Nyquist maximum data transfer rate.

$$C = 2B \log_2 M$$
$$= 2 \times 3100 \times \log_2 8$$
$$= 2 \times 3100 \times 3$$
$$= 18\,600 \text{ bps}$$

In practice, the data transfer rate will be less than this due to the other effects such as noise.

Delay distortion

The rate of propagation of a sinusoidal signal along a transmission line varies with the frequency of the signal. Consequently, when transmitting a digital signal the various frequency components making up the signal arrive at the receiver with varying delays between them. The effect of this is that the received signal is distorted and this is known as **delay distortion**. The amount of distortion increases as the bit rate of the transmitted data increases for the following reason: as the bit rate increases, so some of the frequency components associated with each bit transition are delayed and start to interfere with the frequency components associated with a later bit. Delay distortion is also known therefore as **intersymbol interference** and its effect is to vary the bit transition instants of the received signal. Consequently, since the received signal is normally sampled at the nominal centre of each bit cell, this can lead to incorrect interpretation of the received signal as the bit rate increases.

Noise

In the absence of a signal being transmitted, a transmission line or channel will ideally have zero electrical signal present. In practice, however, there will be random perturbations present on the line even when no signal is being transmitted. This is known as the **line noise level** and, in the limit, as a transmitted signal becomes attenuated, it will reach the same level as the line (background) noise level. An important parameter associated with a transmission medium, therefore, is the ratio of the power in a received signal, S, to the power in the noise level, N. The ratio S/N is known as the **signal-to-noise ratio** and normally it is expressed in decibels or dB as:

$$\frac{S}{N} = 10 \log_{10} \left(\frac{S}{N} \right) \text{ dB}$$

Clearly, a high S/N ratio means a high power signal relative to the prevailing noise level and hence is termed a good quality signal. Conversely, a low S/N ratio means a low quality signal. The theoretical maximum information (data) rate of a transmission medium is related to the S/N ratio and can be determined using a formula attributed to Shannon and Hartley. This formula, known as the **Shannon–Hartley Law**, states:

$$C = B \log_2 \left(1 + \frac{S}{N} \right) \text{ bps}$$

where C is the information rate in bps, B is the bandwidth of the line (or system) in Hz, S is the signal power in watts and N is the random noise power in watts.

EXAMPLE

Assuming that a PSTN has a bandwidth of 3000 Hz and a typical signal-to-noise ratio of 20 dB, determine the maximum theoretical information (data) rate that can be obtained.

$$\frac{S}{N} = 10 \log_{10} \left(\frac{S}{N} \right)$$

Therefore:

$$20 = 10 \log_{10} \left(\frac{S}{N} \right)$$

Hence:

$$\frac{S}{N} = 100$$

Now:

$$C = B \log_2 \left(1 + \frac{S}{N} \right)$$

Therefore:

$$C = 3000 \times \log_2 (1 + 100)$$
$$= 19\,963 \text{ bps}$$

One source of noise, crosstalk, was identified earlier when discussing open-wire and twisted pair transmission lines. It is caused by the unwanted electrical coupling between adjacent lines which has the effect that a signal being transmitted in one line results in a small but finite (noise) signal being picked up in adjacent lines. An example of this type of noise is when one hears another call in the background when using the telephone; even though one is not talking oneself, a signal is still present on the line.

Another related form of noise pick-up is that of **impulse noise**. This, as its name implies, is caused by impulses of electrical energy associated with external activity or equipment being picked up in a signal line. An example is a lightning discharge or, in the case of a telephone network, electrical impulses associated with the switching circuits used in old telephone exchanges. Normally, this takes the form of loud clicks on the line and, although of negligible effect with a telephone conversation, such sources can be particularly troublesome when transmitting data. An impulse (click) of, say, one-half a second might affect (corrupt) 1200 bits of data with a transmission rate of 2400 bps! Fortunately, however, such sources of noise are relatively infrequent.

Both crosstalk and impulse noise are caused by electrical activity that is external to the transmission line. In contrast, a third type of noise, known as **thermal noise**, is present in *all* types of electronic devices and transmission media irrespective of any external effects. It is caused by the thermal agitation of the electrons associated with each atom making up the device or transmission line material. At absolute zero temperature, it is zero but at all other temperatures all forms of transmission media experience thermal noise. It is made up of random frequency components (across the complete frequency spectrum) of continuously varying amplitude. It is also known, therefore, as **white noise**

It should be stressed that the Shannon–Hartley Law gives the theoretical maximum information rate. When considering the effect of noise in practice, it is important to determine the minimum signal level that must be used, relative to the noise level, to achieve a specific minimum bit error rate; that is, an acceptably low probability that a single bit will be misinterpreted by the receiver. For example, a bit error rate of 10^{-4} means that, on average, 1 bit in every 10^4 received will be misinterpreted. The energy (joules = watts × seconds) per bit in a signal is given by the formula:

$$E = ST$$

where S is the signal power in watts and T is the time period for 1 bit in seconds. Now the data transmission rate, R, equals $1/T$ and hence:

$$E = \frac{S}{R} \text{ watts/bit}$$

The level of (thermal) noise in a bandwidth of 1 Hz in any transmission line is given by the formula:

$$N_0 = kT$$

where N_0 is the noise power density in watts/Hz, k is a constant known as Boltzmann's constant $(1.3803 \times 10^{-23}$ joules/°K) and T is the temperature in degrees Kelvin (°K).

To quantify the effect of noise, the energy per bit, E, is then expressed as a ratio of the noise energy per hertz, N_0:

$$\frac{E}{N_0} = \frac{S/R}{N_0} = \frac{S/R}{kT}$$

In practice, the value of E/N_0 used to achieve a particular bit error rate varies for the different modulation schemes. It can readily be deduced from the foregoing, however, that the signal power level required, S, to achieve an acceptable E/N_0 ratio – and hence a minimum bit error rate – increases as both the temperature, T, and the bit rate, R, increase.

2.3.6 Coaxial cable signals

In contrast to the low bandwidth available with a connection through an analogue-switched telephone network, the usable bandwidth with a coaxial cable can be as high as 350 MHz (or higher). This potentially high bandwidth can be utilized in one of two ways:

(1) **Baseband mode**, in which all the available bandwidth is used to derive a single high bit rate (10 Mbps or higher) transmission path (channel).

(2)   **Broadband mode**, in which the available bandwidth is divided to derive a number of lower bandwidth subchannels (and hence transmission paths) on the one cable.

Each mode of working will now be considered separately.

Baseband

With baseband, normally the cable is driven from a single-ended voltage source. Because of the geometry of construction of coaxial cable, however, the effect of external interference is very low. There are a number of matching transmit and receive interface circuits available for use with coaxial cable and a typical connection is shown in Figure 2.13(a). This figure also shows the effect of terminating a line with the correct terminating resistance (that is, Z_0). Such arrangements are suitable for transmitting data at up to 10 Mbps over a distance of several hundred metres.

In some applications, the cable is used exclusively for the transmission of data between two systems – that is, **point-to-point** – while in others the normally high bit rate transmission channel is time shared by a number of systems – referred to as **multipoint** or **multidrop**. The two alternative arrangements are shown in Figure 2.13(b).

The term used to share the available capacity of a baseband transmission channel is **time-division multiplexing** or **TDM**. Two types of TDM are used:

(1)   Synchronous (or fixed cycle): Each user has access to the channel at precisely defined (synchronized) time intervals.

(2)   Asynchronous (or on demand): Users have random access to the channel and, once a user has acquired access, it is the sole user of the channel for the duration of its transmission.

The two alternative forms of TDM are shown diagrammatically in Figure 2.13(c).

As will be described in Chapter 3, data are normally transmitted between two systems (DTEs) in the form of **frames** and, with synchronous TDM, each frame is of a fixed length. To ensure that all systems connected to the (shared) cable transmit data at their allotted time, a special bit pattern, known as the **synchronizing** (or simply **sync**) **pattern**, is transmitted at the beginning of each frame. From this, each system can determine both the start of each frame and the position of the frame (frame number) in a complete cycle of frames. With asynchronous TDM, a mechanism must be employed to ensure that each system can gain access to the channel in a fair way, since each system has random access to the channel. As will be described in Chapter 8, asynchronous TDM is used in certain types of local area network.

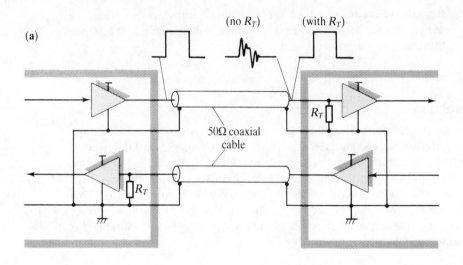

(a)

(no R_T) (with R_T)

50Ω coaxial cable

R_T

R_T

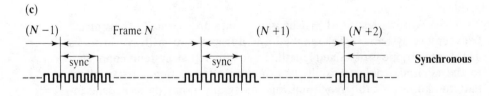

(b)

DTE — DTE **Point to point**

Shared cable

R_T R_T **Multidrop**

DTE DTE ——— DTE

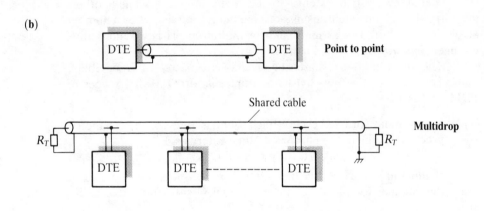

(c)

$(N-1)$ Frame N $(N+1)$ $(N+2)$

sync sync **Synchronous**

Asynchronous

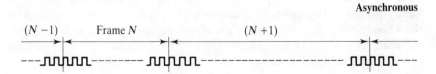

$(N-1)$ Frame N $(N+1)$

FIGURE 2.13

Baseband principles: (a) coaxial cable signals; (b) connection methods; (c) TDM methods.

Broadband

Using broadband, multiple (independent and concurrent) transmission channels are derived from a single distribution (coaxial) cable by using a technique known as **frequency-division multiplexing** or **FDM**. Using FDM, a device known as a **radio frequency** or **rf modem** must be used – cf (audio frequency) modems with the PSTN – between each connected device and the cable. The term radio frequency is utilized because the frequencies used for each channel are in the radio frequency spectrum, but otherwise the principles are the same as those described for baseband in the previous section. Thus, the selected (carrier) frequency for the transmit (forward) direction is modulated with the data to be transmitted and the selected frequency for the receive (reverse) direction is demodulated to obtain the received data.

The amount of bandwidth required for each channel is determined by the desired data (bit) rate and the type of modulation method utilized, typically between 0.25 and 1.0 bits per Hz. Thus, a 9600 bps channel may require in the order of 20 kHz of bandwidth and a 10 Mbps channel in the order of 18 MHz.

The principles of broadband working and the subunits within an rf modem are summarized in Figure 2.14. Normally, the modulation (and demodulation) operation within a modem is carried out in two phases: first, a selected frequency signal is modulated, using phase- or frequency-shift keying, by the data to be transmitted. Then, the resulting modulated signal is *mixed* (multiplied) with a second frequency so the resultant frequency-translated signal is in the assigned frequency band. The filters shown in the figure allow just the signals associated with the assigned frequency band to be transmitted (on output) or processed (on input).

2.3.7 Optical fibre signals

There are a variety of forms of optical signal encoding, one example of which, based on a bipolar encoding scheme, is shown in Figure 2.15. This type of encoding produces three-level optical output which makes it suitable for operating the cable from dc (zero frequency equivalent to a continuous string of binary 0s or 1s) up to 50 Mbps. The three optical power output levels are zero, half-maximum power and maximum power, respectively. The transmit module performs the necessary conversion from the internal binary voltage levels being used to the three-level optical signal that is applied to the fibre using special connectors and a high-speed LED.

At the receiver, the fibre is terminated with a special connector to a high-speed photodiode housed within a special receiver module. This contains the necessary control electronics to convert the electrical signal

(a)

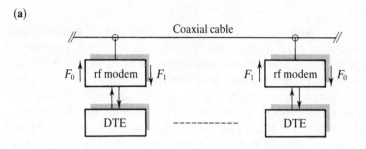

(b)

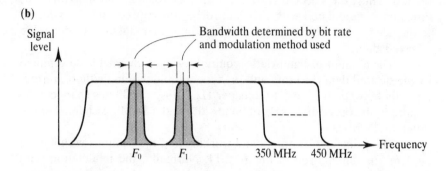

(c)

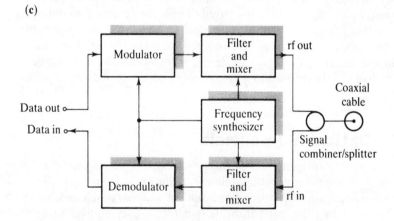

FIGURE 2.14

Broadband principles: (a) cable schematic; (b) bandwidth; (c) rf modem schematic.

output by the photodiode, proportional to the light level, into the internal voltage levels corresponding to binary 1s and 0s.

Currently, optical fibre is used mainly in a point-to-point mode but, as with a baseband coaxial cable, the transmission capacity available may be utilized either for a single high bit rate channel or, with (normally synchronous) TDM, to derive multiple lower bit rate channels using the single link.

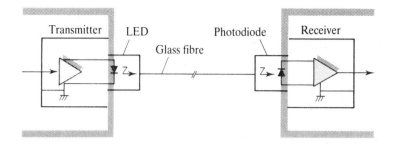

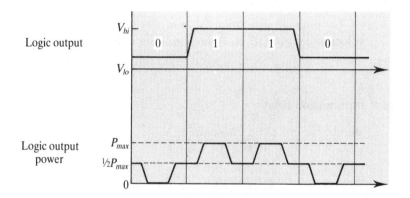

FIGURE 2.15

Optical fibre signals.

2.3.8 Signal propagation delay

Associated with any form of transmission medium there is a short but finite time delay for an electrical (or optical) signal to propagate (travel) from one side of the medium to the other. This is known as the **transmission propagation delay** of the medium. At best, electrical signals propagate (radiate) through free space at the speed of light (3×10^8 m/s). In a physical transmission medium, such as twisted pair wire or coaxial cable, however, the speed of propagation is a fraction of this figure. Typically, it is in the region of 2×10^8 m/s; that is, a signal will take 0.5×10^{-8} s to travel 1 m of the medium. Although this may seem insignificant, in some situations the resulting delay is important.

As will be seen in subsequent chapters, data are normally transmitted in blocks (also known as frames) of bits and, on receipt of a block, an acknowledgement of correct (or otherwise) receipt is returned to the sender. An important parameter associated with a data link, therefore, is the **round-trip delay** associated with the link; that is, the time delay between the first bit of a block being transmitted by the sender and the last bit of its associated acknowledgement being received. Clearly, this will be a function not only of the time taken to transmit the frame at the link bit rate but also on the propagation delay of the link. The relative weighting of the two times will vary for different types of data link and hence the two times are often expressed as a ratio, a, such that:

$$a = \frac{T_p}{T_x}$$

where:

T_p = propagation delay

$$= \frac{\text{physical separation, } S, \text{ in metres}}{\text{velocity of propagation, } V, \text{ in metres per second}}$$

and:

T_x = transmission delay

$$= \frac{\text{number of bits to be transmitted, } N}{\text{link bit rate, } R, \text{ in bits per second}}$$

EXAMPLE

A 1000 bit block of data is to be transmitted between two DTEs. Determine the ratio of the propagation delay to the transmission delay, a, for the following types of data link.

(a)   100 m of twisted pair wire and a transmission rate of 10 kbps.

(b)   10 km of coaxial cable and a transmission rate of 1 Mbps.

(c)   50 000 km of free space (satellite link) and a transmission rate of 10 Mbps.

Assume that the velocity of propagation of an electrical signal with each type of medium is 2×10^8 m/s.

(a) $T_p = \dfrac{S}{V} = \dfrac{100}{2 \times 10^8} = 5 \times 10^{-7} \text{ s}$

$T_x = \dfrac{N}{R} = \dfrac{1000}{10 \times 10^3} = 0.1 \text{ s}$

$a = \dfrac{T_p}{T_x} = \dfrac{5 \times 10^{-7}}{0.1} = 5 \times 10^{-6}$

(b) $\quad T_p = \dfrac{S}{V} = \dfrac{10 \times 10^3}{2 \times 10^8} = 5 \times 10^{-5}\ \text{s}$

$\quad\quad T_x = \dfrac{N}{R} = \dfrac{1000}{1 \times 10^6} = 1 \times 10^{-3}\ \text{s}$

$\quad\quad a = \dfrac{T_p}{T_x} = \dfrac{5 \times 10^{-5}}{1 \times 10^{-3}} = 5 \times 10^{-2}$

(c) $\quad T_p = \dfrac{S}{V} = \dfrac{5 \times 10^7}{2 \times 10^8} = 2.5 \times 10^{-1}\ \text{s}$

$\quad\quad T_x = \dfrac{N}{R} = \dfrac{1000}{10 \times 10^6} = 1 \times 10^{-4}\ \text{s}$

$\quad\quad a = \dfrac{T_p}{T_x} = \dfrac{2.5 \times 10^{-1}}{1 \times 10^{-4}} = 2.5 \times 10^3$

It may be concluded from the foregoing results that:

- if a is less than 1, then the round-trip delay is determined primarily by the transmission delay;
- if a is equal to 1, then both delays have equal effect;
- if a is greater than 1, then the propagation delay dominates.

Furthermore, in case (c), it is interesting to note that, providing blocks are transmitted contiguously, there will be:

$$10 \times 10^6 \times 2.5 \times 10^{-1} = 2.5 \times 10^6\ \text{bits}$$

in transit between the two DTEs at any one time; that is, the sending DTE will have transmitted 2.5×10^6 bits before the first bit arrives at the receiving DTE. The implications of this will be discussed further in later chapters.

2.4 PHYSICAL LAYER INTERFACE STANDARDS

The preceding sections have been concerned with some of the alternative transmission media and the associated electrical signals that may be used to transmit a binary data stream between two DTEs. However, it is important to note that the various standards introduced not only define the form of the electrical signals to be used, but also a complete range of additional signals that control the order and timing of data transfers across the appropriate interfaces. Collectively, these are said to form the **physical layer interface standard**. Although it is not practicable in a book of this type to give a description of the complete range of signal definitions presented in the various standards documents, some of the additional control signals used with the various interface standards introduced previously will now be described.

2.4.1 RS-232C/V.24

As was mentioned earlier, the RS-232C/V.24 standards were originally defined as a standard interface for connecting a DTE to a PTT-supplied (or approved) modem, which is more generally referred to as a data communication-terminating equipment or DCE. A schematic diagram indicating the position of the interface standard with respect to the two pieces of equipment is shown in Figure 2.16(a). Some of the additional control signals that have been defined for use with the RS-232C/V.24 standard are shown in Figure 2.16(b).

The transmit data (TxD) and receive data (RxD) lines are the lines that transmit and receive the data, respectively. The other lines collectively perform the timing and control functions associated with the setting up and clearing of a switched connection through a PSTN. All the lines shown use the same electrical signal levels described earlier. The function and sequence of operation of the various signals is outlined in the example shown in Figure 2.17. To illustrate the function of each line, this example shows how a connection (call) is first established and a half-duplex data interchange carried out. It assumes that the calling DTE is a user at a terminal and that the called DTE is a remote computer with automatic (auto) answering facilities. The latter is normally switch selectable on the modem.

The connection is established by the user dialling the number associated with the remote computer in the usual way and waiting for the call to be answered. Note that **autodial** facilities can also be used. If the remote computer line is free and the computer is ready to communicate, the ringing tone will stop and a single audio tone will be heard by the user. The user then proceeds by pressing a special button, known as the **data button**, on the handset. This initiates the connection of the terminal to the set-up line and the local modem responds by setting the data set ready (DSR) line to on. At this point, a small indicator lamp normally associated with this line comes on, indicating a link has been established with the remote computer.

When the number is dialled, the local modem at the remote

(a)

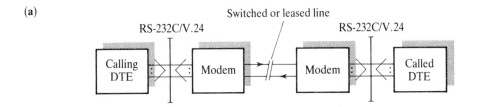

(b)

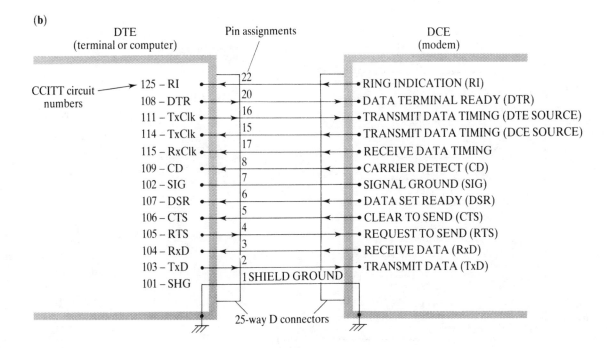

computer sets the ring indicator (RI) line to on and, assuming the computer is ready to receive a call – the data terminal ready (DTR) line is set to on – it responds by setting the request-to-send (RTS) line to on. This has two effects:

(1)   it results in the modem sending a carrier signal (a single audio tone) to the calling modem to indicate that the call has been accepted by the remote computer; and

(2)   after a short delay, to allow the remote modem to prepare to receive data, the modem responds by setting the clear-to-send (CTS) line to on to indicate to the called computer that it may start sending data.

FIGURE 2.16

RS 232C/V.24 signal definitions: (a) interface function: (b) signal definitions.

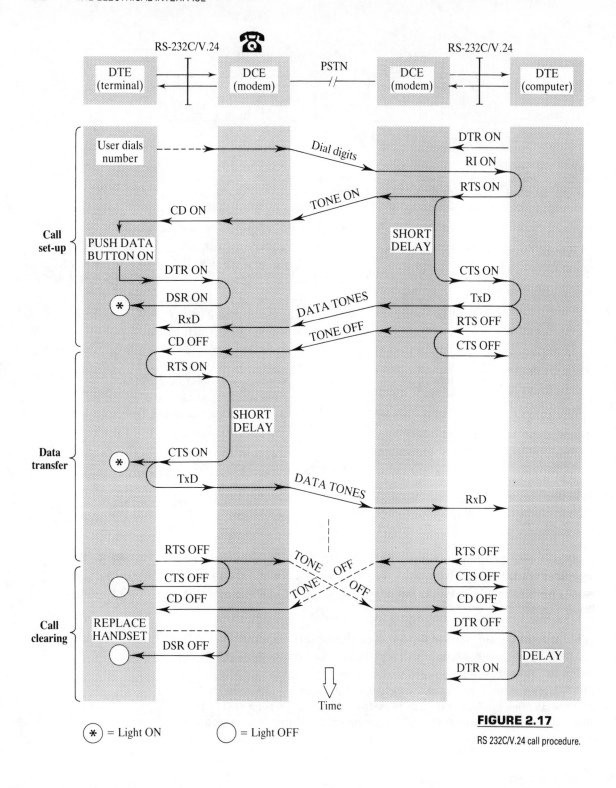

FIGURE 2.17

RS 232C/V.24 call procedure.

Typically, the called computer then responds by sending a short invitation-to-type message or character to the calling terminal via the set-up link. Having done this, the computer then prepares to receive the user's response by switching the RTS line to off, which in turn results in the carrier signal being switched off. When the calling modem detects that the carrier has been switched off, it sets the carrier detect (CD) line to off. The terminal then sets the RTS line to on and, on receipt of the CTS signal from the modem, the user types the response message. (An indicator lamp is normally associated with the CTS signal and hence comes on at this point.) Finally, after the complete transaction has taken place, both carriers are switched off and the set-up link (call) is released (cleared).

The use of a half-duplex switched connection has been selected here to illustrate the meaning and use of some of the control lines available with the RS-232C/V.24 standard. However, it should be noted that in practice the time taken to change from the receive to transmit mode with a half-duplex circuit, known as the **turn-around time**, is not insignificant. Hence, it is preferable to operate with a full-duplex circuit whenever possible, even if only half-duplex working is required. When a full-duplex circuit is used, the transmit and receive functions can, of course, take place simultaneously. In such cases, the RTS line from both devices is normally left permanently set and, under normal operation, both modems maintain the CTS line on and a carrier signal to the remote modem.

When synchronous transmission is used, as will be described in Chapter 3, it is necessary to have a clock signal for bit synchronization purposes. Furthermore, if a synchronous modem is used, the modulation and demodulation functions both require a clock signal to perform the signal encoding and decoding functions. Hence, it is necessary for the modem to supply the transmit and receive clocks to the interface control circuits in the DTEs (terminal and computer). The clock signal is passed from the modem to the DTE using the transmit signal element timing (DCE source) control line and the receive signal element timing line. These are assigned pins 15 and 17, respectively, in the connector. If a single bit per signalling element is used by the modem, then the clock signal supplied to the DTE for control of the transmission and reception rates is the same as the baud rate of the channel. However, if two bits per signalling element are used, then the clock supplied to the DTE is twice the baud rate, and so on.

With an asynchronous modem, on the other hand, the baud and bit rates are the same and no clock is used within the modem. Thus, if synchronous transmission is used, it is necessary for the clock to be extracted by the interface circuits within the DTE from the incoming data stream. The digital phase-lock loop circuit, which will be described in Chapter 3, is an example of a circuit suitable for use with an asynchronous modem. Also, to minimize the additional circuitry required to interface a

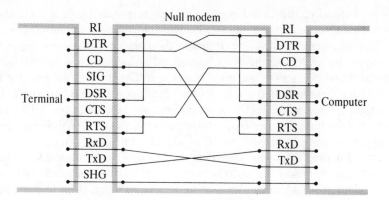

FIGURE 2.18

Null modem connections.

terminal (or computer) to a modem, the interface control circuits (UARTs and USRTs: see Chapter 3) normally have a modem control section that automatically handles the RTS/CTS and DSR/DTR control lines.

The null modem

With the signal assignments shown in Figure 2.16, the terminal and computer both receive and transmit data on the same lines, since the modem provides the same function for both devices. Since its original definition, however, the RS-232C/V.24 standard has been adopted as a standard interface for connecting character-oriented peripherals (VDUs, printers, etc.) to a computer. For this type of use, therefore, it is necessary to decide which of the two devices – peripheral or computer – is going to emulate the modem, since clearly both devices cannot transmit and receive data on the same lines.

There are three possible alternatives in this situation:

(1)   the terminal emulates the modem and the appropriate line definitions are used accordingly;

(2)   the computer emulates the modem; or

(3)   both the terminal and computer remain unchanged and the interconnecting wiring is modified.

The disadvantage of the first two alternatives is that the terminal or computer cannot then be used directly with a modem. Nevertheless, a common approach is for the computer RS-232C port to be wired to emulate a modem, and hence an unmodified terminal can be connected directly to it. The third alternative is also widely used, but this necessitates the use of a **null modem** (or **switch box**) which is inserted between the

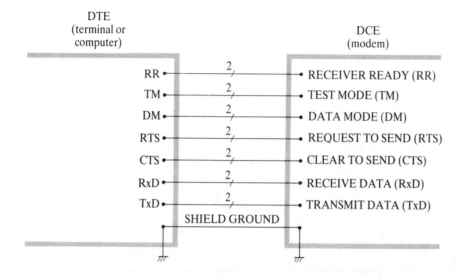

FIGURE 2.19

RS 449/V.35 signal definitions.

terminal and the computer to perform the necessary modifications to the interconnecting lines. The line modifications performed by a null modem are as shown in Figure 2.18.

As can be seen, in addition to reversing the transmit and receive data lines, some of the control lines are also reversed. For example, since a computer and terminal normally operate in a full-duplex mode, the RTS and CTS lines are connected together at each end and this signal is then connected to the CD input line of the other device. Similarly, the DSR and RI lines are connected together at each end and these signals are cross-connected to the DTR inputs. The signal and shield ground lines are of course connected directly.

When the two devices communicate via a synchronous data link, the transmit clock from each device is normally cross-connected and is used as the receive clock by the other device. In some instances, however, neither device contains a clock source and the clock to be used by both devices is generated within the null modem. The latter is then known as a **modem eliminator**.

2.4.2 RS-449/V.35

The interface used when RS-422 electrical signals are used is RS-449/V.35. Some of the control signals used with this standard are shown in Figure 2.19. The differential signals used with RS-422 mean that each line requires a pair of wires. As can be seen, some of the control signals are the same as those used with the RS-232C standard . Also, the data mode and receiver ready lines correspond to the DSR and DTR lines in the RS-232C

CAMROSE LUTHERAN COLLEGE
LIBRARY

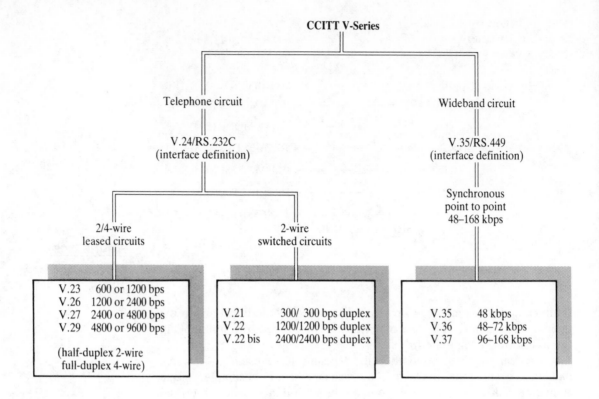

FIGURE 2.20

CCITT V-series standards.

standard. Test mode is a new mandatory signal specific to the RS-449 standard which is intended to provide a means for testing the communication equipment. Essentially, this provides a facility for looping the output of the DTE (terminal or computer) back again through the DCE (modem); that is, the TxD output line is automatically looped back to the RxD input line. In this way, a series of tests can be carried out by the DTE to determine which (if any) piece of communication equipment (DCE) is faulty.

2.4.3 Standards summary

The various standards discussed here are only part of a complete range of standards that have been defined by the CCITT for use with public telephone networks. Collectively, these are known as the V-series standards and a summary of some of the different standards is given in Figure 2.20.

As can be seen from the figure, the two physical interface standards are the V.24 (RS-232C) and the V.35 (RS-449). The first is intended for use with normal (and hence low bit rate) telephone circuits and the second with wider bandwidth (**wide-band**) circuits. The latter are normally leased from the PTT authority and, because they bypass the normal switching circuits, provide a direct point-to-point circuit (link) between two sites. Typically, this can be operated at data rates of from 48 to 168 kbps. As will be described in Chapter 3, a synchronous mode of transmission must be utilized for these circuits because of the relatively high data rates.

The various standards listed in Figure 2.20 are rigidly defined and include a precise definition of both the type of modulation scheme that must be used and the number and use of the additional interface control lines. In this way, a user buying a modem that adheres to, say, the V.21 standard, can readily use it with a V.21 modem from a different manufacturer.

CHAPTER SUMMARY

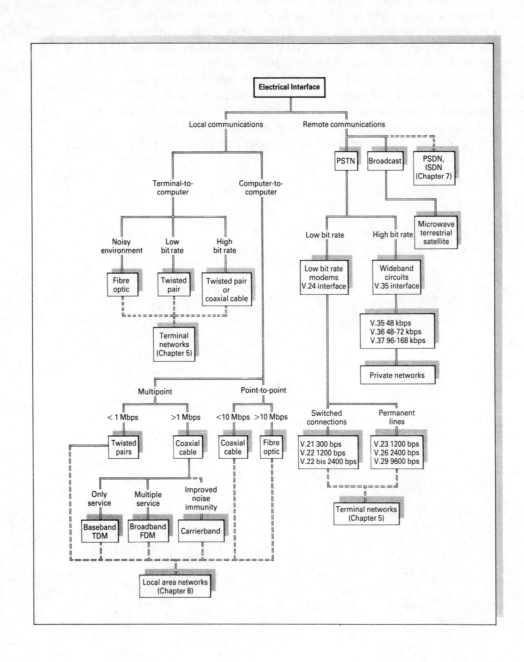

EXERCISES

2.1 Give a brief description of the application and limitations of the following types of transmission medium:

(a) two-wire open lines,

(b) twisted pair lines,

(c) coaxial cable,

(d) optical fibre,

(e) microwaves.

2.2 Make a sketch showing the interface circuits and the associated signal levels used to transmit binary data between two DTEs using the following signal types and transmission media:

(a) RS-232C/V.24 and open lines,

(b) 20 mA current loop and open lines,

(c) RS-422 and twisted pair,

(d) coaxial cable,

(e) optical fibre.

Outline the properties of each signal type.

2.3 (a) Why must a modem be used to transmit binary data through a PSTN? Use sketches and additional text to describe the following modulation methods:

- amplitude modulation,
- frequency modulation,
- phase-coherent PSK,
- differential PSK.

(b) Discuss the factors that influence the choice of carrier frequency and the bandwidth used by the demodulator section of a modem.

2.4 Deduce the maximum theoretical information rates associated with the following transmission channels:

(a) a telex (international message switching) network with a bandwidth of 500 Hz and a signal-to-noise ratio of 5 dB,

(b) a switched telephone network with a bandwidth of 3100 Hz and a signal-to-noise ratio of 20 dB.

2.5 Data are to be transmitted using a modem at 9600 bps. Determine the minimum bandwidth of the system with the following modulation methods:

(a)   FSK,

(b)   AM–PSK.

2.6   Data are to be transmitted through a PSTN at 4800 bps with a minimum bit error rate of 10^{-6} using a PSK modem. If the E/N_0 ratio needed to achieve this error rate is 10 dB with PSK modulation, deduce the minimum received signal level that is required assuming a temperature of 20°C.

2.7   List the main signals used with the RS-232C/V.24 standard interface and state their function. Derive a time sequence diagram to show the use of each line. Use as an example a user at a terminal establishing a half-duplex connection through a PSTN to carry out a transaction involving the exchange of data between the terminal and a remote computer.

2.8   (a)   What is the function of a null modem? Show the internal connections used within a null modem and explain the significance of each connection.

(b)   List the main signals used with the RS-449/V.35 standard interface and state their function.

DATA TRANSMISSION

3

3

CHAPTER OBJECTIVES

When you have completed studying the material in this chapter you should be able to:

- describe the function of the different steps that are necessary to achieve the reliable transfer of data across a point-to-point data link;

- describe the detailed operation of a typical Universal Asynchronous Receiver Transmitter circuit;

- describe the detailed operation of a typical Universal Synchronous Receiver Transmitter circuit;

- explain some of the alternative data encoding and clock synchronization schemes that are used on a synchronous data link;

- understand the operation and limitations of some of the alternative methods that may be employed to detect bit errors occurring during the transmission of data across a data link connecting two DTEs.

3.1 INTRODUCTION

Data communication is concerned with the exchange of digitally encoded information between two DTEs. The physical separation of the two pieces of equipment may vary from a few tens of metres – for example, between a computer and a locally connected terminal – to several hundreds of kilometres, if the two devices are connected using a national data network, for example.

Within the data communication community, the term 'data' is normally reserved for describing a set or block of one or more digitally encoded alphabetic and numerical characters being exchanged between two devices. Typically, these represent a string of numbers or perhaps the contents of a computer file containing a stored document. When using a data communication facility to transfer this type of data, it is also necessary for the two communicating parties (DTEs) to exchange some additional control information (messages); for example, to overcome the effect of transmission errors within the communication facility. Throughout this book, therefore, the more general term **information** will be used to describe any meaningful item, both data and control, being exchanged across the data communication facility.

In any form of digital system, the loss or corruption of a single bit (binary digit) of information can be critical. It is thus essential when designing a communication facility for a distributed system to ensure that adequate precautions are taken to detect and, if necessary, correct for any possible loss or corruption of information during transmission. Data communication is concerned, therefore, not only with the way data are transmitted over the physical transmission medium but also with the techniques that may be adopted to detect and, if necessary, correct transmission errors; with the control of the transfer rate of the data; with the format of the data being transferred; and other related issues.

Both this chapter and the next are concerned with the fundamental concepts associated with data communication and, in particular, with the techniques that are available to achieve the reliable (error free and no losses or duplicates) transfer of information across a data link connecting two DTEs. More specifically, this chapter deals with the basic techniques and circuits used for the transmission of data between two DTEs while Chapter 4 describes the basic techniques employed for the control of data transfer between the two communicating parties. It should be stressed that, irrespective of the type of error-detection (and correction) scheme adopted, it is not possible to detect all possible combinations of transmission errors with 100% certainty. In practice, therefore, the aim of the various error-detection and correction techniques is to make the probability of any undetected errors being present in a received message acceptably low.

3.2 DATA TRANSMISSION BASICS

All electronic digital equipment operate using a fixed number of binary digits to represent a single element of data or **word**. Within a computer, for example, this may be 8, 16 or 32 bits; data requiring more than this precision are represented by multiples of these bits. Because of this range of bits to represent each word, it is usual when communicating data between two pieces of equipment to use multiple fixed-length elements, each of 8 bits. In some applications the 8 bits may represent a binary-encoded alphabetic or numeric (alphanumeric) character while in others it may represent an 8-bit component of a larger value. In the latter case, the component is often referred to as an 8-bit **byte**; but, in general, within the communication facility, each 8-bit element is simply referred to as an **octet**.

3.2.1 Bit-serial transmission

Within a piece of equipment, the distance and hence lengths of wire used to connect each subunit together are short. Thus, it is normal practice to transfer the data between subunits by using a separate piece of wire to carry each bit of the data. This means that there are multiple wires connecting each subunit together and data are said to be exchanged using a **parallel transfer mode**. This mode of operation results in minimal delays in transferring each word.

When transferring information between two physically separate pieces of equipment, especially if the separation is more than several metres, for reasons of cost and varying transmission delays in the individual wires, it is more usual to use just single pair lines and transmit each octet making up the data a single bit at a time using a fixed time interval for each bit. This mode of operation is known as **bit-serial transmission**.

The two alternative modes of operation are shown in diagrammatic form in Figure 3.1. A binary digit is normally represented within a piece of digital electronic equipment as a specific voltage or current level relative to a reference level. Thus, in the figure, a high signal relative to the reference is used to indicate the transmission of a binary 1 while a low signal level, equal to the reference, represents a binary 0.

3.2.2 Communication modes

When a person is giving a lecture or speech, information is primarily conveyed in one direction only. During a conversation between two people, however, it is usual for spoken messages (information) to be

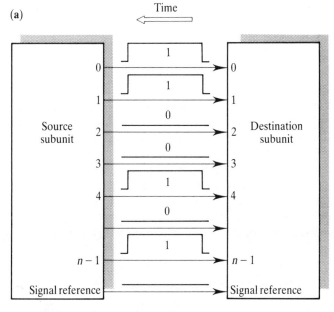

$n = 8, 16, 32$

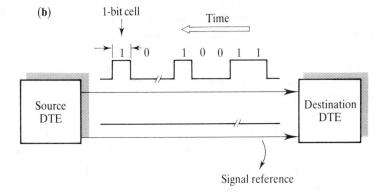

FIGURE 3.1

Transmission modes: (a) parallel; (b) serial.

exchanged in both directions. These messages are normally exchanged alternately but can, of course, be exchanged simultaneously! Similarly, when data are transmitted between two pieces of equipment, there are three analogous modes of operation that may be used:

(1)   **Simplex**: This is used when data are to be transmitted in one direction only; for example, in a data logging system in which a monitoring device returns a reading at regular intervals to the data gathering facility.

(2) **Half-duplex**: This is used when the two interconnected devices wish to exchange information (data) alternately; for example, if one of the devices only returns some data in response to a request from the other. Clearly, it is necessary for the two devices to be able to switch between send and receive modes after each transmission.

(3) **Duplex**: This is also referred to as full-duplex and is used when data are to be exchanged between the two connected devices in both directions simultaneously; for example, if for throughput reasons data can flow in each direction independently.

The alternative communication modes are important since in many distributed systems the circuits (lines) used to provide the necessary communication facilities are often leased from the PTT authorities, and hence it is clearly less expensive to lease a single circuit, rather than two circuits, if only simplex operation is required, for example.

3.2.3 Transmission modes

As has been mentioned, data are normally transmitted between two DTEs in multiples of a fixed-length unit, typically of 8 bits. For example, when a terminal is communicating with a computer, each typed (keyed) character is normally encoded into an 8-bit binary value and the complete message is then made up of a string (block) of similarly encoded characters. Since each character is transmitted bit serially, the receiving DTE receives one of two signal levels which vary according to the bit pattern (and hence character string) making up the message. For the receiving device to decode and interpret this bit pattern correctly, it must know:

(1) the bit rate being used (that is, the time duration of each bit cell),

(2) the start and end of each element (character or byte), and

(3) the start and end of each complete message block or frame.

These three factors are known as **bit** or **clock synchronism**, **byte** or **character synchronism** and **block** or **frame synchronism**, respectively.

In general, synchronization is accomplished in one of two ways, the method used being determined by whether the transmitter and receiver clocks are independent (asynchronous) or synchronized (synchronous). If the data to be transmitted are made up of a string of characters with random (possibly long) time intervals between each character, then each character is normally transmitted independently and the receiver resynchronizes at the start of each new character received. For this type of communication, **asynchronous transmission** is normally used. If, however, the data to be transmitted are made up of complete blocks of data each containing, say, multiple bytes or characters, the transmitter and receiver clocks must be in synchronism over long intervals, and hence **synchronous transmission** is normally used. These two types of transmission will now be considered separately.

Asynchronous transmission

This method of transmission is primarily used when the data to be transmitted are generated at random intervals – for example, by a user at a VDU communicating with a computer. Clearly, with this type of communication, the user keys in each character at an indeterminate rate, with possibly long random time intervals between each successive typed character. This means that the signal on the transmission line will be in the idle (off) state for long time intervals. With this type of communication, therefore, it is necessary for the receiver to be able to resynchronize at the start of each new character received. To accomplish this, each transmitted character or, more generally, item of user data, is encapsulated or framed between an additional start bit and one or more stop bits, as shown in Figure 3.2.

As can be seen from Figure 3.2, the polarity of the start and stop bits is different. This ensures that there is always a minimum of one transition $(1{\rightarrow}0{\rightarrow}1)$ between each successive character, irrespective of the bit sequences in the characters being transmitted. The first $1{\rightarrow}0$ transition after an idle period is then used by the receiving device to determine the start of each new character. In addition, by utilizing a clock whose frequency is N times higher than the transmitted bit rate frequency ($N = 16$ is typical), the receiving device can reliably determine the state of each transmitted bit in the character by sampling the received signal approximately at the centre of each bit cell period. This is shown diagrammatically in Figure 3.2 and will be discussed further in the next section.

It can be deduced from the foregoing that to transmit each item of user data, 10 (one start bit and one stop bit) or possibly 11 (one start bit and two stop bits) bits are utilized. Thus, assuming a single start bit and two stop bits per 8-bit item and a data transmission rate of, say, 1200 bps, the data rate is 1200/11 or approximately 110 bytes per second. The useful data rate is, in fact, less than this for reasons that will be described later.

When defining the transmission rate of a line, the term 'baud' is often used by communication engineers. When correctly used, however, the term baud indicates the number of line signal transitions per second. Thus, if each transmitted signal can be in one of two states, the term baud and bps are equivalent; but, as was described in Chapter 2, in some instances the line signal can take on more than two states, and hence each transmitted cell can be used to convey more than a single binary digit of

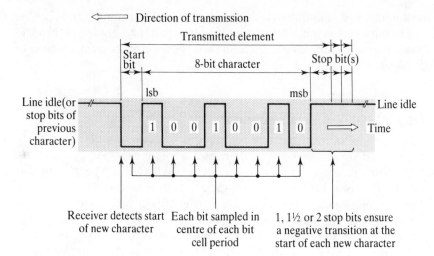

FIGURE 3.2

Asynchronous transmission.

information. To avoid confusion, therefore, the term signalling rate is used to define the number of line signal transitions per second (in baud) while the data or information transfer rate represents the number of information bits per second (in bps). For example, a signalling rate of 300 baud with four bits per signalling element would yield an information rate of 1200 bps. The most common information rates in use on asynchronous lines are 110, 300, 1200, 2400, 4800, 9600 and 19 200 bps.

Synchronous transmission

Asynchronous transmission is normally used when the rate at which characters are generated is indeterminate, and hence the transmission line can be idle for long periods between each transmitted character. The use of additional bits per character for framing purposes is therefore not important. In many applications, however – for example, for computer-to-computer communication – there is often a need to transmit large blocks of data that have already been preassembled ready for transmission – the contents of a disk file, for example. Clearly, the use of additional framing bits per character then becomes wasteful. Also, because of the clock synchronization mechanism used with an asynchronous scheme, asynchronous transmission can only be used reliably at up to 19 200 bps. An alternative and indeed a more efficient approach for the transmission of complete blocks of data is to transmit each complete block (or frame) as a single entity.

Using synchronous transmission, the complete block or frame of data is transmitted as a single bit stream with no delay between each 8-bit

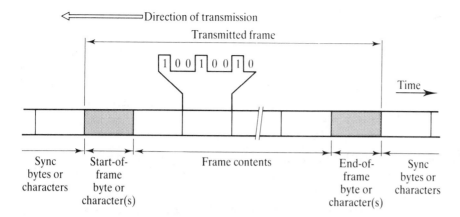

FIGURE 3.3

Synchronous transmission.

element. To enable the receiving device to achieve the various levels of synchronization:

(1)   the transmitted bit stream is suitably encoded so that the receiver can be kept in bit synchronism;

(2)   all frames are preceded by one or more reserved bytes or characters to ensure the receiver reliably interprets the received bit stream on the correct byte or character boundaries (byte/character synchronization; and

(3)   the contents of each frame are encapsulated between a pair of reserved bytes or characters.

The latter ensures that the receiver, on receipt of the opening byte or character after an idle period, can determine that a new frame is being transmitted and, on receipt of the closing byte or character, that this signals the end of the frame. During the period between the transmission of successive frames either idle (sync) bytes or characters are continuously transmitted to allow the receiver to retain bit and byte synchronism, or each frame is preceded by one or more special synchronizing bytes or characters to allow the receiver to regain synchronism. This is shown diagrammatically in Figure 3.3.

The alternative bit-encoding methods that may be employed to achieve bit synchronism will be described in Section 3.4. Also, with synchronous transmission, it is necessary to ensure that the special start and end-of-frame bytes or characters are unique; that is, they are not present in the contents of the frame being transmitted. Clearly, if the frame contains, say, the contents of a binary code file, this cannot be guaranteed, and hence additional steps have to be taken to allow for this possibility. These aspects will be discussed in more detail in later sections.

EXAMPLE

Deduce the number of additional bits required to transmit a message comprising 100 8-bit characters over a data link using each of the following transmission control schemes:

(a)   asynchronous with one start bit and two stop bits per character;

(b)   synchronous with two synchronization characters and a single start and end-of-frame character per message.

(a)   Number of bits per character = 1 + 2 = 3. Therefore, 300 additional bits are required.

(b)   With synchronous transmission, the number of additional bits is simply the two synchronization characters and one start and one end-of-frame character = 4 × 8 = 32 bits.

3.2.4   Transmission error control

During the transmission of a serial bit stream between two DTEs, it is very common – especially when the physical separation is large and, say, the switched telephone network is being used – for the transmitted information to become corrupted; that is, the signal level corresponding to a binary 0 is modified and, in the limit, is interpreted by the receiver as the level for a binary 1, and vice versa. It is normal when data are being transmitted between two devices, therefore, to provide a means for detecting possible transmission errors and, should they arise, a means for correcting for such errors.

There are a number of alternative schemes that may be utilized for this purpose but the one selected is normally determined by the type of transmission method used. When asynchronous transmission is used, for example, it is normal to embed an additional binary digit (bit) within each transmitted character, since each character is treated as a separate entity. The additional digit used is known as a **parity bit** and its function will be described in Section 3.5.1.

In contrast, when synchronous transmission is used, it is more usual to determine possible transmission errors on the complete frame, as the basic unit of transmission is a frame. Moreover, since the contents of a frame may be large, the probability of more than one bit being corrupted increases; hence, a more sophisticated error check sequence must be used. Again, this may take a number of different forms but, in general, the transmitting device computes a sequence of error check digits, based on the contents of the frame being transmitted, and appends these to the tail of the frame before the character or pattern signalling the end of the frame.

Hence, the receiver, during transmission of the frame, can recompute a new set of error check digits based on the received contents and, on receipt of the end-of-frame character or pattern, can compare this with the transmitted check digits. If these are not equal, a transmission error is then assumed.

Both of the schemes just described only allow the receiver to detect the occurrence of transmission errors. Consequently, a scheme is also necessary to enable the receiver to obtain another copy of the transmitted information when errors are detected. Again, a number of schemes are possible. For example, consider the case of a terminal and a computer transmitting data using asynchronous transmission. As the user keys in each character at the keyboard of the terminal, the encoded character is normally transmitted to the computer as already outlined. The character corresponding to the received bit stream is then 'echoed' back by the computer and displayed on the screen of the user terminal. If the displayed character is different from the selected keyed character, the user may send a special (delete) character to inform the computer to ignore the last (erroneous) character received. This in general is referred to as error control and some of the more common error control methods are discussed in Chapter 4.

3.2.5 Flow control

If the amount of data to be transmitted between two devices is small, it is possible for the sending device to transmit all the data immediately, in the knowledge that the receiving device will have sufficient resources (storage space) to hold the data. In many data communication situations, however, this is not the case and so it is often necessary to adopt a method to control the flow of data transfer to ensure that the receiver does not lose any of the transmitted data due to insufficient storage facilities. This is particularly important, for example, when the two devices are communicating through an intermediate data communication network as very often the data network will only buffer a limited amount of data. Hence, if the two devices operate at different data rates, for example, it often becomes necessary to control the mean output rate of the faster device to prevent the communication network from becoming congested. The control of the flow of information between two DTEs is known as flow control and some of the alternative methods used will be introduced in Chapter 4.

3.2.6 Communication protocols

Error and flow control are two essential components of the more general topic of communication protocols. Essentially, a communication protocol is a set of conventions or rules that must be adhered to by both communicating parties to ensure that information being exchanged between the two parties is received and interpreted correctly. Thus, in addition to error and flow control, a communication protocol also defines such things as:

- the format of the data being exchanged – that is, the number of bits per element and the type of encoding scheme being used; and
- the type and order of messages that are to be exchanged in order to achieve a reliable (error free and no duplicates) information transfer between the two communicating parties.

For example, it is normal before transferring any data from one party to another to set up a connection between the two parties to ensure that the receiving party is free and ready to receive the data. This is often accomplished by the sending device transmitting a specific command message – a call or connect request, for example – and the receiver returning a defined response message – a call connected or reject, for example. A number of different communication protocols will be discussed in subsequent chapters of the book.

3.3 TRANSMISSION CONTROL CIRCUITS

As has been outlined, data are normally transmitted between two DTEs bit serially in multiple 8-bit elements using either asynchronous or synchronous transmission. Within the DTEs, however, each element is normally manipulated and stored in a parallel form. Consequently, the transmission control circuits within each DTE, which form the interface between the device and the serial data link, must perform the following functions:

- parallel-to-serial conversion of each element in preparation for transmission of the element on the data link;
- serial-to-parallel conversion of each received element in preparation for storage and processing of the element in the device;
- a means for the receiver to achieve bit, character and, for synchronous transmission, frame synchronization;
- the generation of suitable error check digits for error-detection purposes and the detection of such errors should they occur.

To satisfy these requirements, special integrated circuits are now readily available. A simple point-to-point connection of two DTEs using these circuits is as shown in Figure 3.4. Although different circuits can be used to control asynchronous and synchronous data links, circuits are also

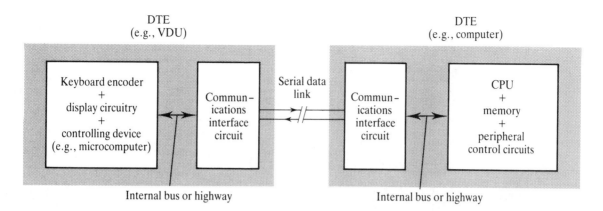

DTE
(e.g., VDU)

DTE
(e.g., computer)

Internal bus or highway

Internal bus or highway

available to support both types of link. The latter are often referred to as **universal communication interface circuits** but, since the two halves of such circuits function independently, each will be considered separately.

FIGURE 3.4

Simple point-to-point link.

3.3.1 Asynchronous transmission

The interface circuit used to support asynchronous transmission is known as a **Universal Asynchronous Receiver and Transmitter**, or simply a **UART**. It is termed universal since it is normally a programmable device and the user can, by simply loading a predefined control word (bit pattern) into the device, specify the required operating characteristics. A schematic diagram of a typical UART is shown in Figure 3.5.

To use such a device, the mode (control) register is first loaded with the required bit pattern to define the required operating characteristics; this is known as initialization. Typically, the user may select 5, 6, 7 or 8 bits per character, odd, even or zero parity, one or more stop bits and a range of transmit and receive bit rates. The latter are selected from a standard range of 50 bps to 19.2 kbps by connecting a clock source of the appropriate frequency to the transmit and receive clock inputs of the UART and defining the ratio of this clock to the required bit rate (x1, x16, x32 or x64) in the mode byte. The use of the latter will be expanded upon later.

Figure 3.6(a) illustrates the meaning of the various mode bits in a typical device. Thus with this device, assuming the bit pattern 01001101 (4D hexadecimal) was loaded into the mode register at start-up, the device would operate with 7 data bits per character, an even parity bit, one stop bit and an external clock source of x16 the bit rate.

After selecting the required operational mode (and prior to transmitting data), a command byte must be loaded into the command register. The individual bits in the command byte perform such functions as enabling the transmitter and receiver sections and, if used, controlling the modem interface.

The controlling device within a DTE determines the current state of

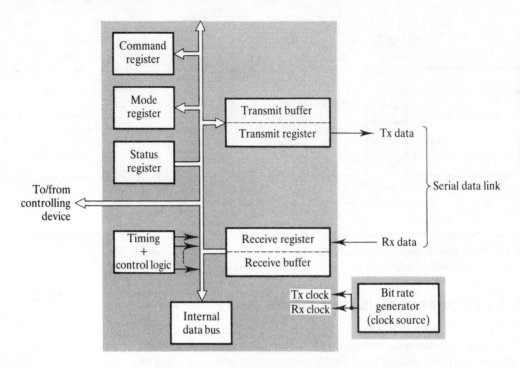

FIGURE 3.5

UART schematic.

the UART by reading the contents of the status register and testing specific bits within it. These are often referred to as **flag bits**. Their use varies for different circuit types but a typical status register composition is as shown in Figure 3.6(b). To use this circuit to transmit a new character, the controlling device first reads the status byte to determine the state of the transmit buffer empty (TxBE) bit. Then, assuming this is logical 1 (true), this signals that the previous character has been transferred from the transmit buffer to the transmit register, from where it is shifted bit serially on to the data link. The buffer is now ready for a new character to be loaded. The controlling device thus loads the character and, in turn, the control logic within the UART transfers it to the transmit register as soon as the final stop bit for the previous character has been transmitted. Each time a new character is loaded into the transmit buffer, the TxBE bit is reset to logical 0 (false). Similarly, when the internal control logic transfers a character from the transmit buffer to the transmit register, the TxBE bit is set, thus allowing the control logic to load a new character, if one is available. In addition, when each character is loaded into the transmit buffer, the control logic automatically computes the appropriate parity bit, if this has been selected. Then, when the complete character (data plus parity) is transferred to the transmit register, a start bit and the specified number of stop bits are inserted and the complete envelope is transmitted bit serially on to the line at a bit rate determined by the externally supplied clock and the ratio setting.

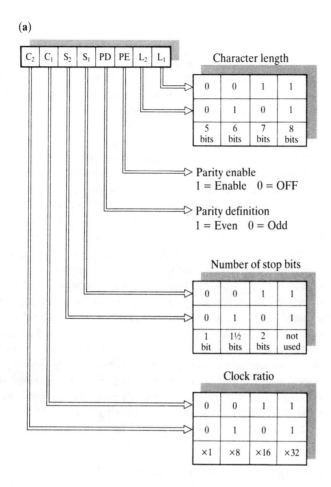

(a)

C_2	C_1	S_2	S_1	PD	PE	L_2	L_1

Character length

0	0	1	1
0	1	0	1
5 bits	6 bits	7 bits	8 bits

Parity enable
1 = Enable   0 = OFF

Parity definition
1 = Even   0 = Odd

Number of stop bits

0	0	1	1
0	1	0	1
1 bit	1½ bits	2 bits	not used

Clock ratio

0	0	1	1
0	1	0	1
×1	×8	×16	×32

(b)

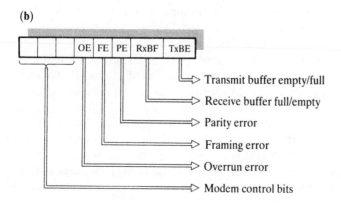

		OE	FE	PE	RxBF	TxBE

Transmit buffer empty/full

Receive buffer full/empty

Parity error

Framing error

Overrun error

Modem control bits

FIGURE 3.6

Typical UART mode and status bit definitions: (a) mode register; (b) status register.

For reception, the receiving UART must be programmed to operate with the same characteristics as the transmitting UART. When the control logic detects the first transition on the receive data line after an idle period (1→0), due to the possibly random intervals between successive characters, the receiver timing logic must be resynchronized. This is accomplished by the control logic presetting the contents of a bit rate counter to one-half of the clock rate ratio setting. Thus, if the UART has been programmed to operate with a x16 external clock rate, a modulo 16 counter would be used, preset initially to 8 on receipt of the first transition. The timing logic then decrements the contents of the counter after each cycle of the external clock. Since there are 16 clock cycles to each bit cell (x16 bit rate), the counter will reach zero approximately at the centre of the start bit. The bit rate counter is then preset to 16 and hence will reach zero at the centre of each bit cell period. Each time the counter reaches zero, this triggers the control circuitry to determine the current state (logical 1 or 0) of the receive data line and the appropriate bit is then shifted into the receive register. This is shown diagrammatically in Figure 3.7. As can be deduced from the figure, the higher the clock rate ratio, the nearer the sampling instant becomes to the nominal bit cell centres.

This process continues until the defined number of data and parity bits have been shifted into the receive register. At this point, the complete character is parallel loaded into the receive buffer. The receive parity bit is then compared with the parity bit recomputed from the received data bits and, if these are different, the parity error (PE) flag bit is set in the status register at the same time as the receive buffer full (RxBF) flag is set. The controlling device can thus determine the following from these bits:

(1)   when a new character has been received, and
(2)   whether any transmission errors have been detected.

The status register contains two additional error flags: namely, the framing and overrun flags. The framing error (FE) flag is set if the control logic determines that a logical 0 (or a valid stop bit) is not present on the receive data line when the last stop bit is expected at the end of a received character. Similarly, the overrun error (OE) flag is set if the controlling device has not read the previously received character from the receive buffer before the next character is received and transferred to the buffer. Normally, the setting of these flags does not inhibit the operation of the UART but rather signals to the controlling device that an error condition has occurred. It is then up to the controlling device to initiate any corrective action should it deem this to be necessary.

As can be seen from Figure 3.5, a UART contains both a transmit and a receive section, both of which operate in an independent way. It is

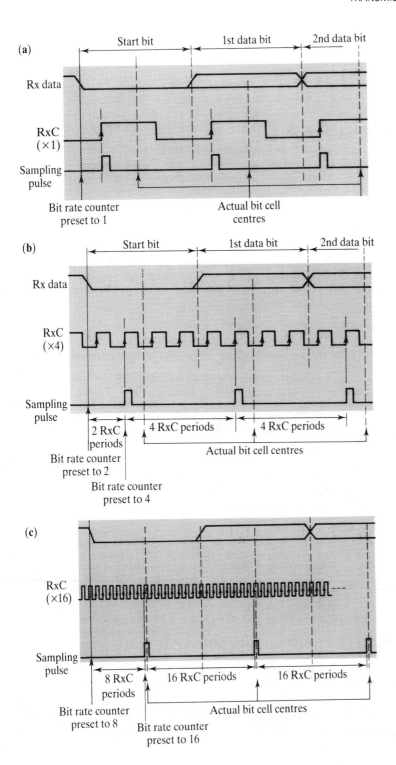

FIGURE 3.7

Receiver timing waveforms:
(a) x1 (RxC); (b) x4 RxC; (c) x16
RxC.

possible with a single UART, therefore, to control a full-duplex data link. Also, most UARTs normally have additional control lines to allow them to be interfaced with a modem directly. The use of these lines was considered in Chapter 2 when modems were discussed.

EXAMPLE

A UART is to be used to transmit data across a data link. If a clock of 19.2 kHz is available at the receiver, deduce the suitable clock rate ratios and estimate the worst-case deviations from the nominal bit cell centres, expressed as a percentage of a bit period, for each of the following data transmission rates:

(a)   1200 bps,

(b)   2400 bps,

(c)   9600 bps.

The worst-case deviation from the nominal bit cell centres is approximately one cycle of the receiver clock. Therefore:

(a)   At 1200 bps, the maximum RxC ratio can be x16. The maximum deviation is thus 6.25%.

(b)   At 2400 bps, the maximum RxC ratio can be x8. The maximum deviation is thus 12.5%.

(c)   At 9600 bps, the maximum RxC ratio can be x2. The maximum deviation is thus 50%.

Clearly, the last case is unacceptable but, with a low quality line, especially one with excessive delay distortion, even the second may be unreliable. It is for this reason that an x16 clock ratio is used whenever possible.

3.3.2   Synchronous transmission

Although the type of framing (character or block) is often used to discriminate between asynchronous and synchronous transmission, the fundamental difference between the two methods is that with asynchronous transmission the transmitter and receiver clocks are unsynchronized while with synchronous transmission both clocks are synchronized.

Clearly, the latter may be accomplished by having an additional line linking the two pieces of equipment to carry the transmit clock, so that the receiving device can reliably determine when each new bit is being sent. In practice, however, it is more common to use a single data line with the clock (timing) information embedded within the transmitted waveform. With this method, the receiver sampling clock must be extracted from the incoming data stream using a suitable **clock extraction circuit**. The different methods used to achieve this will be discussed later.

There are two alternative ways of organizing a synchronous data link: character (or byte) oriented and bit oriented. The essential difference between these two methods is in the way the start and end of a frame is determined. With a bit-oriented system, it is possible for the receiver to detect the end of a frame at any bit instant and not just on an 8-bit (byte) boundary. This implies that a frame may be N bits in length where N is an arbitrary number. In practice, however, this feature is not often used, since the majority of applications tend to use frames that are multiples of 8-bit bytes. Nevertheless, a bit-oriented system offers the potential of up to a two times increase in throughput over a character-oriented system, and hence is the preferred mode of operation. Since character-oriented systems are still in widespread use, however, both will be described here.

Character oriented

With a character-oriented scheme, each frame to be transmitted is made up of a variable number of 7- or 8-bit characters which are transmitted as a contiguous string of binary bits with no delay between them. The receiving device, therefore, having achieved clock (bit) synchronism must be able to:

(1)   detect the start and end of each character – character synchronism, and

(2)   detect the start and end of each complete frame – frame synchronism.

A number of schemes have been devised to achieve this, the main aim of which is to make the synchronization process independent of the actual contents of a frame. This type of synchronization scheme is said to be **transparent** to the frame contents or simply **data transparent**.

The most common character-oriented scheme is that used in the binary synchronous control protocol known as **Basic Mode**. (Basic Mode protocols will be discussed in more detail in Chapter 5. They are used primarily for the transfer of alphanumeric characters between communities of intelligent terminals and a computer.) A number of alternative forms of this protocol are in use but an example of the frame format used in one of these is shown in Figure 3.8(a). The format selected is the one normally

(a)

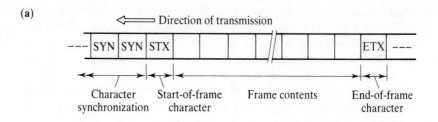

(b)

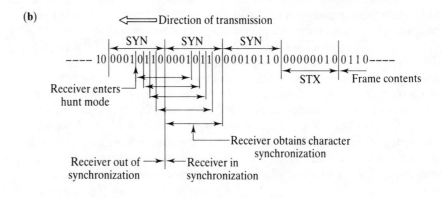

(c)

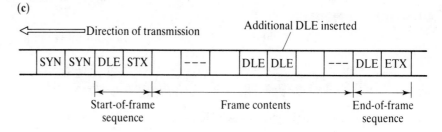

FIGURE 3.8

Character-oriented link: (a) basic
frame format; (b) character
synchronization; (c) data
transparency.

used to transmit a block of data – an information frame.

When using Basic Mode, character synchronism is achieved by the transmitting device sending two or more special synchronizing characters (known as SYN) immediately before each transmitted frame. The receiver, at start-up or after an idle period, then scans (hunts) the received bit stream one bit at a time until it detects the known pattern of the SYN character. This results in the receiver achieving character synchronism and the subsequent string of binary bits is then treated as a contiguous sequence of 7- or 8-bit characters as defined at set-up time. This is illustrated in Figure 3.8(b).

With the Basic Mode protocol, the SYN character (00010110) is one of the reserved characters from the ISO defined set of character codes. Similarly, the characters used to signal the start and end of each frame are from this set. In the example, the start-of-text (STX) character is used to signal the start of a frame and the end-of-text (ETX) character is used to signal the end of a frame. Thus, as each character in the frame is received, following the STX character, it is compared with the ETX character. If the character is not an ETX character it is simply stored. If it is an ETX character, however, the frame contents are processed. This scheme is satisfactory provided the data (information) transmitted are made up of strings of printable characters entered at a keyboard, for example, since then there is no possibility of an ETX control character being present within the frame contents. Clearly, if the latter did occur, this would cause the receiver to terminate the reception process abnormally.

In some applications, however, the contents of frames may not be character strings but rather the binary contents of a file, for example. For this type of application it is necessary to take additional steps to ensure that the end-of-frame termination character is not present within the frame contents; that is, it must be data transparent. To achieve this with a character-oriented transmission control scheme, a pair of characters is used both to signal the start of a frame and also the end of a frame. This is shown in Figure 3.8(c). A pair of characters is necessary to achieve data transparency: to avoid the abnormal termination of a frame due to the frame contents containing the end-of-frame character sequence, the transmitter inserts a second data link escape (DLE) character into the transmitted data stream whenever it detects a DLE character in the contents of the frame. This is often referred to as **character** (or **byte**) **stuffing**. The receiver can thus detect the end of a frame by the unique DLE–ETX sequence and, whenever it receives a DLE character followed by a second DLE, it discards the second character. (The DLE character will be discussed further in Chapter 5.) As has been mentioned, with a frame-oriented scheme, transmission errors are normally detected by the use of additional error-detection digits computed from the contents of the frame and transmitted at the end of the frame. To maintain transparency, therefore, the error check characters are transmitted after the closing frame sequence. The different error-detection methods will be expanded on in a later section.

Bit oriented

With a bit-oriented scheme, each transmitted frame may contain an arbitrary number of bits, which is not necessarily a multiple of 8. A typical frame format used with a bit-oriented scheme is shown in Figure 3.9. As can be seen, the opening and closing flag fields indicating the start and end of the frame are the same (01111110). Thus, to achieve data transparency with this scheme it is necessary to ensure that the flag sequence is not present in the frame contents. This is accomplished by the use of a technique known as **zero bit insertion** or **bit stuffing**. As the frame contents

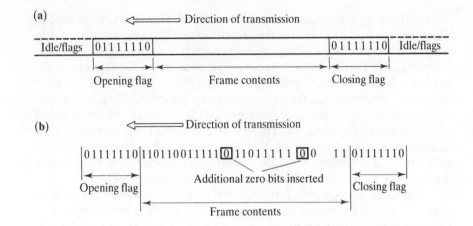

FIGURE 3.9

Bit-oriented link: (a) frame
format; (b) zero bit insertion.

are transmitted to line, the transmitter detects whenever there is a sequence of five contiguous binary 1 digits and automatically inserts an additional binary 0. In this way, the flag sequence 01111110 can never be transmitted between the opening and closing flags. Similarly, the receiver, after detecting the opening flag of a frame, monitors the incoming bit stream and, whenever it detects a binary 0 after five contiguous binary 1s, removes (deletes) it from the frame contents. As with a byte-oriented scheme, each frame will normally contain additional error-detection digits at the end of the frame, but the inserted and deleted 0s are not included in the error-detection processing.

The USRT

As already mentioned, special integrated circuits are available for the control of both character-oriented and bit-oriented synchronous transmission lines. The interface circuit used for the control of a character-oriented line is known as a **Universal Synchronous Receiver and Transmitter** or **USRT**. Again, the term universal is used as the device is programmable and its detailed operational characteristics can be changed under the control of the user. A schematic diagram of a typical USRT is shown in Figure 3.10.

As with a UART, to use such a device the mode (control) register is first loaded to define the required operating characteristics. Figure 3.11(a) illustrates the meaning of some of the bits used in a typical device. The length and parity bits have the same effect and meaning as with a UART. The sync character select (SCS) bit is provided to allow the user to operate the device, and hence data link, with either a single or double SYN

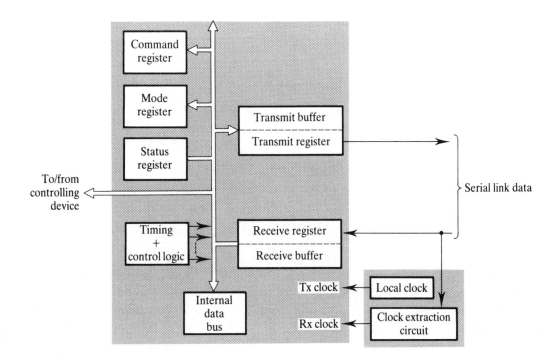

FIGURE 3.10

USRT schematic.

character preceding each transmitted frame. (In fact, the actual sync character used can normally be selected at start-up also.) The controlling device determines the current state of the USRT by reading the contents of the status register and testing specific bits within it – for example, the TxBE bit, the RxBF bit, etc.

At the start of transmission, the controlling device initiates the transmission of several SYN characters to allow the receiving device to achieve character sychronism. This is achieved by loading SYN characters into the transmit buffer each time the TxBE bit becomes set (logical 1). The contents of the frame to be transmitted are then transferred by the controlling device to the transmit buffer a single character at a time, the rate again being controlled by the state of the TxBE bit. After the last character of the frame has been transmitted, the USRT automatically starts to transmit SYN characters until the controlling device is ready to transmit a new frame. These are referred to as **interframe time-fill characters** and they allow the receiver to maintain character synchronism between successive frames.

At the destination, the controlling device first sets the receiving USRT into **hunt mode**, which causes the control logic to compare the contents of the receive buffer with the SYN character, after each new bit is received. When a match is found, the sync detect (SYNDET) bit in the

(a)

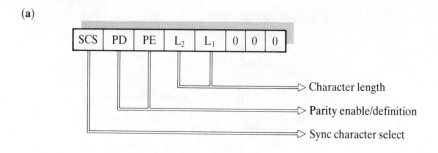

(b)

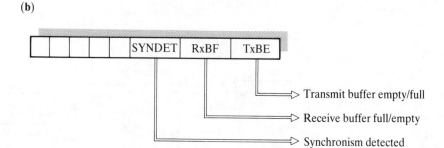

FIGURE 3.11

Typical USRT mode and status
bit definitions: (a) mode register;
(b) status register.

status register is set to indicate to the controlling device that character synchronism has been obtained. The latter then waits for the start-of-frame character (STX) to indicate that a new frame is being received. Each character of the frame is then received by the controlling device, under the control of the RxBF bit, until the end-of-frame character (ETX) is detected. In the synchronous mode, all data are transmitted and received at a rate determined by the transmit and receive clocks, respectively. The latter, as will be described in the next section, is normally derived from the incoming bit stream using a suitable clock extraction circuit.

The circuits available for the control of a bit-oriented line normally contain features that perform frame synchronization and zero bit insertion and deletion. In addition, as for a character-oriented USRT, they also include features for such functions as the generation and detection of transmission errors. These will be expanded upon later.

3.4 CLOCK (BIT) SYNCHRONIZATION

It has been shown that with asynchronous transmission a separate clock is utilized at the receiver whose frequency is typically several times higher than the transmitted bit rate. Then, on receipt of the leading edge of the start bit of each character envelope, the receiver uses this, together with its local clock, to estimate the centre of each bit cell period. This approach is acceptable for asynchronous transmission since:

(1) the maximum bit rate used with an asynchronous scheme is relatively low (less than 19.2 kbps), and

(2) the encoding method ensures that there is a guaranteed synchronizing edge at the start of each character.

With synchronous transmission, however, start and stop bits are not used. Instead, each frame is transmitted as a contiguous stream of binary digits. It is necessary, therefore, to utilize a different clock (bit) synchronization method. One approach, of course, is to have two pairs of lines between the transmitter and receiver: one to carry the transmitted bit stream and the other to carry the associated clock (timing) signal. The receiver could then utilize the latter to clock the incoming bit stream into, say, the receiver register within the USRT. In practice, however, this is very rarely possible, since if a switched telephone network is used, for example, only a single pair of lines is normally available.

Two alternative methods are used to overcome this dilemma: either the clocking information (signal) is embedded into the transmitted bit stream and subsequently extracted by the receiver, or the information to be transmitted is encoded in such a way that there are sufficient guaranteed transitions in the transmitted bit stream to synchronize a separate clock held at the receiver. Both of these approaches will now be considered.

3.4.1 Clock encoding and extraction

Two alternative methods of embedding timing (clock) information into a transmitted bit stream are shown in Figure 3.12. In (a), the bit stream to be transmitted is encoded so that a binary 1 is represented by a positive pulse and a binary 0 as a negative pulse. The encoding method is thus known as **bipolar encoding**. Clearly, each bit cell contains clocking information and, by means of a simple rectifier and delay circuit, the clock can readily be extracted from the received waveform. Since the waveform returns to zero after each encoded bit (positive or negative) with this method, the encoded signal is referred to as a **return-to-zero**, or simply **RZ**, **waveform**. As can be seen from Figure 3.12(a), three distinct amplitude levels are required with an RZ waveform to represent the transmitted bit stream.

In contrast, the scheme illustrated in Figure 3.12(b) only requires two levels. The resulting waveform is referred to as a **non-return-to-zero (NRZ) waveform** and the method **phase-** or **Manchester-encoding (PE)**. Although the associated clock extraction circuitry required for use with this

(a)

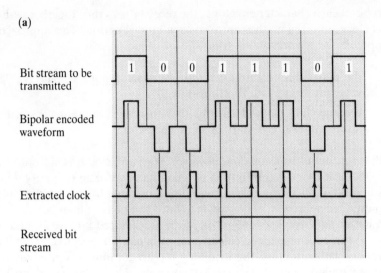

Bit stream to be
transmitted

Bipolar encoded
waveform

Extracted clock

Received bit
stream

(b)

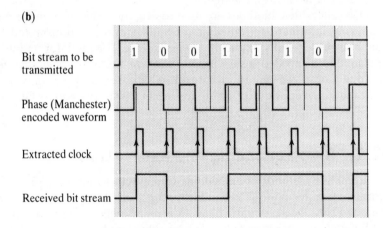

Bit stream to be
transmitted

Phase (Manchester)
encoded waveform

Extracted clock

Received bit stream

FIGURE 3.12

Clock-encoding methods:
(a) bipolar encoding: (b) phase
(Manchester) encoding.

method is a little more complicated than with bipolar encoding, the
presence of a positive or negative transition at the centre of each bit cell
period means that the extraction of the clock can be readily accomplished.
Thus, with bipolar encoding the extracted clock is used to sample (clock)
the incoming bit stream at the centre of each bit cell while with phase
encoding the bit stream is sampled during the second half of each bit cell.

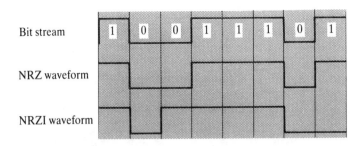

FIGURE 3.13
NRZI (differential) encoding.

3.4.2 Data encoding and clock synchronization

An alternative approach to encoding the clock in the transmitted bit stream is to utilize a stable clock source at the receiver which is kept in time synchronism with the incoming bit stream. However, as there are no start and stop bits with a synchronous transmission scheme, it is necessary to encode the information in such a way that there are always sufficient bit transitions (1→0 or 0→1) in the transmitted waveform to enable the receiver clock to be resynchronized at frequent intervals. One approach is to pass the data to be transmitted through a **scrambler** which has the effect of randomizing the transmitted bit stream and hence removing contiguous strings of 1s or 0s. Alternatively, the data may be encoded in such a way that suitable transitions are always naturally present.

The bit pattern to be transmitted is first encoded as shown in Figure 3.13, the resulting encoded signal being referred to as a **non-return-to-zero-inverted (NRZI)** waveform. With NRZI encoding (also known as **differential encoding**), the signal level (1 or 0) does not change for the transmission of a binary 1 whereas a binary 0 does cause a change. This means that there will always be bit transitions in the incoming signal of an NRZI waveform, providing there are no contiguous streams of binary 1s. On the surface, this may seem no different from the normal NRZ waveform but, as was described previously, if a bit-oriented scheme with zero bit insertion is adopted, an active line will always have a binary 0 in the transmitted bit stream at least every five bit cells. Consequently, the resulting waveform will contain a guaranteed number of transitions, since long strings of 0s cause a transition every bit cell, and this enables the receiver to adjust its clock so that it is in synchronism with the incoming bit stream.

The circuit used to maintain bit synchronism is known as a **digital phase-locked loop (DPLL)**. To utilize a DPLL, a **crystal-controlled oscillator** (clock source), which can hold its frequency sufficiently constant to require only very small adjustments at irregular intervals, is connected to the DPLL. Typically, the frequency of the clock is 32 times the bit rate used on the data link and this in turn is used by the DPLL to derive the timing interval between successive samples of the received bit stream.

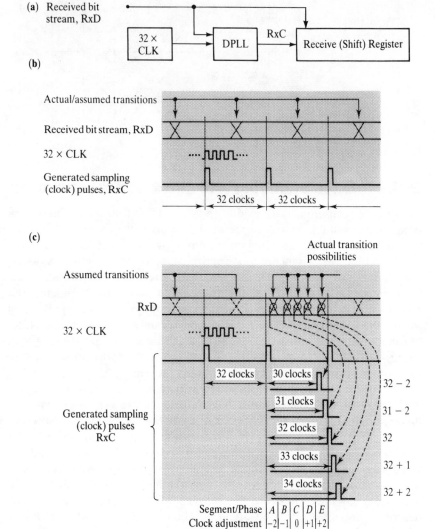

FIGURE 3.14

DPLL operation: (a) schematic; (b) in phase; (c) clock adjustment rules.

Hence, assuming the incoming bit stream and the local clock are in synchronism, the state (1 or 0) of the incoming signal on the line will be sampled (clocked) at the centre of each bit cell with exactly 32 clock periods between each sample. This is shown in Figure 3.14(a).

Now assume that the incoming bit stream and local clock drift out of synchronism. The adjustment of the sampling instant is carried out in discrete increments as shown in Figure 3.14(b). If there are no transitions on the line, the DPLL simply generates a sampling pulse every 32 clock periods after the previous one. Whenever a transition (1→0 or 0→1) is detected, however, the time interval between the previously generated sampling pulse and the next is determined according to the position of the transition relative to where the DPLL thought it should occur. To achieve this, each bit period is divided into five segments, shown as A, B, C, D and E in the figure. Then if, for example, a transition occurs during segment A, this indicates that the last sampling pulse was in fact too close and hence late. The time period to the next pulse is therefore shortened to 30 clock periods. Similarly, if a transition occurs in segment E, this indicates that the previous sampling pulse was too early. The time period to the next pulse is therefore lengthened to 34 clock periods. Transitions in segments B and D are clearly nearer to the assumed transition and hence the relative adjustments are less (-1 and $+1$, respectively). Finally, a transition in segment C will be deemed to be close enough to the assumed transition to warrant no adjustment.

In this way, successive adjustments keep the generated sampling pulses close to the centre of each bit cell. In practice, the widths of each segment (in terms of clock periods) are not equal; the outer segments (A and E), being further away from the nominal centre, are made longer than the three inner segments. Thus for the circuit shown, a typical division might be $A = E = 10$ and $B = C = D = 4$. It can then be readily deduced that in the worst case the DPLL will require 10 bit transitions to converge to the nominal bit centre of a waveform: five bit periods of coarse adjustments (±2) and five bit periods of fine adjustments (±1). Hence, when using a DPLL, it is usual before transmitting the first frame on a line, or following an idle period between frames, to transmit a number of characters to provide a minimum of 10 bit transitions. Two characters each composed of all 0s, for example, will provide 16 transitions with NRZI encoding. This ensures that the DPLL will generate sampling pulses at the nominal centre of each bit cell by the time the opening flag of a frame is received. It should be stressed, however, that once in synchronism (lock) only minor adjustments will normally take place during the reception of a frame. Further information relating to the DPLL can be found in the list of references at the end of the book.

3.5   ERROR-DETECTION METHODS

When data are being transmitted between two DTEs it is very common, especially if the transmission lines are in an electrically noisy environment such as the switched telephone network, for the electrical signals representing the transmitted bit stream to be changed by electromagnetic interference induced in the lines by neighbouring electrical devices. This means that the signals representing a binary 1 may be interpreted by the receiver as a binary 0 signal and vice versa. To ensure that information received by a destination device has a high probability of being the same as that transmitted by a sending device, therefore, there must be some means for the receiver to deduce, to a high probability, when received information contains errors. Furthermore, should errors be detected, a mechanism is needed for obtaining a copy of the (hopefully) correct information.

There are two approaches available for achieving this:

(1) **Forward error control**, in which each transmitted character or frame contains additional (redundant) information so that the receiver cannot only detect when errors are present but also infer from the received bit stream what it thinks the correct information should be.

(2) **Feedback error control**, in which each character or frame includes only sufficient additional information to enable the receiver to detect when errors are present and then to employ a retransmission scheme to request that another, hopefully correct, copy of the erroneous information be sent.

In practice, the number of additional bits required to achieve reliable forward error control increases rapidly as the number of information bits increases; hence, feedback error control is the predominant method used in the types of distributed system discussed in this book. Nevertheless, a brief introduction to the subject of forward error control is given in Appendix A.

As has been indicated, feedback error control can be divided into two parts: firstly, the techniques that may be used to achieve reliable error detection; and secondly, the control algorithms that are available to perform the associated retransmission schemes. This section is concerned with the most common error-detection techniques currently in use. Some of the alternative retransmission control algorithms are discussed in Chapter 4.

3.5.1 Parity

The most common method employed for detecting errors when the number of information bits is small and the probability of an error being present is low is by the use of a single additional parity bit per transmitted element. This method is particularly suitable with asynchronous transmission, for example, since, as will be seen in Chapter 5, use of the standard coding methods results in each transmitted character containing either 7 or 8 data bits plus the parity bit itself.

Using the parity method, the data bits in each character are inspected prior to transmission and the parity bit computed. This is then added so that the total number of binary 1s in the complete envelope is either odd or even according to whether *odd* or *even* parity is used. The receiver can then recompute the parity for the received character and determine whether any transmission errors have occurred. The format of a transmitted envelope is as shown in Figure 3.15(a).

The ability of a particular type of error-detection scheme to reveal errors depends strongly on the types of error that can arise on the data link used. For example, it can be readily deduced that the inclusion of a single parity bit with each character will only reliably safeguard against single bits being in error (odd errors), since if two bits are corrupted the transmitted parity bit will not indicate the error. In practice, however, if two or more (even) errors occur, and hence remain undetected by the line transmission control circuitry, the retransmission control schemes used with character-oriented transmission provide a means for detecting this.

Since parity is used with both asynchronous transmission control schemes and character-oriented synchronous transmission schemes, both UARTs and USRTs (collectively referred to as USARTs) also contain facilities to:

(1)   compute and insert the appropriate parity bit into each transmitted character automatically prior to transmission, and

(2)   recompute the parity, on reception, for each received character and to signal when an error is detected.

The circuitry integrated into the USARTs to perform these functions is relatively simple. It comprises a string of **exclusive-OR (XOR) gates** connected as shown in Figure 3.15(c). The XOR gate is also known as a **modulo 2 adder** since, as shown by the **truth table** in Figure 3.15(b), the output of the exclusive-OR operation between two binary digits is the same as the addition of the two digits without a carry bit. The least significant pair of bits are first XORed together and the output of this gate is then XORed with the next (more significant) bit, and so on. The output of the final gate is the required parity bit and this is loaded into the transmit register of the USART prior to transmission of the character. Similarly, on receipt, the recomputed parity bit is compared with the expected parity bit and, if different, the PE bit in the USART status register is set, thus indicating to the controlling device that a transmission error has been detected.

3.5.2   Block sum check

With a block (frame)-oriented transmission scheme, an extension to the error-detecting capabilities obtained with the use of a single parity bit per character can be obtained by the use of an additional set of parity bits computed from the complete string of characters in the frame. With this method, each character in the frame is assigned a parity bit as before by the

(a)

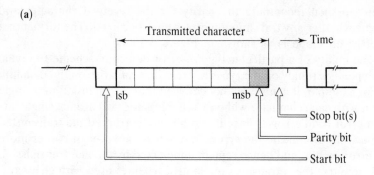

(b)

Bit 1	Bit 2	XOR
0	0	0
0	1	1
1	0	1
1	1	0

(c)

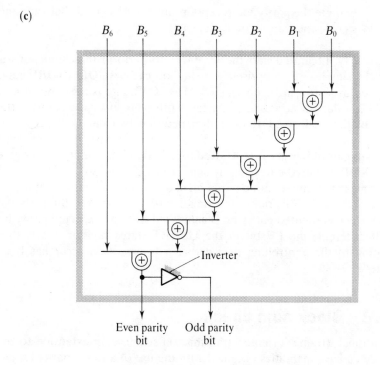

FIGURE 3.15

Parity generation and checking:
(a) character envelope; (b) XOR
truth table; (c) circuit;
(d) examples.

(d)

1001001	1	(Even parity)
1001001	0	(Odd parity)

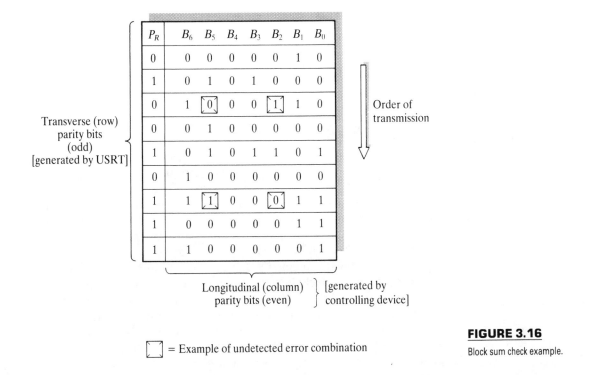

Transverse (row) parity bits (odd) [generated by USRT]

Order of transmission

Longitudinal (column) parity bits (even) } [generated by controlling device]

☐ = Example of undetected error combination

FIGURE 3.16

Block sum check example.

USRT but, in addition, an extra parity bit is generated by the controlling device for each bit position (column) in the complete frame. The resulting set of parity bits for each column is referred to as the **block sum check** and an example is illustrated in Figure 3.16.

To discriminate between the parity bits generated for each character by the USART and the additional set of parity bits generated for each column by the controlling device, the former are known as the **row** or **transverse parity bits** whereas the latter are known as the **column** or **longitudinal parity bits**. Since the final set of column parity bits are each computed by summing (modulo 2) the bits in each column, the final character in the block is known as the block sum check.

The example illustrated in Figure 3.16 uses odd parity for the row and even parity for the column parity bits. It can be readily seen from this example that although two-bit errors in a character may escape the row parity check, they will be detected by the column parity check bits. This is true, of course, only if no two-bit errors occur in the same column at the same time. As the probability of this occurring is not insignificant on some types of line, this method is used only when a frame transmission scheme is being used on transmission lines with only a low error probability rate. For more error-prone (noisy) lines, the more rigorous polynomial type of error-detection method is used.

3.5.3 Polynomial codes

The most common type of error that arises when data are transmitted over lines from the switched telephone network are those caused by a burst of electrical interference due, for example, to noise impulses caused by the switching elements within the exchanges. These, in turn, can cause a string or burst of consecutive bits in a frame to be corrupted; hence, this type of error is known as an **error burst**. An error burst begins and ends with an erroneous bit, although the bits in between may or may not be corrupted. Thus, an error burst is defined as the number of bits between two successive erroneous bits including the two bits in error. Furthermore, when determining the length of an error burst, the last erroneous bit in a burst and the first erroneous bit in the following burst must be separated by B or more correct bits, where B is the length of the error burst. An example showing two different error burst lengths is shown in Figure 3.17. Notice that the first and third bit errors could not be used to define a single 11-bit error burst since an error occurs within the next 11 bits.

Parity, or its derivative block sum check, does not provide a reliable detection scheme against error bursts. In such cases, the most common alternative is based on the use of **polynomial codes**. Polynomial codes are used with frame (or block) transmission schemes; that is, a single set of check digits are generated (computed) for each frame transmitted. These digits, which are based on the actual contents of the frame, are appended by the transmitter at the tail of the frame. The receiver then performs a computation on the complete frame and check digits and, if no errors have been induced, a known result should always be obtained; if a different answer is found, this indicates an error.

The number of check digits per frame varies to suit the worst-case type of transmission errors anticipated, although 16 and 32 bits are the most common. The computed check digits are referred to as the **frame check sequence (FCS)** or the **cyclic redundancy check (CRC)**.

The underlying mathematical theory of polynomial codes is beyond the scope of this book but, essentially, the method exploits the following property of binary numbers if modulo 2 arithmetic is used. Let:

M = a k-bit number (the Message to be transmitted)

R = an n-bit number such that k is greater than n (the Remainder)

G = an $(n + 1)$-bit number (the Divisor or Generator)

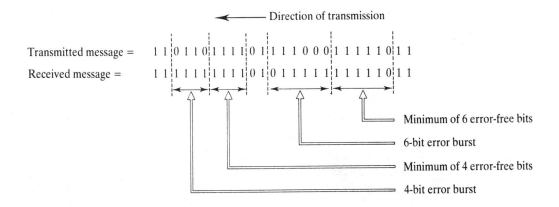

FIGURE 3.17

Error burst examples.

Then if:

$$\frac{M \times 2^n}{G} = Q + \frac{R}{G}, \text{ where } Q \text{ is the quotient,}$$

$$\frac{M \times 2^n + R}{G} = Q, \text{ assuming modulo 2 arithmetic.}$$

This result can readily be confirmed by substituting the expression for $M \times 2^n/G$ into the last equation, giving:

$$\frac{M \times 2^n + R}{G} = Q + \frac{R}{G} + \frac{R}{G}$$

which is equal to Q since any number added to itself modulo 2 will result in zero; that is, the resulting remainder is zero.

To exploit this, the complete frame contents, M, together with an appended set of zeros equal in number to the number of FCS digits to be generated (which is equivalent to mulitplying the message by 2^n where n is the number of FCS digits) are divided modulo 2 by a second binary number G, the **generator polynomial**, containing one more digit than the FCS. The division operation is equivalent to performing the exclusive-OR operation bit by bit in parallel as each bit in the frame is processed. The resulting remainder, R, is then the FCS. This is then transmitted at the tail of the information digits. Similarly, on receipt, the received bit stream including the FCS digits is again divided by the same generator polynomial – that is, $(M \times 2^n + R)/G$ – and, if no errors are present, the resulting remainder is all zeros. If an error is present, however, the remainder is non-zero.

EXAMPLE

A series of 8-bit message blocks (frames) are to be transmitted across a data link using a CRC for error-detection purposes. A generator polynomial of 11001 is to be used. Use an example to illustrate the following:

(a)   the FCS generation process,

(b)   the FCS checking process.

The generation of the FCS for the message 1100110 is shown in Figure 3.18(a). First, four zeros are appended to the message, which is equivalent to multiplying the message by 2^4, since the FCS will be four bits. This is then divided (modulo 2) by the generator polynomial (binary number). The modulo 2 division operation is equivalent to performing the exclusive-OR operation bit by bit in parallel as each bit in the dividend is processed. Also, with modulo 2 arithmetic, a division can be performed, into each partial remainder, providing the two numbers are of the same length; that is, the most significant bits are both 1s. The relative magnitude of both numbers is not considered. The resulting 4-bit remainder (0110) is the FCS, which is then appended at the tail of the original message when the latter is transmitted. The quotient is not used.

At the receiver, the complete received bit sequence is divided by the same generator polynomial used at the transmitter. Two examples are shown in Figure 3.18(b). In the first, no errors are assumed to be present, so the remainder obtained is zero – the quotient is again not used. In the second, however, an error burst of four bits at the tail of the transmitted bit sequence is assumed, and so the resulting remainder is non-zero, indicating a transmission error has occurred.

The choice of generator polynomial is important since it determines the types of error that are detected. For example, an error pattern that is identical, or has a factor identical, to the generator polynomial will generate the same check bits as the correct transmission, and hence will be undetectable. A polynomial which is prime, in the modulo 2 sense, is therefore normally chosen.

EXAMPLE

Assuming the same requirements as were used in the previous example, deduce an example of a received frame that will not be detected.

Any number multiplied by another number will give zero remainder when subsequently divided by the same number:

```
     11100110  =  Arbitrary message (multiplicand)
        11001  =  Generator polynomial (multiplier)
  111001100000 ⎤
   11100110000 ⎬  Partial products
      11100110 ⎦
  100110110110  =  Final product (modulo 2 sum of partial products)
```

Thus, if a received frame (information plus FCS bits) is 100110110110, this will yield zero remainder when divided by 11001, irrespective of the contents of the transmitted frame.

An important characteristic of the polynomial code method is that all bursts of errors with fewer terms than the generator polynomial are detected. As an example, the generator polynomial defined by the CCITT for use on the switched telephone network is:

$$x^{16} + x^{12} + x^5 + x^0$$

In binary form, this is equivalent to 10001000000100001, the power in x being represented as a 1 or 0. In this case, 16 zeros would be appended to the frame contents prior to the generation of the FCS. The latter would then be the 16-bit remainder. The generator polynomial selected will, therefore, detect any one error burst not exceeding 16 bits in length, in addition to all odd errors, any 2-bit errors and any two error bursts not exceeding two bits.

As this type of error-detection method is now very prevalent, especially with the more recent bit-oriented transmission control schemes, all of the integrated circuits available for use with this scheme support this type of error-detection method. Although the requirement to perform multiple division operations to compute the FCS digits may seem difficult to implement at a fast transmitter bit rate in practice, since the arithmetic is all performed modulo 2, it is possible to implement an FCS generator checker very readily in hardware using just a combination of shift registers and exclusive-OR gates (modulo 2 adders). A typical arrangement for the example shown earlier in Figure 3.18 is as shown in Figure 3.19.

In the example, since four FCS digits are to be generated, just a 4-bit shift register is sufficient to represent bits x^3, x^2, x^1 and x^0 in

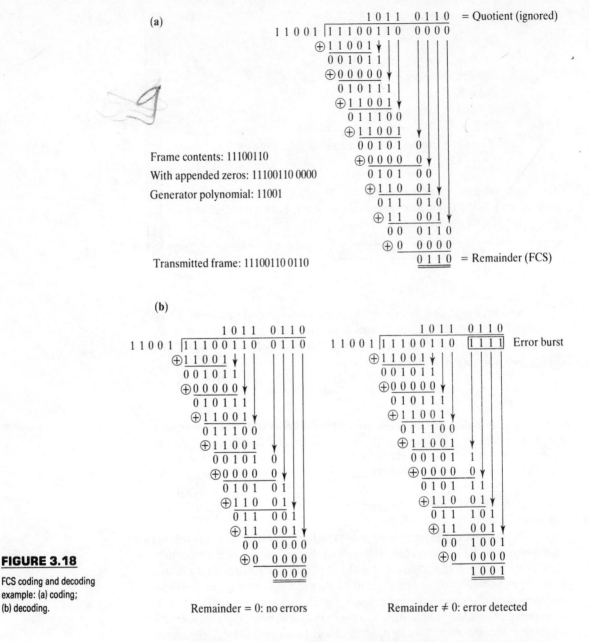

Frame contents: 11100110

With appended zeros: 11100110 0000

Generator polynomial: 11001

Transmitted frame: 11100110 0110

FIGURE 3.18

FCS coding and decoding example: (a) coding; (b) decoding.

Remainder = 0: no errors   Remainder ≠ 0: error detected

the generator polynomial. These are often referred to as the **active bits** of the generator. Thus, with an active generator polynomial of $x^3 + x^0 - 1001$ binary, the two XOR gates between the intermediate shift register elements x^1 and x^2 simply pass on the existing contents of x^0 and x^1, respectively, unmodified while the new states of x^0 and x^3 are determined by the intermediate XOR gate connections.

(a)

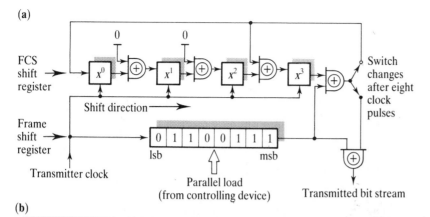

(b)

Transmitter clock (shift) pulses	Frame shift register (SR) contents								FCS SR contents			
	lsb							msb	x^0	x^1	x^2	x^3
0	0	1	1	0	0	1	1	1	0	0	0	0
1	0	0	1	1	0	0	1	1	1	0	0	1
2	0	0	0	1	1	0	0	1	0	1	0	0
3	0	0	0	0	1	1	0	0	1	0	1	1
4	0	0	0	0	0	1	1	0	1	1	0	0
5		0	0	0	0	0	1	1	0	1	1	0
6			0	0	0	0	0	1	1	0	1	0
7				0	0	0	0	0	1	1	0	0
8					0	0	0	0	0	1	1	0
9						0	0	0		0	1	1
10							0	0			0	1
11								0				0

FIGURE 3.19

FCS generator checker hardware.

The frame contents to be transmitted are simultaneously passed from the frame shift register unmodified to the transmission line and the FCS shift register, with the most significant bit first and at a rate determined by the required transmitter bit frequency. An additional bit counter (not shown) is used to determine when all the frame contents bits have been transmitted (8) and at this point switches the output to be the output of element x^3 of the FCS shift register. In the figure, for clarity, the frame shift register is shown to contain the same number of bits as there are bits in the frame. In practice, however, only a, say, 4-bit shift register would need to be used with the example selected and this would be (parallel) loaded with successive 4-bit groups after each preceding 4-bit group had been transmitted to the line. Thus, the first group would be 1110 and the second 0110 in this example.

CHAPTER SUMMARY

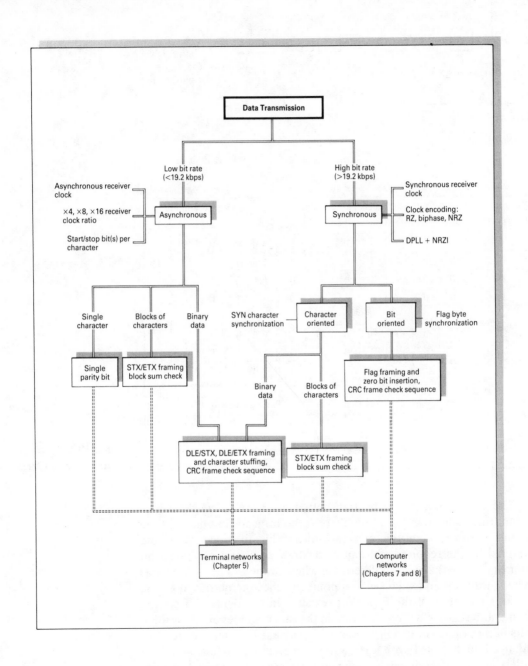

EXERCISES

3.1 (a) Explain the difference between asynchronous and synchronous transmission.

(b) Assuming asynchronous transmission, one start bit, two stop bits, one parity bit and two bits per signalling element, derive the useful information transfer rate in bps for each of the following signalling (baud) rates;

- 300,
- 600,
- 1200,
- 4800.

3.2 (a) With the aid of a diagram, explain the clock (bit) and character synchronization methods used with an asynchronous transmission control scheme.

(b) Draw a schematic diagram showing the arrangement of the various registers used in a UART. Outline the operation of the device and the use of the various bits in the mode and status registers.

3.3 Assuming a synchronous transmission control scheme, explain how character and frame synchronization are achieved:

(a) with a character-oriented link,
(b) with a bit-oriented link.

3.4 (a) Explain what is meant by data transparency and how it may be achieved using:

- character stuffing,
- zero bit insertion.

(b) Draw a schematic diagram showing the arrangement of the various registers used in a USRT. Outline the operation of the device and the use of the various bits in the mode and status registers.

3.5 (a) With the aid of diagrams, explain how clock synchronization may be achieved using:

- bipolar encoding,
- phase (Manchester) encoding.

(b) Explain under what circumstances data encoding and a DPLL circuit may be used to achieve clock synchronization. Also, with the aid of a diagram, explain the operation of the DPLL circuit.

(c) Assuming the receiver is initially out of synchronism, derive the minimum number of bit transitions required for a DPLL circuit to converge to the nominal bit centre of a transmitted waveform. How may this be achieved in practice?

3.6 (a) What are the two basic methods of error control used on a data transmission link? What is the most prevalent method and why?

(b) Explain the operation and application areas of the following error-detection methods:

- parity,
- block sum check,
- polynomial codes.

Give examples showing how each check sequence is derived.

3.7 (a) With the aid of an example, illustrate the type of transmission errors that are not detected with a block sum check. Clearly identify the row and column parity bits used assuming an odd and even parity, respectively.

(b) Sketch a schematic circuit diagram showing how the frame check sequence bits for a transmitted block of information may be generated using a generator polynomial of $x^4 + x^3 + 1$.

(c) Use an example to show how an error pattern equal to the generator polynomial used in (b) will not be detected. List other error patterns that would not be detected with this polynomial.

3.8 (a) Distinguish between an asynchronous and a synchronous transmission control scheme.

(b) A message block comprising a string of ASCII characters is to be transmitted across a data link using a character-oriented transmission control scheme and a block sum check as the error-detection method.

- Produce a sketch showing the format of each message block, including any additional frame control characters, and the position and use of the error-detection bits.
- Explain how clock (bit) and character synchronization would be achieved assuming:
    - an asynchronous transmission control scheme and a receiver clock ratio of x4 of the nominal bit rate,
    - a synchronous transmission control scheme and a Manchester-encoded clocking scheme.

(c) If the requirements of the system were to be changed to allow message blocks comprising pure binary data to be transmitted, outline the changes that would be necessary to the frame synchronization and error-detection methods used.

DATA LINK
PROTOCOLS

4

CHAPTER CONTENTS

CHAPTER OBJECTIVES

When you have completed studying the material in this chapter you should be able to:

- appreciate that a communication protocol is made up of a number of functional components which include error control, flow control and connection management;

- understand the meaning and application areas of echo checking and the X-ON/X-OFF flow control mechanism;

- draw and explain typical frame sequences for both idle RQ and continuous RQ frame-oriented error control schemes;

- understand the differences between selective retransmission and go-back-N control strategies, and draw typical frame sequences to illustrate their operation;

- explain the reason for having a timeout mechanism associated with a protocol and draw typical frame sequences to illustrate its operation;

- describe the operation of a window flow control mechanism and its effect on the range of sequence numbers required;

- understand the various phases associated with the overall management of data transfer across a logical data link.

4.1   INTRODUCTION

Chapter 3 described the circuits and techniques that may be employed to transmit a character or frame of information between two DTEs across a point-to-point data link. In addition, the various error-detection schemes were described which allow the receiving DTE to determine, to a known probability, the presence of any errors in the transmitted bit stream. Alternatively, if forward error correction is used, the receiver can deduce from the received bit stream, again to a known probability, the actual information being transmitted even when errors are present.

In general, however, the techniques described provide only the basic mechanism for transmitting information so, in addition, it is necessary to define a set of rules or control procedures that must be adopted by both communicating parties to ensure the reliable (that is, to a high probability, free of errors and duplicates) exchange of meaningful messages. For example, the various error-detection schemes described in Chapter 3 only allow the receiver to detect when errors have been induced in the transmitted bit stream; they do not provide a means for correcting the erroneous character or frame. Normally, this is accomplished by the controlling device at the destination informing the source that an error has been detected; hence, another copy of the affected character or frame should be sent. The combined error detection/correction cycle is known as **error control**. It is worth noting here that this mechanism necessitates the two controlling devices at each end of a link exchanging an agreed set of defined characters or frames to achieve the reliable transfer of each element. In addition to this type of control, there are often other control mechanisms that must be observed by the two communicating parties, and collectively these constitute the **communication protocol** for the link in question. Some of the basic components of a communication protocol will now be considered.

4.2   ERROR CONTROL

There are two basic strategies in common use to enable a sending DTE to determine whether the receiving DTE has correctly received a transmitted element: **echo checking** and **automatic repeat request (ARQ)**. Each is applicable to a different set of application requirements and hence will be considered separately.

4.2.1   Echo checking

Echo checking is primarily used with character-oriented asynchronous transmission between, for example, a terminal communicating with a remote computer. Normally, terminals have a facility to allow them to be used in either **local** or **remote mode**. In local mode, a character is transmitted to the remote computer and simultaneously printed or displayed on the terminal screen when a key is depressed on the terminal keyboard. In remote mode, however, when a key is selected, the character is transmitted to the remote computer but is not displayed on the terminal screen. Instead, the character received by the computer is retransmitted or *echoed* back to the terminal, when it is then displayed on the terminal screen. If the displayed character does not match the character selected on the keyboard, the user assumes that a transmission error has occurred and, as a result, transmits an agreed control character – a DELete, for example – to inform the computer to ignore the previously transmitted (and hence echoed) character. On receipt of this character, the computer performs the necessary deletion and again echoes the character back to the terminal, at which point the user can confirm that the previous character has been ignored. In fact, the transmission error may have corrupted the echoed character rather than the originally transmitted character, but the control scheme outlined allows for this possibility.

Clearly, echo checking transmits each character at least twice and hence it is relatively inefficient in its use of transmission bandwidth. However, this is not an important consideration in this type of application environment and hence this mechanism is in widespread use for this type of application.

4.2.2   Automatic repeat request

Clearly, echo checking relies on the intelligence of the user for its correct operation. In many data communication situations, however, a user is not involved and so the information is transmitted between two pieces of equipment automatically with no user intervention. Consequently, although it is possible to program one of the pieces of equipment to function as a terminal and use echo checking, in practice there are a number of more efficient alternatives that may be considered. In general, these alternative schemes necessitate the return of only a small control message or frame to acknowledge correct receipt (or otherwise) of each transmitted frame, rather than retransmission of a complete copy of each transmitted frame. This is particularly significant with a frame-oriented transmission scheme as each transmitted element may contain a substantial number of bytes or characters. The use of an acknowledgement scheme in this way is known as automatic repeat request (ARQ). A number of derivatives of the basic scheme are possible, the choice being determined by the relative importance assigned to the use of buffer storage compared with the efficiency of utilization of the available transmission capacity. The two most common alternatives are **idle RQ** (send-and-wait) and **continuous RQ**, the latter employing either a selective retransmission strategy or a go-back-N mechanism. Each of these schemes will now be considered separately.

Idle RQ

This is the simplest ARQ scheme. It requires a minimum of buffer storage for its implementation but, as can be deduced from the example shown in Figure 4.1, it is also the least efficient in its use of transmission capacity.

In many data communication situations, information frames (I-frames) flow in both directions simultaneously. Thus, to discriminate between the sender (source) and receiver (sink) of I-frames at each side of a link, the notion of a **primary** (*P*) and a **secondary** (*S*) are used, respectively. For clarity, only a unidirectional flow of I-frames will be considered initially.

The following points should be noted when interpreting the operation of the example in Figure 4.1:

- *P* can have only one I-frame outstanding (awaiting an acknowledgement or ACK-frame) at a time;
- when *P* initiates the transmission of a frame it starts a timer;
- if *S* receives an I-frame or *P* receives an ACK-frame containing transmission errors, the frame is discarded;
- on receipt of an error-free I-frame, *S* returns an ACK-frame to *P*;
- on receipt of an error-free ACK-frame, *P* can transmit another I-frame;
- if *P* does not receive an ACK-frame within a predefined time interval, known as the **timeout interval**, *P* retransmits the waiting I-frame (Figure 4.1(b)).

The scheme just outlined is also known as **send-and-wait** or **stop-and-wait** and it ensures that *S* receives at least one copy of each frame transmitted by *P*. Clearly, however, if an ACK-frame is itself corrupted and hence ignored by *P* (Figure 4.1(c)), it is possible for *S* to receive two (or more) copies of a particular I-frame. These are known as **duplicates** and, to allow *S* to discriminate between a valid I-frame and a duplicate, each frame transmitted by *P* contains a unique identifier (N, $N + 1$, etc.). *S* thus retains a record of the identifier contained within the last frame it correctly received and discards any frames already correctly received. To allow *P* to resynchronize, *S* returns an ACK-frame for each correctly received frame.

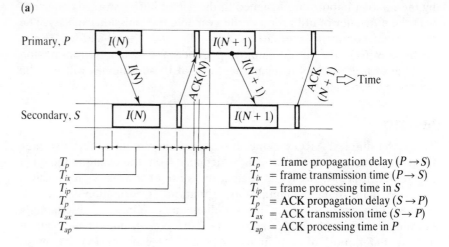

(a)

T_p = frame propagation delay ($P \rightarrow S$)
T_{ix} = frame transmission time ($P \rightarrow S$)
T_{ip} = frame processing time in S
T_p = ACK propagation delay ($S \rightarrow P$)
T_{ax} = ACK transmission time ($S \rightarrow P$)
T_{ap} = ACK processing time in P

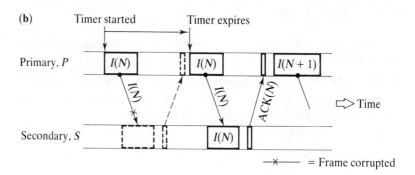

(b)

$-\!\!\times\!\!-$ = Frame corrupted

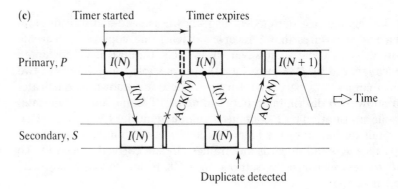

(c)

FIGURE 4.1

Idle RQ frame sequences: (a) no transmission errors; (b) I-frame corrupted; (c) ACK-frame corrupted.

It can be seen from Figure 4.1 that the idle RQ method is inefficient in its use of the available transmission capacity since, in the best case, P must wait a total time, T_t, of:

$$T_t = T_{ix} + T_{ip} + T_{ax} + T_{ap} + 2T_p$$

before transmitting the next I-frame, even if the previous I-frame was correctly received by S. In the worst case, the delay is the total time plus the timeout interval, which clearly must be selected to be longer than the worst-case delay anticipated for P to receive a valid ACK-frame from S. It is for this reason that some idle RQ schemes utilize an additional **negative acknowledgement (NAK) frame** to allow S to report the receipt of a corrupted I-frame immediately, rather than waiting for the timeout mechanism to initiate the retransmission of another copy of the frame. An example of such a scheme is the binary synchronous control protocol which is described in Chapter 5.

The relative magnitude of each component making up T_t varies for different types of data link. It is determined by such factors as the physical separation of the two communicating systems (P and S) and the data transmission rate of the link. In practice, the time to process an I-frame, T_{ip}, and its associated ACK-frame, T_{ap}, are both short compared with their transmission times. Also, since an ACK-frame is much shorter than an I-frame, T_{ax} is negligible compared with T_{ix}. The total time before another frame can be transmitted, therefore, is often approximated to $T_{ix} + 2T_p$.

The efficiency of utilization of the available link capacity, U, is defined as:

$$U = \frac{\text{time for transmitter to transmit a frame}}{\text{time before next frame can be transmitted}}$$

If no transmission errors are assumed:

$$U = \frac{T_{ix}}{T_{ix} + 2T_p} \quad \text{or} \quad U = \frac{1}{1 + \dfrac{2T_p}{T_{ix}}}$$

As was explained in Chapter 2, the propagation delay, T_p, is the time an electrical signal takes to propagate from one side of a link to the other. Thus, it will be the same in both directions and for both I- and ACK-frames. At best, the velocity of propagation is the same as the speed of light, but in most physical media it is actually less than this, 2×10^8 m/s being a typical figure. The propagation delay is then the physical separation, S, divided by the velocity of propagation, V.

The ratio T_p/T_{ix} is important since it relates the signal propagation delay time, and hence the physical separation of the primary and secondary, to the time to transmit the frame, and hence the data transmission rate of the link. Normally, this is given the symbol a and, as was shown in Chapter 2, it can range from a small fraction for short links and relatively low data rates to a large integer value for long links and high data rates. Thus for idle RQ:

$$U = 1$$

for $(1 + 2a)$ less than or equal to 1, and

$$U = \frac{1}{1 + 2a}$$

for $(1 + 2a)$ greater than 1.

EXAMPLE

A series of 1000 bit frames are to be transmitted using an idle RQ protocol. Determine the link efficiency for the following types of data link assuming a data transmission rate of (i) 1 kbps and (ii) 1 Mbps. The velocity of propagation of the link is 2×10^8 m/s and the bit error rate is negligible.

(a)   a twisted pair cable 1 km in length,

(b)   a leased line 200 km in length,

(c)   a satellite link of 50 000 km.

The time taken to transmit a frame, T_{ix}, is given by:

$$T_{ix} = \frac{\text{number of bits in frame, } N_i}{\text{bit rate, } R, \text{ in bps}}$$

At 1 kbps:

$$T_{ix} = \frac{1000}{10^3} = 1 \text{ s}$$

At 1 Mbps:

$$T_{ix} = \frac{1000}{10^6} = 10^{-3} \text{ s}$$

$$T_p = \frac{S}{V} \quad \text{and} \quad U = \frac{1}{1 + \dfrac{2T_p}{T_{ix}}} = \frac{1}{1 + 2a}$$

(a) $$T_p = \frac{10^3}{2 \times 10^8} = 5 \times 10^{-6} \text{ s}$$

(i) $$a = \frac{5 \times 10^{-6}}{1} = 5 \times 10^{-6} \quad \text{and hence } (1 + 2a) \simeq 1 \text{ and } U = 1$$

(ii) $\quad a = \dfrac{5 \times 10^{-6}}{10^{-3}} = 5 \times 10^{-6}$ and hence $(1 + 2a) \simeq 1$ and $U = 1$

(b) $\quad T_p = \dfrac{200 \times 10^3}{2 \times 10^8} = 1 \times 10^{-3}\,\text{s}$

(i) $\quad a = \dfrac{1 \times 10^{-3}}{1} = 1 \times 10^{-3}$ and hence $(1 + 2a) \simeq 1$ and $U = 1$

(ii) $\quad a = \dfrac{1 \times 10^{-3}}{10^{-3}} = 1$ and hence $(1 + 2a) > 1$ and $U = \dfrac{1}{1 + 2} = 0.33$

(c) $\quad T_p = \dfrac{50 \times 10^6}{2 \times 10^8} = 0.25\,\text{s}$

(i) $\quad a = \dfrac{0.25}{1} = 0.25$ and hence $(1 + 2a) > 1$ and $U = \dfrac{1}{1 + 0.5} = 0.67$

(ii) $\quad a = \dfrac{0.25}{10^{-3}} = 250$ and hence $(1 + 2a) > 1$ and $U = \dfrac{1}{1 + 500} = 0.002$

A summary of the results for this example is shown in diagrammatic form in Figure 4.2, from which some interesting observations may be made. Firstly, for relatively short links for which a is less than 1, the link efficiency is (to a good approximation) 100% and is independent of the data rate used. This means that an idle RQ protocol is perfectly adequate for short links and modest data rates. Secondly, for longer terrestrial links, the link efficiency is high for low data rates (and hence values of a) but falls off significantly as the data rate (and hence a) increases. Thirdly, for satellite links, the link efficiency is poor, even for low data rates. It can be concluded, therefore, that an idle RQ protocol is unsuitable for such applications and also for those that involve high bit rate terrestrial links.

The link efficiencies calculated in the example assumed no transmission errors. In practice, however, the links used will have a non-zero bit error rate; hence, to successfully transmit a frame, on average, a number of retransmission attempts, N_r will be required. The expression for link efficiency can be modified, therefore, to give:

$$U = \dfrac{T_{ix}}{N_r T_{ix} + 2 N_r T_p} = \dfrac{1}{N_r\left(1 + \dfrac{2T_p}{T}\right)}$$

(a)

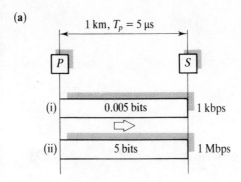

(b)

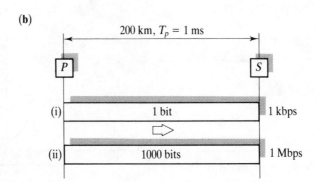

(c)

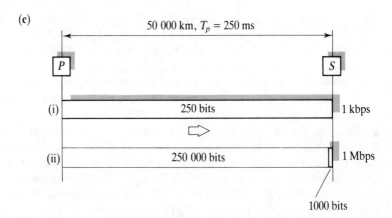

FIGURE 4.2

Effect of propagation delay as a
function of data transmission
rate.

The value of N_r can be derived from a knowledge of the bit error
rate of the link, P. If P is the probability that a bit will be corrupted, then
N_iP is the probability that a frame will be corrupted. For example, a bit
error rate of 10^{-4} means that, on average, 1 bit in 10^4 will be
corrupted. Hence, for, say, 1000 bit frames, the frame error rate will be

$10^3 \times 10^{-4} = 10^{-1}$ or 1 frame in 10. Now, if N_iP is the probability that a frame will be corrupted, then $(1 - N_iP)$ is the probability that an uncorrupted frame will be received. Hence:

$$N_r = \frac{1}{(1 - N_iP)}$$

For example, if $N_iP = 0.5$, $N_r = 2$; that is, if on average 50% of the frames are corrupted, then on average each frame will have to be transmitted twice. This assumes, of course, that ACK-frames are not corrupted but, because of their short length relative to I-frames, this is a reasonable assumption. In practice, therefore, all the link efficiency values must be divided by N_r.

The major advantage of the idle RQ mechanism is that it requires a minimum of buffer storage for its implementation, since both P and S need only contain sufficient storage for one frame. In addition, S must retain only a record of the identifier of the last correctly received frame to enable it to detect duplicates. In general, the various retransmission schemes trade buffer storage requirements for transmission efficiency. Because of its minimum storage requirements, however, idle RQ is used extensively in applications that involve a relatively simple device (such as a terminal or instrument) at one end of the link.

Protocol specification methods

Although the three frame sequence diagrams shown in Figure 4.1, coupled with the descriptive text, are probably sufficient to illustrate the operation of an idle RQ protocol, with more sophisticated protocols it is often not practicable to describe fully the operation of the protocol using just this method. Indeed, as will be seen in this and later chapters of the book, to define the operation of a protocol allowing for all the possible events and error conditions that may arise can be very complex. In general, therefore, protocols are specified using one of a number of more precise methods and formalisms, and frame sequence diagrams of the type shown in Figure 4.1 are normally used simply to illustrate selected aspects of a protocol, rather than as a means of specifying the protocol.

The three most common methods used for specifying a communication protocol are: state-transition diagrams, event-state tables and high-level structured programs. In many instances, however, a protocol is defined as a combination of these and is coupled, where appropriate, with frame (or, more generally, time) sequence diagrams to highlight selected aspects of its operation.

Irrespective of the specification method used, a protocol is treated

(a)

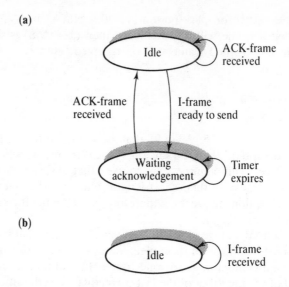

FIGURE 4.3

Idle RQ state-transition diagram:
(a) primary; (b) secondary.

as a **finite-state machine** or **automaton** that can assume, at any instant of time, just one of a number of defined **states**; for example, 'waiting to send a frame' or 'waiting to receive an acknowledgement'. Transitions between states take place as a result of an **event** occurring; for example, a frame becoming ready to send, a frame received or a timer expiring. The various specification methods use different techniques to define the states and transitions associated with the automaton. The principles of the three methods will now be described.

State-transition diagrams   The traditional method used to define the operation of a communication protocol is the **state-transition diagram**. Using this method, the various possible states of the automaton are given names and are shown in the form of circles. Directional arrows are then used to indicate the possible transitions between the states with the incoming event causing the transition stated alongside it. As an example, a state-transition diagram for the primary and secondary side of a link operating with an idle RQ protocol is shown in Figure 4.3(a) and (b), respectively.

As can be seen from the figure, the primary has two defined states: idle (that is, there are no new I-frames ready to be sent and the previous frame has been correctly acknowledged) and waiting acknowledgement, which is self-explanatory. If the automaton is in the idle state and an I-frame becomes ready to be sent, for example, the frame will be transmitted and the automaton will enter the waiting acknowledgement state. (Transmission of a frame is known as the outgoing event or **action** and is often not shown on the diagram for space reasons.) It is important to note here that an incoming event need not necessarily result in a change of state. Typically, such events will cause a certain action to occur (for example, the timer expiring will result in an I-frame being retransmitted) but the automaton will remain in the same state.

Although a state-transition diagram provides a convenient method for diagrammatically representing the possible states, transitions and enabling events associated with a protocol, considerable additional explanatory information is required to define the protocol completely. This includes not only a description of the actions that take place as a result of certain events but also a definition of any additional conditions that are associated with a state and which must be met before a particular transition can occur. Also, if the protocol is complex, the state-transition diagram(s) can become very cluttered, especially if all the possible events are shown. It is for these reasons that, when using a state-transition diagram to define a protocol, a substantial amount of supplementary documentation must be provided.

Event-state tables   A development of the state-transition diagram that effectively presents the same information but in a more concise way is the **event-state table** which, because of its origin, is also known as the **state-transition table**. Using this method, the various automaton states and interface (incoming) events are represented in the form of a table: each possible event is assigned to a specific column in the table while each possible state is assigned to a row. An event-state table thus contains entries corresponding to all the possible automaton states and, for each state, entries for each possible interface (incoming) event. Each entry in the table then defines:

(1)   any conditions that must be satisfied,

(2)   the necessary action to be performed as a result of the event, and

(3)   the new state the automaton will enter.

As an example, an event-state table defining the operation of the primary and secondary with an idle RQ link protocol is shown in Figure 4.4.

This example can be interpreted as follows. The automaton is in the idle state (first row) with an I-frame ready to be sent (second column). The entry in the table indicates that the frame should be transmitted (the action or outgoing event) and that the automaton should enter the waiting acknowledgement state (the new state). Similarly, if the automaton is in the idle state and an ACK-frame is received, this indicates an error condition. Typically, the occurrence of an error condition is noted in an **error log** and the automaton will remain in the same state.

(a)

Present State \ Event	Timer expires	I-frame ready to send	ACK-frame received	
Idle	NA	TxFrame	Error	Action
(0)	0	1	0	New state
Waiting acknowledgement	RetxFrame	Delay	ProcAck	Action
(1)	1	1	0	New state

TxFrame = Transmit frame
RetxFrame = Retransmit frame
ProcAck = Process acknowledgement
NA = No action
Delay = Wait for a defined time delay

(b)

Present State \ Event	I-frame received	
Idle	ProcFrame	Action
(0)	(0)	New state

FIGURE 4.4

Idle RQ event-state tables.

ProcFrame = Process frame

Clearly, an event-state table contains more information about the operation of a protocol than a simple state-transition diagram. Moreover, since the information is in tabular form, it is easy to assimilate and hence understand. However, a set of variables that hold information relating to the current state of the automaton are normally associated with the automaton (**protocol entity**); for example, the identifier to be assigned to the next in-sequence I-frame. As certain incoming events and resulting actions will cause these variables to change, it is therefore also necessary to define precisely the effect of each event and action on them. This is done using either additional descriptive comments or, more usually, structured programs, which define unambiguously the steps to be taken to implement each action.

Structured programs Structured programs are frequently used in protocol specification documents, in collaboration with event-state tables, to describe the detailed actions identified in the state-transition table. This has the advantage that not only can the actions be precisely defined, but also the implementation of the actions in actual program code is made more straightforward. In addition to using a structured programming language to specify the actions associated with the state-transition table, it is also possible to represent the complete contents of the event-state table in the form of a high-level data structure. This has the added advantage that the complete protocol specification is in a form that is readily implemented in program code.

Figure 4.5 shows how the primary side of the idle RQ protocol may be specified in the form of a structured program and Figure 4.6 the secondary side. The programming language used is a form of Pascal; this has been selected because of its general acceptance and relative clarity. To improve readability, however, as is the case in many specification documents, a high-level pseudo-code is used rather than pure code. This means that the implementor normally must make additional refinements to produce the executable code. Wherever possible, however, the names used in the various pseudo-code program segments are the same as those used in the accompanying event-state tables.

For the primary, it is assumed that the main body of the program is executed whenever one of the defined events occurs – *FrameToSend*, *AckReceived* or *Timeout* – and, once activated, the program runs to completion. Furthermore, it is assumed that the various variables associated with the program have been initialized prior to the first event occurring. Thus, the contents of the *EventStateTable* array are assumed to be initialized to contain the appropriate actions and new states as defined in Figure 4.4, and *PresentState* is set to the idle state.

The event causing the program to be run is first assigned to *EventType* before the main body is run. Hence, on receipt of each event, the current contents of *PresentState* and *EventType* are used as indices to the *EventStateTable* array to allow the required action and new state to be accessed from the array. A *Case* statement is then used to initiate the execution of the selected action from the list of action procedures. For clarity, the latter have also been defined in the form of descriptive pseudo-code.

The listing of the secondary is perhaps self-explanatory: whenever an I-frame is received, an ACK-frame is first created with the same identifier as that contained within the received I-frame and this is output to the line. The identifier from the I-frame is then compared with the identifier from the last correctly received frame (*LastIdentifier*). If they are equal, the frame is discarded as a duplicate; if they are not equal, the frame is passed on for further processing and *LastIdentifier* is updated to be the same as the identifier from the accepted frame.

```
program    IdleRQ_Primary;

type       Events = (FrameToSend, AckReceived, Timeout);{List of possible events}
           States = (Idle, WaitAck); {List of automaton states}
           Actions = (NA, TxFrame, Error, RetxFrame, Delay, ProcAck);{List of actions}

var        EventStateTable = array [States, Events] of {Contains the Event State Table}
                              record Action: Actions;
                                         Newstate: States
                              end;
           PresentState: States; {Holds the current automaton state}
           EventType: Events; {Specifies the event that has invoked the program}
           NextIdentifier; {The next in-sequence identifier}
           RetxPointer; {Pointer to the frame buffer containing the I-frame awaiting acknowledgement}
           ErrorLog; {Holds a count of the number of error conditions that have occurred}

procedure Initialize;
           begin Initialize state variables and EventStateTable contents end;

procedure NoAction;
           begin Do nothing end;

procedure TransmitFrame;
           begin Insert NextIdentifier into frame; Output frame to line;
                    Save frame pointer in RetxPointer; Start timer end;

procedure ErrorCondition;
           begin Add 1 to EventLog end;

procedure RetransmitFrame;
           begin Get frame pointer from RetxPointer; Output frame to line; Start timer end;

procedure WaitAwhile
           begin Delay a short time interval end;

procedure ProcessAcknowledgement;
           begin Remove frame pointer from RetxPointer; Increment NextIdentifier; Reset timer end;

begin      {Start of main body}
           Initialize;
           repeat Wait for an incoming event to occur;
                   EventType := type of event;
                   with EventStateTable [PresentState, EventType] do
                      begin case Action of {List of possible actions}
                               NA : NoAction;
                               TxFrame : TransmitFrame;
                               Error : ErrorConditions;
                               RetxFrame : RetransmitFrame;
                               Delay : WaitAwhile;
                               ProcAck : ProcessAcknowledgement
                           end; {Case}
                           PresentState := NewState  {Present state is updated}
                   end
           until Forever
end.
```

List of action procedures

FIGURE 4.5

Specification of the idle RQ primary in the form of a structured program.

```
program    IdleRQ_Secondary;

var        LastIdentifier; {Identifier contained within the last correctly received I-frame}

begin      {Start of main body}
           Initialize LastIdentifier;
           repeat Wait for an I-frame to be received;
                  Create ACK-frame with Identifier = Identifier from received I-frame;
                  Output ACK-frame to line;
                  if Identifier = LastIdentifier then Discard the received I-frame;
                      else begin LastIdentifier := Identifier from the received I-frame;
                                 Pass on frame for further processing
                      end
           until Forever
end.
```

FIGURE 4.6

Program specification of the idle RQ secondary.

Continuous RQ

With a continuous RQ scheme the link utilization is much improved at the expense of increased buffer storage requirements. An example illustrating the transmission of a sequence of I-frames and their returned ACK-frames is shown in Figure 4.7.

The following points should be noted when interpreting the operation of the example in Figure 4.7:

- *P* sends I-frames continuously without waiting for an ACK-frame to be returned;
- *P* retains a copy of each I-frame transmitted in a **retransmission list**;
- the retransmission list operates on a first-in, first-out (FIFO) queue discipline;
- *S* returns an ACK-frame for each correctly received I-frame;
- each I-frame contains a unique identifier which is returned in the corresponding ACK-frame;
- *S* retains an ordered list, the **receive list**, containing the identifiers from the last correctly received I-frames;
- on receipt of an ACK-frame the corresponding I-frame is removed from the retransmission list by *P*.

It can be readily concluded from Figure 4.7 that, in the absence of transmission errors, the link efficiency of a continuous RQ scheme (to a reasonable level of approximation) will always be 100% providing the

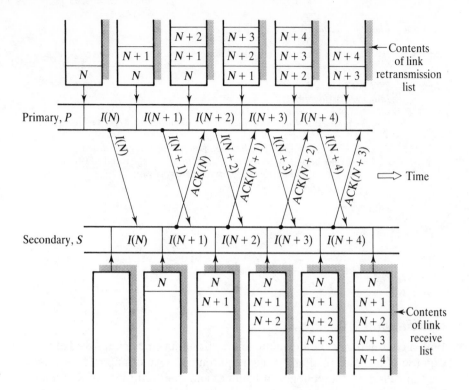

FIGURE 4.7

Continuous RQ frame sequence.

sending of I-frames by P is unrestricted. As will be seen later, however, this is not necessarily the case, as normally there is a limit set on the number of I-frames that P can send before an ACK-frame relating to them is received. Further discussion of the link efficiency with a continuous RQ scheme will, therefore, be delayed until later in the chapter.

A more precise definition of the continuous RQ protocol can now be derived and this is shown in Figures 4.8 (primary) and 4.9 (secondary). Again, a form of descriptive pseudo-code is used to improve readability. Also, as will be expanded upon later, a timeout mechanism similar to that used with an idle RQ protocol must be associated with each frame, and hence this is shown as one of the possible events.

The example illustrated assumes that no transmission errors occur. When an error does occur, two alternative procedures may be followed;

(1) **Selective retransmission**: P detects the out-of-sequence ACK-frame and retransmits just the unacknowledged frame(s).

(2) **Go-back-N**: S detects the receipt of an out-of-sequence I-frame and requests P to retransmit all outstanding unacknowledged I-frames from the last correctly received, and therefore acknowledged, frame.

(a)

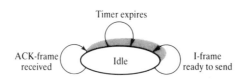

Timer expires

ACK-frame
received

Idle

I-frame
ready to send

(b)

Event Present State	I-frame ready to send	ACK-frame received	Timer expires	
Idle	TxFrame	ProcAck	RetxFrame	Action
(0)	0	0	0	New state

(c)

program *ContinuousRQ_Primary;*

type *Events = (FrameToSend, AckReceived, Timeout); {List of possible events}*
Actions = (TxFrame, ProcAck, RetxFrame); {List of actions}

var *EventStateTable =* **array** *[Events]* **of**
Action : Actions;
EventType : Events ; {Specifies the event that has invoked the program}
NextIdentifier ; {The next in-sequence identifier}
RetxList ; {FIFO queue holding the pointers to the frame buffers of the-I-frames awaiting acknowledgement}

procedure *Initialize;*
  begin *Initialize state variables and EventStateTable contents*
  end;

procedure *TransmitFrame;*
  begin *Insert NextIdentifier into frame;*
    Increment NextIdentifier;
    Output frame to line;
    Insert frame pointer at tail of RetxList;
    Start timer for frame
  end;

procedure *ProcessAcknowledgement;*
  begin *Remove frame pointer from head of RetxList;*
    Reset timer for the frame
  end;

⎫ List of action procedures

procedure *RetransmitFrame;*
  begin *Retransmit the I-frame which has timed out;*
    Start timer
  end;

begin *{Start of main body}*
    Initialize;
    repeat *Wait for an incoming event to occur;*
        EventType := type of event;
        with *EventStateTable [EventType]* **do**
            begin case *Action* **of** *{List of possible actions}*
                TxFrame : TransmitFrame;
                ProcAck : ProcessAcknowledgement;
                RetxFrame : RetransmitFrame
            end *{Case}*
        end
    until *Forever*
end.

FIGURE 4.8

Continuous RQ protocol –
primary: (a) state-transition
diagram; (b) event-state table;
(c) program segment.

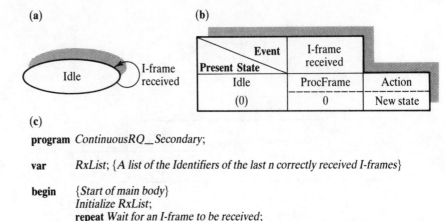

(a)

(b)

(c)

program *ContinuousRQ_Secondary*;

var *RxList; {A list of the Identifiers of the last n correctly received I-frames}*

begin *{Start of main body}*
Initialize RxList;
repeat *Wait for an I-frame to be received;*
Create ACK-frame with Identifier = Identifier from received I-frame;
Output ACK-frame to line;
Add Identifier from received frame to RxList;
Pass frame on for further processing
until *Forever*
end.

FIGURE 4.9

Continuous RQ protocol –
secondary: (a) state-transition
diagram; (b) event-state table;
(c) program segment.

Selective retransmission An example illustrating the effect of a corrupted I-frame with a selective retransmission control strategy is shown in Figure 4.10(a). Its operation is as follows:

- assume I-frame $N + 1$ is corrupted;
- S returns an ACK-frame for each correctly received I-frame as before;
- S returns an ACK for frames $N - 1$, N, $N + 2$, . . .;
- on receipt of the ACK for frame $N + 2$, P detects this is out of sequence and that frame $N + 1$ has not been acknowledged;
- P removes I-frame $N + 2$ from the retransmission list and retransmits I-frame $N + 1$ before transmitting frame $N + 5$.

The effect of the above on the general protocol description presented earlier in Figure 4.8 is that the *ProcessAcknowledgement* procedure must be expanded to determine if there are any frames awaiting acknowledgement ahead of the acknowledged frame and, if there are, to initiate their retransmission. The appropriate additions are thus as shown in Figure 4.10(b).

The last example assumed that an I-frame was corrupted and that the acknowledgement frames were received correctly. Clearly, it is possible for the I-frames to be received correctly by S but for the subsequent ACK-frame(s) to be corrupted. An example illustrating the

(a)

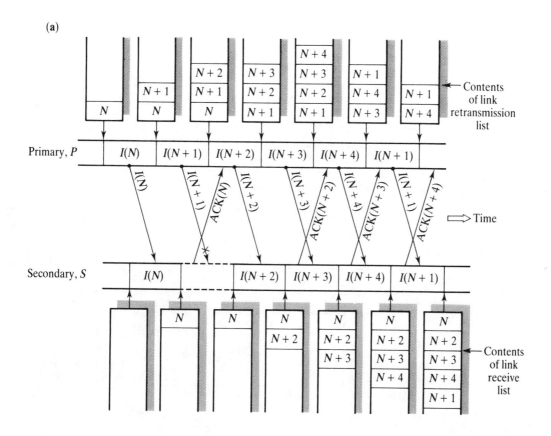

(b)

> **procedure** *ProcessAcknowledgement*; {*Initiates retransmission of unacknowledged frames*}
>
> **begin**   **repeat** *Read Identifier from the frame at the head of the RetxList;*
>   **if** *Identifier = Identifier in ACK-frame*
>   **then** *Remove frame from RetxList*
>   **else begin** *Retransmit the frame;*
>   *Start timer for the frame;*
>   *Insert frame pointer at tail of RetxList*
>   **end**
>   **until** *Identifier = Identifier in ACK-frame*
> **end;**

effect of this on the frame transmission sequence is shown in Figure 4.11(a). The following points should be noted concerning its operation:

- *S* receives each transmitted I-frame correctly;
- assume ACK-frame *N* is corrupted;

FIGURE 4.10

Selective retransmission:
(a) corrupted I-frame [*Note:* ✳ indicates frame corrupted during transmission];
(b) protocol modification I.

(a)

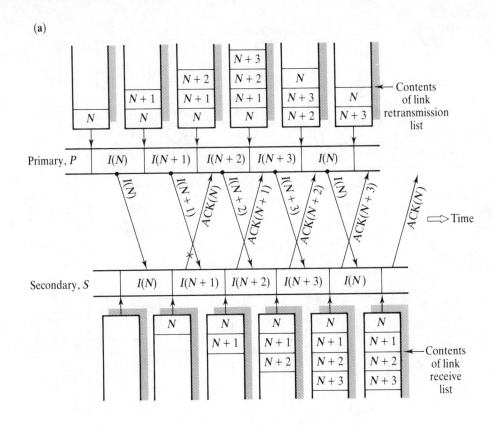

(b)

```
program  ContinuousRQ_Secondary;

var      RxList; {A list of Identifiers of the last n correctly received I-frames}

begin    {Start of main body}
         Initialize RxList;
         repeat Wait for an I-frame to be received;
                Create ACK-frame with Identifier = Identifier from received I-frame;
                Output ACK-frame to line;
                if Identifier from received frame is in the RxList then Discard the frame
                    else begin Add Identifier from received frame to RxList
                                Pass frame on for further processing
                    end

         until Forever

end.
```

FIGURE 4.11

Selective retransmission II:
(a) corrupted ACK-frame [*Note*:
✗ indicates frame corrupted
during transmission];
(b) protocol modification II.

- on receipt of ACK-frame $N + 1$, P detects that there is an outstanding I-frame in the retransmision list (N) and hence retransmits it;

- in the example, on receipt of the retransmitted frame (N), S searches the receive list and determines that N has already been correctly received and is therefore a duplicate;

- S discards the frame but returns an acknowledgement to P to ensure that N is removed from the retransmission list.

The effect of the above on the protocol description presented earlier in Figure 4.9 is that the secondary, on receipt of each I-frame, must search the receive list to determine if the frame is a valid new frame or a duplicate. The necessary addition is readily achieved and is shown in Figure 4.11(b).

It is apparent from the first example that although S receives a correct copy of each frame sent by P, the order of reception is not maintained; for example, S receives I-frames $N + 2$, $N + 3$ and $N + 4$ before frame $N + 1$. This approach, therefore, is primarily used when the frames being transmitted are self-contained entities; that is, the order of reception is not important. As will be seen in later chapters, however, this is not always the case, since large messages are often broken into smaller frame segments for transmission through a communication network. The frames relating to each message must therefore be reassembled in the correct sequence prior to delivery of the complete message to the higher level software within the destination DTE. To achieve this with a selective retransmission control scheme, it is necessary for S to buffer any frames it receives out of sequence until the missing frame(s) is received. Since this may have to be performed for a number of messages simultaneously, the number of frame buffers required can become large and is of course nondeterministic. For this type of communication requirement, therefore, it is more usual to adopt the alternative go-back-N retransmission control scheme.

Go-back-N An example illustrating a typical frame sequence using a go-back-N scheme is shown in Figure 4.12(a). The following points should be noted when interpreting its operation:

- assume I-frame $N + 1$ is corrupted;

- S receives I-frame $N + 2$ out of sequence;

- on receipt of I-frame $N + 2$, S returns a NAK – NAK(N) – frame indicating the identity of the last correctly received I-frame (N);

- S discards I-frame $N + 2$ and all other I-frames received ($N + 3$ and $N + 4$) until the next in-sequence I-frame is received ($N + 1$);

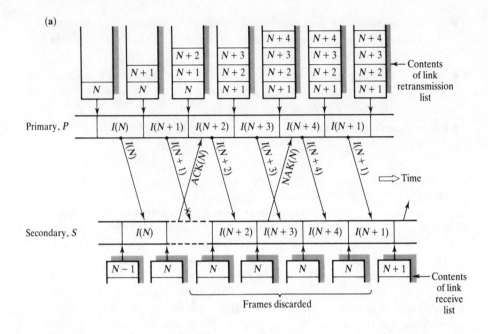

(a)

(b)

```
procedure ProcessAcknowledgement; {Allows for both ACK and NAK frames}

begin      FrameType := Type of acknowledgement frame received;

           case FrameType of
               ACK: {As Figure 4.7 }
               NAK: repeat Read Identifier from frame at head of RetxList
                          if Identifier > Identifier in NAK-frame
                             then begin Retransmit the frame;
                                        Start timer for frame  end
                          until All entries in RetxList have been processed
               end  {Case}
end;
```

(c)

```
program ContinuousRQ_Secondary; {Creates either an ACK or a NAK-frame}

var      RxList; {Holds Identifier of last in-sequence I-frame accepted}

begin    Initialize RxList;
         repeat Wait for an I-frame to be received;
                Read Identifier from received frame
                if Identifier = Identifier in the RxList + 1
                   then begin Create ACK-frame with Identifier = Identifier from RxList;
                              Output ACK-frame to line;
                              Put Identifier into link RxList;
                              Pass frame on for further processing  end
                   else begin Create NAK-frame with Identifier = Identifier from RxList;
                              Output NAK-frame to line;
                              Discard received frame  end
         until Forever
end.
```

FIGURE 4.12

Go-back-N I: (a) corrupted I-frame; (b) modification to primary; (c) modification to secondary.

- on receipt of I-frame $N + 1$, S continues as before.

The effect of the above on the general protocol descriptions presented earlier in Figures 4.8 and 4.9 are as follows:

(1) the *ProcessAcknowledgement* procedure in the primary must be expanded to allow for the received acknowledgement frame being either a positive acknowledgement (ACK) or a negative acknowledgement (NAK); and

(2) the secondary must be modified to allow a NAK-frame to be generated whenever an out-of-sequence I-frame is received.

The two modifications are as shown in Figure 4.12(b) and (c).

Again, it has been assumed in this example that an I-frame was corrupted and that the acknowledgement frames were received correctly. An example illustrating the effect of a corrupted acknowledgement on the frame transmission sequence is shown in Figure 4.13(a). The following points should be noted regarding its operation:

- S receives each transmitted I-frame correctly;
- assume ACK-frames N and $N + 1$ are both corrupted;
- on receipt of ACK-frame $N + 2$, P detects that there are two outstanding I-frames in the retransmission list (N and $N + 1$);
- since it is an ACK-frame rather than a NAK-frame, P implies that the two ACK-frames for I-frames N and $N + 1$ have both been corrupted and hence also accepts ACK ($N + 2$) as an acknowledgement for the two outstanding frames.

It can be deduced from this that the procedure *ProcessAcknowledgement* in the general protocol description defined earlier in Figure 4.8 must be modified to allow a number of I-frames to be acknowledged by a single ACK-frame. The necessary change is given in Figure 4.13(b).

This example shows that with a go-back-N strategy the correct frame sequence is maintained, thus minimizing the amount of buffer storage required for its implementation. But, since some already correctly received frames must be retransmitted, it is less efficient than a selective retransmission scheme in its use of the available transmission capacity.

4.2.3 Sequence numbers I

The three retransmission schemes just described all assume that each I-frame transmitted can be both uniquely identified and its correct sequence relative to other I-frames deduced. In addition, the ACK- and NAK-

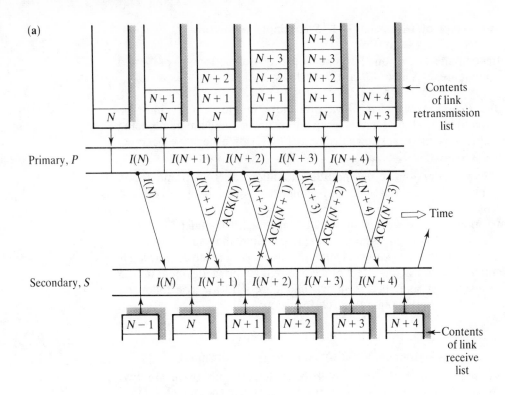

(a)

(b)

procedure *ProcessAcknowledgement;* {*Allows a single ACK-frame to acknowledge multiple frames*}

```
begin        FrameType := Type of acknowledgement frame received;
             case FrameType of
                 ACK: repeat Read Identifier from the frame at the head of the RetxList;
                             Remove frame from RetxList
                       until  Identifier = Identifier in ACK-frame;
                 NAK: repeat Read Identifier from frame at head of RetxList
                              if Identifier > Identifier in NAK-frame
                              then begin Retransmit the frame;
                                          Start timer for the frame  end
                       until All entries in RetxList have been processed
             end  {Case}
end;
```

FIGURE 4.13

Go-back-N II: (a) corrupted ACK-frame; (b) modification to primary.

(where appropriate) frames are assumed to carry similar identification information. This was accomplished in the examples by the use of arbitrary identifiers N, $N + 1$, $N + 2$, etc. In practice these are known as **sequence numbers** since, as the examples illustrate, their main function is to allow the primary and secondary to deduce from the identifier the position or sequence of a frame relative to other frames.

To implement the control functions performed at each side of a link, it is also necessary for both the primary and secondary to retain, in addition to the sequence numbers contained within each frame, a record of the identifiers of the previously correctly received frames on the link. Thus, the primary maintains a send state variable, $V(S)$, which indicates the sequence number it will assign to the next I-frame to be transmitted, and the secondary maintains a receive state variable, $V(R)$, which indicates the next in-sequence I-frame it expects to receive. Their use is as follows:

- each I-frame transmitted by P is assigned a send sequence number, $N(S)$, which is equal to its current $V(S)$;
- each I-frame received by S with an $N(S)$ equal to its current $V(R)$ is accepted by S, which then increments its $V(R)$ by 1;
- when S returns an ACK- or NAK-frame it contains a receive sequence number, $N(R)$, which is equal to its current $V(R)$;
- since $V(R)$ is incremented at S prior to the ACK- or NAK-frame being transmitted, on receipt of an ACK or NAK by P, the $N(R)$ contained within it acknowledges those I-frames in the retransmission list up to and including $N(R) - 1$.

To illustrate the implementation of the above in a diagrammatic form, consider the frame sequence shown in Figure 4.14(a), which is based on a go-back-N control strategy. The following additional points should be noted:

- the two state variables $V(S)$ and $V(R)$ are initialized to zero prior to the transmission of any frames on the link;
- no transmission errors are assumed to have occurred.

Now consider the same example but this time assume that the I-frame with $N(S) = 1$ is corrupted, and therefore ignored (discarded) by S. The new frame sequence is shown in Figure 4.14(b). The following points should be noted:

- since the I-frame with $N(S) = 1$ ($I[N(S) = 1]$) is corrupted, the $V(R)$ at S is not incremented;
- on receipt of $I[N(S) = 2]$, $N(S)$ is not equal to $V(R)$ and hence the frame is discarded by S and a NAK ($[N(R) = 1]$) is returned to P;
- on receipt of NAK$[N(R) = 1]$, the two outstanding unacknowledged I-frames in the retransmission list ($I[N(S) = 1]$ and $I[N(S) = 2]$) are retransmitted by P;
- in the example, each is assumed to be received correctly and acknowledged in the normal way.

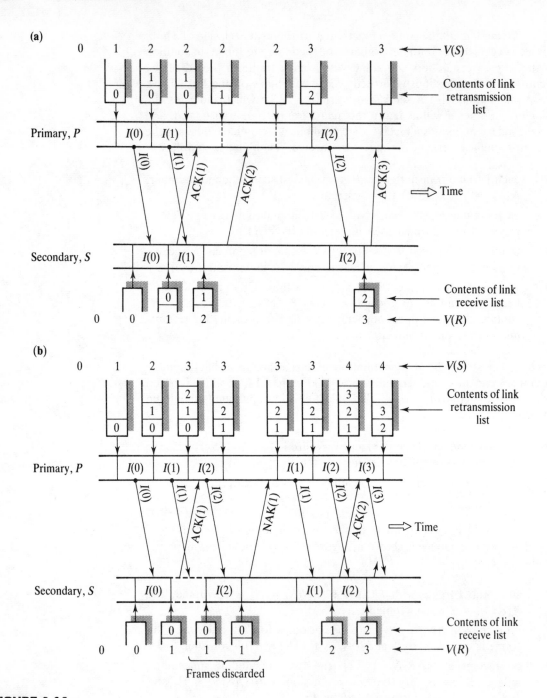

FIGURE 4.14

Sequence numbers: (a) normal
operation; (b) corrupted I-frame.

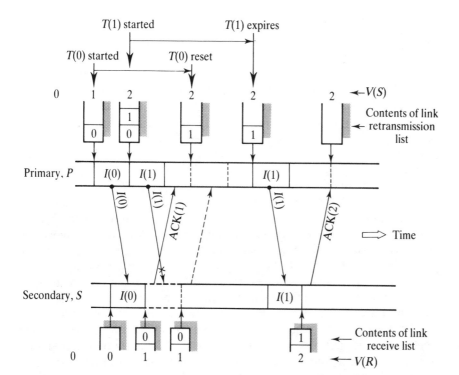

FIGURE 4.15

Timeout mechanism [*Note*: ✕ indicates frame corrupted during transmission].

It can be deduced from the example illustrated in Figure 4.14 that the loss of the frame $I[N(S) = 1]$ was detected only after the next (out-of-sequence) frame $I[N(S) = 2]$ was correctly received by S. Clearly, this necessitates other frames waiting and therefore being transmitted on the link since, if P did not have another frame awaiting transmission, S would not know that frame $I[N(S) = 1]$ was corrupted until another I-frame became ready and was successfully transmitted to S.

To allow for this possibility, P normally employs an additional timeout mechanism similar to the one outlined earlier with the idle RQ control scheme. A number of alternative timeout schemes are possible but the one selected in the earlier protocol definitions assumes a separate timer is started each time an I-frame is transmitted by P, and this is stopped (reset) when an acknowledgement indicating its correct receipt is received. Then, if an acknowledgement for a frame is not received before the timeout interval expires, the frame is retransmitted. This is shown diagrammatically in Figure 4.15.

Clearly, the timeout interval selected must be greater than the worst-case propagation delay between transmitting a frame and receiving the associated acknowledgement. Also, with a timeout mechanism, as was indicated earlier, it is possible for S to receive duplicate copies of a frame in the following way: the frame may be successfully received by S but the resulting acknowledgement frame may be corrupted on its return to P; then, in the absence of an acknowledgement, P assumes that the initial frame has been corrupted and erroneously retransmits another copy. With a go-back-N control scheme, this does not create a problem since the $N(S)$ in the duplicate frame(s) will not be equal to the current $V(R)$ held by S and so it will be discarded automatically. With a selective retransmission scheme, however, the possibility of one or more duplicate frames being sent by P is allowed for by S retaining an ordered list (the receive list) of the sequence numbers of the last N correctly received I-frames. In this way, it can check if a received frame is a duplicate of an already correctly received (and therefore acknowledged) frame or a new frame. The number of frames to be retained, N, is influenced by the flow control algorithm employed, which will be considered in more detail in the next section.

For clarity, all of the foregoing examples have assumed that information frames flow in one direction only and that the return path is used simply for acknowledgement purposes. Normally, however, most communication links carry information frames in both directions. To accommodate for this, each side of such links contains both a primary and a secondary: the first controlling the sequence of I-frames transmitted and the second controlling the sequence of I-frames received. Thus, each side of the link contains both a $V(S)$, which is controlled by the primary, and a $V(R)$, which is controlled by the secondary. Also, although separate ACK- and NAK-frames are utilized, since there is the possibility of an I-frame awaiting transmission in the reverse direction when an ACK or NAK is to be returned, to improve link efficiency some protocols utilize the I-frames flowing in the return direction to carry acknowledgement information relating to the transmission of I-frames in the forward direction. Each I-frame transmitted then contains both an $N(S)$, indicating the send sequence number as was described previously, and an $N(R)$, containing acknowledgement information for the reverse direction. This set-up is referred to as a **piggyback acknowledgement** and an example of a protocol that uses this technique is the high-level data link control protocol, which will be described in Chapter 5.

4.3 FLOW CONTROL

As was indicated earlier, error control is only one component of a communication protocol. Another important and related component is **flow control**. This, as the name implies, is concerned with the control of the rate of transmission of elements (characters or frames) on a link so that the receiver always has sufficient buffer storage resources to accept each element prior to processing. With a character-oriented terminal-to-computer link, for example, if it is servicing many terminals, the remote computer may become temporarily overloaded and hence it will be unable to process all the characters sent to it at the available transmission rates. Similarly, with a frame-oriented selective retransmission scheme, the receiver may run out of buffer storage capacity if it is endeavouring to buffer an indeterminate number of frames. Two of the more common flow control schemes will now be considered.

4.3.1 X-ON/X-OFF

It may be deduced from the discussion in Section 4.2.1 that echo checking is in many ways self-regulating since, if the remote computer runs out of buffer storage, it will cease echoing characters back to the terminal screen and hence the user will automatically stop keying in further characters. Normally, however, the lack of echoed characters from the computer is due to the computer becoming temporarily overloaded. Hence, if the user does not cease transmitting new characters, the computer will incur further and unnecessary processing overheads by simply reading each character and then discarding it.

It is for this reason that an additional automatic flow control facility is often invoked to ensure that a terminal does not send any further characters until an overload condition is cleared. This mechanism is achieved by the computer returning a special control character, X-OFF, to the controlling device within the terminal instructing it to cease transmission. On receipt of the X-OFF character, the terminal then either ignores any further characters entered at the keyboard or it buffers them into a local buffer until the overload is cleared. In this way, the computer does not incur any unnecessary processing overheads associated with them. Then, when the overload condition decays and the computer becomes able to accept further characters, it returns a companion control character, X-ON, to indicate to the terminal control device that it may restart sending characters. This mechanism is also used when a computer is sending characters to a printer or other terminal that cannot sustain the same rate of output as the computer. In such cases, however, it is the controlling device within the printer (or terminal) that controls the flow of characters.

4.3.2 Window mechanisms

Recall that with a frame-oriented link, an idle RQ error control scheme, although inefficient in its use of transmission bandwidth, requires a minimum of buffer storage capacity for its implementation since, after a frame is transmitted by P, it must wait until an acknowledgement is returned by S before transmitting the next frame. The flow of I-frames across the link is therefore automatically tightly controlled.

With a continuous RQ error control scheme, however, P may send I-frames continuously before receiving any acknowledgements. Hence, with this type of scheme, it is clearly possible for the destination to run out of available buffer storage if, for example, it is unable to pass on the frames at the rate they are received. To allow for this possibility, therefore, it is usual to introduce an additional regulating action into such schemes. The approach has many similarities to the one inherent in the idle RQ control scheme in that it essentially sets a limit on the number of I-frames that P may send before receiving an acknowledgement. This is accomplished by P monitoring the number of outstanding (unacknowledged) I-frames currently held in the retransmission list. Then, if the destination side of a link becomes unable to pass on the frames sent to it, S will stop returning acknowledgement frames, the retransmission list at P will build up and this in turn can be interpreted as a signal for P to stop transmitting further frames until acknowledgements start to flow again.

To implement this scheme, a maximum limit is set on the number of I-frames that can be outstanding in the retransmission list. This limit is referred to as the **send window** for the link. Clearly, if this is set to 1, the transmission control scheme reverts to idle RQ with the consequential drop in transmission efficiency. The limit is normally selected, therefore, so that, providing the destination is able to pass on or absorb all frames it receives, the send window does not impair the flow of I-frames across the link. Factors such as the maximum frame size, the amount of buffer storage available and the transmission bit rate must all be considered when selecting the send window.

The operation of this scheme is shown in diagrammatic form in Figure 4.16(a). A record of the number of I-frames awaiting acknowledgement in the retransmission list is maintained by the primary. This is known as the **retransmission count** and, as each I-frame is transmitted, it is incremented by 1. Similarly, as each I-frame is acknowledged, and hence removed from the retransmission list, the retransmission count is decremented by 1. The flow of I-frames is stopped if the retransmission count becomes equal to the send window.

Before describing the additional steps in program pseudo-code, it is perhaps helpful to consider how the higher level (user) software normally communicates with the communication protocol software. Until now, it has been assumed that whenever the higher level software has an I-frame ready to send, the primary is run. Similarly, whenever the secondary receives a valid in-sequence I-frame, this is simply passed on to the higher level software for further processing.

In practice, the interface between the higher level software and the communication protocol software normally takes the form of two FIFO queues, similar to those used for the retransmission list. This is shown in schematic form in Figure 4.16(b). Again, only a unidirectional flow of I-frames is considered for clarity.

Whenever the higher level software wishes to send a frame, it simply inserts the address pointer to where the frame contents are stored in memory into the primary input queue. This, in turn, is interpreted as an event – frame ready to send – and the communication protocol software of the primary is run. Similarly, whenever a received frame is to be passed to the higher level software by the secondary, the latter inserts the frame address pointer at the tail of the output queue which, in turn, causes the higher level software to be run.

The necessary additions to the pseudo-code program for the primary are as shown in Figure 4.16(c). Whenever a new frame pointer is placed in the primary input queue, before initiating the transmission of the frame, the program first determines if the current number of frame pointers in the retransmission list awaiting acknowledgement (RetxCount) is less than the send window for the link. If it is, the frame is transmitted and the frame pointer is transferred to the retransmission list; if it is not, the frame is not transmitted and the pointer is left in the input queue. Then, whenever an ACK-frame is received, a check is made, in addition to the normal acknowledgement processing, to determine if there are any frames awaiting transmission in the link input queue. If there are, one of the queued frames is sent for each frame pointer that is removed from the retransmission list.

As was indicated previously, the use of a timeout mechanism to overcome the problem of lost (corrupted) acknowledgements can also result in duplicate frames being received by S. Hence, to allow for this possibility, S must retain a list of the identifiers of the last N frames correctly received so that, on receipt of each frame, it can deduce whether a correct copy of the frame has previously been received. The number of identifiers, n, is referred to as the **receive window** for the link.

With a go-back-N control scheme, n need only be 1 since, if any out-of-sequence frames are received, S will simply discard them and wait until it receives the next in-sequence frame. With a selective retransmission scheme, however, n must be large enough to ensure that S can determine if a frame has already been received. It may be deduced that the adoption of a maximum limit on the number of I-frames that P may send before receiving any acknowledgements (the send window) means that the number of identifiers to be retained by S need only be the same. Thus, with selective retransmission, it is normal to operate the link with equal send and receive windows so that, in the worst case, S can always determine if a received frame is a valid retransmitted frame or a duplicate.

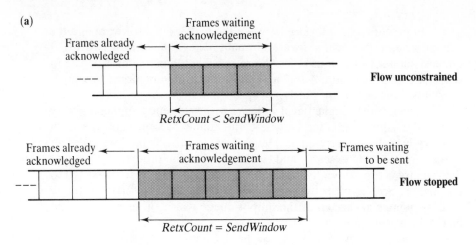

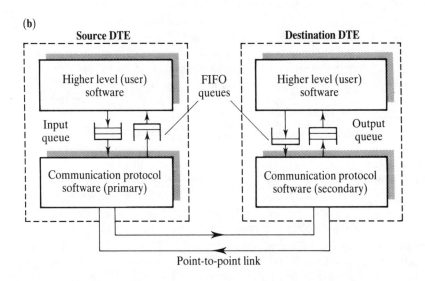

FIGURE 4.16

Implementation of the send
window mechanism.

4.3.3 Sequence numbers II

Until now, it has been assumed that the sequence number inserted into
each frame by P is simply the previous sequence number plus one and that
the range of numbers available is infinite. Another effect of defining a
maximum limit to the number of I-frames that may be in the process of

(c)
.
.
.

procedure *TransmitFrame*; {*Transmits a frame only if Send Window still open*}

    begin if *RetxCount < SendWindow* **then**
                begin *Transmit frame at head of InputQueue; Start timer;*
                    Transfer frame pointer to RetxList;
                    Increment RetxCount **end**

    end;

procedure *ProcessAcknowledgement*; {*Transmits any frame(s) held up by Send Window*}
        Remove acknowledged frame from RetxList;
    begin *Reset timer for frame;*
        Decrement RetxCount
        if *InputQueue non-empty* **then**
                begin *Transmit frame from top of InputQueue;*
                    Start timer;
                    Transfer frame pointer to RetxList;
                    Increment RetxCount **end**

    end;
.
.
.

FIGURE 4.16 (cont.)

Implementation of the send window mechanism.

being transferred across a link, however, is that it then becomes possible to limit the range of sequence numbers required to uniquely identify each frame. The number of identifiers required is a function of both the type of retransmission control scheme used and the size of the send and receive windows.

For example, with an idle RQ control scheme, the send and receive windows are both 1 and hence only two identifiers are required to allow S to determine whether a particular I-frame received is a new frame or a duplicate. Typically, the two identifiers would be 0 and 1, thereby requiring just a single binary digit for its implementation, and the send and receive variables would then be incremented modulo 2 by P and S, respectively.

With a go-back-N control scheme and a send window of, say, K, the number of identifiers must be at least $K + 1$. This can best be seen by considering the example shown in Figure 4.17.

The following should be noted when interpreting this example:

- the send window used in the example is 3;
- P sends its full window of three I-frames;
- the three I-frames are correctly received by S;
- the three ACK-frames returned by S are all corrupted;

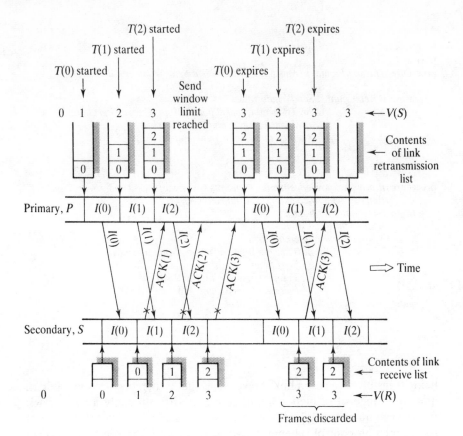

FIGURE 4.17

Window mechanism [*Note*: ✗ indicates frame corrupted during transmission].

- P times out each I-frame and retransmits them;
- S discards each duplicate I-frame and acknowledges all of them with a single ACK-frame.

Now, if only three identifiers are used – that is, the same number as the send window – S would not be able to determine whether I-frame $I[0]$ was a new frame or a duplicate, since 0 would then be the next in-sequence identifier. Hence, with four identifiers (the send window + 1), S would know that the next in-sequence I-frame would have an identifier of 3, whereas the retransmitted (duplicate) frame would have an identifier of 0. It would, therefore, correctly discard the latter.

With a selective retransmission scheme and a send and receive window of K, the number of identifiers must not be less than $2K + 1$. Again, this can be deduced by considering the case when P sends a full window of K frames and all the subsequent acknowledgements are corrupted. S must be able to determine if any of the next K frames are new frames or retransmissions of the previous batch of correctly received frames. The only way of ensuring that S can deduce this is to assign a completely new set of K identifiers to the next window of I-frames transmitted, thus necessitating at least $2K + 1$ identifiers.

In practice, since the identifier of a frame is in binary form, a set number of binary digits must be reserved for its use. For example, with a send window of, say, 7 and a go-back-N control scheme, three binary digits would be required for the send and receive sequence numbers yielding eight possible identifiers: 0 through 7. The send and receive variables would then be incremented modulo 8 by P and S, respectively.

4.3.4 Link efficiency

During the discussion of the idle RQ protocol, it was shown that the link efficiency, U, to a good approximation, is a function of the time to transmit an I-frame, T_{ix}, and the propagation delay of the link, T_p. However, for links with a T_p greater than T_{ix}, the link efficiency is also influenced by the send window, K.

Recall that the example in the section on idle RQ (Figure 4.2) showed that with a typical satellite link T_p is often much greater than T_{ix}. In this example, T_{ix} was derived to be 1 ms and T_p in the order of 250 ms, for a 1 Mbps channel and 1000 bit frames. Theoretically, therefore, it is possible for 250 such frames to be in transmission between P and S at any one time. Hence, to achieve a link efficiency of 100%, a send window in excess of 500 is required, since an ACK-frame for the first frame in the sequence will not be received until 500 ms ($2T_p$) later.

In general, the link efficiency, U, for a send window of K, is given by:

$$U = 1$$

providing K is greater than $1 + 2a$ and:

$$U = \frac{KT_{ix}}{T_{ix} + 2T_p} = \frac{K}{1 + \dfrac{2T_p}{T_{ix}}} = \frac{K}{1 + 2a}$$

providing K is less than $1 + 2a$.

This can best be seen by considering the case when $T_p = T_{ix}$. In this case, the last bit of a frame sent by P will not be received until $2T_p$ (and hence $2T_{ix}$) later. The associated ACK-frame will then take a further T_p (and hence T_{ix}) to be received by P. If $K = 1$ (idle RQ), then K is less than (idle RQ), then K is less than $1 + 2a$ and $U = \frac{1}{3}$. To raise this to 100% (K greater than $1 + 2a$), K must be in excess of 3; that is, three or more frames must be sent by P before an ACK is received.

EXAMPLE

A series of 1000 bit frames are to be transmitted using a continuous RQ protocol. Determine the link efficiency for the following types of data link if the velocity of propagation is 2×10^8 m/s and the bit error rates of the links are all negligibly low.

(a)   a 1-km link of 1 Mbps and a send window $K = 2$,

(b)   a 10-km link of 200 Mbps and a send window $K = 7$,

(c)   a 50 000-km satellite link of 2 Mbps and a send window $K = 127$.

$$T_p = \frac{S}{V} \qquad T_{ix} = \frac{N_i}{R} \qquad a = \frac{T_p}{T_{ix}}$$

(a) $T_p = \dfrac{10^3}{2 \times 10^8} = 5 \times 10^{-6} \text{ s}$

$T_{ix} = \dfrac{1000}{1 \times 10^6} = 10^{-3} \text{ s}$

Hence:

$$a = \frac{5 \times 10^{-6}}{1 \times 10^{-3}} = 5 \times 10^{-3}$$

Now $K = 2$ is greater than $1 + 2a$ and hence $U = 1$.

(b) $T_p = \dfrac{10 \times 10^3}{2 \times 10^8} = 5 \times 10^{-5} \text{ s}$

$T_{ix} = \dfrac{1000}{200 \times 10^6} = 5 \times 10^{-6} \text{ s}$

Hence:

$$a = \frac{5 \times 10^{-5}}{5 \times 10^{-6}} = 10$$

Now $K = 7$ is less than $1 + 2a$ and hence:

$$U = \frac{K}{1 + 2a} = \frac{7}{1 + 20} = 0.33$$

(c) $\quad T_p = \frac{50 \times 10^6}{2 \times 10^8} = 0.25 \text{ s}$

$\quad\quad T_{ix} = \frac{1000}{2 \times 10^6} = 5 \times 10^{-4} \text{ s}$

Hence:

$$a = \frac{0.25}{5 \times 10^{-4}} = 500$$

Now $K = 127$ is less than $1 + 2a$ and hence:

$$U = \frac{K}{1 + 2a} = \frac{127}{1 + 1000} = 0.127$$

It can be deduced from these results that the choice of K has a strong impact on the link efficiency in certain cases. As can be seen, even with a K of 127 the link efficiency of a satellite link is still very low. It is for this reason that a large K (and hence sequence number range) is utilized. This also applies equally to terrestrial links operating at high bit rates, but this will be expanded upon in later chapters.

The results calculated in the example assumed no transmission errors. The effect of such errors is to reduce the link efficiency further, since some frames must be retransmitted. However, the effect differs slightly for the two types of retransmission scheme. For example, with a selective retransmission scheme, U is reduced simply by the number of retransmission attempts to transmit each frame, N_r, since only the corrupted frame is retransmitted. As was shown earlier in the chapter, if P is the bit error rate of the link and N_i is the average length of an I-frame, then:

$$N_r = \frac{1}{1 - N_i P}$$

The modified value of U is thus:

$$U = \frac{1}{N_r} = (1 - N_iP)$$

for K greater than $1 + 2a$ and:

$$U = \frac{K}{N_r(1 + 2a)} = \frac{K(1 - N_iP)}{1 + 2a}$$

for K less than $1 + 2a$.

With a go-back-N scheme, the link efficiency is reduced further since, if a frame is corrupted, then more than one frame must be retransmitted. Again, the number of additional frames to be retransmitted will be determined by the magnitude of K relative to $1 + 2a$.

For K greater than $1 + 2a$, U will be reduced in a similar way to that in selective retransmission except that when an error does occur, then $(2a + 2)$ frames must be retransmitted. This can be deduced by determining the time expired before P is informed that a corrupted frame has been received by S: a corrupted frame is detected by S after $T_p + 2T_{ix}$ (that is, after the following error-free frame has been received), the resulting NAK frame then takes a further T_p to propagate back to P, giving a total time of $2T_p + 2T_{ix}$. In time T_p, P has sent a frames and hence in time $2T_p + 2T_{ix}$, P has sent $2a + 2$ frames.

If K is less than $1 + 2a$, then, in the limit, K frames must be retransmitted whenever a frame is corrupted. This will only occur, however, when one of the frames within a window is corrupted. The probability of a frame within a window of K frames being corrupted is KN_iP. For example, if the probability of a frame being corrupted is $\frac{1}{6}$ and $K = 6$, then on average every window will have a corrupted frame; if $K = 3$, however, only every other window will be affected. Thus:

$$U = 1 - 2N_iP(a + 1)$$

for K greater than $1 + 2a$ and:

$$U = \frac{K(1 - KN_iP)}{1 + 2a}$$

for K less than $1 + 2a$.

It should be stressed that the formulae given are only approximations since, in addition to the earlier approximations, they do not take into account the effect of retransmitted frames also being corrupted. Nevertheless, they give a good guide both to the type of performance that can be expected and to the relative performance of each method.

EXAMPLE

A series of 1000 bit frames are to be transmitted across a data link 100 km in length at 20 Mbps. If the link has a velocity of propagation of 2×10^8 m/s and a bit error rate of 4×10^{-5}, determine the link utilization (efficiency) using the following link protocols:

(a)   idle RQ,

(b)   selective retransmission and a send window of 10,

(c)   go-back-N and a send window of 10.

$$T_p = \frac{S}{V} = \frac{100 \times 10^3}{2 \times 10^8} = 5 \times 10^{-4} \text{ s}$$

$$T_{ix} = \frac{N_i}{R} = \frac{1000}{20 \times 10^6} = 5 \times 10^{-5} \text{ s}$$

$$a = \frac{T_p}{T_{ix}} = \frac{5 \times 10^{-4}}{5 \times 10^{-5}} = 10$$

Hence:

$$1 + 2a = 21$$

Now:

$$N_i P = 1000 \times 4 \times 10^{-5} = 4 \times 10^{-2}$$

Hence:

$$1 - N_i P = 96 \times 10^{-2} \quad \text{and} \quad 1 + K N_i P = 1 + 10 \times 4 \times 10^{-2} = 1.4$$

(a) $$U = \frac{(1 - N_i P)}{1 + 2a} = \frac{96 \times 10^{-2}}{21} = 0.046$$

(b)   For K less than $1 + 2a$:

$$U = \frac{K(1 - N_i P)}{1 + 2a} = \frac{10 \times 96 \times 10^{-2}}{21} = 0.46$$

(c)   For K less than $1 + 2a$:

$$U = \frac{K(1 - K N_i P)}{1 + 2a} = \frac{10 \times 6 \times 10^{-1}}{21} = 0.286$$

4.4 LINK MANAGEMENT

Error and flow control are both concerned with the correct transfer (in sequence and without error or duplication) of characters or frames across an imperfect communication link. For the schemes outlined to function correctly, it has been assumed that both communicating parties have been primed so that they are ready to exchange information. With a frame-oriented link, for example, it is necessary to ensure that both sides of the link start with the same send and receive variables before any information frames are transmitted. In general, this is known as the initialization or **link set-up** phase and, after all data has been exchanged across a link, this is normally followed by the **link disconnection phase**. Since the link set-up and disconnection phases are not concerned with the actual transfer of user data, they are collectively referred to as **link management** and some aspects of this will now be described.

For a link between a terminal and a computer with a relatively short separation (up to, say, 20 m), the management functions can be achieved by exchanging signals on additional (control) lines to those used for data. This is often known as a **handshake procedure**: when the user wishes to open a dialogue with the computer, the user first switches the terminal on and this results in one of the control lines becoming set (active), thus indicating to the computer that the terminal is ready to send characters. The terminal must then wait until the computer responds by setting a corresponding response control line to indicate that it is ready to receive characters. The exchange of characters as outlined previously can then commence. There are, in fact, internationally agreed standards laid down for this type of interconnection. An example is the RS-232C (V.24) interface, which was discussed in Chapter 2.

When the two communicating devices are, say, computers using a frame-oriented link, the link is established (set up) by the link-level protocol within each computer exchanging an agreed set of **control** or **supervisory frames**. In the previous example, the link was established by the user switching on the terminal. In the case of a computer-to-computer link, however, the setting up of a link is normally initiated as a result of some higher level software (an application program for example) in one of the computers signalling to the communication software that it wishes to open a dialogue with a remote computer. Typically, this might take the form of a send or transfer request primitive being executed in the application program which, in turn, causes the communication software to be invoked. In practice, as will be seen in later chapters, the communication software is normally made up of a number of separate protocol layers, each responsible for a specific function in the overall communication

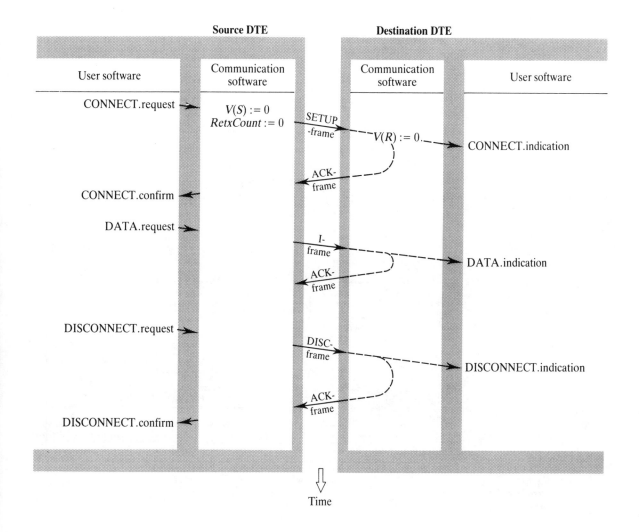

Source DTE

Destination DTE

User software Communication software Communication software User software

CONNECT.request →

$V(S) := 0$
$RetxCount := 0$

SETUP-frame

$V(R) := 0.$

CONNECT.indication

ACK-frame

CONNECT.confirm ←

DATA.request →

I-frame

DATA.indication

ACK-frame

DISCONNECT.request →

DISC-frame

DISCONNECT.indication

ACK-frame

DISCONNECT.confirm ←

Time

FIGURE 4.18

Time (frame) sequence diagram including link set-up.

strategy. A typical set of messages used by a higher (user) software layer together with their interpretation by the lower communication (link-level protocol) software is shown in Figure 4.18.

In the figure, the initial primitive issued by the user software is assumed to be a connect request, which results firstly in a connect request message being passed to the communication software. On receipt of this, the latter first initializes the $V(S)$ and RetxCount state variables to zero and then sends a (link) SETUP frame to the communication software in the destination DTE. On receipt of this, the latter first initializes $V(R)$ to

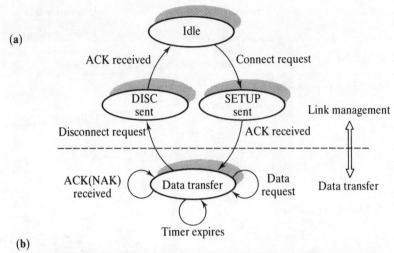

(a)

(b)

Present State ＼ Event	Connect request	Data request	Disconnect request	ACK received	Timer expires	
Idle	Setup					Action
(0)	1					New state
SETUP sent				ProcAck	RetxFrame	Action
(1)				2	1	New state
Data transfer		TxFrame	Disc	ProcAck	RetxFrame	Action
(2)		2	3	2	2	New state
DISC sent				ProcAck	RetxFrame	Action
(3)				0	3	New state

⎵⎵⎵⎵⎵⎵ Messages from user interface   Frames received from link   Internal event

FIGURE 4.19

Communication protocol specification: (a) state-transition diagram: (b) event-state table.

zero and then passes a connect indication message to the user software in the destination DTE. It then returns an ACK-frame to the source DTE and, in turn, the communication software passes a connect confirmation message to the user software. A logical communication path between the two user software layers has now been established and the various variables associated with the underlying link-level protocol initialized.

Next, the data associated with the message are transferred by the communication software within one or more I-frames, as described earlier, using one of the selected link-level protocols. Finally, after all the data have been transferred, the logical communication path between the two

```
program ContinuousRQ_ Primary; {Modifications to incorporate link management}

type     Events = (ConnectRequest, DataRequest, DisconnectRequest,
         ACKReceived, Timeout );
         States = (Idle, SetupSent, DataTransfer, DiscSent);
         Actions = (NA, Setup, Disc, TxFrame, ProcAck, RetxFrame);
         IncomingMessage = (Connect, Data, Disconnect); {List of user messages}

var      {As Figure 4.5}
         .
         .
         .

         {List of Action and Initialize procedures }
         .
         .
         .



begin    {Start of main body}
         Initialize;
         repeat Wait for an incoming event to occur;
                EventType := type of event
                with EventStateTable [PresentState, EventType] do
                     begin case Action of {List of action procedure calls}
                         NA :
                        Setup :
                      TxFrame :
                        Disc :
                      ProcAck :
                    RetxFrame :
                         end; {Case }
                         PresentState := NewState
                end
         until Forever
end.
```

FIGURE 4.20

Protocol specification in pseudo-code form.

user software layers is disconnected in a manner similar to that outlined for the set-up phase. (Note here that unidirectional flow is assumed for clarity.)

The addition of a link set-up and disconnection phase into state-transition diagrams and tables is readily achieved and the updated versions for the primary are shown in Figure 4.19. A continuous RQ protocol is assumed, although the link management section is in many ways indepen-dent of the type of protocol used to control the flow of I-frames. For clarity, only those entries in the event-state table that result in an action taking place are shown. Typically, all the other entries would correspond to no action taking place and the protocol entity remaining in the same state.

As has been shown earlier, it is also possible to derive a specification for the protocol from the event-state table definition in a high-level programming language. Since in this instance the user software must, in addition to originating requests (connect, data and disconnect), also receive the corresponding responses (connect and disconnect confirmation) from the communication software, two queues are required: an input queue for the requests and an output queue for the responses. Typically, the user request would be written into a message buffer in memory by the user software and the address pointer of the buffer inserted into the input queue. Then, when the communication software is invoked, the type of request would first be decoded, before consulting the array containing the event-state table definitions, to determine the necessary action and new state. Similarly, whenever a response is to be passed from the communication software to the user software, the address pointer of the memory buffer containing the response message would be inserted into the output queue. An outline structure of the pseudo-code definition of the primary is given in Figure 4.20. Since in practice I-frames often flow in both directions simultaneously, the software must, on receipt of a frame from the communication link, first determine the type of frame before consulting the event-state table array.

It can be concluded from these descriptions that the user and communication software in each computer is organized into layers and that each layer operates independently. Thus, in the example, the higher software layers communicate by exchanging messages using the well-defined set of services provided by the lower communication layer. Furthermore, the types of frames and messages used by each layer vary, since they each perform a different and complementary function. The function and operation of the various protocol layers normally used for computer-to-computer communication will be described in later chapters.

CHAPTER SUMMARY

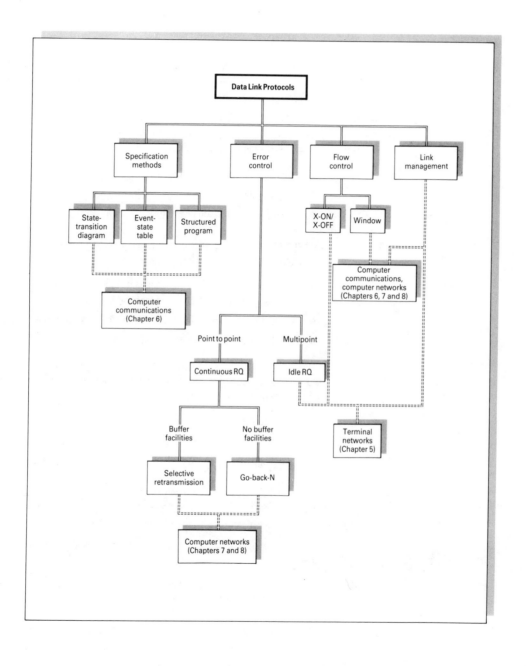

EXERCISES

4.1   Assume a terminal is connected to a computer. Explain the two techniques that are used to achieve error control and flow control. Clearly outline the effect of each mechanism on the user of the terminal.

4.2   (a)   With the aid of frame sequence diagrams, describe the difference between an idle RQ and a continuous RQ error control procedure. For clarity, assume that no frames are corrupted during transmission.

(b)   Using a continuous RQ error control scheme as an example, describe how the operation of the primary and secondary side of a link may be defined in the form of a finite-state machine and:

- a state-transition diagram,
- a state-transition table,
- a high-level language program segment written in pseudo-code.

4.3   (a)   With the aid of frame sequence diagrams and assuming an idle RQ error control procedure, describe the following:

- the factors influencing the minimum time delay between the transmission of two consecutive information frames,
- how the loss of a corrupted information frame is overcome,
- how the loss of a corrupted acknowledgement frame is overcome.

(b)   Use the frame sequence diagrams of (a) to define the operation of the primary and secondary sides of a link that is operating with an idle RQ error control scheme using:

- a state-transition diagram,
- a state-transition table,
- a program segment written in a pseudo high-level language.

4.4   A series of information frames with a mean length of 1000 bits are to be transmitted across the following data links using an idle RQ protocol. If the velocity of propagation of the links is 2×10^8 m/s, determine the link efficiency (utilization) for each type of link.

(a)   A 10-km link with a bit error rate of 10^{-4} and a data transmission rate of 9600 bps.

(b)   A 500-m link with a bit error rate of 10^{-6} and a data transmission rate of 10 Mbps.

4.5   (a)   With the aid of frame sequence diagrams and assuming a selective retransmission error control scheme, describe how the following are overcome:

- a corrupted information frame,

- a corrupted acknowledgement frame.

(b)   Use the frame sequence diagrams of (a) to define the operation of the primary and secondary sides of a link that is operating with a continuous RQ and selective retransmission error control scheme using:

- a state-transition diagram,
- a state-transition table,
- a program segment written in pseudo high-level code.

Deduce the factors that influence the maximum size of the link receive list with a selective retransmission strategy.

4.6   With the aid of frame sequence diagrams and assuming a go-back-N error control scheme, describe how the following are overcome:

(a)   a corrupted information frame,

(b)   a corrupted acknowledgement frame,

(c)   a corrupted NAK-frame.

Include in these diagrams the contents of the link retransmission and receive lists in addition to the state of the send and receive sequence variables as each frame is transmitted and received.

4.7   What is the function of a timeout mechanism? Use frame sequence diagrams to illustrate how a timeout interval may be used to overcome the effect of a corrupted information frame assuming:

(a)   a selective retransmission control scheme,

(b)   a go-back-N control scheme.

Deduce the factors that determine the duration of the timeout interval to be used for a link. How are duplicates handled with each scheme?

4.8   (a)   Discriminate between the send window and receive window for a link and how they are related with:

- a selective retransmission scheme,
- a go-back-N control scheme.

(b)   With the aid of frame sequence diagrams, illustrate the effect of a send window flow control limit being reached. Assume a send window of 2 and a go-back-N error control procedure.

4.9   Assuming a send window of K, deduce the minimum range of sequence numbers (frame identifiers) required with each of the following error control schemes:

(a)   idle RQ,

(b)   selective retransmission,

(c)   go-back-N.

Clearly identify the condition when the maximum number of identifiers is in use.

4.10   A series of information frames with a mean length of 1000 bits is to be transmitted across a data link of 4000 km length at a data rate of 2 Mbps. If the link has a velocity of propagation of 2×10^8 m/s and a bit error rate of 10^{-4}, determine the link efficiency using the following link protocols:

(a)   idle RQ,

(b)   selective retransmission and a send window of 7,

(c)   go-back-N and a send window of 127.

4.11   (a)   Explain what is meant by the term link management. Use an example set of user primitives and a time sequence diagram to show how a logical communication path is established (set up) between two systems and subsequently cleared (disconnected).

        (b)   Assuming the user primitives used in (a) and an idle RQ error and flow control mechanism, derive:

                •   a state-transition diagram,

                •   a state-transition table,

        for the protocol. Outline how the protocol could be defined in a pseudo high-level programming language.

TERMINAL NETWORKS

5

CHAPTER CONTENTS

5

CHAPTER OBJECTIVES

When you have completed studying the material in this chapter you should be able to:

- describe the most commonly used information codes in terminal-based networks;

- understand the role of the additional communication devices that are used in interactive character-mode terminal networks and explain their operation;

- understand the role of the additional communication devices that are used in block-mode terminal networks and explain their operation;

- describe the binary synchronous control protocol as used in poll–select networks and appreciate its limitations;

- understand the alternative modes of operation of the high-level data link control protocol and describe selected aspects of its operation.

5.1 INTRODUCTION

Terminal-based networks in their various forms are probably the most prevalent type of distributed system in use today. They range from systems comprising a small number of relatively unintelligent character-mode terminals linked directly to a locally situated computer, to systems containing a large number of sophisticated block-mode terminals linked through a network of additional communication equipment to a powerful central computing complex. There is a common thread that links the different forms of system together, however; that is, there is normally just a single central computer, or computing complex, to which all the terminals in the network require access. In addition, because of the limited intelligence associated with a terminal, the communication protocols are relatively simple, certainly in comparison with those used in computer-to-computer communication networks. This chapter is concerned with the range of communication equipment used in such networks and also with the communication protocols used for their operation.

5.2 TERMINAL CHARACTERISTICS

Since the advent of the microprocessor in the mid 1970s all terminals have had a degree of local intelligence, or processing capability, associated with them. The level of intelligence varies, however, from one type of terminal to another. It is determined by the amount of local processing to be performed and also the type of communication protocol being used to control the flow of information to and from the terminal. Essentially, therefore, the local processor performs two functions:

(1) It controls the operation of the terminal; that is, the reception and processing of characters entered at the terminal keyboard and the output of characters to the terminal display screen.

(2) It controls the exchange of characters or blocks of characters between the terminal and the remote computer, or its agent.

The diagrammatic form of a terminal is as shown in Figure 5.1.

The different classes of terminal in common use, listed in order of increasing processing capability, are:

- single-character (also known as scroll-mode) interactive terminals,
- screen-mode interactive terminals,

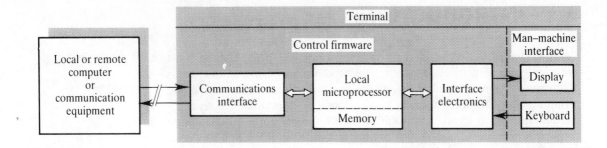

FIGURE 5.1

Generalized terminal schematic.

- data entry/point-of-sale terminals,
- remote job entry terminals.

For the purpose of this chapter, however, terminals are perhaps best classified according to the type of communication protocol they are able to support. In general, both scroll- and screen-mode interactive terminals incorporate just a basic UART and utilize a simple asynchronous character-mode protocol, normally with an echo checking error control procedure. Furthermore, since interactive screen-mode terminals may at times generate a complete string of characters rather than a single character, an X-ON/X-OFF flow control mechanism is often used to enable the central computer to regulate the flow of characters from the terminal. On the other hand, data entry and remote job entry terminals normally utilize a more sophisticated synchronous block-mode protocol with an ARQ error control procedure. Both character-oriented and bit-oriented protocols are in widespread use. Also, as will be seen later, many character-mode terminal networks incorporate additional communication equipment that uses a block-mode protocol.

5.3 INFORMATION EXCHANGE CODES

A feature of terminal-based systems is that most of the information is exchanged in the form of single strings (blocks) of characters. There are two main character codes that have been adopted for this function. They are the American Standards Committee for Information Interchange (**ASCII**) code and the Extended Binary Coded Decimal Interchange Code (**EBCDIC**). A third code, called the International Alphabet Number 5 (**IA5**), is the standard code defined by the CCITT and recommended by the ISO (as ISO 646). In practice, IA5 is almost exactly the same as ASCII

					B7:	0	0	0	0	1	1	1	1
					B6:	0	0	1	1	0	0	1	1
					B5:	0	1	0	1	0	1	0	1
Bits B_4	B_3	B_2	B_1	Row									
0	0	0	0	0		NUL	(TC$_7$) DLE	SP	0	@	P		p
0	0	0	1	1		(TC$_1$) SOH	DC$_1$	!	1	A	Q	a	q
0	0	1	0	2		(TC$_2$) STX	DC$_2$	"	2	B	R	b	r
0	0	1	1	3		(TC$_3$) ETX	DC$_3$	£	3	C	S	c	s
0	1	0	0	4		(TC$_4$) EOT	DC$_4$	$	4	D	T	d	t
0	1	0	1	5		(TC$_5$) ENQ	(TC$_8$) NAK	%	5	E	U	e	u
0	1	1	0	6		(TC$_6$) ACK	(TC$_9$) SYN	&	6	F	V	f	v
0	1	1	1	7		BEL	(TC$_{10}$) ETB	'	7	G	W	g	w
1	0	0	0	8		FE$_0$ (BS)	CAN	(	8	H	X	h	x
1	0	0	1	9		FE$_1$ (HT)	EM	)	9	I	Y	i	y
1	0	1	0	10		FE$_2$ (LF)	SUB	*	:	J	Z	j	z
1	0	1	1	11		FE$_3$ (VT)	ESC	+	;	K		k	
1	1	0	0	12		FE$_4$ (FF)	IS$_4$ (FS)	,	<	L		l	
1	1	0	1	13		FE$_5$ (CR)	IS$_3$ (GS)	−	=	M		m	
1	1	1	0	14		SO	IS$_2$ (RS)	.	>	N	^	n	
1	1	1	1	15		SI	IS$_1$ (US)	/	?	O	_	o	DEL

FIGURE 5.2

ASCII/IA5 code.

since the latter is basically the American national version of IA5.

The ASCII/IA5 code is a 7-bit code and the bit pattern definitions used are shown in Figure 5.2. As can be seen, the code caters for all the normal alphabetic and numeric (collectively referred to as **alphanumeric** or **printable**) characters plus a range of additional control characters.

The EBCDIC code is an 8-bit code used with all equipment manufactured by IBM. As such, it is a proprietary code but, owing to the widespread use of IBM equipment in the computer industry, it is frequently used. The bit pattern definitions used are shown in Figure 5.3. As can be seen, EBCDIC covers most of the characters used in ASCII/IA5. However, because of the large number of possible bit combinations (256), a number of combinations are not defined in EBCDIC.

5.4 CHARACTER-MODE NETWORKS

An example of a very simple character-mode terminal network is shown in Figure 5.4(a). Typically, the terminals would be VDUs, each connected to a locally situated central computing complex by means of a point-to-point (direct) data link. Each terminal would be either a character or screen-mode device operating in an interactive mode. The data link would be a

EBCDIC	Bit Configuration		EBCDIC	Bit Configuration		EDCBIC	Bit Configuration		EDCBIC	Bit Configuration	
NUL	0000	0000	SP	0100	0000		1000	0000		1100	0000
SOH	0000	0001		0100	0001	a	1000	0001	A	1100	0001
STX	0000	0010		0100	0010	b	1000	0010	B	1100	0010
ETX	0000	0011		0100	0011	c	1000	0011	C	1100	0011
PF	0000	0100		0100	0100	d	1000	0100	D	1100	0100
HT	0000	0101		0100	0101	e	1000	0101	E	1100	0101
LC	0000	0110		0100	0110	f	1000	0110	F	1100	0110
DEL	0000	0111		0100	0111	g	1000	0111	G	1100	0111
	0000	1000		0100	1000	h	1000	1000	H	1100	1000
RLF	0000	1001		0100	1001	i	1000	1001	I	1100	1001
SMM	0000	1010	[	0100	1010		1000	1010		1100	1010
VT	0000	1011	.	0100	1011		1000	1011		1100	1011
FF	0000	1100	<	0100	1100		1000	1100		1100	1100
CR	0000	1101	(	0100	1101		1000	1101		1100	1101
SO	0000	1110	+	0100	1110		1000	1110	–	1100	1110
SI	0000	1111			0100	1111		1000	1111		1100	1111
DLE	0001	0000	&	0101	0000		1001	0000		1101	0000
DC1	0001	0001		0101	0001	j	1001	0001	J	1101	0001
DC2	0001	0010		0101	0010	k	1001	0010	K	1101	0010
TM	0001	0011		0101	0011	l	1001	0011	L	1101	0011
RES	0001	0100		0101	0100	m	1001	0100	M	1101	0100
NL	0001	0101		0101	0101	n	1001	0101	N	1101	0101
BS	0001	0110		0101	0110	o	1001	0110	O	1101	0110
IL	0001	0111		0101	0111	p	1001	0111	P	1101	0111
CAN	0001	1000		0101	1000	q	1001	1000	Q	1101	1000
EM	0001	1001		0101	1001	r	1001	1001	R	1101	1001
CC	0001	1010	]	0101	1010		1001	1010		1101	1010
CU1	0001	1011	$	0101	1011		1001	1011		1101	1011
IFS	0001	1100	*	0101	1100		1001	1100		1101	1100
IGS	0001	1101	)	0101	1101		1001	1101		1101	1101
IRS	0001	1110	;	0101	1110		1001	1110		1101	1110
IUS	0001	1111		0101	1111		1001	1111		1101	1111
DS	0010	0000	–	0110	0000		1010	0000		1110	0000
SOS	0010	0001	/	0110	0001		1010	0001		1110	0001
FS	0010	0010		0110	0010	s	1010	0010	S	1110	0010
	0010	0011		0110	0011	t	1010	0011	T	1110	0011
BYP	0010	0100		0110	0100	u	1010	0100	U	1110	0100
LF	0010	0101		0110	0101	v	1010	0101	V	1110	0101
ETB	0010	0110		0110	0110	w	1010	0110	W	1110	0110
ESC	0010	0111		0110	0111	x	1010	0111	X	1110	0111
	0010	1000		0110	1000	y	1010	1000	Y	1110	1000
	0010	1001		0110	1001	z	1010	1001	Z	1110	1001
SM	0010	1010		0110	1010		1010	1010		1110	1010
CU2	0010	1011	,	0110	1011		1010	1011		1110	1011
	0010	1100	%	0110	1100		1010	1100		1110	1100
ENQ	0010	1101	–	0110	1101		1010	1101		1110	1101
ACK	0010	1110	>	0110	1110		1010	1110		1110	1110
BEL	0010	1111	?	0110	1111		1010	1111		1110	1111
	0011	0000		0111	0000		1011	0000	0	1111	0000
	0011	0001		0111	0001		1011	0001	1	1111	0001
SYN	0011	0010		0111	0010		1011	0010	2	1111	0010
	0011	0011		0111	0011		1011	0011	3	1111	0011
PN	0011	0100		0111	0100		1011	0100	4	1111	0100
RS	0011	0101		0111	0101		1011	0101	5	1111	0101
UC	0011	0110		0111	0110		1011	0110	6	1111	0110
EOT	0011	0111		0111	0111		1011	0111	7	1111	0111
	0011	1000		0111	1000		1011	1000	8	1111	1000
	0011	1001		0111	1001		1011	1001	9	1111	1001
	0011	1010	:	0111	1010		1011	1010		1111	1010
CU3	0011	1011	#	0111	1011		1011	1011		1111	1011
DC4	0011	1100	@	0111	1100		1011	1100		1111	1100
NAK	0011	1101	'	0111	1101		1011	1101		1111	1101
	0011	1110	=	0111	1110		1011	1110		1111	1110
SUB	0011	1111	"	0111	1111		1011	1111		1111	1111

FIGURE 5.3

EBCDIC code.

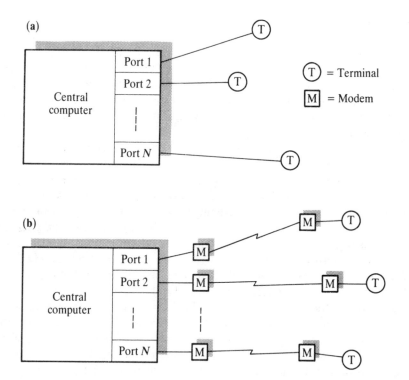

FIGURE 5.4

Simple terminal networks:
(a) local; (b) remote.

low bit rate (typically less than 9600 bps) asynchronous link that operates using simple echo checking and an X-ON/X-OFF flow control protocol similar to that described in Chapter 4. This type of organization is perfectly adequate when the terminals are all locally situated relative to the central computer or if there is a single terminal at each remote location. However, if the terminals are remotely situated, then either simple line drivers are required or, if the terminals are in a different establishment, PTT-approved modems. This is shown in Figure 5.4(b).

In a large establishment, a common requirement is to have more than one terminal at each remote location. Clearly, an architecture similar to that shown in Figure 5.4 could be used with additional communication lines for each terminal. However, a more efficient, and ultimately more flexible, arrangement is to provide a single high bit rate line between each remote location and the central computer and to share its data bandwidth between the various lower bit rate terminals. If all the terminals are within the same establishment, a device known as a **terminal multiplexer** may be used. Alternatively, if the remote terminals are in a different establishment and modems are required, a device known as a **statistical multiplexer** is often more appropriate. These and other types of communication equipment used in this type of network will now be described.

5.4.1 Terminal multiplexer

A schematic diagram illustrating a typical application of a terminal multiplexer is shown in Figure 5.5(a). As can be seen, a similar multiplexer is normally used at both ends of the link, which has the effect that each terminal operates as if it were connected directly to a terminal port on the computer. It is therefore said to be transparent to both the terminal user and the computer.

A schematic of the internal organization of a terminal multiplexer is shown in Figure 5.5(b). As can be seen, each terminal is allocated a separate UART and the controlling microprocessor continuously 'polls' each UART in turn to determine if a character has been received from the terminal; that is, the status byte in each UART is read to determine if the RxBF status bit is set. If it is, the received character is read and prepared for transmission on the outgoing data link to the remote computer; if it is not, the status byte in the next UART is read, and so on. Similarly, on receipt of each character from the data link, it is transferred to the transmit buffer register of the appropriate UART for forwarding to the terminal.

With a terminal multiplexer, the bit rate of the common data link must be at least N times that used for each terminal, where N is the number of terminals. For example, if the bit rate used for each terminal is 1200 bps and the multiplexer is servicing eight such terminals, the bit rate of the common data link must be greater than eight times 1200; that is, greater than 9600 bps.

Since the controlling microprocessor polls each UART in turn, it automatically knows from which terminal or computer port any received characters have come. As characters are received from the data link, however, it must be able to determine for which UART, and hence terminal or computer port, they are intended. This may be achieved in a number of ways but a typical arrangement is as shown in Figure 5.5(c). In this scheme, each UART is assigned a specific character slot relative to the start of each frame. Typically, each frame has the same number of character slots as there are UARTs and, to allow the controlling microprocessor to determine the start of each slot, each frame is preceded by a synchronizing control character such as SYN. It is for this reason that the bit rate of the common data link must be greater than the aggregate bit rate of each terminal. This type of multiplexing arrangement is known as **time-division multiplexing (TDM)** since the available transmission capacity of the data link is time-shared between the various terminals.

If the multiplexer is servicing only a small number of low bit rate terminals – for example, four VDUs each operating at 1200 bps – the aggregate bit rate of the common data link is still only low and hence an asynchronous transmission control scheme can be used. As the aggregate data rate increases, however, a synchronous control scheme must be used. In fact, terminal multiplexers of the type just described can be purchased

(a)

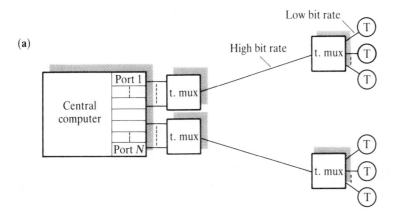

(b)

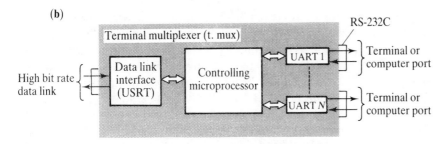

(c)

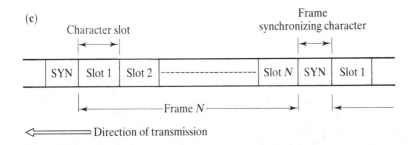

FIGURE 5.5

Terminal multiplexer principles:
(a) network schematic;
(b) multiplexer schematic;
(c) data link organization.

to service up to 32 terminals, each operating at up to 9600 bps. Clearly, in such cases, the aggregate data rate is in excess of 300 kbps; hence, this type of multiplexer can only be used where special high bit rate data links can be laid and transmission media such as fibre optics used. This type of multiplexer is normally constrained for use, therefore, within a single private establishment.

5.4.2 Statistical multiplexer

As already mentioned, each terminal in a terminal multiplexer is allocated a fixed character slot in each frame. If the terminal or computer has no character ready to transmit when the controlling microprocessor polls the associated UART, therefore, the microprocessor must insert a NULL character in this slot, thus leading to inefficiencies in the use of the available transmission bandwidth. If the data link used is a private line, this action is not necessarily important but, if PTT-supplied lines are used, it can be very costly. An alternative and more efficient method is to use a statistical multiplexer, or stat mux.

Statistical multiplexers operate on the principle that the mean data rate of characters entered at a terminal keyboard is often much lower than the nominal available transmission capacity of the line – this is certainly the case with a human user, for example. Hence, if the mean user data rate is used rather than the transmission line rate, the bit rate of the common data link can be much lower, with the effect that transmission line costs are substantially reduced. For example, suppose a remote location has eight terminals that need to be connected to a single remote central computer by means of a PTT-supplied line, which has a maximum line rate of, say, 4800 bps. Using a basic multiplexer and a single line, the nominal operating rate of each terminal would therefore have to be less than 600 bps – say 300 bps. The effect of this limit is that the response time of the computer to each character keyed in at the terminal would be relatively slow or, if a block of characters was being transmitted to the terminal, the delay would be very noticeable. Alternatively, if the mean data rate of the terminal is, say, 300 bps, then with a statistical multiplexer the data could be transmitted by a terminal at the maximum available bit rate of 4800 bps. Thus, the average response time to each keyed character is much improved.

To implement the scheme just outlined, the controlling microprocessor within the statistical multiplexer, in addition to performing the normal polling function associated with the terminal UARTs, must also provide and manage a limited amount of buffer storage facilities to allow for possible transient overload conditions on the common data link when a number of terminals are active simultaneously. Also, because characters are being transmitted on the common data link on a statistical rather than a preallocated basis, each character or group of characters transmitted must also carry some identification information.

Another function that must be performed by the microprocessor in a statistical multiplexer is related to error control. With a normal terminal multiplexer, simple echo checking is often a perfectly acceptable mode of working, since each terminal and computer port is allocated a fixed character slot in each frame. However, due to the statistical mode of working of a statistical multiplexer, it is more common to introduce a separate ARQ-based error control scheme on the shared data link. A

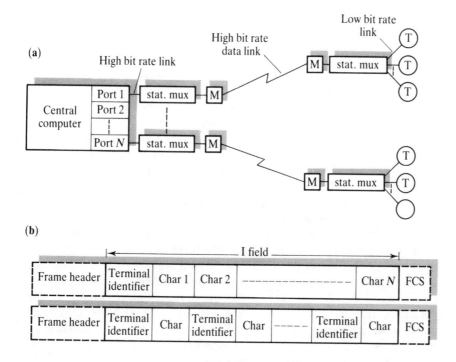

FIGURE 5.6

Statistical multiplexer principles:
(a) network schematic;
(b) framing alternatives.

typical statistical multiplexer arrangement is shown in Figure 5.6(a). In this example, the link between the statistical multiplexer and the computer is shown as a single high-speed link since, if echo checking is not used, there is no advantage in performing a demultiplexing function on behalf of the computer.

Recall that with an ARQ error control scheme each block of data transmitted is separately identified for retransmission purposes. Hence, to reduce the overheads associated with each transmitted character, it is usual to group a number of characters together for transmission on the shared data link. This can be done in a number of ways, two examples of which are shown in Figure 5.6(b). In the first, the controlling microprocessor waits until it has a number of characters from a single terminal – a string of characters making up a single line, for example – and it then transmits them as a complete block with a single terminal (channel) identifier at the head. In the second, each block contains a mix of characters from all currently active terminals with a separate terminal identifier associated with each. Also, as can be seen from the figure, the assembled characters collectively occupy the I-field of each block or frame transmitted on the shared data link. The communication protocol used on the link is normally either a character-oriented or a bit-oriented synchronous protocol and details of both of these will be described in more detail later in the chapter.

5.4.3   Terminal switching exchange

Although most terminal networks contain a single central computer to which all the terminals require access, it is rapidly becoming common practice in many larger establishments to have a number of computers physically distributed around the establishment and for users to have access to more than one of them. This is the case, for example, if the various computers each offer different user services, such as word processing, electronic mail, special application packages and so on. To meet this type of requirement, a device known as a **terminal switching exchange (TSE)** is often used. A typical character-mode terminal network based on such a device is shown in Figure 5.7.

Essentially, a TSE has a number of asynchronous terminal access ports and asynchronous computer ports. To gain access to a particular computer (port), the user first keys in the address of the required computer at the terminal keyboard. Then, assuming there is a free port available on the required computer, the TSE establishes a logical connection and the user goes through the normal logging-in procedure for that computer. The presence of the TSE, and indeed the terminal multiplexer should this be present, is transparent to the user and computer alike. Finally, at the end of the transaction, the user initiates the clearing of the connection by pressing a specific control character on the keyboard, thereby releasing the computer port and making it available to another user.

5.5   BLOCK-MODE NETWORKS

As was mentioned earlier, more sophisticated terminals, such as those used in a bank for data entry or point-of-sale terminals as used in a department store, normally operate in a block mode rather than a character mode; that is, as each character is keyed in at the terminal it is echoed to the display screen directly by the local processor within the terminal. The data are then passed to the central computing complex for processing only when a complete block of data (a message) has been assembled. Because of this, such terminals normally support a more sophisticated block-oriented communication protocol to control the transfer of messages. Also, because the acceptable response time to each transmitted message can often be much slower than that expected with an interactive character-mode network, equipment aimed at reducing the communication line costs at the expense of the response time is often used in block-mode terminal networks. Some of the techniques and equipment used in such networks will now be described.

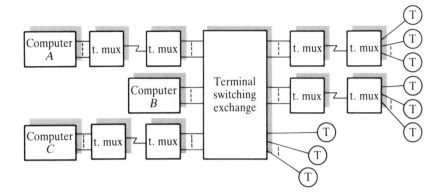

FIGURE 5.7

Terminal switching exchange.

5.5.1   Multidrop lines

A common method used to reduce transmission line costs in block-mode terminal networks is that employing **multidrop** (also known as **multipoint**) **lines**. A schematic of a network that uses multidrop lines is shown in Figure 5.8(a). As can be seen, instead of each terminal being connected directly to the central computer by a separate line, a number of terminals share the same line. In this way, the number of lines and hence modems, or line drivers depending on the geographical scope of the network, is much reduced. Clearly, however, with only one line for each community of terminals, only one message block at a time can be sent, either by a terminal or the central computer. To achieve this, all transmissions on each line are controlled by the central computer itself and an arbitration procedure known as **poll–select** is used.

5.5.2   Poll–select

To ensure that only one message is transmitted at any instant on each shared communication line, the central computer, or its agent, either **polls** or **selects** each terminal connected to the line in a particular sequence. As each terminal connected to the shared line is allocated a unique identifier, the central computer communicates with a terminal by sending it messages with the identity of the terminal at the head. Messages can be of two types: control or data.

   At periodic intervals, the central computer sends each terminal, in turn, a poll control message, which effectively invites the polled terminal to send a message should it have one waiting. If it has, it is returned in a data message; if it has not, it responds with a nothing-to-send control message. Similarly, whenever the central computer wishes to send a message to a terminal, it first sends a select control message addressed to the particular

(a)

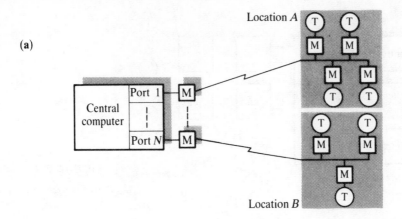

(b)

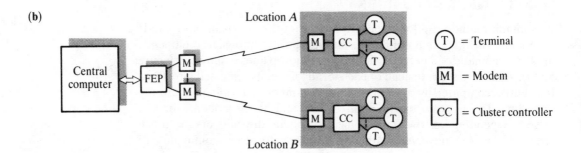

(c)

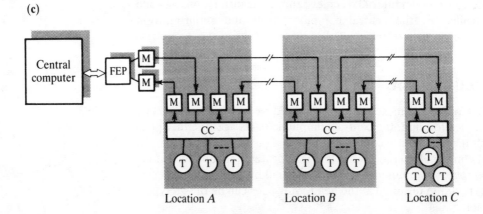

FIGURE 5.8

Polling network alternatives:
(a) multidrop; (b) cluster
controllers; (c) hub polling.

terminal and, assuming the selected terminal is able to receive a message, it responds by returning a ready-to-receive control message. The central computer then continues by sending the data message. Finally, the terminal acknowledges correct receipt of the data message and the central computer continues by either polling or selecting another terminal. This type of polling, known as **roll call polling**, results in quite long response times for larger networks since each terminal in the network must be polled or selected before it can send or receive a message. The communication overheads imposed on the central computer can also be very high.

To overcome these problems, a more common type of multidrop network uses, firstly, a device known as a **cluster controller** to reduce the response time of the network and, secondly, a device known as a **front-end processor** (**FEP**) to reduce the communication overheads on the central computer. An example of such a network is as shown in Figure 5.8(b). Effectively, each cluster controller acts as an agent for the central computer by polling and selecting the terminals connected to it, thereby managing all message transfers to and from the terminals. Thus, the central computer, or the FEP in practice, needs only poll or select each controller.

An FEP is typically a small computer that is closely coupled to the central computer. It is programmed to handle all the polling and selection procedures, allowing the central computer to devote its time to the main task of application processing.

The advantage of an FEP is that the central computer need only be involved when a data message has been received or is to be sent. Furthermore, since all the communication overheads associated with each message transfer are handled by the FEP, the central computer need only initiate the transfer of each message to and from the FEP.

If very large physical distances separate each terminal cluster, an alternative mechanism known as **hub polling** is sometimes cost justified. This is shown in diagrammatic form in Figure 5.8(c). As can be seen, each cluster controller is connected to its nearest neighbour rather than to the central computer directly. As before, the central computer manages all transfers to and from the cluster controllers. The central computer selects and sends a data message to any of the controllers at any time by means of the top line in the figure.

To receive messages from the controllers, the central computer first sends a poll control message to the furthest controller. The latter then responds by sending either a data message or a nothing-to-send control message on the bottom (return) line to its nearest neighbouring controller. On receipt of this message, the next controller interprets this as a poll message and, if it has a message waiting, it responds by adding its own data message to the tail of the received message from its upstream neighbour. The composite message is then forwarded to its own downstream neighbour, again on the return line. This procedure continues down the chain, each controller adding its own response message as it relays the message towards the central computer. Finally, on receipt of the composite response message, the FEP disassembles the message and passes on any valid data messages contained within it to the central computer for further processing.

5.6 TERMINAL NETWORK PROTOCOLS

In a character-mode terminal network, all transmissions on the link between the terminal and the remote computer or communication device are normally carried out using an asynchronous transmission control scheme. Furthermore, because the terminals in such networks are normally used in an interactive mode, an echo checking error control procedure is used with an X-ON/X-OFF flow control mechanism. However, in a block-mode terminal network, the terminals communicate using complete messages; hence, they must be able to support a more sophisticated block-oriented link control protocol. There are two such protocols in widespread use: **binary synchronous control** (also known as **bisync** or simply **BSC**), which is a character-oriented protocol, and **high-level data link control** (**HDLC**), which is a bit-oriented protocol. Both of these protocols have been designed to control the exchange of blocks of data (information) across a synchronous transmission line, although the character definitions and sequences used in BSC are also sometimes used to transfer message blocks across an asynchronous line. Before describing aspects of these protocols, however, it is important first to define the user interface to the link layer to form a clear distinction between the user (application-oriented) software and the software (and hardware) within the communication subsystem.

Recall from Chapter 4 that any link-level protocol can be considered as being comprised of two components:

(1)   link management, which is concerned with the initial setting up of a (logical) link between both parties to ensure they are ready to exchange information and also with the orderly termination or clearing of the link; and

(2)   data transfer, which is concerned with the ordered exchange of data blocks (messages) across the link.

A typical set of user services (primitives) for the link layer is as shown in Figure 5.9.

As will be seen in the following sections, the confirm primitives relating to both the L.CONNECT.request and the L.DISCONNECT.request primitives may be generated as a result of either an acknowledgement being received from the remote link layer (as shown) or by the local link layer directly. In both cases, however, the service (L.CONNECT or L.DISCONNECT) is known as a **confirmed service**. In contrast, the L.DATA service is known as an **unconfirmed service** since, although the protocol associated with the link layer will endeavour to

Calling (Master) Station   **Called (Slave) Station**

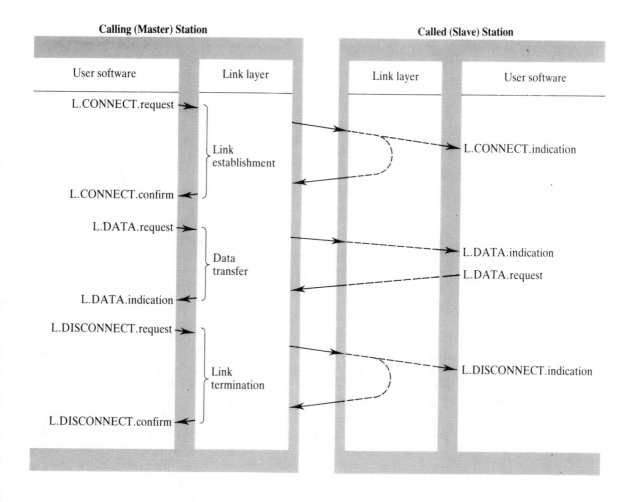

transfer the data (information) across the link correctly, the *user* is not
informed of the success (or failure) of the transfer request.

    Normally, a set of parameters are associated with each primitive and
these convey additional information relating to the primitive. For example,
a parameter indicating the address of the called station is associated with
the L.CONNECT.request primitive; similarly, the L.DATA.request primitive has a parameter specifying a memory address pointer to where the
block of user data is located.

    It should be stressed that these services are independent of the type
of link-level protocol used, and so any changes relating to the latter should
have no effect on the user software. The relationship between these
services and the various message units associated with each protocol will be
shown after each protocol has been described.

FIGURE 5.9

Link layer user services.

5.6.1 Binary synchronous control

BSC is in fact the terminology adopted by IBM for the ISO character-oriented link-level protocol known as Basic Mode. Because of the prevalence of IBM equipment, however, BSC is the term most widely used and hence will be used in this chapter to refer to the ISO Basic Mode protocol. It is a practical example of the idle RQ protocol discussed earlier in Chapter 4 but with the addition of a negative acknowledgement to improve the link efficiency.

It may be remembered from Chapter 4 that any link-level protocol can be considered as being made up of three sections:

- The first is concerned with the initial setting up of the link to ensure both parties are ready to exchange information.

- The second is concerned with the ordered exchange of data blocks or messages across the link.

- The third is concerned with the orderly release or clearing of the link.

To perform the various functions associated with link management, a number of control messages are needed, in addition to normal data blocks or messages. Also, it may be remembered that, with a synchronous link, it is necessary for the receiver to be able to achieve both character (byte) and frame synchronization.

With a character-oriented protocol like BSC, some of the control characters defined in ASCII/IA5 (or EBCDIC if this is being used) are provided to achieve these functions. These characters are referred to as **transmission control (TC) characters**. The role of some of these characters was described earlier in Chapter 3 but a more complete list of those used with BSC, together with their function, is shown in Table 5.1.

Block formats

Some examples of the different types of data block used in BSC, illustrating the use of some of the TC characters, are shown in Figure 5.10(a). All blocks transmitted are preceded by at least two SYN characters to allow the receiver to achieve character synchronization. Short messages (less than the defined maximum length) are transmitted in a single data block while longer messages are transmitted in multiple blocks. The header field, when present, is for general use and normally defines how the data field is to be interpreted. In addition, all data blocks have a **block check character (BCC)** after the end-of-block delimiter (ETX or ETB), which is a longitudinal (column) parity check (see Chapter 3). It starts the check with the STX character and ends with the particular end-of-block delimiter character being used. Parity has, of course, only limited

Table 5.1 Transmission control characters used with BSC.

Character	Function
SOH (TC1)	Start of heading: used to indicate the start of the header (if one is present) of an information message (block)
STX (TC2)	Start of text: used both to terminate a heading (if one is present) and to signal the start of a text string
ETX (TC3)	End of text: used to signal the end of a text string
EOT (TC4)	End of transmission: used to indicate the end of the transmission of one or more text (information) blocks and to terminate (clear) the connection
ENQ (TC5)	Enquiry: used as a request for a response from a remote station – the response may include the identity and/or status of the station
ACK (TC6)	Acknowledge: positive acknowledgement transmitted by a receiver in response to a message from the sender
DLE (TC7)	Data link escape: used to change the meaning of other selected transmission control characters
NAK (TC8)	Negative acknowledge: negative response transmitted by a receiver to a message from the sender
SYN (TC9)	Synchronous idle: used to provide the means for a receiver to achieve or retain (idle condition) character synchronization with a synchronous transmission control scheme
ETB (TC10)	End of transmission block: used to indicate the end of a block of data when a message is divided into a number of such blocks

error-detection properties, so there is a limit to the number of characters allowed in each transmitted data block – this is determined by the bit error rate of the link being used. Longer messages must, therefore, be transmitted as a sequence of shorter fixed-sized data blocks, each terminated with an ETB control character and with the last data block of such a sequence terminating with an ETX control character.

Four different control messages associated with the BSC protocol are shown in Figure 5.10(b). The ACK and NAK control characters have two functions:

(1)   The first is for acknowledgement purposes: one or other is returned in response to a previously transmitted data block and hence contains an identifier (sequence number).

(2)   The second is as a response to a select control message: an ACK indicates that the selected station is able to receive a data block and a NAK indicates that it is not.

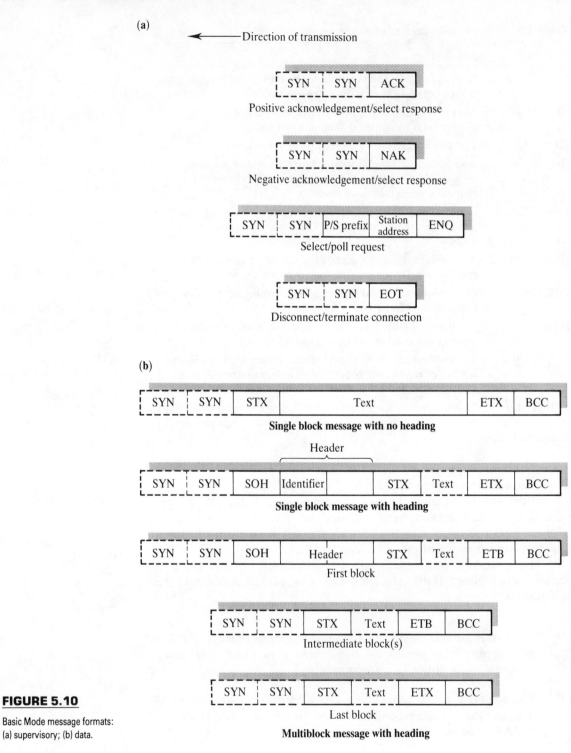

FIGURE 5.10

Basic Mode message formats:
(a) supervisory; (b) data.

The ENQ control character is used as both a poll and a select control message. In a multidrop configuration, the address of the polled or selected terminal precedes the ENQ character; uppercase characters are used for polling and lowercase for selection.

Finally, the EOT control character has two functions:

(1) The first signals the end of a complete message exchange sequence and effectively clears the logical link between the two communicating parties.

(2) The second provides a means of resetting the link to the idle state.

The use of the DLE character to achieve data transparency when transmitting pure binary data rather than character strings was described in Chapter 3. Essentially, the various framing character sequences shown in Figure 5.10 are modified to be DLE.STX, DLE.ETX, etc. Also, whenever a binary pattern corresponding to a DLE character is detected in the text by the transmitter, it adds (inserts) an extra DLE. The receiver then performs a similar check and, whenever it detects two consecutive DLEs, it removes the inserted DLE before passing the data on for further processing.

A further difference when operating in the transparent mode is concerned with error control. Under normal operation, the eighth bit of each transmitted character is used as a parity bit and hence features in the error-detection procedure. Clearly, therefore, if a block contains a transparent sequence of 8-bit binary values, this cannot be used. Hence, when transmitting binary data in the transparent mode, an alternative error-detection procedure is normally used: instead of a simple 8- bit longitudinal parity check per block, a more sophisticated polynomial code is used. Each block is thus terminated with a 16-bit CRC rather than an 8- bit BCC.

Protocol operation

As was described earlier, the central computer (or **master station**) in terminal networks is responsible for scheduling all transmissions on each shared data link. The poll control message is used to request a specific terminal (or cluster controller) to send any waiting data message(s) it may have, and the select control message is used to ask the selected terminal whether it is ready to receive a data message(s). Each terminal or cluster controller is normally referred to therefore as a **slave station**.

A typical sequence of messages exchanged on a multidrop line is shown in Figure 5.11. In Figure 5.11(a), both a successful and an unsuccessful sequence associated with a select operation are shown. In Figure 5.11(b), two sequences associated with a poll operation are shown.

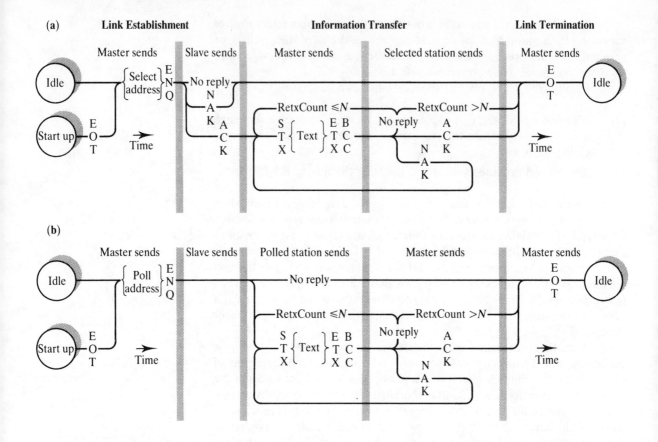

FIGURE 5.11

Some BSC message sequences:
(a) select; (b) poll.

For clarity, only single-block data messages are considered.

To select a particular slave station, the master station sends an ENQ select control message with the address of the slave station preceding the ENQ character. Assuming the selected station is ready to receive a message, it responds with an ACK control message. The master station then sends the message either as a single data block (as shown in the figure) or as a sequence of data blocks with the last block terminating with an ETX character. As each data block is received and stored, the slave station recomputes the parity check sequence and, assuming there are no transmission errors, responds with an ACK control message for each block. Finally, after the complete message has been sent, the master station sends an EOT control message, which effectively terminates the message transfer and clears the logical connection.

In some situations, when selecting a terminal, it is not always necessary to wait for an acknowledgement to the ENQ control message before sending a message; for example, if a terminal has been previously selected and the logical connection has not been closed. In such cases, therefore, the master station sends the message immediately after the select control message, without waiting for an ACK (or NAK) response. Such a procedure is known as a **fast select sequence**.

During the polling phase, the master station first sends an ENQ poll control messsage with the address of the polled slave station preceding the ENQ character. Then, assuming the polled station has a message awaiting transmission, it responds by sending the message. The master station, on receipt of the data block, recomputes the parity check sequence and, assuming no transmission errors, acknowledges its correct receipt. Finally, after the complete message has been transferred and acknowledged, the logical connection is cleared with an EOT control message.

Figure 5.11 clearly illustrates the fact that BSC is an example of an idle RQ protocol because, after sending each data block, the transmitter waits for either an ACK or a NAK control message before sending the next block and, in the case of the latter, the sending station retransmits the corrupted block. The use of an additional NAK control message means that a corrupted data block will be retransmitted sooner; that is, on receipt of the NAK message rather than after the timeout interval, as is the case with the basic idle RQ protocol. As was described in Chapter 4, if the transmitted block is completely corrupted, an additional timeout mechanism is still required to ensure the affected block is retransmitted. A single identifier, which alternates between 0 and 1, is then used in each data block to allow the receiver to detect duplicates.

User interface

As was indicated earlier, it is important to discriminate between the services provided by the link layer and the detailed operation of the link-layer protocol. To illustrate this, the relationship between the user services shown in Figure 5.9 and the various message blocks (control and data) associated with the BSC protocol are shown in Figure 5.12(a) and (b). As can be seen, the initial ENQ control message is acknowledged in the select sequence and hence this may be used as a confirmation that the remote station is ready to accept a message. With the poll sequence, however, an ACK is not returned in response to the initial ENQ message and so the confirm primitive has to be generated by the local protocol entity after the ENQ message has been transmitted. A similar procedure is also followed with the link disconnection procedure. In both examples shown, it is assumed that the first attempt at sending the data block fails (due, for example, to a BCC failure) and hence has to be retransmitted.

Because BSC is effectively a half-duplex protocol, it is very inefficient in its use of transmission bandwidth; even if the physical link supports full-duplex transmission, BSC cannot exploit this. Nevertheless, as it needs a minimum of buffer storage facilities for its implementation, it is still in widespread use for terminal networks of the type considered in

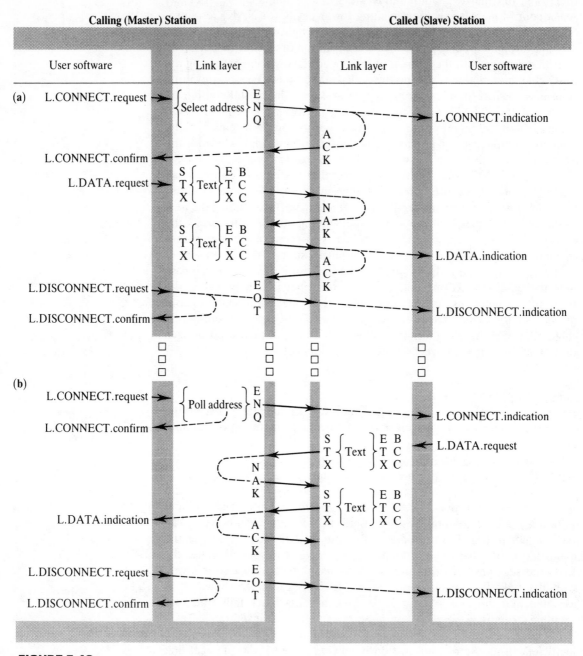

FIGURE 5.12

User/link layer interaction:
(a) select; (b) poll.

this chapter. But there has been a shift towards the more flexible and potentially more efficient HDLC protocol over recent years due to the falling costs of computer hardware and the increased level of sophistication of terminals. This is certainly the case for computer-to- computer communication networks which normally require full-duplex, transparent working.

Protocol performance

Before describing the HDLC protocol, it is perhaps helpful to quantify the performance of BSC. The basic link efficiency (utilization) obtained with the idle RQ protocol was discussed in the previous chapter. As has been outlined, however, the major use of BSC is in applications where there is a single master (primary) station that sends and receives messages to and from multiple slave (secondary) stations. An important additional performance parameter with such configurations, therefore, is the average time taken to poll or select all the slave stations on a link.

In practice, because of the low-link utilization of idle RQ relative to continuous RQ, idle RQ protocols are used primarily with relatively short multidrop links operating at relatively low data rates of up to, say, 64 kbps. As was seen in the last chapter, the time to transmit a message with such links dominates the other times contributing to a poll or select sequence. For example, if an average message is 1000 bits and the data rate is 10 kbps, then the time to transmit a message is 0.1 s. In contrast, the control messages associated with a poll (or select) sequence are short (say 30 bits) and hence the time to transmit these messages is also short (0.003 s at 10 kbps). Hence, even allowing a small additional time of, say, 0.001 s to process these messages, the total time for each poll (or select) sequence (0.004 s) is still small compared with the time to transmit a message.

In the absence of any messages to send, the minimum time to poll all secondaries is N times the time to poll a single secondary, where N is the number of secondaries on the link. As messages become ready to transmit, however, the average time to poll all secondaries increases and depends on the average rate at which messages are generated. Clearly, the maximum poll time occurs when the average rate at which messages are generated approaches the link bit rate since, beyond this rate, the link becomes overloaded and delays progressively increase.

In general, the average time to poll each secondary can be expressed as:

$$T_{avr} = \frac{T_{min}}{1 - M_r T_{ix}}$$

where T_{min} is the minimum time to poll all secondaries, M_r is the average rate at which messages are generated and T_{ix} is the time to transmit an average-sized message. If M_r is low compared with T_{ix}, then T_{avr} is approximately T_{min}; as M_r increases, however, so T_{avr} increases.

EXAMPLE

A BSC protocol is to be used to control the flow of messages between a computer (master station) and 10 block-mode terminals (secondaries) over a multipoint data link. The link data rate is 10 kbps and the average length of a message is 1000 bits. If a poll message and its associated ACK is 30 bits and the total time to process these messages is 1 ms, determine the average time each terminal will be polled if the average rate at which messages are generated is:

(a)   one message per minute,

(b)   six messages per second.

The bit error rate and signal propagation delay times of the link can be assumed to be negligible.

The time to transmit an average message is:

$$\frac{N_i}{R} = \frac{1000}{10^4} = 100 \text{ ms}$$

The time to transmit a poll and its ACK is:

$$\frac{30}{10^4} = 3 \text{ ms}$$

The time to poll a single secondary is:

$$3 + 1 = 4 \text{ ms}$$

The minimum time to poll all secondaries is:

$$T_{min} = 10 \times 4 = 40 \text{ ms}$$

Now:

$$T_{avr} = \frac{T_{min}}{1 - M_r T_{ix}}$$

(a) M_r = one message per minute = $\dfrac{10^{-3}}{60}$ messages/ms. Hence:

$$T_{avr} = \frac{40}{1 - \dfrac{10^{-3}}{60} \times 100} = 40 \text{ ms}$$

(b) M_r = six messages per second = 6×10^{-3} messages/ms. Hence:

$$T_{avr} = \frac{40}{1 - 6 \times 10^{-3} \times 100} = \frac{40}{0.4} = 100 \text{ ms}$$

5.6.2 High-level data link control

Like BSC, HDLC is a link-level protocol that has been defined by the ISO for use on both point-to-point and multipoint (multidrop) data links. It supports full-duplex, transparent-mode operation and is now extensively used in both terminal-based networks and computer networks. Although the acronym HDLC is now widely accepted, a number of large manufacturers and other standards bodies still use their own acronym. These include SDLC (synchronous data link control) by IBM and ADCCP (advanced data communications control procedure), which is used by the American National Standards Institute (ANSI).

Because HDLC has been defined as a general-purpose data link control protocol, a specific mode of operation is selected when the data link is first set up. The two most prevalent modes are:

(1)   **Unbalanced normal response mode (NRM):** This is mainly used in terminal-based networks since in this mode slave stations (or secondaries) can only transmit when specifically instructed by the master (primary) station. The link may be point to point or multidrop but in the case of the latter only one primary station is allowed.

(2)   **Asynchronous balanced mode (ABM):** This is mainly used on point-to-point links for computer-to-computer communication or for connections between, say, statistical multiplexers. In this mode, each station has an equal status and performs both primary and secondary functions.

Frame formats

Unlike BSC, HDLC is a bit-oriented protocol which, for reasons given in Chapter 3, is more efficient than a character-oriented protocol. With HDLC, both data and control messages are carried in a standard format block that is referred to as a frame. The standard format of a frame is shown in Figure 5.13 together with the different frame types that are defined in the control field of the frame header. There are three different classes of frame used in HDLC:

(1) **Unnumbered frames**: These are used for such functions as link set-up and disconnection and hence do not contain any acknowledgement information. Since the latter is contained in sequence numbers, these frames are known as unnumbered frames.

(2) **Information frames**: These are used to carry the actual information or data and are normally referred to as simply I-frames. Also, as will be seen, I-frames may be used to piggyback acknowledgement information relating to the flow of I-frames in the reverse direction when the link is being operated in ABM.

(3) **Supervisory frames**: These are used for error and flow control purposes and hence contain send and receive sequence numbers.

The use of the flag field as a start- and end-of-frame delimiter, together with zero bit insertion and deletion to achieve data transparency, was described in Chapter 3 and hence will not be repeated here.

The frame check sequence (FCS) is a 16-bit cyclic redundancy check for the complete frame contents enclosed between the two flag delimiters. The generator polynomial used with HDLC is:

$$x^{16} + x^{12} + x^5 + 1$$

The FCS is generated by the procedure described in Chapter 3 except that additional procedures, such as adding 16 ones to the tail of the dividend prior to division (instead of zeros) and inverting the remainder, are used to make the check more robust. This has the effect that the remainder when computed by the receiver is not all zeros but a special bit pattern – 0001 1101 0000 1111.

The contents of the address field depend on the mode of operation used. In NRM, as used on a multidrop line, for example, every secondary station is assigned a unique address and, whenever the primary station communicates with a particular secondary, the address field contains the address of the secondary. In addition, certain addresses may be assigned to more than one secondary station. These are known as **group addresses** and all frames transmitted with a group address are received by all stations in that group. Also, an address containing all ones is known as a **broadcast**

(a)

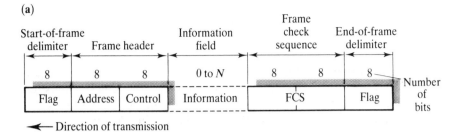

Direction of transmission

(b)

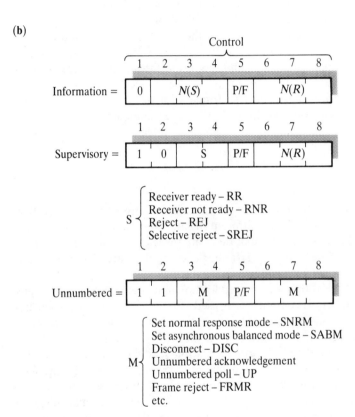

FIGURE 5.13

HDLC frame format and types:
(a) standard frame format;
(b) control field bit definitions.

address, since it is used to transmit a frame to all secondary stations on the link.

When a particular secondary station returns a response message (frame) to the primary, the address field always contains the unique address of the secondary. Also, for large networks containing possibly a large number of secondaries, the address field may be extended beyond eight bits. The least significant bit (lsb) of each 8-bit field is then used to indicate whether there is another octet to follow (l.s. bit = 0) or whether it is the last or only octet (lsb = 1). Note that the address field is not used in this way in ABM because only direct point-to-point links are involved. Instead, it is used to indicate the direction of commands and their associated responses. This will be expanded upon later.

The various control field bit definitions are defined in Figure 5.13(b). The S-field in supervisory frames and the M-field in unnumbered frames are used to define the specific frame type. The send and receive sequence numbers ($N(S)$ and $N(R)$) are used in conjunction with the error and flow control procedures and will be expanded upon later.

The P/F bit is known as the poll/final bit. A frame of any type is called a **command frame** if it is sent by the primary station and a **response frame** if it is sent by a secondary station. The P/F bit is called the poll bit when used in a command frame and, if set, indicates that the receiver must acknowledge this frame. The receiver acknowledges this frame by returning an appropriate response frame with the P/F bit set; it is then known as the final bit. Again, this will be expanded upon later.

Frame types

Before describing the operation of the HDLC protocol, it is perhaps helpful to list some of the different frame types and to outline their function. As has been mentioned, there are three classes of frame used and some of the different types of frame in each class are listed in Figure 5.13(b).

Unnumbered frames are used for link management purposes. Thus, the SNRM and SABM frames are used, firstly, to set up a logical link between the primary and a secondary station and, secondly, to inform the secondary station of the mode of operation to be used. A logical link is subsequently cleared by the primary station sending a DISC frame. The UA frame is used as an acknowledgement to the other frames in this class.

Although there are four different types of supervisory frame, only RR and RNR are used in both NRM and ABM. These frames are used, firstly, to indicate the willingness or otherwise of a secondary station to receive an I-frame(s) from the primary station and, secondly, for acknowledgement purposes. The REJ and SREJ frames are used only in ABM. This mode permits two-way simultaneous communication across a point-to-point link and the two frames are used to indicate to the other station that a sequence error has occurred; that is, an I-frame containing an out-of-sequence $N(S)$ has been received. The SREJ frame is used when a selective retransmission procedure is used whereas the REJ frame is used when a go-back-N procedure is used. The use of some of the different types of frame will now be illustrated as some aspects of the operation of the protocol are described.

Protocol operation

The aim of this section is to highlight some of the more important features of the HDLC protocol, rather than to give a full description of its operation. The two basic functions are link management and data transfer (including error and flow control) and these will now be considered.

Link management Before any information (data) may be transmitted, either between the primary and a secondary station on a multidrop link or between two stations connected by a point-to-point link, a logical connection between the two communicating parties must be established. This is accomplished by the exchange of two unnumbered frames as shown in Figure 5.14.

In a multidrop link (Figure 5.14(b)), an SNRM frame is first sent by the primary station with the poll bit set to 1 and the address of the appropriate secondary in the address field. The secondary then responds with a UA frame with the final bit set and its own address in the address field. Also, as can be seen, the set-up procedure has the effect of initializing the sequence variables held by each station. These, as will be described, are used in the error and flow control procedures. Finally, after all data have been transferred, the link is cleared by the primary sending a DISC frame and the secondary responding with a UA.

The procedure followed to set up a point-to-point link is the same as that used for a multidrop link. In the example shown in Figure 5.14(b), however, ABM has been selected and hence an SABM frame is first sent. In this mode, both sides of the link may initiate the transfer of I-frames independently and hence each station is often referred to as a **combined station**, since it must act as both a primary and a secondary. For this mode, either station may initiate the setting up or clearing of the link. In the example, station A initiates the set-up of the link and station B initiates the clearing of the (logical) connection. A single exchange of frames sets up the link in both directions. Also, as can be seen, the address field is used to indicate the direction of the command frame (SABM/DISC) and its associated response.

If the receiver wishes to refuse a set-up command in either mode, a disconnected mode (DM) frame is returned in response to the initial mode setting frame (SNRM or SABM).

Data transfer In NRM, all data (I-frames) are transferred under the control of the primary station. The unnumbered poll (UP) frame with the P bit set to 1 is normally used by the primary to poll a secondary. If the secondary has no data to transmit, it returns an RNR frame with the F bit set. If it has data waiting, it transmits the data, typically as a sequence of I-frames, with the F bit set to 1 in the last frame of the sequence.

(a)

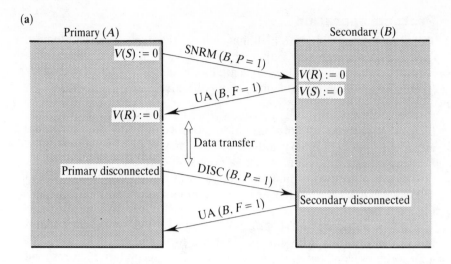

(b)

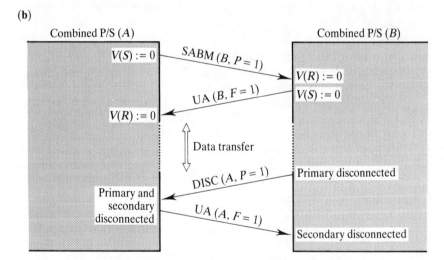

FIGURE 5.14

Link management procedure:
(a) normal response mode –
multidrop link; (b) asynchronous
balanced mode – point-to-point
link.

The two more important aspects associated with the data transfer phase are error control and flow control. Essentially, error control is accomplished by means of a continuous RQ procedure with either a selective retransmission or a go-back-N retransmission strategy, while flow control is accomplished by means of a window mechanism. The basic operation of both these procedures was described in Chapter 4 and hence only typical frame sequences will be given here to illustrate the use of the different frame types.

An example illustrating the basic acknowledgement and retransmission procedure is given in Figure 5.15, which assumes a go-back-N

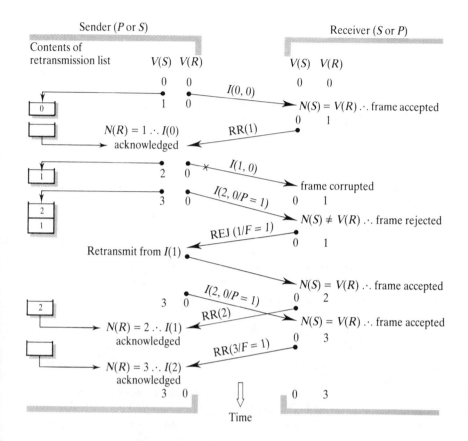

FIGURE 5.15

Use of acknowledgement frames.

strategy. In the figure, only a unidirectional flow of information frames is shown and hence all acknowledgement information must be returned using specific acknowledgement supervisory frames. As can be seen, each side of the link maintains both a send and a receive sequence variable, respectively. The $V(S)$ indicates the next send sequence number, $N(S)$, which is allocated to an I-frame transmitted by that station, and $V(R)$ the send sequence number of the next in-sequence I-frame expected by that station.

Each RR (positive acknowledgement) supervisory frame contains a receive sequence number, $N(R)$, which acknowledges correct receipt of all previously transmitted I-frames up to and including that with an $N(S)$ equal to $[N(R) - 1]$. Similarly, each REJ (negative acknowledgement) supervisory frame contains an $N(R)$ which indicates that an out-of-sequence I-frame has been received and the sender must start to retransmit from the I-frame with $N(S)$ equal to $N(R)$.

As can be seen from the example, the sequence numbers are incremented modulo 8. Also, when the receiver detects that frame $I(2, 0) -$

that is, the last frame in the sequence with $P = 1$ – is out of sequence, it returns an REJ frame with the F bit set. The sender then retransmits frames $I(1, 0)$ and $I(2, 0)$ with the P bit again set to 1 in frame $I(2, 0)$. The receiver acknowledges correct receipt of each frame with the F bit set to 1 in the last RR frame. If selective retransmission were being used, then frame $I(2, 0)$ would be accepted and an SREJ frame returned to request that frame $I(1, 0)$ be retransmitted.

The frame sequence shown in Figure 5.15 is typical of an information transfer over a multidrop link operating in NRM. For a point-to-point link in ABM, however, a bidirectional flow of I-frames is possible and hence acknowledgement information relating to the flow of I-frames in one direction can be piggybacked in I-frames flowing in the reverse direction. An example illustrating this is given in Figure 5.16. For clarity, no transmission errors are shown.

As each I-frame is received, both the $N(S)$ and $N(R)$ contained within it are read. The $N(S)$ is first compared with the receiver's $V(R)$ and, if they are equal, the frame is in the correct sequence and hence is accepted; if they were not equal, the frame would be discarded and an REJ or SREJ frame returned. The $N(R)$ is then examined and this is used to acknowledge any outstanding frames in the retransmission list. Finally, as no further I-frames are awaiting transmission, an RR frame is used to acknowledge the outstanding unacknowledged frames in each retransmission list.

Flow control is particularly important when two-way simultaneous working is used and hence the link is being operated in ABM. Clearly, with NRM, if the primary experiences some transient overload conditions, it can simply suspend the polling operation, thereby allowing the overload to subside. When both sides of the link are operating independently, however, an alternative mechanism must be used. The flow control procedure used in HDLC is based on a window mechanism similar to that already discussed in Chapter 4.

As has been seen in the examples, the send and receive sequence numbers are incremented modulo 8 and hence the maximum send window, K, that can be used is 7; that is, the maximum number of I-frames that can be awaiting acknowledgement in the retransmission list at any time is 7. Each side of the link maintains a separate variable known as the retransmission count (RetxCount) which is initialized to zero when the logical link is first set up. It is incremented each time an I-frame is transmitted, and hence each time a frame is placed in the retransmission list, and is decremented whenever a positive acknowledgement is received, and hence each time a frame is removed from the retransmission list. The primary stops sending I-frames when the retransmission count reaches K and does not resume until a positive acknowledgement is received, either as a separate RR supervisory frame or piggybacked in an I-frame flowing in the reverse direction. It can be concluded, therefore, that transmission of I-

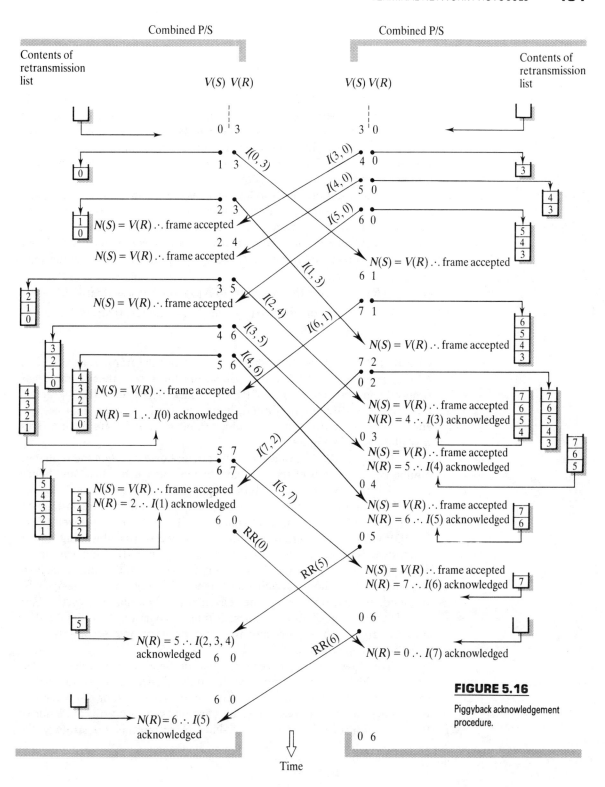

FIGURE 5.16

Piggyback acknowledgement procedure.

frames is stopped when:

$$V(S) = \text{last } N(R) \text{ received} + K$$

It should be noted that the window mechanism controls the flow of I-frames in only one direction and also that supervisory and unnumbered frames are not affected by the mechanism. Hence, these frames may still be transmitted when the window is operating. An example illustrating this is shown in Figure 5.17. In the example, for clarity, only the flow of I-frames in one direction is affected.

The application of a window mechanism means that the sequence numbers in all incoming frames must lie within certain boundaries. On receipt of each frame, therefore, the secondary may check to establish that this is the case and, if not, take corrective action. It can be readily deduced that each received $N(S)$ and $N(R)$ must satisfy the following conditions:

(1) $V(R) - 1$ is less than or equal to $N(S)$ which is less than $V(R) + K$.
(2) $V(S)$ is greater than $N(R)$ which is greater than or equal to $V(S) - \text{RetxCount}$.

Clearly, if $N(S)$ equals $V(R)$, then all is well and the frame is accepted. If $N(S)$ is not equal to $V(R)$ but is still within the range, then a frame has simply been corrupted and an REJ (go-back-N) or an SREJ (selective retransmission) frame is returned, indicating to the primary that a sequence error has occurred and from which frame to start retransmission. This was illustrated in Figure 5.15.

If $N(S)$ or $N(R)$ is outside of the range; however, then the sequence numbers at both ends of the link have become unsynchronized and hence the link must be reinitialized (set up). This is accomplished by the secondary, on detecting an out-of-range sequence number, discarding the received frame and returning a frame reject (FRMR) or a command reject (CMDR) frame to the primary. The latter then discards all waiting frames and proceeds to set up the link again by sending an SABM and waiting for a UA response. On receipt of the latter, both sides of the link reset their sequence and window variables and hence the flow of I-frames can be resumed. In fact, this is only one reason why a link may be reset; others include the receipt of an unnumbered frame such as a UA during the data transfer phase which indicates that the primary and secondary have become unsynchronized.

The flow control procedure just outlined is controlled by the primary side of the link controlling the flow of I-frames according to the send window. In addition, however, it may be necessary for the secondary to stop the flow of I-frames as a result of some event occurring at its side of the link. For example, with a go-back-N retransmission strategy the

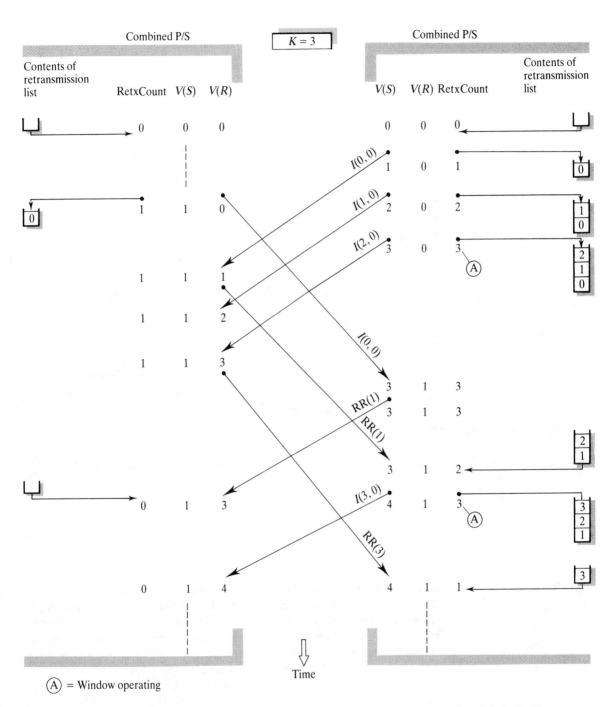

FIGURE 5.17

Window flow control procedure.

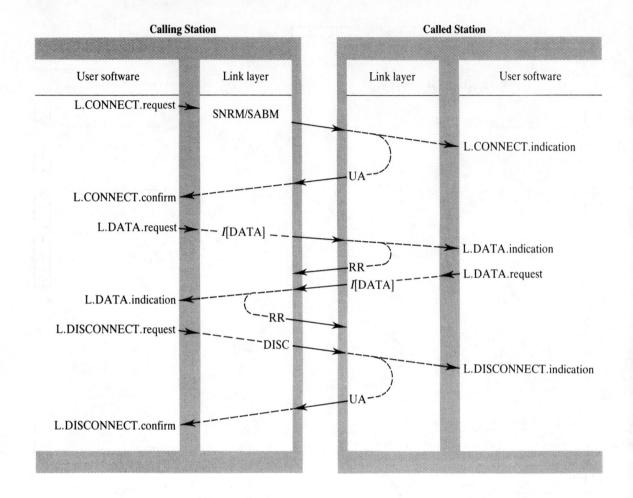

FIGURE 5.18

User/link layer interaction.

receive window is 1 and hence it is reasonably straightforward to ensure that there are sufficient memory buffers available at the receiver. If selective retransmission is used, however, it is possible for the secondary to run out of free buffers to store any new frames. Hence, when the secondary approaches a point at which all its buffers are likely to become full, it returns an RNR supervisory frame to the primary to instruct the latter to stop sending any more I-frames. Acknowledgement frames are not affected, of course, and hence when the number of full buffers drops below another preset limit, the secondary returns an RR frame to the primary with an $N(R)$ indicating from which frame to restart transmission.

(a)

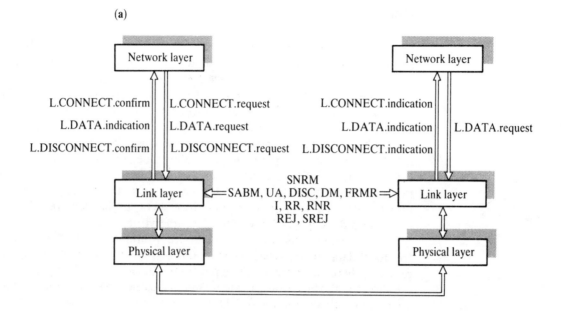

(b)

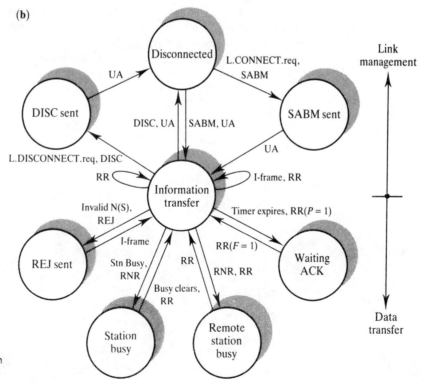

FIGURE 5.19

HDLC summary: (a) service primitives; (b) state-transition diagram (ABM).

User interface

The relationship between the link layer user services shown earlier in Figure 5.9 and the various protocol message units associated with HDLC can now be established. These are shown in the diagram of Figure 5.18.

On receipt of the initial L.CONNECT.request from the user, the link layer protocol entity in the calling system first sends an SABM supervisory frame to the link layer protocol entity in the called system. Then, on receipt of this, the latter creates and passes an L.CONNECT.indication primitive to the called user. In addition, it creates a UA frame and returns this to the calling side. On receipt of this, an L.CONNECT.confirm primitive is created and passed to the user so that the transfer of user data can then commence using the L.DATA service. Finally, after all data (information) have been exchanged, the link is disconnected using the DISC and UA supervisory frames.

A summary of the various service primitives and frame types (protocol data units) associated with HDLC is given in Figure 5.19(a). In practice, there are more unnumbered frames associated with HDLC than are shown in the figure but, as was mentioned earlier, the aim here is not to give a complete description of HDLC but rather highlight selected aspects of its operation. To further reinforce understanding, however, a (simplified) state-transition diagram for HDLC is given in Figure 5.19(b). The first entry alongside each arc is the incoming event causing the transition (if any) and the second entry the resulting action. Note that a state-transition diagram shows only the correct operation of the protocol entity and so normally this would be accompanied by a more complete definition in the form of an event-state table.

CHAPTER SUMMARY

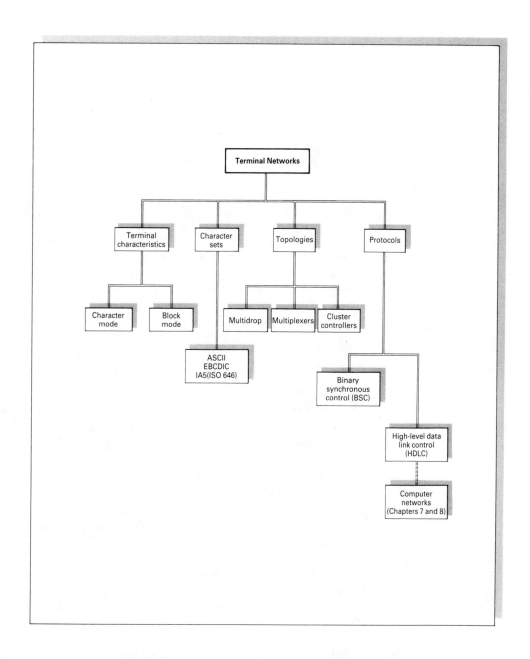

EXERCISES

5.1 (a) Explain the principle of operation of a terminal multiplexer and make a sketch of a terminal network that uses a number of such devices.

(b) Produce a sketch showing the internal organization of a terminal multiplexer and explain its operation. Describe the organization of the shared data link and explain how the controlling device determines the destination of each received character.

5.2 Explain the principle of operation of a statistical multiplexer and make a sketch of a terminal network that uses such a device. Derive typical data rates for both the user links and the shared data link and list the advantages and disadvantages of such a device as compared to a basic terminal multiplexer.

5.3 Outline the function of a terminal switching exchange and make a sketch of a typical terminal network that is based on such a device.

5.4 Make a sketch of a typical block-mode terminal network that uses multidrop lines and a poll–select control protocol. Explain the operation of the network and describe how the computer sends and receives messages to and from each terminal.

5.5 (a) Explain the function of:

- a cluster controller
- a front-end processor

as used in block-mode terminal networks and make a sketch of a typical network that uses such devices. List the advantages of using these devices.

(b) Distinguish between roll call polling and hub polling. Make a sketch of a typical network for each polling method and explain their operation.

5.6 (a) List the main transmission control characters used in the BSC protocol and explain their function.

(b) Show how the various characters listed in (a) are incorporated into BSC messages and illustrate typical message sequences to show their use in both the poll and select modes.

5.7 Assuming an HDLC protocol, distinguish between the NRM and ABM modes of working. Sketch typical frame sequences to show how a link is first set up (established) and then cleared (disconnected) for each mode. Clearly show the different frame types used and the use of the address and poll/final bit in each frame.

5.8 Define the supervisory frames used for acknowledgement purposes in the HDLC protocol. Assuming a unidirectional flow of I-frames, sketch a typical frame sequence to illustrate the acknowledgement procedure used in the HDLC protocol. Include in the diagram the contents of the link retransmission list and the state of the send and receive sequence variables as each frame is transmitted and received. Also show the send and receive sequence numbers contained within each frame and the state of the poll/final bit, where appropriate.

5.9   What is understood by a piggyback acknowledgement? Sketch a typical frame sequence to illustrate how piggyback acknowledgements are used in the HDLC protocol. Clearly show the send and receive sequence numbers contained within each frame transmitted and the contents of the retransmission lists and send and receive variables at each side of the link.

5.10 (a)   Outline the operation of a window flow control mechanism. Assuming a send window of K and a send window variable $V(W)$, deduce the range within which the send and receive sequence numbers contained within each received frame should be, assuming both sides of the link are in synchronism.

   (b)   Assuming a send window of 3 and a unidirectional flow of I-frames, sketch a frame sequence to illustrate the operation of the window flow control mechanism used with the HDLC protocol.

PART TWO
COMPUTER NETWORKS

Part Two of this book is concerned with the mode of operation of different types of data network used for computer-to-computer communication and the various interface standards and protocols associated with them.

Chapter 6 first presents an overview of the international standard protocols that have now been defined to allow computers from different manufacturers to communicate in an open way and how such protocols are specified. It then identifies those standards relating to the different types of data network and how the detailed operation of the different network types is masked from the higher, application-oriented protocols.

Chapter 7 then describes the operation and interface protocols associated with the different types of public data network.

Chapter 8 describes the operation and interface protocols associated with the different types of private (local area) networks. International standards are emphasized throughout.

COMPUTER COMMUNICATION

6

CHAPTER OBJECTIVES

When you have completed studying the material in this chapter you should be able to:

- appreciate the structure and aims of the ISO Reference Model for open systems interconnection;

- understand the basic function of each protocol layer in the reference model;

- understand the methodology that is used in the ISO standards documents to describe the services provided by a protocol layer;

- understand the methodology that is used in the ISO standards documents to define the operation and specification of a protocol entity;

- describe the services and operation of the transport layer;

- understand the formal specification of the transport protocol entity and a methodology for its implementation in structured program code.

6.1 INTRODUCTION

Communication between distributed communities of computers is required for many reasons. At a national level, for example, computers located in different parts of the country use public communication services to exchange electronic messages (mail) and to transfer files of information from one computer to another. Similarly, at a local level within, say, a single building or establishment, distributed communities of computer-based workstations use local communication networks to access expensive shared resources – for example, printers, copiers, disks and tapes, etc. – that are also managed by computers. Clearly, as the range of computer-based products and associated public and local communication networks proliferate, computer-to-computer communication will expand rapidly and ultimately dominate the field of distributed systems.

Although the physical separation of the communicating computers may vary considerably from one type of application to another, in general a computer communication network can be represented diagrammatically as shown in Figure 6.1. At the heart of any computer communication network is the data communication facility which, as has just been outlined, may be a PSDN, a private LAN or perhaps a number of such networks interconnected together. However, irrespective of the type of data communication facility, an amount of hardware and software is required within each attached computer to handle the appropriate network-dependent protocols. Typically, these are concerned with the establishment of a communication channel across the network and with the control of the flow of messages across this channel. The provision of such facilities is only part of the network requirements, however, since in many applications the communicating computers may be of different types. This means that they may use different programming languages and, more importantly, different forms of data representation. Also, the computers may use different operating systems; hence, the interface between user (application) programs, normally referred to as **application processes** or **APs**, and the underlying communication services may be different. For example, one computer may be a small single-user computer, while another may be a large multi-user system.

In the earlier days of computer communication, these issues meant that only *closed* communities of computers (that is, from the same manufacturer) could communicate with each other in a meaningful way. IBM's Systems Network Architecture (SNA) and DEC's Digital Network Architecture (DNA) are just two examples of communication software packages produced by manufacturers to allow their systems to be interconnected together. These proprietary packages, however, of which there are still many in existence, do not address the problem of universal interconnectability, or open systems interconnection. In an attempt to alleviate this

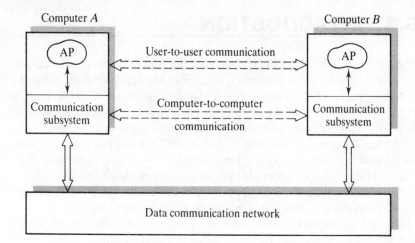

FIGURE 6.1

Computer communication
schematic.

problem, the ISO, in the late 1970s, formulated a reference model to
provide a common basis for the coordination of standards developments
and to allow existing and evolving standards activities to be placed into
perspective with one another. The ultimate aim was to allow an application
process in any computer that supported the applicable standards to freely
communicate with an application process in any other computer supporting
the same standard, irrespective of its origin of manufacture. This model
was termed the **ISO Reference Model for Open Systems Interconnection**. It
should be stressed, however, that this model is not concerned with specific
applications of computer communication networks. Rather, it is concerned
with the structuring of the communication software that is needed to
provide a reliable, data transparent, communication service (which is
independent of any specific manufacturers equipment or conventions) to
support a wide range of applications.

Some examples of application processes that may wish to communicate in an open way are:

- a process in a banking terminal that may wish to initiate a debit or
  credit operation on a remote system;

- a process (program) executing in a computer and accessing a remote
  file system;

- a process acting as a centralized file server to a distributed community of (client) processes;

- a process controlling a piece of equipment and linked to a manufacturing or plant control supervisory system;

- a process in an office workstation accessing an electronic mail
  service;

- a process acting as an electronic mail server to a distributed
  community of (client) processes.

Open systems interconnection (or OSI) is concerned with the exchange of information between such application processes and its objective is to enable such processes in real systems to cooperate in achieving a common (distributed) information processing goal.

6.2 ISO REFERENCE MODEL

A communication subsystem is a complex piece of software. Early attempts at implementing such software were often based on a single, complex, unstructured program (normally written in assembly language) with many interacting components. The resulting communication subsystem was thus difficult to test and often very difficult to modify.

To overcome this problem, the ISO have adopted a layered approach for the reference model. The complete communication subsystem is broken down into a number of layers each of which performs a well-defined function. Conceptually, these layers can be considered as performing one of two overall functions: network-dependent functions or application-oriented functions. This in turn gives rise to three distinct operational environments:

(1)   The **network environment**, which is concerned with the protocols and standards relating to the different types of underlying data communication networks.

(2)   The **OSI environment**, which embraces the network environment and adds additional application-oriented protocols and standards to allow end systems (computers) to communicate with one another in an open way.

(3)   The **real systems environment**, which builds on the OSI environment and is concerned with a manufacturer's own proprietary software and services, which have been produced to meet a particular distributed information processing task.

This is shown in diagrammatic form in Figure 6.2.

Both the network-dependent and application-oriented (network-independent) components of the OSI model are in turn implemented in the form of a number of **protocol layers**. The boundaries between each protocol layer, and hence the functions performed by each layer, have been selected as a result of the experience gained by earlier standards activity.

Each layer performs a well-defined function in the context of the overall communication strategy. It operates according to a defined protocol by exchanging messages, both user data and additional control

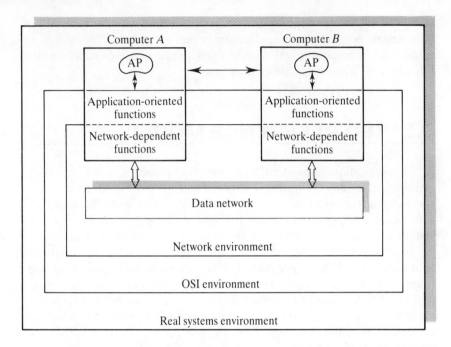

FIGURE 6.2

Operational environments.

information, with a corresponding (correspondent) layer in a remote system. Each layer has a well-defined interface between itself and the layer immediately above and below it, and as a result the implementation of a particular protocol layer is independent of all other layers.

The logical structure of the ISO Reference Model is as shown in Figure 6.3. As can be seen, it is made up of seven protocol layers. The lowest three layers (1–3) are network dependent and are concerned with the protocols associated with the data communication network being used to link the two communicating computers together. In contrast, the upper three layers (5–7) are application oriented and are concerned with the protocols that allow two end user application processes to interact with each other, normally through a range of services offered by the local operating system. The intermediate transport layer masks the upper application-oriented layers from the detailed operation of the lower network-dependent layers. Essentially, it builds on the services provided by the latter to provide the application-oriented layers with a network-independent message interchange service.

The function of each layer is specified formally in the form of a protocol that defines the set of rules and conventions used by the layer to communicate with a similar (**peer**) layer in another (remote) system. Each layer provides a defined set of services to the layer immediately above it and, in turn, uses the services provided by the layer immediately below it to transport the message units associated with the protocol to the remote

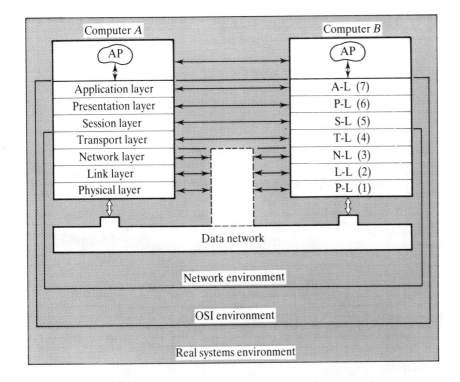

FIGURE 6.3

Overall structure of the ISO Reference Model.

peer layer. Thus, the transport layer, for example, provides a reliable, network-independent message transport service to the session layer above it and uses the services provided by the network layer below it to transfer the set of message units associated with the transport protocol to a peer transport layer in another system. Conceptually, therefore, each layer communicates with a similar peer layer in a remote system according to a defined protocol, but in practice the resulting protocol message units of the layer are passed by means of the services provided by the next lower layer. The basic function of each layer is summarized in Figure 6.4.

6.2.1 The application-oriented layers

The application layer

The **application layer** provides the user interface to a range of network-wide distributed information services. These include file transfer access and management, and general document and message interchange services such as electronic mail. A number of standard protocols are either available or are being developed for these and other types of service.

Access to application services is normally achieved through a

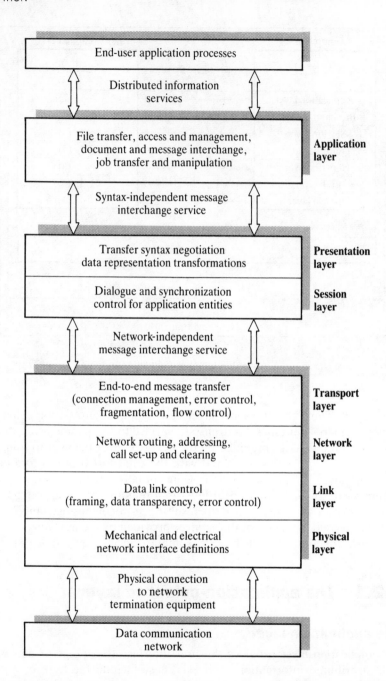

FIGURE 6.4

Protocol layer summary.

defined set of primitives, each with associated parameters, which are supported by the local operating system. The access primitives are the same as other operating system calls (as used for access to, say, a local file system) and result in an appropriate operating system procedure (process) being activated. These operating system procedures utilize the communication subsystem (software and hardware) as if it is a local device – similar to a disk controller, for example. The detailed operation and implementation of the communication subsystem is thus transparent to the (user) application process and, normally, when the application process making the call is rescheduled (run), one (or more) status parameters are returned indicating the success (or otherwise) of the network transaction that has been attempted.

In addition to information transfer, the application layer also provides such services as:

- identification of the intended communication partner(s) by name or by address;
- determination of the current availability of an intended communication partner;
- establishment of authority to communicate;
- agreement on privacy (encryption) mechanisms;
- authentication of an intended communication partner;
- selection of the dialogue discipline, including the initiation and release procedures;
- agreement on responsibility for error recovery;
- identification of constraints on data syntax (character sets, data structures, etc.).

The presentation layer

The **presentation layer** is concerned with the representation (syntax) of the data during transfer between two correspondent application layer protocol entities. To achieve true open systems interconnection, a number of common **abstract data syntax** forms have been defined for use by application entities together with associated **transfer** (or **concrete**) **syntaxes**. The presentation layer thus negotiates and selects the appropriate transfer syntax(es) to be used during a transaction so that the syntax (structure) of the messages being exchanged between two application entities is maintained. Then, if this form of representation is different from the internal abstract form, the presentation entity performs the necessary conversions.

To illustrate the services provided by the presentation layer, consider a telephone conversation taking place between, say, a French speaking person and a Spanish speaking person. Assume each uses an interpreter and that the only common language understood by both interpreters is English. Hence, each interpreter must translate both to and from English and to their local language. The two correspondents are thus analogous to application layer entities, the two interpreters representing presentation layer entities, French and Spanish the local syntaxes, and English the transfer or concrete syntax. Note also that there must be a universally understood language which must be defined to allow the agreed transfer language (syntax) to be negotiated and also that the interpreters do not necessarily understand the meaning (semantics) of the conversation.

Another function of the presentation layer is concerned with data security. In some applications, data sent by an application entity are first encrypted (enciphered) using a **key**, which is (hopefully) known only by the intended recipient presentation layer. The latter then decrypts (deciphers) any received data using the corresponding key before passing it on to the application entity. Although this is not currently part of the standard, the subject of encryption is discussed in Appendix B.

The session layer

The **session layer** provides the means necessary for two application layer protocol entities to organize and synchronize their dialogue and to manage their data exchange. It is thus responsible for setting up (and clearing) a communication (dialogue) channel between two correspondent application layer protocol entities (presentation layer protocol entities in practice) for the duration of the complete network transaction. A number of optional services are then provided including:

- Interaction management: The data exchange associated with a dialogue may be duplex or half-duplex. If it is the latter, this provides a means for controlling the exchange of data (dialogue units) in a synchronized way.

- Synchronization: For network transactions over a long period of time the user (through the services provided by the session layer) may choose to periodically establish synchronization points associated with the transfer with the correspondent user. Then, should a fault develop during a transaction, the dialogue may be restarted at an agreed (earlier) synchronization point.

- Exception reporting: Non-recoverable exceptions arising during a transaction can be signalled to the application layer by the session layer.

The transport layer

The **transport layer** forms the interface between the higher application-oriented layers and the underlying network-dependent protocol layers. It provides the session layer with a reliable message transfer facility that is independent of the underlying network type. The transport layer thus masks the detailed operation of the underlying network from the session layer and simply provides the latter with a defined set of message transfer facilities.

To cater for a range of different network types, the transport layer offers a number of **classes of service**. The alternative classes of service cater for the varying **quality of service (QOS)** provided by the different network types. There are five classes of service ranging from:

- class 0, which provides only the basic functions needed for connection establishment and data transfer, to
- class 4, which provides full error control and flow control procedures.

As an example, class 0 may be selected for use with a PSDN and class 4 may be used with a PSTN. This will be expanded upon later.

6.2.2 The network-dependent layers

As the lowest three layers of the reference model are network dependent, their detailed operation varies from one network type to another. In general, however, the **network layer** is responsible for the establishment and clearing of a network-wide connection between two transport layer protocol entities. It includes such facilities as network routing (addressing) and, in some instances, flow control across the computer-to-network interface.

The **link layer** builds on the physical connection provided by the particular network to provide the network layer with a reliable information transfer facility. It is thus responsible for such functions as error detection and, in the event of transmission errors, the retransmission of messages. Normally, two types of service are provided:

(1) **Connectionless** (also known as datagram), which treats each information frame as a self-contained entity that is transferred using a best-try approach.

(2) **Connection oriented**, which endeavours to provide an error-free information transfer facility.

Finally, the **physical layer** is concerned with both the physical and electrical interface between the user equipment and the network terminating equipment. It provides the link layer with a means of transmitting a serial bit stream between two correspondent systems.

6.3   STANDARDS ACTIVITIES

As has been stated, the ISO Reference Model has been proposed to act simply as a template for the structure of a communication subsystem against which standards activities associated with each layer may be based. Moreover, it is not intended that there should be just a single standard protocol associated with each layer. Rather, a set of standards is associated with each layer, each of which offers different levels of functionality. Then, for a specific open systems interconnection environment, such as that for linking a wide range of computer-based systems in a large, fully automated manufacturing plant, a selected set of standards is defined for use by all systems in that environment.

The three major international bodies actively producing standards for computer communications are the ISO, the American Institution of Electrical and Electronic Engineers (IEEE) and the CCITT. Essentially, the ISO and the IEEE are concerned with producing standards for use by computer manufacturers while the CCITT is concerned with producing standards for connecting equipment to the different types of national and international PTT networks. As the degree of overlap between the computer and telecommunications industries increases, however, so there is an increasing level of cooperation and commonality between the standards produced by each body.

A summary of some of the standards associated with each layer in the reference model is presented in Figure 6.5. As has been stated, the lower three layers vary for different network types. Those produced by the CCITT for use with PTT networks, for example, are the X- and the I-series; the X-series relate to existing networks whereas the I-series are intended for use with the emerging integrated services digital networks. Descriptions of these standards are presented in Chapter 7 when public data networks are discussed. Those produced by the ISO/IEEE are intended for use primarily with privately owned and run LANs and these are discussed in Chapter 8.

Although different numbering systems are used by the ISO and CCITT, the function and specification of the transport, session and presentation layers are almost identical. There is then a range of application layer standards, some defined by the ISO for use in private networks and others by the CCITT for use with PTT-supported services. The function and operation of the application-oriented (network-independent) protocol layers will be described in Chapter 9.

Before describing the function and operation of each layer, it is necessary first to gain an understanding of the terms and the methodology adopted by the various standards bodies for describing the overall operation and specification of a protocol layer. The remainder of this chapter, therefore, describes the methodology that is used and, as an example,

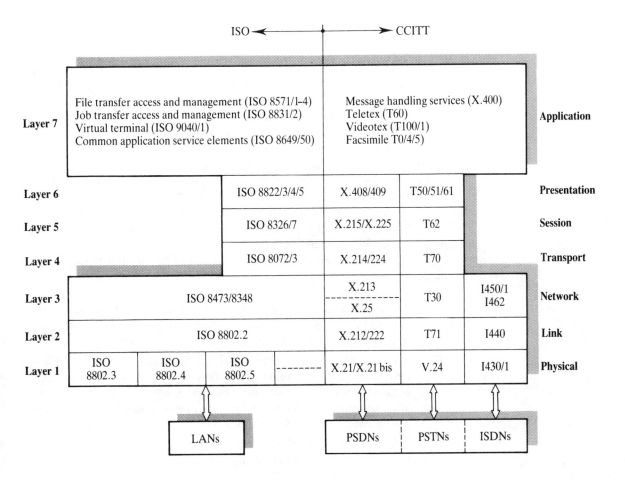

	ISO ◄─────────┼─────────► CCITT					
Layer 7	File transfer access and management (ISO 8571/1–4) Job transfer access and management (ISO 8831/2) Virtual terminal (ISO 9040/1) Common application service elements (ISO 8649/50)			Message handling services (X.400) Teletex (T60) Videotex (T100/1) Facsimile T0/4/5)		Application
Layer 6		ISO 8822/3/4/5	X.408/409	T50/51/61		Presentation
Layer 5		ISO 8326/7	X.215/X.225	T62		Session
Layer 4		ISO 8072/3	X.214/224	T70		Transport
Layer 3	ISO 8473/8348		X.213 --------- X.25	T30	I450/1 I462	Network
Layer 2	ISO 8802.2		X.212/222	T71	I440	Link
Layer 1	ISO 8802.3 | ISO 8802.4 | ISO 8802.5 | - - - - -		X.21/X.21 bis	V.24	I430/1	Physical
	LANs		PSDNs ¦ PSTNs ¦ ISDNs			

FIGURE 6.5

Standards summary.

describes the operation and specification of the transport layer. It should be stressed, however, that the descriptions that follow in this and subsequent chapters are not intended to be interpreted as being complete. Rather, the descriptions are presented in a tutorial form and are intended to give the reader an insight into the operation of each layer and the specification of specific protocols that have been defined for use within each layer. It should then be straightforward for the reader to consult a specific standards document and to readily understand and interpret its meaning.

6.4 PROTOCOL LAYERS

When describing the operation of any of the protocol layers, it is important from the outset to discriminate between the services provided by the layer, the internal operation (that is, the protocol) of the layer and the services used by the layer. This is important because only then can the function of each layer be defined in the context of the other layers. This also has the effect that a person (programmer) who is implementing just a single protocol layer needs only have a knowledge of the services the layer is to provide to the layer above, the internal protocol of the layer, and the services that are provided by the layer below to transfer the appropriate items of information associated with the protocol to the similar layer in a remote system; it should not be necessary for the implementor to have any further knowledge of the other layers.

For example, to describe the function of the transport layer, it is necessary only to consider:

(1) The defined set of services the transport layer is to provide to the session layer (for the purpose of transporting session layer message units to a peer session layer in a remote system).

(2) The internal operation (protocol) of the transport layer. (This is concerned with such functions as establishing and managing logical connections with a similar peer transport layer in a remote system, and the error and flow control of transport layer message units across established connections.)

(3) The services provided by the (lower) network layer to transfer these message units to a peer transport layer.

When describing the functions of each protocol layer, therefore, these three aspects will be treated separately; that is, the services provided by the layer, the internal operation (the protocol) of the layer and the services used by the layer.

The specification of each protocol layer comprises two sets of documents: a **service definition document** and a **protocol specification document**. The service definition document contains a specification of the services provided by the layer to the layer above it – that is, the **user services**. Normally, these are in the form of a defined set of **service primitives** each with an associated set of **service parameters**. As will be seen, it is through the service parameters that the layer above initiates the transfer of information to a similar **correspondent layer** in a remote system.

The protocol specification document contains:

(1) A precise definition of the **protocol data units** (**PDUs**) used by the

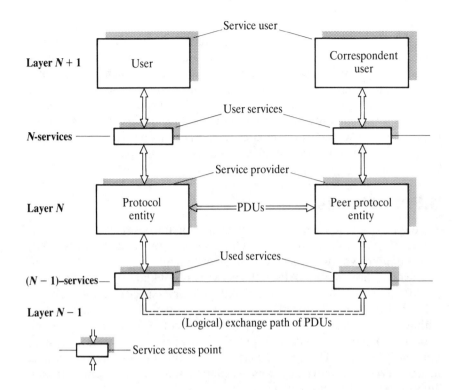

FIGURE 6.6

Protocol layer model.

protocol entity of that layer to communicate with a similar (peer)
protocol entity in a remote system.

(2)   A specification of the services used by the layer (that is, the services
provided by the layer immediately below it) to transfer each PDU
type.

(3)   A precise definition of the operation of the protocol entity presented in one of the formal specification methods.

Some of the terms just introduced are summarized in diagrammatic form in
Figure 6.6.

6.5   SERVICE DEFINITION

In any networking system it is important to discriminate between the
identity of a user application process and the *location* on the network where
the user application process currently resides. The identity of a user
application process is normally in the form of a symbolic *name* or *title* while

the location on the network is in the form of an *address*. This is similar to the use of names and addresses when sending a letter via the postal system: a name is used to indicate the identity of the intended recipient of the letter while the address is used to indicate where the recipient is currently resident. Also, because a number of application processes may be resident in the same computer, the address must contain, in addition to the physical address of the computer within the network, additional addressing information for use within the computer itself. This is analogous to, say, the floor and room numbers within a block of flats or apartments.

6.5.1 Names

Since symbolic names are used for identification purposes at the user level, it is necessary for the names utilized for each user application process (AP) to be unique within a specific OSI environment. Normally, the actual physical location of other APs in the network is not known by an AP and so an AP communicates with another AP by simply specifying the name or title of the intended correspondent. To ensure that names are unique within a particular (OSI) environment, some means of managing the allocation of names to APs (user processes and service provider processes) must be provided. The system that provides this function is known as a **name server** and normally this is maintained by the administration authority of the environment.

For a relatively small environment comprising, say, a distributed community of computer-based systems connected to a single LAN, it is usually sufficient to maintain a single name server for the complete system. For larger environments, however, comprising perhaps several thousand systems interconnected by a number of LANs and WANs, a single name server often becomes unmanageable. Therefore, a separate name server is used for each subnetwork. Then, to ensure that each name is unique within the complete environment, the name associated with a user on one subnetwork is prefaced by the identity of the subnetwork within the complete OSI environment.

6.5.2 Addresses

Although names are used at the user level, addresses are used within the OSI environment itself to ascertain, firstly, the physical location of the computer within the network in which the required AP is currently resident and, secondly, the identity of the application layer protocol entity to which the AP is currently said to be attached. It is, thus, the responsibility of the OSI environment to relate the required correspondent symbolic name specified by a user AP into a specific network-wide address. The list of relationships or mappings between symbolic names and addresses is contained in a **system directory** and hence, in principle, the actual physical location of an AP may vary simply by changing its entry in the system directory.

The addresses used in the OSI environment comprise a concatenation of a number of subaddresses known as **service access points (SAPs)**. The latter are used at the interface between each protocol layer in the system to which the AP is currently attached; that is, the address of an AP is made up of:

AP address = PSAP + SSAP + TSAP + NSAP

where PSAP is the service access point subaddress between the application layer protocol entity to which the AP is attached and the presentation layer, SSAP is the service access point subaddress between the presentation layer and the session layer, and so on. In practice, as will be seen, the PSAP and SSAP are one and the same. Also, it is the NSAP that contains the physical network-wide address of the system in which the AP is resident. The P/SSAP and TSAP addresses are then used within the system to determine the specific application layer protocol entity to which the user AP is currently attached. This is shown diagrammatically in Figure 6.7. The topic of addresses will be expanded upon in Chapters 9 and 10.

In the event of multiple transactions involving the same application entity being in progress concurrently – for example, multiple transactions involving an AP acting as a server such as a file server – it is an implementation-dependent (local) matter for each protocol layer within that system to know the identity of the particular transaction to which messages relate. That is, this is not part of the SAP address structure and, to allow for this, a **connection (endpoint) identifier** or **instance number** is associated with the appropriate PDUs exchanged. This will be expanded upon later when the transport layer is described.

6.5.3 Service primitives

The user services provided by a layer are specified by a set of service primitives. The services associated with a layer can be of two types: confirmed or unconfirmed. A schematic diagram illustrating the difference between the two types is shown in Figure 6.8(a) and (b).

Normally, a particular transfer starts by the user of the layer passing a **request primitive** across the layer interface. This, in turn, results in an associated PDU being generated by the local protocol entity within the layer and this being passed, using the services provided by the underlying layer, to a correspondent (peer) protocol entity in a remote system. Then, on receipt of the PDU, the peer protocol entity in the remote system creates an associated **indication primitive** and passes this up to the correspondent user. In the case of an unconfirmed service this completes

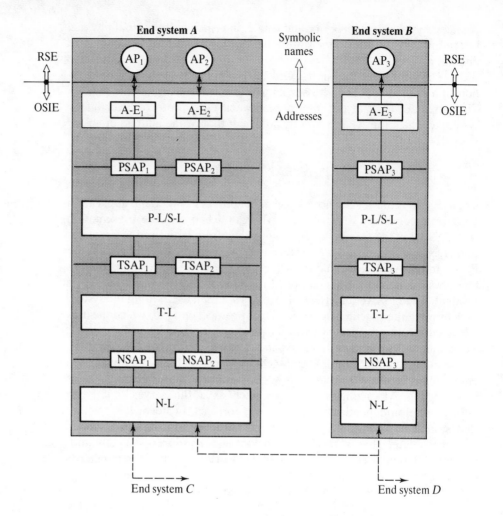

FIGURE 6.7

Address structure.

the transfer, but with a confirmed service this is followed by the correspon-dent user issuing a **response primitive**. Again, this results in an associated PDU being generated by the local protocol entity which is then sent back to the originating protocol entity, using the services provided by the underlying layer. On receipt of this, the originating protocol entity then creates a **confirmation primitive** and passes this up to the user to complete the transfer.

It can be concluded from the foregoing discussion that there is a logical relationship between the various service primitives and also that these relationships are related in time. The interrelationship of the service primitives within a layer are often illustrated, therefore, in the form of a **time sequence diagram**. As an example, Figure 6.8(b) is a time sequence diagram showing the interrelationship of the four primitives just described.

(a)

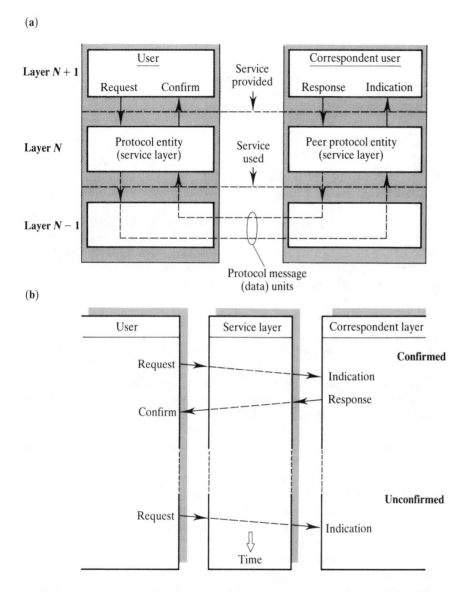

(b)

FIGURE 6.8

Service primitives: (a) space representation; (b) time sequence representation.

It should be apparent from this figure that a time sequence diagram is only an abstract way of representing the logical relationships between the service primitives of a layer and does not indicate how the specified services are implemented by the layer.

Normally, the type of primitive and the identity of the layer providing the service are included with the primitive name. Thus:

● T.CONNECT.request is a request primitive, issued by the transport service user (TS-user) – that is, the session layer – to set up a (logical) transport connection with a remote TS-user (session layer).

- S.DATA.indication is an indication primitive issued by a peer (correspondent) session layer to the presentation layer above it and is concerned with the transfer of data received from a remote presentation layer.

6.5.4 Service parameters and layer interactions

Associated with each service primitive is a defined set of parameters. As will be seen, it is through these parameters that adjacent layers within the same system pass information and also how two correspondent user layers in different systems exchange PDUs. For example, the parameters associated with the previous service primitives may include:

T.CONNECT.request (called address, calling address, . . . , user data)

S.DATA.indication (connection identifier, user data)

In the first example, the called address and calling address parameters are concatenations of the relevant service access point subaddresses associated with the particular logical connection being established. Normally, the user data field parameter is an address pointer to a memory buffer containing a PDU generated by the protocol entity in the user layer above to be passed to a correspondent protocol entity in the user layer in the remote system. Thus, although the term 'user data' is used, this does not necessarily imply it is data as generated by a user application process. Rather, it means that it is data with meaning only to the user layer above and, as will be seen, it may contain protocol control information being exchanged between two correspondent user layers.

The user data parameter associated with a service primitive is known as a **service data unit** (**SDU**) by the recipient layer. Since this contains a PDU relating to the layer above, a $(N + 1)$-PDU is the same as a (N)-SDU. Typically, on receipt of a service primitive, the protocol entity of the layer reads selected parameters associated with the primitive and combines them with additional **protocol control information** (**PCI**) to form a PDU for that layer. The resulting PDU is then passed to the layer below in the user data field of a suitable primitive with additional parameters as appropriate. This is shown in diagrammatic form in Figure 6.9(a).

It may be concluded from this discussion that the user data field (parameter) associated with the service primitive at each layer interface grows as it passes down through the layers, with each layer adding its own PCI to it. Also, once the link layer protocol entity has added its own PCI, it is this that is encoded and transmitted to the remote system. Conversely, at the remote system, the user data field reduces at each layer interface as it passes up through the layers and the protocol entity in each layer reads and interprets the PCI relating to it. This is shown in diagrammatic form in Figure 6.9(b) and will be expanded upon in Chapter 10 after the detailed operation of each layer has been described.

6.5.5 Sequencing of primitives

Associated with each layer there is a range of primitives to provide such services as connection establishment, data transfer, and so on. On receipt of a service primitive at the interface of a layer, therefore, it is necessary first to determine whether the primitive is in the correct sequence; for example, normally it is not possible to issue a data transfer request primitive before a connection has been established. Within the standards documents, therefore, the acceptable sequence of service primitives associated with a layer is illustrated either in the form of a state-transition diagram or in the form of a **sequence table**. An example of each is shown in Figure 6.10.

In the example, the user services supported are intended to allow a user first to establish a logical connection with a remote (correspondent) user, then to transfer data across this connection and finally to disconnect (clear) the connection. For clarity, however, only the connect and data transfer primitives are included. Normally, the state-transition diagram is used simply to show the correct sequence of primitives that are allowed at the user interface. The sequence table, in contrast, is a more precise definition, as it shows all possible sequences, both valid and invalid. The sequence diagram is used, therefore, for implementation purposes to ascertain whether a received primitive is in the permitted sequence. Normally, receipt of an out-of-sequence primitive is a protocol violation and results in the associated connection being cleared (disconnected).

6.6 PROTOCOL SPECIFICATION

The protocol specification document for a layer comprises:

- A qualitative description of the types of PDU associated with the protocol entity and their purpose, together with a description of the fields present in each PDU and their use.

(a)

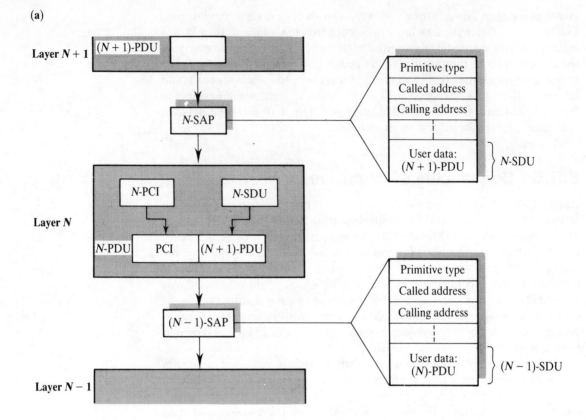

FIGURE 6.9

Layer interactions: (a) single
layer; (b) multiple layers.

- A description of the procedures followed during the various phases of operation of the protocol entity and the services it uses to transfer each PDU type.
- A formal definition of the structure of each PDU type.
- A precise definition of the operation of the protocol entity in one of the formal specification methods.

6.6.1 PDU definition

Two peer protocol entities communicate with each other by exchanging messages or PDUs. Typically, a PDU contains user data and PCI generated by the layer (protocol entity) itself. Since the parameters associated

(b)

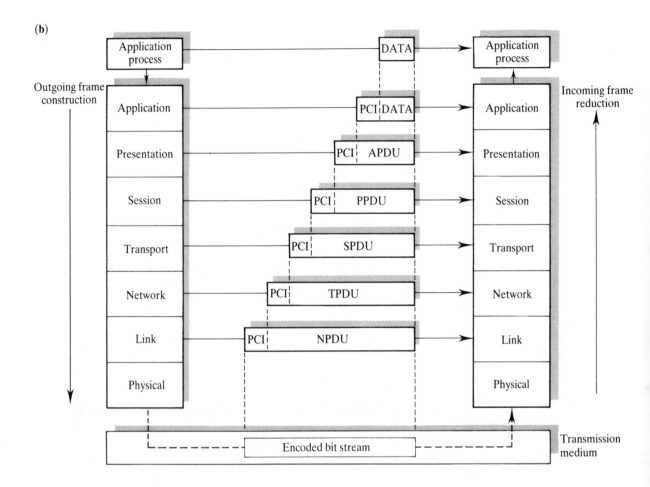

FIGURE 6.9 (cont.)

Layer interactions: (a) single layer; (b) multiple layers.

with a service primitive have only local significance (meaning), they are normally defined in terms of abstract data types, such as *INTEGER*, *BOOLEAN*, etc. In contrast, the PDUs generated by a protocol entity are passed *between* systems and hence, to avoid ambiguity, these must be defined in a precise way so that they have a common meaning in both systems.

   To achieve this, the PDUs associated with a protocol entity are defined in the standards documents in a precise way using either a specific bit string form or in an abstract data type form (known as Abstract Syntax Notation Number One or ASN.1) coupled with an associated set of **encoding rules**. An example of a PDU defined in each form is given in Figure 6.11. The example shown in Figure 6.11(a) is a PDU used by a transport layer protocol entity. It is a connect-request TPDU (transport protocol data unit). This, as will be described later in the chapter, is

(a)

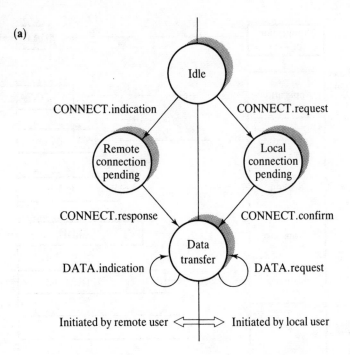

(b)

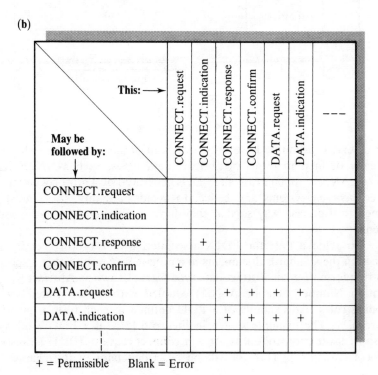

May be followed by: \ This: →	CONNECT.request	CONNECT.indication	CONNECT.response	CONNECT.confirm	DATA.request	DATA.indication	---
CONNECT.request							
CONNECT.indication							
CONNECT.response		+					
CONNECT.confirm	+						
DATA.request		+	+	+	+		
DATA.indication		+	+	+	+		

+ = Permissible   Blank = Error

FIGURE 6.10

Service primitives: (a) state-transition diagram; (b) sequence table.

(a)

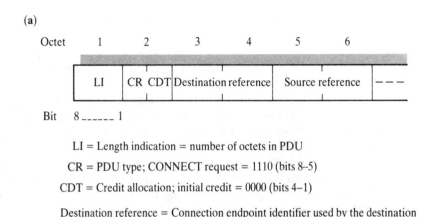

Octet   1   2   3   4   5   6

| LI | CR CDT | Destination reference | Source reference | – – – |

Bit   8 ‒‒‒‒‒‒ 1

LI = Length indication = number of octets in PDU

CR = PDU type; CONNECT request = 1110 (bits 8–5)

CDT = Credit allocation; initial credit = 0000 (bits 4–1)

Destination reference = Connection endpoint identifier used by the destination
for this connection; set initially to zero

Source reference = Connection endpoint identifier used by the source for this connection

(b)

```
FINITIALIZErequest ::= SEQUENCE {
        protocolId [0] INTEGER { isoFTAM (0) },
        versionNumber [1] IMPLICIT SEQUENCE {
                major INTEGER, minor INTEGER },
                – – initially { major 0, minor 0 }
        serviceType [2] INTEGER {
                reliable (0), user correctable (1) },
        serviceClass [3] INTEGER { transfer (0),
                access (1), management (2) },
        functionalUnits [4] BITSTRING {
                read (0),
                write (1),
                fileAccess (2),
                limitedFileManagement (3),
                enhancedFileManagement (4),
                grouping (5),
                recovery (6),
                restartDataTransfer (7) }
        attributeGroups [5] BITSTRING {
                storage (0),
                security (1) }
        rollbackAvailability [6] BOOLEAN DEFAULT FALSE,
        presentationContextName, [7] IMPLICIT ISO646String { "ISO8822"},
        identityOfInitiator [8] ISO646String OPTIONAL,
        currentAccount [9] ISO646String OPTIONAL,
        filestorePassword [10] OCTETSTRING OPTIONAL,
        checkpointWindow [11] INTEGER OPTIONAL}
```

FIGURE 6.11

Example PDU definition: (a) bit
string form; (b) ASN.1 form.

generated by a transport layer protocol entity to initiate the establishment of a logical connection with a peer transport entity as a result of a T.CONNECT.request service primitive at its user interface. The PDU in Figure 6.11(b) is associated with the application protocol entity FTAM, which will be described in Chapter 9.

As can be seen from Figure 6.11(a), the bit string form of each PDU is made up of a number of octets and the intended use and format of each octet is precisely defined. Although this form of definition has been used with all the lower network-dependent layers, ASN.1 is the method adopted for use with most of the application-oriented layers. Essentially, as can be deduced from Figure 6.11(b), ASN.1 is based on data typing as is used with most high-level programming languages. Thus, a PDU defined using ASN.1 is comprised of a number of typed data elements. Both simple (primitive) types (*INTEGER* and *BOOLEAN*) and structured types (*SET* and *SEQUENCE*) are used, the latter being similar to the **record** type in Pascal.

As the name implies, ASN.1 is an abstract syntax, which means that although a data element may be of a defined type (*INTEGER*, for example), its absolute syntax in terms of the number of bits and the order of the bits used is not implied. Thus, to produce the absolute or concrete syntax for a PDU defined in ASN.1, a set of encoding rules must be used. The resulting PDUs are then simply strings of octets that are interpreted in the same (fixed) way in each system. A more complete description of ASN.1 will be given in Chapter 9 when the application-oriented protocols associated with the ISO Reference Model are discussed.

6.6.2 Protocol operation – Overview

The operation of a protocol entity was first introduced in Chapter 4 when link-level protocols were described. A protocol entity is modelled in the form of a finite-state machine or automaton. This means that a protocol entity can only be in one of a finite number of states at any one time. The current operational state of the automaton, together with other related protocol state information, is retained in a set of state variables maintained by the automaton.

A transition from one state to another is prompted by a valid incoming event occurring at one of the automaton interfaces; for example:

- receipt of a service primitive from the interface with the layer above;
- receipt of a service primitive from the interface with the layer below;
- receipt of a service primitive from the interface with a **local entity** such as a **timer** or **management sublayer**.

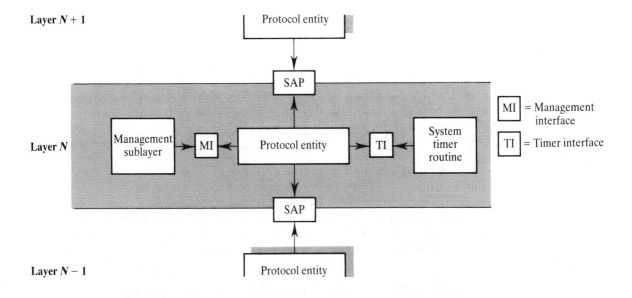

Layer N + 1

Protocol entity

Layer N

Management sublayer → MI ← Protocol entity → TI ← System timer routine

SAP

MI = Management interface

TI = Timer interface

Layer N − 1

Protocol entity

FIGURE 6.12

Incoming event interfaces.

This is shown in diagrammatic form in Figure 6.12. Normally, the occurrence of a valid incoming event results in a PDU being generated by the protocol entity, which is output in the form of an outgoing event (action) at one of the layer interfaces. Typically, this is associated with a change of state of the automaton and, possibly, a specific internal action, such as the starting of a timer, with an associated change to one or more of the automaton state variables.

All incoming events are assumed to be **atomic**; that is, a protocol entity (automaton) carries out all the operations associated with an event (outgoing event, specific actions, change of state) before another incoming event is processed. Thus, to ensure that each incoming event is processed in an atomic way, local events such as the occurrence of timeouts are passed to the protocol entity in the same way as other incoming events. Normally, the various interfaces shown in Figure 6.12 are each implemented in the form of a pair of queues (mailboxes): one for input to the protocol entity and the other for output. The queues are then serviced by the protocol entity in a prescribed way. This will be expanded upon later in the chapter.

In some instances, the operations performed by a protocol entity and the new state (if any) assumed by it depend on the current state of one or more **enabling conditions** or **predicates**. A predicate is a Boolean variable that depends on a combination of the values of the parameters associated with an incoming event and the current values of one or more of the automaton state variables. Normally, predicates are given the symbol P with an additional numeric qualifier. For example:

P0: T.CONNECT.request is acceptable;

P2: Retransmission count = Maximum.

Typical examples of their use are:

P5& (Not P1): Outgoing event *A*
    New state *X*;

P0: Outgoing event *B*
    New state *Y*.

If a predicate condition is not satisfied and the alternative state is not defined, a protocol error condition is said to have occurred and a predefined outgoing event and new automaton state are generated.

6.6.3   Protocol specification method

The standards documents present the formal specification of a protocol entity as follows:

- a definition of all the possible incoming events at each interface;
- a definition of the possible automaton states;
- a definition of all the possible outgoing events generated by the protocol entity together with a list of any specific actions to be carried out;
- a definition of the state variables and predicates (enabling conditions) associated with the operation of the automaton;
- an event-state table defining, for all possible incoming event and present state combinations, the outgoing event (and any specific actions) and the new automaton state together with any alternative event and new state combinations that depend on predicates.

The format of the event-state table used by the ISO is similar to that described in Chapter 4 and an example is shown in Figure 6.13(a). Each entry in the table specifies the appropriate outgoing event (together with any specific actions) and the new state of the automaton for that particular (incoming) event-(present) state combination. Normally, only valid event-state combinations have an entry in the table, all other combinations being left blank. A blank entry is a protocol error and will always be treated in a defined way.

Each entry in the table is specified in one of two ways, as shown in Figure 6.13(b). As can be seen, the entry either contains a specification of the actual outgoing event and the new state in the cell itself or the entry

(a)

Incoming Event \ Present State	S_0	S_1	S_2	---	S_N	
IE_1						⎫ Incoming events (from user layer – service primitives)
⋮						
IE_x						
IE_{x+1}						⎫ Incoming events (from layer below – PDUs received)
⋮						
IE_y						
IE_{y+1}						⎫ Local events (e.g., timer)
⋮						
IE_z						

(b)

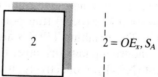

OE_x
S_A

OE_x = Outgoing event x
S_A = New state A

2

$2 = OE_x, S_A$

(c)

$P0: OE_x$
$S_A;$
$P2: OE_y$
S_B

OE_y

$OE_x[2]$
S_A

FIGURE 6.13

Event-state tables: (a) table format; (b), (c) alternative entry formats.

contains a reference number that refers to an entry in a separate list of outgoing event/new state specifications.

If the outgoing event and the new state are determined by predicates, these are included in the entry. An example is shown in Figure 6.13(c). Again, if none of the predicates are satisfied, a protocol error is assumed. Furthermore, if there is no state transition associated with an entry (that is, the automaton remains in the same state), only an outgoing event is specified. Similarly, if there is a specific action associated with an entry, a reference to the action in the list of actions is given. In the last example shown in Figure 6.13(c), the specific action [2] may mean, say, stop the associated timer.

6.7   TRANSPORT LAYER

The aims of this section are two-fold: firstly, to give an example of the application of the specification methodology introduced in the previous sections and, secondly, to describe the operation and specification of the transport layer in the context of the ISO Reference Model.

6.7.1   Overview

In keeping with the methodology outlined, a model of the transport layer is as shown in Figure 6.14. A user of the transport service (the TS-user) communicates with its underlying transport entity (or service provider) through a **transport service access point** (**TSAP**) using a defined set of user service primitives. The TSAP used is that associated with the initiating application entity. Service primitives cause, or are the result of, the exchange of **transport protocol data units** (**TPDUs**) between the two correspondent (peer) transport entities involved in a **transport connection** (**TC**). The resulting TPDUs are exchanged using the services provided by the underlying network layer through an associated **network service access point** (**NSAP**). Collectively, it is the TSAP and NSAP addresses that help to identify, uniquely, the application entity (and hence the attached AP) involved in the connection.

As already mentioned, the function of the transport layer is to provide the session layer with a reliable (error-free, in-sequence, with no loss or duplication) message transport facility that is independent of the quality of service provided by the underlying network. To cater for the different types of network, five classes of service are provided to the user:

• Class 0: Simple class (normally used with a network offering a high QOS such as the Telex network or a PSDN).

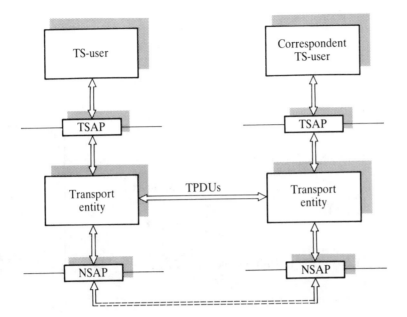

FIGURE 6.14

Model of transport layer.

- Class 1: Basic error recovery class.
- Class 2: Multiplexing class.
- Class 3: Error recovery and multiplexing class.
- Class 4: Error detection and recovery class. This contains the maximum control functions, such as error detection and retransmission, flow control, etc., and is intended for low-quality networks such as a PSTN or a WAN or an LAN operating with a connectionless network layer.

All the classes of service assume a connection-oriented mode of operation; that is, a logical TC is established between the two correspondent transport entities prior to any data transfers being made. Although this is the preferred mode of working in most applications, it inevitably involves a certain level of protocol overheads in connection with the setting up and clearing of the TC. For certain selected application environments in which overheads are important, therefore, a more efficient (but less reliable) class of service based on a connectionless mode of working has been proposed. As will be seen, in this mode, data may be transferred between two correspondent entities without a TC first being established.

It should be noted that it is not necessary for the transport layer to support all the different classes of service available. Normally, for a particular OSIE, the controlling authority of the environment specifies

(a)

Primitive	Parameters
T.CONNECT.request .indication	Calling address Called address Expedited data option Quality of service TS user data
T.CONNECT.response .confirm	Responding address Quality of service Expedited data option TS user data
T.DATA.request .indication	TS user data
T.EXPEDITED_DATA.request .indication	TS user data
T.DISCONNECT.request	TS user data
T.DISCONNECT.indication	Disconnect reason TS user data

(b)

Primitive	Parameters
T.UNIT_DATA.request .indication	Calling address Called address Quality of service TS user data

FIGURE 6.15

User service primitives and
associated parameters:
(a) connection oriented;
(b) connectionless.

which class of service is to be used. All systems would then be expected to utilize that class, which would be chosen to best suit the QOS provided by the underlying network(s) being used.

6.7.2 User services

The services provided by the transport layer can be divided into two categories: connection oriented and connectionless. In turn, the connection-oriented services can be divided into two subsets: those concerned with connection management and those concerned with data transfer. The connection management services allow a TS-user to establish and maintain a logical connection to a correspondent TS-user in a remote system. The data transfer services provide the means for exchanging data (messages) between the two correspondent users over this connection. A list of the service primitives associated with the transport layer, together with their parameters, is given in Figure 6.15 and a time sequence diagram showing the order of their use is given in Figure 6.16.

The called and calling address parameters associated with the T.CONNECT service are concatenations of the TSAP and NSAP addresses associated with the called and calling application entities involved in the connection. The QOS parameter refers to certain characteristics expected from the TC, such as throughput and error rates. Normally, these are defined for a particular network type.

The additional T.EXPEDITED_DATA service can only be used during the data transfer phase, after a connection has been established and on the proviso that the two correspondent TS-users have agreed on the use of this service when the TC is first established. It is provided to allow a TS-user to send an item of data that bypasses the flow control procedure associated with the T.DATA service of class 4. An example of its use will be identified when the higher, application-oriented (network-independent) layers are described in Chapter 9.

The sequence of primitives shown in Figure 6.16 assumes a successful connection establishment phase but, should the request for a connection be unacceptable by the correspondent TS-user, then the latter would issue a T.DISCONNECT.request primitive, instead of a T.CONNECT.response primitive, with the reason for the rejection given as a parameter. Once a TC has been established, either user can initiate its release at any time by issuing a T.DISCONNECT.request at the user interface with the reason as a parameter. Also, should the underlying network connection become disconnected, the transport entity would initiate the release of the TC using a T.DISCONNECT.indication primitive.

The two primitives associated with the connectionless mode of working, T.UNIT_DATA.request and T.UNIT_DATA.indication, enable a TS-user to initiate the transfer of an item of user data without first establishing a TC. With this service, however, there is no guarantee that the transfer has been successful and it is left to the higher application-oriented layers to recover from such eventualities. Inevitably, the protocol associated with the connection-oriented services is more complex than that associated with the connectionless mode; hence, the remainder of this chapter will concentrate on the connection-oriented mode of operation.

A state-transition diagram and an associated sequence table relating to the user services with the connection-oriented mode is given in Figure 6.17 and, as can be seen, the sequence table gives a more complete specification of the acceptable sequence of primitives by each user.

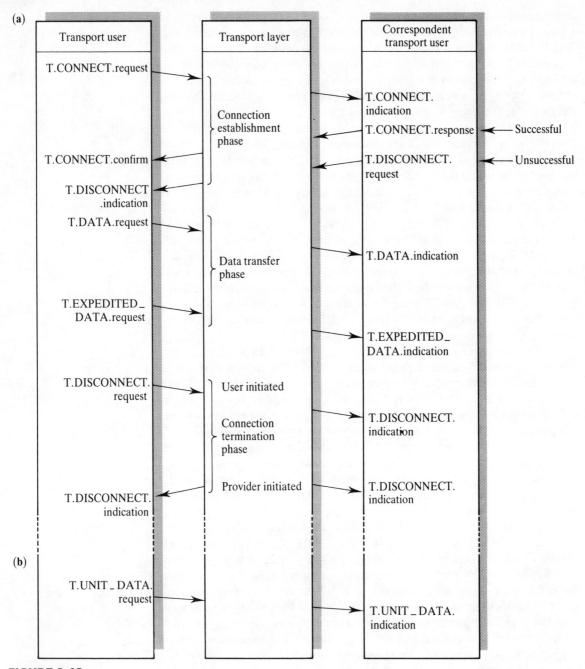

(a)

(b)

FIGURE 6.16

Time sequence diagram for user
services: (a) connection oriented,
(b) connectionless.

(a)

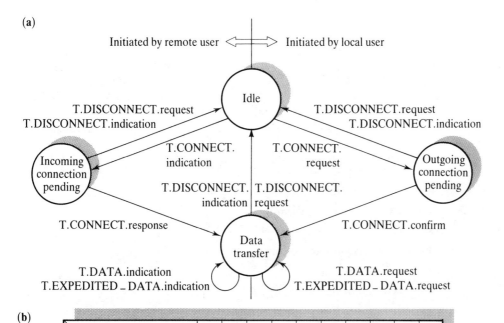

(b)

May be followed by: \ This:	T.CONNECT.request	T.CONNECT.indication	T.CONNECT.response	T.CONNECT.confirm	T.DATA.request	T.DATA.indication	T.EXPEDITED_DATA. request	T.EXPEDITED_DATA. indication	T.DISCONNECT.request	T.DISCONNECT. indication
T.CONNECT.request										
T.CONNECT.indication										
T.CONNECT.response		+								
T.CONNECT.confirm	+									
T.DATA.request			+	+	+	+	+	+		
T.DATA.indication			+	+	+	+	+	+		
T.EXPEDITED_DATA. request			+	+	+	+	+	+		
T.EXPEDITED_DATA. indication			+	+	+	+	+	+		
T.DISCONNECT.request	+	+	+	+	+	+	+	+		
T.DISCONNECT. indication	+	+	+	+	+	+	+	+		

+ : Possible   Blank : Not permitted

FIGURE 6.17

User services: (a) state-transition diagram; (b) sequence table.

6.7.3   Protocol operation

On receipt of a valid incoming service primitive (either from the TS-user or the network provider), the transport protocol entity generates an associated TPDU. Typically, assuming the incoming primitive is from the TS-user, the TPDU comprises the user data associated with the primitive together with additional PCI added by the transport entity. The generated TPDU is then transferred to the correspondent transport entity using the services provided by the underlying network layer.

The TPDUs associated with the transport protocol are as follows:

- CR: Connect request,
- CC: Connect confirm,
- DR: Disconnect request,
- DC: Disconnect confirm,
- DT: Data,
- AK: Data acknowledge,
- ED: Expedited data,
- EA: Expedited acknowledge,
- RJ: Reject,
- ER: Error.

Each of these TPDU types has a number of associated fields and the precise format and contents of each field is shown in Figure 6.18. The LI (length indicator) field indicates the number of octets in the header excluding the LI octet; the class field specifies the protocol class to be used with this connection (0–4); and the option field specifies whether normal (7-bit sequence numbers and 4-bit credit values) or extended (31-bit sequence and 16-bit credit) sequence and credit (CDT) fields are to be used.

The fields shown constitute what is termed as the **fixed header** part of each PDU. Some PDUs also contain a **variable header** part. For example, CR- and CC-PDUs contain fields for the calling and called TSAPs, the TPDU size to be used, and so on. Also, as will be seen later, if class 4 is used, then each TPDU contains a 16-bit check sum field. The use of some of the TPDUs will now be described as the various operational phases are discussed.

Connection establishment

The establishment of a TC begins when a TS-user issues a T.CONNECT.request primitive. The local transport protocol entity responds by creating a CR-TPDU and sends this to its peer transport protocol

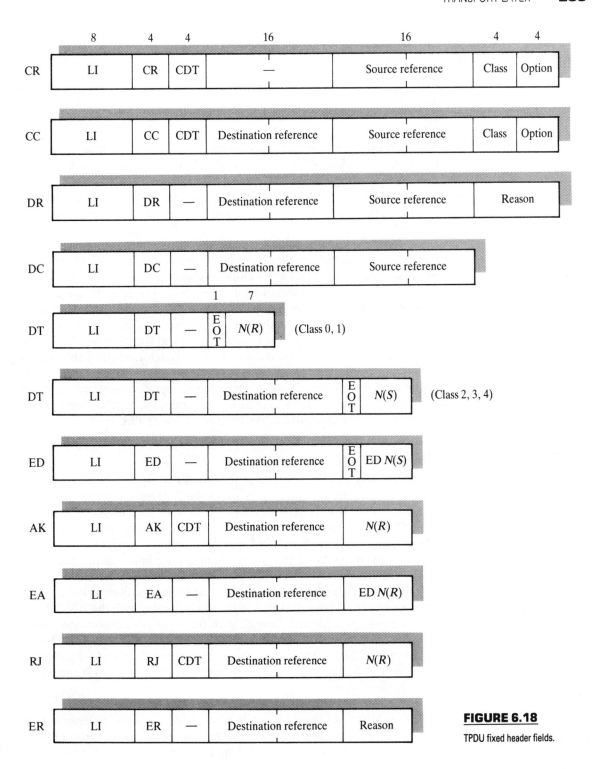

FIGURE 6.18

TPDU fixed header fields.

entity in the called system. On receipt of this, the latter notifies the designated user in its own system of the connection request by means of a T.CONNECT.indication primitive. Then, providing the correspondent user is prepared to accept the call, it responds by issuing a T.CONNECT.response primitive. Alternatively, if the correspondent user does not wish to accept the call, it issues a T.DISCONNECT.request primitive with the reason for the rejection as a parameter. The peer transport protocol entity then relays the appropriate response in either a CC-TPDU or a DR-TPDU, respectively. Finally, the response is relayed by the initiating protocol entity to the user by means of the T.CONNECT.confirm primitive or the T.DISCONNECT.indication primitive, respectively, the latter containing the reason for the rejection as a parameter.

The parameters contained in the CR- and CC-TPDUs relay information relating to the connection being established which both transport protocol entities must know in order to manage the subsequent data transfers across the established connection. This includes such information as the connection (endpoint) identifiers (references) to be associated with the TC by both the calling (source) and called (destination) transport entity, the class of service required and the maximum length of subsequent DT-TPDUs. Typically, the latter is determined by the type of underlying network being used and may range from 128 octets to 8192 octets increasing in powers of 2. Once the transport connection has been established, data can be accepted by the transport entities for transfer across the established logical connection in either direction.

Data transfer

A TS-user initiates the transfer of data to a correspondent user across a previously established connection using the T.DATA.request primitive. The local transport entity then transfers the user data (TSDU) in one or more DT-TPDUs depending on the amount of user data in the TSDU and the maximum size of the TPDU specified for the connection. Each DT-TPDU contains a marker (EOT) which, when set, indicates that this is the last TPDU in a sequence making up a single TSDU. Also, each DT-TPDU contains a send sequence number, $N(S)$, which is used both to indicate the order of the TPDU in a sequence and, in conjunction with the AK-TPDU, for acknowledgement and flow control purposes. When the destination transport entity has received, and acknowledged, all the DT-TPDUs making up a TSDU, it then passes the reassembled block of data (that is, the TSDU) to the correspondent user using a T.DATA.indication primitive.

The acknowledgement and flow control mechanisms used vary for different classes of service, which in turn are determined by the quality of service of the underlying data network being used to transport the TPDUs. With an X.25 PSDN, for example, the integrity and order of transmitted

TPDUs is maintained by the network layer; hence, only minimal acknowledgement and flow control mechanisms are needed in the transport protocol. With other types of network, however, this is not the case and so more sophisticated mechanisms, similar to those described in Chapter 4, must be used.

The acknowledgement procedure with class 4 is based on a go-back-N strategy (see Chapter 4) and works as follows. The receiver, on receipt of the next in-sequence DT-TPDU or, if the TPDU completes a contiguous sequence of TPDUs, returns an AK-TPDU that contains a receive sequence number, $N(R)$, that positively acknowledges correct receipt of those DT-TPDUs up to and including that with a send sequence number of $N(R) - 1$. On receipt of an out-of-sequence DT-TPDU (that is, with an $N(S)$ exceeding the next in-sequence DT-TPDU expected), the receiving transport entity returns an RJ (negative acknowledgement) TPDU with an $N(R)$ indicating the $N(S)$ of the next in-sequence DT-TPDU expected. Also, to overcome the loss of an AK- or RJ-TPDU, a timeout mechanism is employed for both these TPDUs.

If the network layer does not ensure that DT-TPDUs always arrive in sequence, the receiving transport entity uses the sequence numbers contained in each DT-TPDU to reassemble them into the correct order. In such cases, therefore, it is only when a DT-TPDU arrives in sequence or completes a contiguous sequence of outstanding TPDUs that the receiver returns an AK-TPDU indicating their correct receipt. A typical sequence of TPDUs to implement a user data transfer request is shown in Figure 6.19.

Another factor that must be considered is that if the service provided by the network layer is of a low quality, it may lose TPDUs without notifying the sender or intended receiver, or it may pass on TPDUs containing transmission errors. To allow for these possibilities, the user may specify a class of service at connection establishment that invokes a timeout and retransmission procedure, to allow for the possibility of lost TPDUs, and also computed check sums and error-detection mechanisms to ensure the integrity of each transmitted TPDU.

The protocol mechanism used to implement the timeout and retransmission scheme works as follows. When a transport entity sends a TPDU that requires a response, it sets a timer. Then, if the timer expires before the appropriate response is received, the TPDU is retransmitted and the timer reset. This cycle is repeated a number of times and, if the appropriate response is still not received, the transport entity assumes that communication with its peer has been lost. It then notifies the user by means of a T.DISCONNECT.indication primitive with the reason for the disconnection being passed as a parameter. The use of timeouts means that duplicates may be generated – for example, TPDU received correctly but acknowledgement lost. If a DT-TPDU is found to be a duplicate of a previously received TPDU, which is determined by its sequence number, an AK-TPDU is returned but the duplicate is discarded.

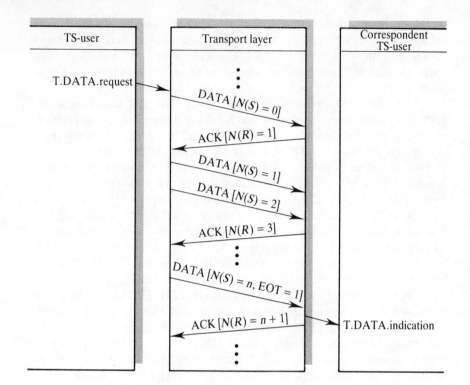

FIGURE 6.19

Data transfer example.

Data integrity is accomplished by generating and including a 16-bit check sum as a parameter in the header of each TPDU transmitted. The receiver then uses a similar algorithm to compute a check sum for the complete TPDU including the check sum parameter. This check sum should be zero if the TPDU does not contain any errors. If the computed check sum is not zero, the TPDU is discarded, but the timeout and retransmission schemes ensure that a new copy of the TPDU is sent.

A check sum is used with all CC- and CR-TPDUs and also with all other TPDUs if class 4 is selected. The check sum is intended to detect any TPDUs having residual (undetected) errors after their transfer across the network. The algorithm in the standards document has been chosen to minimize the amount of processing required per TPDU. The algorithm calculates two check sum octets, X and Y, such that:

$$X = -C1 + C0$$
$$Y = C1 - 2C0$$

where:

$$C0 = \sum_{i=1}^{L} a_i \quad \text{(modulo 255)}$$

$$C1 = \sum_{i=1}^{L} ia_i \quad \text{(modulo 255)}$$

n is the position of the first check sum octet, L is the number of octets in the complete TPDU and a is the value of the ith octet in the TPDU.

An example showing the check sum generation and checking procedures is shown in Figure 6.20. The contents of the TPDU are assumed to be comprised of a string of unsigned 8-bit integers with the two check sum octets (X and Y) initially zero. The two check sum octets are then computed as follows:

(1) Initialize C0 and C1 to zero.

(2) Process each octet sequentially from $i = 1$ to L.

(3) At each stage:
     (a) add the value of the octet to C0,
     (b) add the new C0 to C1.

(4) Calculate X and Y such that:
$$X = -C1 + C0$$
$$Y = C1 - 2C0$$

It should be noted that this procedure produces the same C1 as that produced by summing ia_i. Once computed, the two check sum octets (X and Y) are inserted into the TPDU prior to transmission, and a similar sequence of steps is followed at the receiver during the checking phase. Then, if *either* C0 or C1 is zero, no error is assumed. If C0 and C1 are *both* non-zero, however, an error is assumed and the TPDU is ignored. It is for this reason that a timeout is incorporated into the protocol.

During the computation of C0 and C1, modulo 255 arithmetic is used; that is, unsigned arithmetic (no overflow and carry ignored) and the results are assumed to be in the range [0..255]. Also, to compute the two check sum octets (X and Y), one's complement arithmetic is used. This implies the use of an end-around-carry and also a result of 255 is regarded as being zero.

The objective of a flow control mechanism is to limit the amount of data (or DT-TPDUs) transmitted by the sending transport entity to a level that the receiver can accommodate. Clearly, therefore, if the transport entity is only servicing a single user, the appropriate amount of buffer storage required to process the subsequent user TSDUs may be reserved in advance, when the transport connection is being established, and hence no

Assume TPDU contents are:

$$i = \begin{array}{ccccc} 1 & 2 & 3 & 4 & 5 \\ \hline 5 & 9 & 6 & X & Y \end{array} \qquad L = 5$$

Check sum generation:

$$
\begin{array}{lll}
i = 0 & C0 = C1 = 0 & X = Y = 0 \\
i = 1 & C0 := 0 + 5 = 5 & C1 := 0 + 5 = 5 \\
i = 2 & C0 := 5 + 9 = 14 & C1 := 5 + 14 = 19 \\
i = 3 & C0 := 14 + 6 = 20 & C1 := 19 + 20 = 39 \\
i = 4 & C0 := 20 + 0 = 20 & C1 := 39 + 20 = 59 \\
i = 5 & C0 := 20 + 0 = 20 & C1 := 59 + 20 = 79 \\
\end{array}
$$
$$X = -79 + 1.20 = -59 \, (196)$$
$$Y = +79 - 2.20 = +39 \, (39)$$

FIGURE 6.20

Transport protocol check sum
example.

Check sum checking:

$$
\begin{array}{lll}
i = 0 & C0 = C1 = 0 & X = -59 \, (196) \quad Y = +39 \, (39) \\
i = 1 & C0 := 0 + 5 = 5 & C1 := 0 + 5 = 5 \\
i = 2 & C0 := 5 + 9 = 14 & C1 := 5 + 14 = 19 \\
i = 3 & C0 := 14 + 6 = 20 & C1 := 19 + 20 = 39 \\
i = 4 & C0 := 20 - 59 = -39 \, (216) & C1 := 39 - 39 = 0 \, (255) \\
i = 5 & C0 := -39 + 39 = 0 \, (255) & C1 := 0 + 0 = 0 \, (255) \\
\end{array}
$$

flow control mechanism need be provided. If the transport entity is servicing multiple users, however, and buffer storage is reserved on a statistical basis, then a flow control mechanism must be supported by the protocol. This again is determined by the class of service provided by the transport entity.

The flow control mechanism used with class 4 is based on a (sliding) **window protocol**: an initial credit value, equal to the number of outstanding (unacknowledged) DT-TPDUs, for each direction of transmission is specified in the CDT field of each CR-TPDU and the CC-TPDU exchanged during connection establishment. The initial sequence number for each direction of transmission is set to zero when the connection is first established and this becomes the **lower window edge (LWE)**. The sender can continuously compute the **upper window edge (UWE)** by adding, modulo the size of the sequence field, the credit value for the connection to the LWE. The flow of DT-TPDUs is then stopped if the UWE becomes equal to the CDT value. The LWE is continuously incremented as AK-TPDUs for outstanding DT-TPDUs are received. This is shown in diagrammatic form in Figure 6.21.

The actual number of new DT-TPDUs that can be transmitted by the sender may vary during the lifetime of a connection since this is completely under the control of the receiver. Each AK-TPDU contains, in

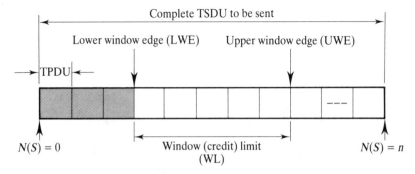

Complete TSDU to be sent

Lower window edge (LWE)   Upper window edge (UWE)

TPDU

$N(S) = 0$ Window (credit) limit
(WL) $N(S) = n$

Note

LWE is initialized to zero and is incremented
as each TPDU is sent.

UWE is initialized to the CDT value agreed when
the connection is established and is subsequently
incremented by the CDT value in each AK
TPDU received.

Flow is stopped if LWE reaches UWE.

FIGURE 6.21

Flow control mechanism.

addition to a receive sequence number, a new credit value which specifies
the number of new TPDUs that the receiver is prepared to accept after the
one being acknowledged. If this is zero, the sender must cease transmission
of DT-TPDUs over the connection. Normally, however, the credit value is
used in the situation where the receiver allocates a fixed number of buffers
for the connection, then, as each TPDU is received, this progressively
reduces the number of new TPDUs it is prepared to accept (the UWE) as
the transfer proceeds and buffers start to be used up.

Connection termination

Connection termination (or release) is initiated by either of the TS-users
issuing a T.DISCONNECT.request primitive to its local transport entity
with the reason for the clearing as a parameter. With class 0, termination of
the TC also implies termination of the associated network connection
(NC), while with the other classes the TC may be terminated independently of the NC. On receipt of the T.DISCONNECT primitive, the
transport entity sends a DR-TPDU. It then ignores all subsequently
received TPDUs until it receives a DC-TPDU. The peer entity, on receipt
of the DR-TPDU, returns a DC-TPDU and issues a
T.DISCONNECT.indication to the correspondent TS-user. The TC is
then assumed closed.

(a)

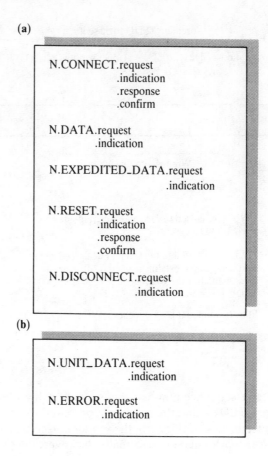

N.CONNECT.request
            .indication
            .response
            .confirm

N.DATA.request
         .indication

N.EXPEDITED_DATA.request
                  .indication

N.RESET.request
          .indication
          .response
          .confirm

N.DISCONNECT.request
                .indication

(b)

N.UNIT_DATA.request
              .indication

N.ERROR.request
         .indication

FIGURE 6.22

Network services: (a) connection oriented; (b) connectionless.

6.7.4 Network services

The transport layer uses the services provided by the network layer to exchange TPDUs with a correspondent transport layer in a remote system. The network layer can operate in either a connectionless or a connection-oriented mode. As will be described in subsequent chapters, LANs normally operate with a connectionless network layer while WANs normally operate with a connection-oriented network layer. The set of service primitives associated with each mode are shown in Figure 6.22. As can be seen from Figure 6.22(b), just a single (unconfirmed) service primitive (N.UNIT_DATA) is provided for the transfer of all information with a connectionless mode.

To illustrate the added overheads associated with a connection-oriented service, Figure 6.23 shows the network layer primitives necessary to establish a transport connection using (a) a connection-oriented service

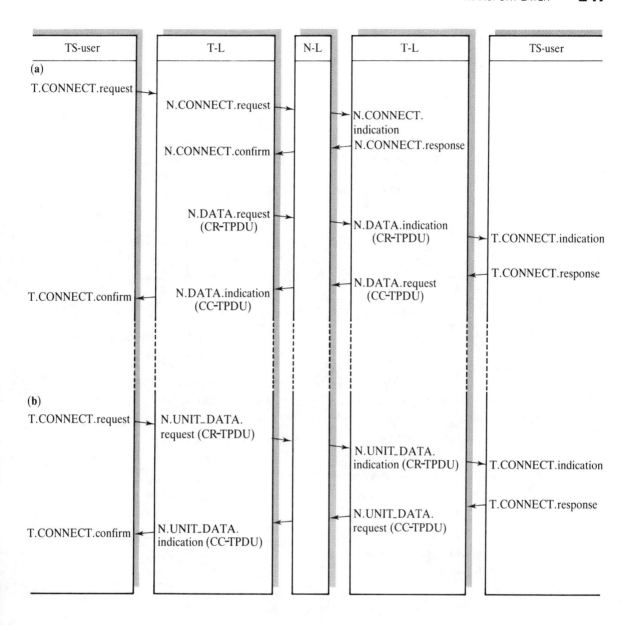

FIGURE 6.23

Network services for connection establishment: (a) connection oriented; (b) connectionless.

and (b) a connectionless service. As can be seen, the CR-TPDU is transferred directly using the N.UNIT_DATA service in the connectionless service while with a connection-oriented service a (network) connection must first be established before the CR-TPDU can be transferred as NS-user data. Clearly, however, the quality of service associated with a

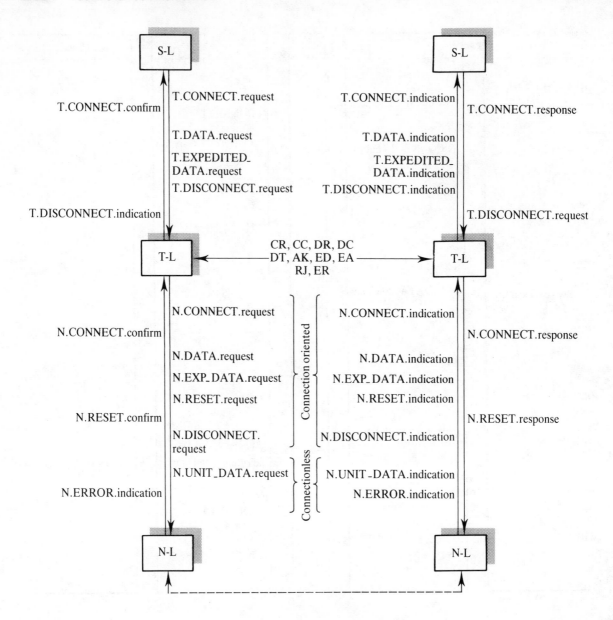

FIGURE 6.24

Transport layer summary.

connectionless service is much lower than that with a connection-oriented service.

A summary of the various services provided and the services used by the transport layer is given in Figure 6.24 together with a list of the various TPDU types exchanged between two correspondent (peer) layers. This style of presentation will also be used with the other protocol layers to be discussed.

6.7.5 Protocol specification

As was described earlier, in the ISO standards documents the formal specification of a protocol entity is specified in the form of an event-state table. This defines, for all possible incoming event-present state combinations, the appropriate outgoing event (together with any specific actions) and the new state. Furthermore, if predicates are involved, all the alternative outgoing event-new state possibilities are defined.

Normally, the event-state table(s) associated with a protocol are preceded by lists of the (abbreviated) names used for the possible:

- incoming events,
- automaton states,
- outgoing events,
- predicates,
- specific actions.

To illustrate the protocol specification technique used by ISO, a list of these names for the connection establishment phase of the transport entity are given in Figure 6.25. Since the network service primitives used to transfer the different TPDU types differ for both the type of network service and the type of TPDU being exchanged, only N-provider is normally specified in the various tables. The specific service to be used is then specified as the different TPDUs are defined.

Two alternative forms of the event-state table definition associated with the connection establishment phase are shown in Figure 6.26. In Figure 6.26(a), each entry in the table specifies the actual outgoing event and the new state combination(s) whereas in Figure 6.26(b) the entry is simply an indirection pointer to a table that contains the list of event-state combinations. All blanks in the table in (a) are error conditions and are the same as the zero entries in (b). Also, if none of the predicates associated with an entry are satisfied, then this also constitutes an error condition. The latter are all treated in the defined way.

6.7.6 Protocol implementation

A basic methodology for implementing a protocol entity was introduced in Chapter 4 when link-level protocols were discussed. The aim here, therefore, is simply to illustrate how the basic methodology may be extended to allow for the fact that the transport layer is one of a number of such layers.

It was stressed in the earlier sections of this chapter that when describing the operation of a communication subsystem, which has been

(a)

Name	Interface	Meaning
TCONreq	TS-user	T.CONNECT.request received
TCONresp	TS-user	T.CONNECT.response received
NCONconf	N-provider	N.CONNECT.confirm received
CR	N-provider	CONNECT.request TPDU received
CC	N-provider	CONNECT.confirm TPDU received

(b)

Name	Meaning
CLOSED	Transport connection is closed
WFNC	Waiting for a network connection
WFCC	Waiting for the CC-TPDU
OPEN	Transport connection is open and ready for data transfer
WFTRESP	Waiting for the T.CONNECT.response from the TS-user

(c)

Name	Interface	Meaning
TCONind	TS-user	Send T.CONNECT.indication
TCONconf	TS-user	Send T.CONNECT.confirm
TDISind	TS-user	Send T.DISCONNECT.indication
NCONreq	N-provider	Send N.CONNECT.request
CR	N-provider	Send CONNECT.request TPDU
CC	N-provider	Send CONNECT.confirm TPDU
DR	N-provider	Send DISCONNECT.request TPDU
NDISreq	N-provider	Send N.DISCONNECT.request

(d)

Name	Meaning
P0	T.CONNECT.request from TS-user unacceptable
P1	Unacceptable CR-TPDU received
P2	No network connection available
P3	Network connection available and open
P4	Network connection available and open and in progress
P5	Unacceptable CC-TPDU received

FIGURE 6.25

Abbreviated names for
connection establishment of the
transport entity: (a) incoming
events; (b) automaton states;
(c) outgoing events;
(d) predicates.

(a)

State / Event	CLOSED	WFTRESP	WFNC	WFCC	OPEN ---
TCONreq	P0: TDISind CLOSED; P2: NCONreq WFNC; P3: CR WFCC; P4: WFNC				
TCONresp		CC OPEN			
NCONconf			CR WFCC		
CR	P1: DR CLOSED; NOT P1: TCONind WFTRESP				
CC	DR CLOSED			NOT P5: TCONconf OPEN; P5: TDISind NDISreq CLOSED	

(b)

State / Event	CLOSED	WFTRESP	WFNC	WFCC	OPEN ---
TCONreq	1	0	0	0	
TCONresp	0	2	0	0	
NCONconf	0	0	3	0	
CR	4	0	0	0	
CC	5	0	0	6	

0 = TDISind, NDISreq, CLOSED (Error condition)

1 = P0: TDISind, CLOSED;
P2: NCONreq, WFNC;
P3: CR, WFCC;
P4: WFNC

2 = CC, OPEN

3 = CR, WFCC

4 = P1: DR, CLOSED;
NOT P1: TCONind, WFTRESP

5 = DR, CLOSED

6 = NOT P5: TCONconf, OPEN;
P5: TDISind, NDISreq, CLOSED

FIGURE 6.26

Event-state table formats for connection establishment.

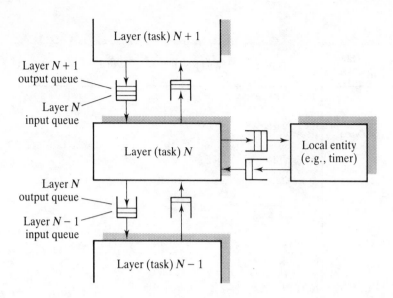

Layer $N + 1$ output queue

Layer N input queue

Layer N output queue

Layer $N - 1$ input queue

Local entity (e.g., timer)

FIGURE 6.27

Intertask queue structure.

structured according to the ISO Reference Model, it is essential to treat each protocol layer as an autonomous entity; that is, it provides a defined set of (user) services to the layer above it and, in turn, uses the services provided by the layer below it to transport the protocol data units generated by the layer to a similar peer layer in a remote system. In the same way, when implementing the various protocol layers in the software, it is essential to retain the same approach, otherwise the benefits gained by the adoption of a layered architecture are, of course, lost.

Normally, therefore, a complete communication subsystem is implemented as a suite of task (process) modules, one per protocol layer, with additional tasks to perform local management and timer functions. Tasks communicate with each other through a set of FIFO queues or mailboxes as shown in Figure 6.27. As will be expanded upon in Chapter 10, a communication subsystem is normally implemented using a separate processing subsystem, due to the relatively high processing overheads associated with a complete communication subsystem. Intertask communication is then managed by the local (real-time) kernel associated with the processing subsystem which also handles such functions as task scheduling and interrupt handling – for the timers associated with each protocol entity, for example.

As has been described, a protocol layer communicates with an adjacent layer by means of the service primitives associated with that layer. Each service primitive, together with its associated parameters, is first created in the defined (local) format in a **memory buffer** known as an **event control block** (**ECB**). Unlike the rigid structure (syntax) associated with PDUs, many of the parameters associated with each service primitive are

```
const  octet      = 0..255;
       maxSSAP  = 2;
       maxTSAP  = 2;
       maxNSAP = 11;

type   SSAPaddrtype  = array [1..maxSSAP] of octet;
       TSAPaddrtype  = array [1..maxTSAP] of octet;
       NSAPaddrtype = array [1..maxNSAP] of octet;
       TransportECBtype =

       record  EventType:      integer;
               UDBpointer:      ↑ UDB;
               UDBlength:      integer;
               CallingSSAP:     SSAPaddrtype;
               CallingTSAP:     TSAPaddrtype;
               CallingNSAP:     NSAPaddrtype;
               CalledSSAP:      SSAPaddrtype;
               CalledTSAP:      TSAPaddrtype;
               CalledNSAP:      NSAPaddrtype;
               DestinationId:   integer;
               SourceId:        integer;
               QOS:             integer
       end;

var    TransportECB : TransportECBtype;
```

FIGURE 6.28

Interlayer data structure example: transport ECB.

in the form of a list of abstract data types. Hence, assuming a high-level language is being used for the implementation of each protocol entity (and hence task), a language-dependent typed data structure is used when passing parameters between tasks.

In general, the number and type of parameters associated with each primitive varies but, to avoid the necessity of having a different data structure for each primitive type, there is normally just a single-typed data structure (the ECB) associated with each protocol layer. At the head of the ECB is a primitive type field. This is followed by an additional (typed) field for all the possible parameters associated with the complete set of service primitives of that layer. When passing primitives between layers, the sending task indicates the type of primitive being passed at the head of the ECB and, as will be seen later, the receiving task then uses this to determine the particular outgoing event procedure to be invoked. The latter then reads only those parameters related to it and hence those having meaningful values assigned to them.

The structure of a typical ECB is shown in Figure 6.28. The example selected relates to the transport layer and is thus used for all communications between the session and transport layers; that is, for all transport request, indication, response and confirm service primitives. The complete ECB is a **record** structure and the type of the service primitive is assigned to *EventType*. The use of the *UDBpointer* and its associated *UDBlength* will be expanded upon later. The calling and called SSAP, TSAP and NSAP fields are used with the T.CONNECT primitives while the *DestinationID* and *SourceId* are used with subsequent T.DATA primitives to relate the user data associated with the primitive to a specific TC.

Service primitives are passed between layers (tasks) by the initiating task simply invoking an intertask communication primitive (to the local kernel) with the address pointer of the ECB as a parameter. This results in the pointer being inserted by the kernel at the tail of the appropriate interlayer queue. Then, when a task is scheduled to run, it examines each of its input queues – with the layer above and below and with the timer and management tasks – to determine if an ECB is awaiting processing. If it is, it first reads the pointer from the head of the appropriate queue and proceeds to process the incoming event. Typically, this results in a PDU being generated and a suitably formatted message (ECB) being created and passed to one of its output queues.

The mechanism just outlined is suitable providing there is only a single application layer activity, and hence service request, being processed at one time. In many instances, however, there may be a number of different activities (service requests) being processed concurrently. In such cases, either all interlayer messages are passed using a single set of queues or there is a separate set of queues associated with each active service access point (channel). The problem with the former alternative is that, since there are often conditions associated with the state of a protocol entity (layer) that must be met before a particular action can be carried out (for example, the send window associated with a flow control mechanism being closed), it is sometimes necessary to suspend the processing of a message until the inhibiting condition is cleared. Normally, of course, the latter only affects a single channel and hence any other channels that may be active should not be affected.

The management of such issues can in fact become quite complicated (especially when expedited data is present, for example) and hence, to alleviate this, it is common practice to have a set of queues associated with each access point. Then, if a channel becomes temporarily closed, this is readily controlled by simply suspending the processing of entries in the affected queue until the inhibiting condition is cleared. In this way, the flow of messages through the other channels (queues) is unaffected.

As was described earlier, each service primitive normally has user data associated with it which, in general, is a concatenation of the PCI relating to the higher protocol layers. Thus, on receipt of a service primitive (ECB), the protocol entity uses the parameters associated with the primitive, together with the current protocol state information associated with the connection, to create the PCI for this layer. This is then added to the user data associated with the incoming primitive to form the layer PDU and it is this that is then passed down to the next lower layer in the user data field associated with a suitable primitive. This was shown earlier in diagrammatic form in Figure 6.9.

The user data associated with a primitive is held in a separate buffer known as the **user data buffer** (**UDB**). As can be deduced from the preceding paragraph, it is the UDB that contains the accumulated PCI (PDUs) for each of the higher layers and hence it is the contents of the UDB that are eventually transmitted by the physical layer. As was indicated earlier in Section 6.6.1, the PCI associated with each layer is defined in a rigid or concrete syntax, since it must be interpreted in the same way by two, possibly different, systems. Irrespective of the way the PDUs are defined, this is in the form of a string of octets and so each UDB is declared simply as an array of octets. The UDB-pointer field in each ECB is the address pointer to the UDB containing the user data associated with the primitive. The UDB-length is used to indicate the number of octets currently in the buffer and, as each layer adds its own PCI to the existing contents, it increments the UDB-length by the appropriate amount. Then, on receiving the UDB at the physical layer, the specified number of octets are transmitted from the UDB.

The outline structure of a single protocol layer in the context of a complete communication package is as shown in Figure 6.29. Since the ECBs and associated UDBs must be accessible by each layer, they are each declared as global data structures. Normally, a pool of ECBs (for each layer) and UDBs is created when the system is first initialized and the pointers to these buffers are then linked in the form of a free list. Hence, whenever a new buffer is required, a free buffer pointer is obtained from the free list and, whenever a buffer is finished with, it is returned to the free list.

Although there is a single *EventStateTable* array associated with each layer (task), there will be a separate set of state variables associated with each active channel if the layer can handle multiple service requests concurrently. For clarity, however, only a single set is shown in the figure. The example layer selected relates to the transport layer and hence the various event types, automaton states, outgoing event procedures and predicates are as was shown earlier in the event-state table of Figure 6.26.

As already mentioned, the scheduling of tasks is normally managed by the local real-time kernel; hence, if a task is idle (waiting for an incoming event to occur) and an ECB pointer is transferred to one of its input queues, the kernel automatically schedules the task to be run. The type of event (from the ECB) is first assigned to *EventType* and this, coupled with the current *PresentState*, is used to access the *EventStateTable* array. The entry in the table then defines the appropriate outgoing event procedure to be invoked and the new *PresentState*; alternatively, if predicates are involved, the list of alternative outgoing event-new state combinations are defined. Normally, the predicates relate to a number of different conditions; hence, they are set/reset either at the appropriate points during the processing of each event or by invoking specially written Boolean functions that compute the predicate state.

```
program    Communications_Subsystem;
global     Intertask queues (mailboxes);
           Event Control Blocks;
           User Data Buffers;
                  |
                  |

    task   Transport_Layer;
    local type  Events = (TCONreq, TCONresp, NCONconf, CR, CC, ---);
                States = (CLOSED, WFNC, WFCC, OPEN, WFTRESP, ---);
                  |
                  |

        var    EventStateTable = array [Events, States] of 0..N;
               PresentState:  States;
               EventType:  Events;
               ECB: ↑  ECB Buffer;
               UDB: ↑  UDB Buffer;


                  |
                  |

        procedure   Initialize; {Initialize EventStateTable contents and state variables}
        procedure   TCONind;  ⎫
        procedure   TCONconf; ⎬  List of outgoing event procedures
        procedure   TDISind;  ⎭
                  |
                  |

        function P0: boolean;  ⎫
        function P1: boolean;  ⎬  List of predicate functions
                               ⎭

        begin  Initialize;
            repeat   Wait for an ECB to arrive at an input interface queue;
                     EventType := type of event in ECB;
                     case  EventStateTable [PresentState, EventType] of
                         0: begin TDISind, NDISreq, PresentState := CLOSED end;
                         1: begin if P0 then begin TDISind; PresentState := CLOSED end
                            else if P2 then begin NCONreq; PresentState := WFNC end
                            else if P3 then begin CR; PresentState := WFCC end
                            else if P4 then PresentState := WFNC
                            else begin TDISind; NDISreq; PresentState := CLOSED end
                            end;
                         2:
                            |
                            |
            until Forever

        end.
                  |
                  |
```

FIGURE 6.29

Outline program structure of a
protocol layer.

CHAPTER SUMMARY

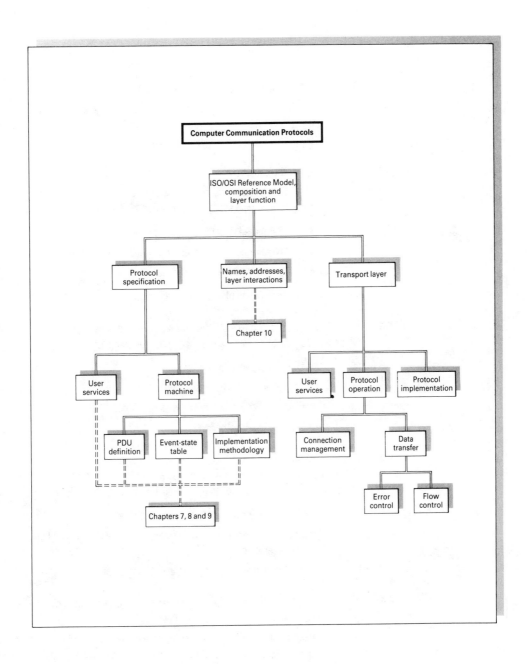

EXERCISES

6.1 In the context of the ISO Reference Model for OSI, explain briefly, with the aid of sketches where appropriate:

(a) The meaning and interrelationship of the terms network environment, open systems environment and real systems environment.

(b) The difference between a user name (title) and a fully qualified address.

(c) How the overheads associated with a user message increase as the message passes down through each protocol layer prior to transmission and decrease as it passes up through the layers on reception.

6.2 (a) What is the aim of the ISO Reference Model for OSI?

(b) Make a sketch summarizing the structure of the reference model and indicate where the following services are provided:

- distributed information services,
- syntax-independent message interchange service,
- network-independent message interchange service.

(c) Outline the function of each protocol layer.

6.3 Make a sketch of a model of a protocol layer, together with additional descriptions where appropriate, to explain the meaning of the following terms:

(a) The services provided by the layer.

(b) The service access points associated with the layer.

(c) The PDUs exchanged between two peer protocol entities.

(d) The services used by the layer.

6.4 Outline the structure of the event-state table used in the methodology adopted by the ISO to specify a protocol entity with particular emphasis on the meaning of each row and column. Give an example of an entry in such a table that has:

(a) A single outgoing event and new state combination.

(b) A number of alternative outgoing event and new state combinations determined by predicates.

(c) A specific action associated with the outgoing event.

6.5 (a) Use a time sequence diagram to illustrate a typical set of user services for the transport layer and describe their function.

(b) Define a set of TPDUs to implement these services and hence derive a time sequence diagram showing a typical sequence of TPDUs exchanged to implement the services in (a).

(c)   Define a set of network service primitives and hence derive a time sequence diagram showing how the TPDUs defined in (b) are transferred using these services.

6.6   Describe the following in relation to the data transfer phase of the transport layer:

(a)   The acknowledgement procedure.

(b)   The error-detection method used and an example of its use.

(c)   The flow control mechanism.

6.7   The connection establishment phase of the transport layer is to be implemented.

(a)   Produce a list of the incoming events, automaton states, outgoing events and predicates associated with this phase.

(b)   Derive an event-state table for the protocol entity showing clearly the outgoing event-new state possibilities for each incoming event-present state combination.

6.8   Outline a methodology for the implementation of a protocol entity. Include in the description:

(a)   The structure and use of an ECB.

(b)   The structure and use of a UDB.

PUBLIC DATA NETWORKS

7

CHAPTER CONTENTS

7

CHAPTER OBJECTIVES

When you have completed studying the material in this chapter you should be able to:

- describe the different types of public data network;

- understand the difference between a circuit-switched and a packet-switched network and the relative advantages and disadvantages of each type;

- describe the structure of the X.25 protocol as used in packet-switched networks and the operation of the packet (network) layer in the context of the ISO Reference Model;

- describe the function of a packet assembly and disassembly device and the various protocols associated with its use and operation;

- explain how a call is established and cleared using the X.21 protocol and a circuit-switched data network;

- understand the aims of an integrated services digital network and the various user interfaces and protocols associated with these networks.

7.1 INTRODUCTION

In Chapter 2 and later in Chapter 5, the use of the PSTN for the transmission of data was considered. Indeed, prior to the advent of public data networks, this was the only method available for the transmission of data between user equipment belonging to different establishments. As was indicated, however, a switched connection made through the PSTN currently supports only a modest user data rate, typically less than 4800 bps. Furthermore, as telephone calls are charged on a time and distance basis, the cost of a typical transaction can be very expensive owing to the often long distances and times involved, especially when a human user is involved.

It was for these reasons that many large organizations established their own proprietary nation-wide private data networks. Typically, these used dedicated lines leased from the telephone authorities to interconnect a number of privately owned switching nodes or exchanges. Although networks of this type offer the user security, flexibility and ultimate control, they also involve high investment costs in purchasing or leasing the equipment. Such networks are therefore generally owned by large organizations, such as the major clearing banks, who can both afford the initial capital outlay and also generate sufficient traffic to justify this level of investment.

At the time of introduction of the many private data networks, the PTT authorities would only lease lines to an organization to enable it to build its own private data network; that is, the PTTs would not supply lines to allow such networks to be connected together. The demand and subsequent establishment of public data networks stemmed, therefore, from the ever-increasing demands from users of these private networks for facilities to enable them to communicate with each other.

7.2 CHARACTERISTICS OF PUBLIC DATA NETWORKS

A **public data network (PDN)** is a network established and operated by a national network administration authority specifically for the transmission of data. A primary requirement for a PDN is the capability to facilitate the interworking of equipment from a number of different manufacturers, which in turn requires the establishment of agreed standards for the access and use of these networks. After much discussion and experimentation firstly at national and later at international level, a set of internationally

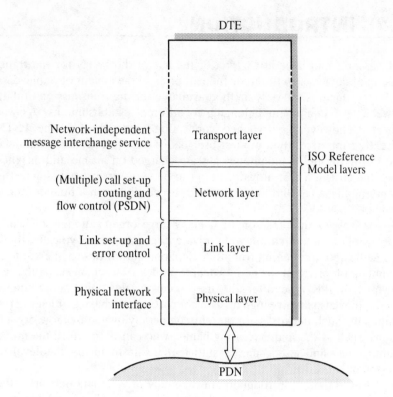

DTE

Network-independent
message interchange service → Transport layer

ISO Reference
Model layers

(Multiple) call set-up
routing and → Network layer
flow control (PSDN)

Link set-up and
error control → Link layer

Physical network
interface → Physical layer

PDN

FIGURE 7.1

Network-dependent protocol
layers in PDNs.

agreed standards have been accepted by the CCITT for use with a range of
PDNs. These standards are known as the X-series and I-series recommendations and include standards for user data signalling rates and also user
interfaces with such networks.

There are two main types of PDN: **packet-switched data networks
(PSDNs)** and **circuit-switched data networks (CSDNs)**, and different
standards have been defined for each type. Since the PSTN is still widely
used for the transmission of data, standards have also been established for
interfacing to this type of network. In general, the standards for each of
these networks refer to the lowest three layers of the ISO Reference Model
and the functions of each of these layers is as shown in Figure 7.1. It should
be remembered that the characteristics of the network-dependent layers in
the ISO Reference Model are made transparent to the higher protocol
layers by the transport layer, which offers the higher layers a network-
independent message transport service. This chapter is concerned with the
different types of PDN and the various interface protocols that have been
defined for use with each type.

7.2.1 Circuit and packet switching

Before describing the various interface standards associated with PDNs, it is necessary to first outline the differences between the two types of switching used in these networks. Each connection established through a circuit-switched network results in a specific physical communication channel being set up through the network from the calling to the called subscriber equipment, which is then used exclusively by the two subscribers for the duration of the call. An example of a circuit-switched network is the PSTN and indeed all connections established using the PSTN are of the circuit-switched type.

In the context of data transmission, a feature of a circuit-switched connection is that it effectively provides a fixed data rate channel and hence both subscribers must operate at this rate. Also, before any data can be transmitted over such a connection, it is necessary to first set up or establish the connection through the network. Currently, the time required to set up a call through the PSTN is relatively long (tens of seconds), owing to the type of equipment used in each exchange. Normally, therefore, when transmitting data, a connection is first established and this is then kept open for the duration of the transaction. However, the introduction of new computer-controlled switching exchanges, coupled with the adoption of digital transmission throughout the network, will mean that the set-up time of a connection through the PSTN will be much shorter (tens of milliseconds). Furthermore, the extension of digital transmission to the subscriber's equipment will mean that a high bit rate (typically 64 kbps or higher) switched transmission path will be available at each subscriber outlet. It will then be possible to use this facility for transmitting data without the necessity of modems. The resulting digital PSTN can then also be regarded as a public CSDN or, since such networks can support both digitized voice and data, integrated services digital networks (ISDNs). Further details relating to ISDNs will be presented later in the chapter.

Although the connection set-up time associated with an all-digital circuit-switched network is relatively fast, the resulting connection still only provides a fixed data rate path that both subscribers must transmit and receive at. In contrast, with a packet-switched network, it is possible for two communicating subscribers (DTEs) to operate at different data rates, since the rate at which data are passed at the two interfaces to the network is separately regulated by each subscriber equipment. Also, no physical connections are established through the network with a packet-switched network. Instead, all data to be transmitted are first assembled into one or more message units called **packets** by the source DTE, which include both the source and destination DTE network addresses. These are then passed bit serially by the source DTE to its local **packet-switching exchange (PSE)**. The latter, on receipt of each packet, first stores the packet and then inspects the required destination address contained within it. Each

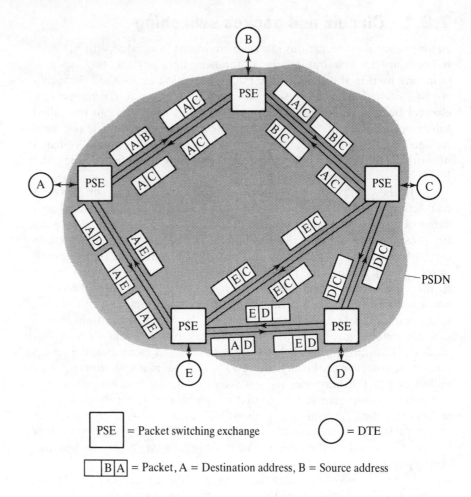

FIGURE 7.2

Packet-switching schematic.

PSE = Packet switching exchange   ◯ = DTE

☐ B A = Packet, A = Destination address, B = Source address

PSE contains a **routing directory** specifying the outgoing link(s) (transmission path(s)) to be used for each network address. On receipt of a packet, therefore, the PSE forwards the packet on the appropriate link at the maximum available bit rate. This mode of working is often referred to as the **packet store-and-forward mode**.

Similarly, as each packet is received (and stored) at each intermediate PSE along the route taken, it is forwarded on the appropriate link interspersed with other packets being forwarded on that link. Then, at the appropriate destination PSE, determined from the destination address within the packet, the packet is finally passed to the destination DTE.

This procedure is shown in diagrammatic form in Figure 7.2. As can be seen, each overall transaction occupies only a (random) portion of the available bandwidth on each link, since packets from different sources are interspersed with packets from other sources on the various network links. In the limit, this will vary from zero when the user is not transmitting any data to the full bandwidth if it is transmitting packets continuously.

It can also be deduced from the figure that it is possible for a number of packets to arrive simultaneously at a PSE on different incoming links and for each to require forwarding on the same outgoing link. Clearly, therefore, if a number of particularly long packets are waiting to be transmitted on the same link, other packets may experience unpredictably long delays. Consequently, to avoid this happening and hence ensure that the network has a reliably fast response time, there is a maximum length allowed for each packet. It is for this reason that when a packet-switched network is being used, a message as submitted to the transport layer within the DTE may first have to be divided by the source transport protocol entity into a number of smaller packet units before transmission and, in turn, reassembled into a single message by the correspondent transport protocol entity at the destination DTE. This is, of course, transparent to the transport layer user.

Another difference between a CSDN and a PSDN is that with a CSDN there is no error or flow control applied by the network on the transmitted data and hence this must be performed by the user. With a PSDN, however, sophisticated error and flow control procedures are applied on each link by the network PSEs, and hence the class of service provided by a PSDN is normally much higher than that provided by a CSDN.

It can be concluded from the foregoing that circuit and packet switching offer the user two different types of service. Hence, even with the advent of all-digitial networks, both types of service will still be supported and it will then be up to the user to select the particular service to be used.

7.2.2 Datagrams and virtual circuits

With a PSDN, two types of service are normally supported: **datagram** and **virtual call (circuit)**. The difference between the two types of service can be explained by the analogy between exchanging messages by means of letters and by means of a telephone call. In the first case, the letter containing each message is treated as a self-contained entity by the postal authorities and its delivery is independent of any other letters. In the case of a telephone call, however, a communication path is first established through the network and the subsequent message exchange takes place.

The datagram service is analogous to sending a message by means of a letter, since each packet entering the network is treated as a separate, self-contained entity with no relationship to other packets. Each packet is

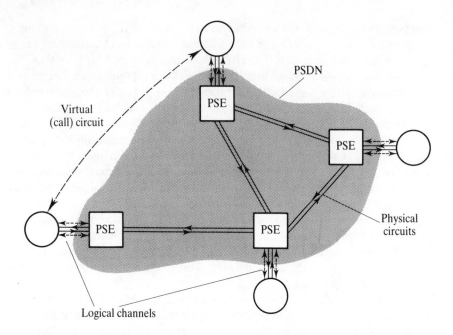

FIGURE 7.3

Logical channels and virtual calls.

simply received and forwarded in the way just outlined, and hence the datagram service is primarily used for the transfer of short, single-packet messages.

If a message contains multiple packets, the virtual call service is normally selected. This is analogous to sending a message by means of a telephone call, since when using this service, prior to sending any information (data packets) associated with a call, the source DTE sends a special call request packet to its local PSE containing, in addition to the required destination DTE network address, a reference number called the **logical channel identifier (LCI)**. This is noted by the PSE and the packet is then forwarded through the network as before. At the destination PSE, a second LCI is assigned to the call request packet before it is forwarded on the outgoing link to the required destination DTE. Then, assuming the call is accepted, an appropriate response packet is returned to the calling DTE. At this point, a virtual call is said to exist between the two DTEs. The information transfer phase is then entered and all subsequent data packets relating to this call are assigned the same reference numbers on each interface link to the network. In this way, both the source and destination DTEs can readily distinguish between packets arriving on the same link but relating to different calls. Hence, packets belonging to the same call can be passed to the user (the transport layer) in the same sequence as they were entered. The relationship between a logical channel and a virtual circuit is shown diagrammatically in Figure 7.3.

(a)

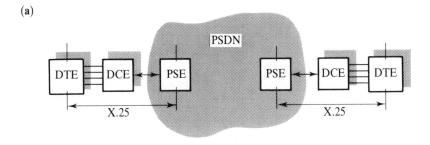

(b)

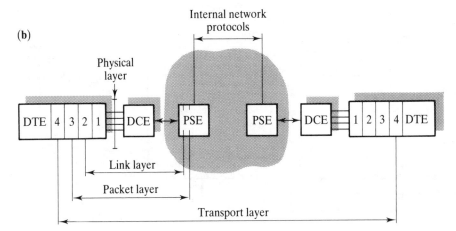

FIGURE 7.4

X.25 network access protocol: (a) applicability; (b) protocol components.

It should be noted that although a virtual circuit may appear to the user to be similar to a connection established through a circuit-switched network, a virtual circuit, as the name implies, is purely conceptual. Moreover, since the PSDN is able to apply additional error and flow control procedures at the packet level as well as those used at the link level, the class of service supported by a virtual circuit is very high; that is, the probability of all the packets relating to a particular call being delivered free of errors and in the correct sequence without duplicates is very high.

Normally, a virtual circuit is cleared and the appropriate logical channel identifiers released after all data relating to a call have been exchanged. However, it is possible for the virtual circuit to be left permanently established, so that a user who requires to communicate with another user very frequently does not have to set up a new virtual circuit for each individual call. This is then known as a **permanent virtual circuit** and, although the user must pay for this facility, the cost of each call is based only on the quantity of data transferred. As has been mentioned in

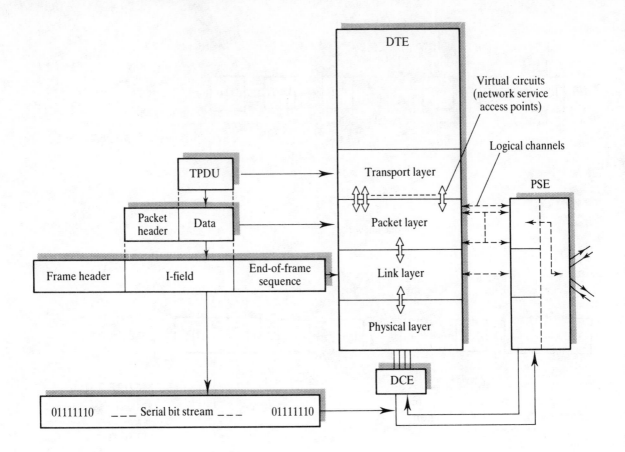

FIGURE 7.5

X.25 message units and layer
interactions.

connection with a circuit-switched network, charges are normally made on
a distance and call duration basis.

7.3 PACKET-SWITCHED DATA NETWORKS

The internationally agreed network access protocol that has been defined
to interface a DTE to a PSDN is X.25. X.25 is, in fact, a set of protocols
and the various protocol layers making up X.25 are shown in Figure 7.4.
As can be seen, the three protocols making up X.25 have only local
significance, which is in contrast to the transport layer which operates on
an end-to-end basis.

At the lowest layer, the X.21 interface standard is used to define the physical interface between the DTE and the PTT-supplied local DCE. The link layer protocol used with X.25 is a version of the HDLC protocol known as LAPB and its function is to provide the packet layer with an error-free packet transport facility over the physical link between the DTE and its local PSE. Finally, the packet layer is concerned with the reliable transfer of TPDUs and with the multiplexing of one or more virtual calls (TSAPs) on to the single physical link controlled by the link layer. The message units and interactions between the various layers are shown in Figure 7.5. Each layer will now be considered separately.

7.3.1 Physical interface

The physical interface between the DTE and the local PTT-supplied DCE is defined in recommendation X.21. The DCE plays an analogous role to a synchronous modem since its function is to provide a full-duplex, bit-serial, synchronous transmission path between the DTE and the local PSE. It can operate at data rates from 600 bps to 48 kbps. As will be seen in Section 7.4, X.21 is in fact the same interface as that used with an all-digital circuit-switched network. Note also that a second standard known as X.21 bis has been defined for use with existing (analogue) networks, which is in turn a subset of RS-232C/V.24; hence, existing user equipment can be readily interfaced using this standard. The various interchange circuits associated with X.21 and X.21 (bis) are defined in recommendation X.24 and are shown in Figure 7.6. The use of each line will be described in more detail in Section 7.4 when CSDNs are discussed.

7.3.2 Link layer

The aim of the link layer, which is often referred to as level 2 because of its position in the ISO Reference Model, is to provide the packet layer with a reliable (error free and no duplicates) packet transport facility across the physical link between the DTE and the local PSE. The link layer has no knowledge of the logical channel to which a packet may belong – this is only known by the packet layer. The error and flow control procedures used by the link layer apply, therefore, to all packets irrespective of the virtual circuits to which they belong.

The frame structure and error and flow control procedures used by the link layer are based on the HDLC protocol. Since the basic operation of the HDLC was described in Chapter 5, it will not be repeated again here. It uses the ABM of operation, which is also referred to as LAPB in the CCITT X.25 standards documents. This stands for Link Access Procedure Version B since it superseded the earlier Version A link access procedure.

In the context of the ISO Reference Model, the services provided by

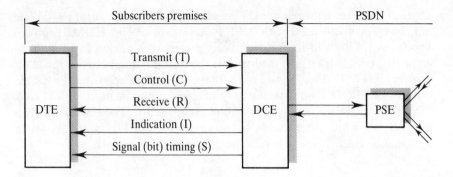

FIGURE 7.6

X.21 physical layer interface circuits.

the link layer to the network (packet) layer above it, together with a list of the PDUs associated with the operation of the link layer protocol entity, are summarized in Figure 7.7(a). The service primitives are shown in the order they can be issued with the initiating and corresponding reply primitives on the same line. It should be remembered, however, that either of the packet layers can initiate the three service requests shown.

Using ABM, both the DTE and PSE operate asynchronously, and hence both can initiate the transmission of commands and responses at any time. Also, since the protocol only controls the flow of I-frames across a point-to-point link – that is, across the link between the DTE and its local PSE – the address field in each frame is not used to convey network-wide address information; this is carried in the I-field since network addressing is handled by the packet layer. Instead, the address field contains either the DTE or DCE (PSE) address: if the frame is a command frame, the address specifies the recipient's address; if the frame is a response frame, the address specifies the sender's address. This is shown in diagrammatic form in Figure 7.7(b).

7.3.3 Packet (network) layer

In the context of the ISO Reference Model, the packet layer is the same as the network layer. Also, because of its position in the reference model, the packet layer is often referred to simply as level 3. The transport layer thus uses the services provided by the packet layer to enable it to exchange TPDUs with one or more remote transport layers.

User services

The user services provided by the network (packet) layer are shown in the time sequence diagram of Figure 7.8. As can be seen, a further service primitive (N.EXPEDITED_DATA) is provided in addition to the normal

(a)

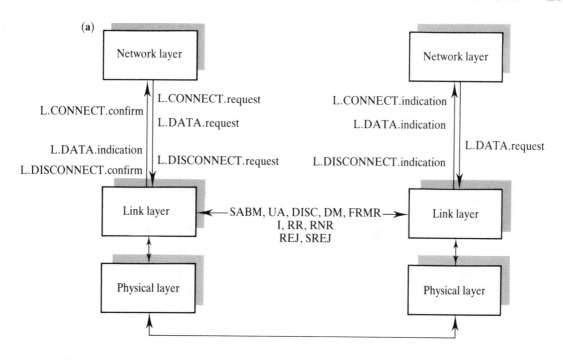

(b)

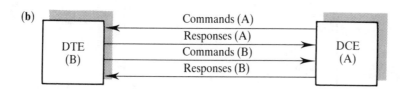

data transfer service primitive (N.DATA). This, as will be expanded upon later, is an optional service that allows the user to send a single data packet over a connection (logical channel) even though the normal flow of data packets may be stopped by flow control constraints. Another optional service (N.DATA_ACKNOWLEDGE) allows the user to specifically acknowledge receipt of a previously transmitted item of user data sent using the N.DATA service. Finally, the RESET service allows two users to resynchronize should the flow of packets over a logical channel become out of synchronism.

All of the primitives shown in the figure have parameters associated with them. For example, the parameters associated with the N.CONNECT

FIGURE 7.7

Link layer: (a) summary;
(b) address usage.

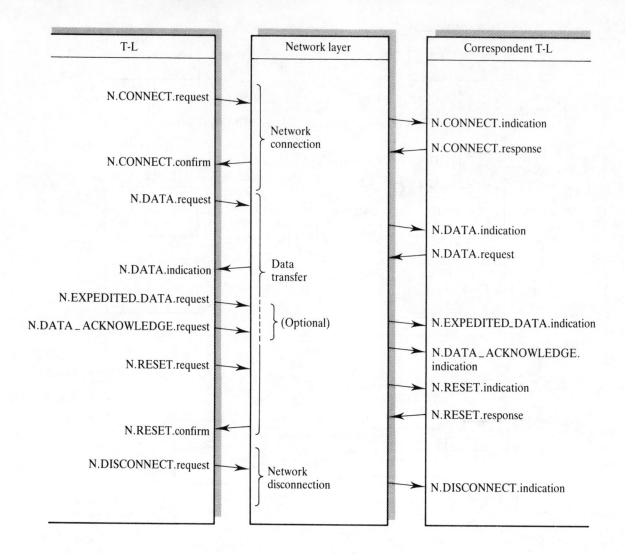

FIGURE 7.8

Network layer services.

primitives include:

- Called DTE network address
- Called DTE address extension
- Calling DTE network address
- Calling DTE address extension
- Quality of service
- Expedited data selection
- Receipt confirmation selection

Packet (PPDU) Types		Protocol Usage
DTE → DCE	DCE → DTE	
Call request Call accepted	Incoming call Call confirmation	Call set-up
Clear request DTE clear confirmation	Clear indication DCE clear confirmation	Call clearing
DTE data	DCE data	Data transfer
DTE RR DTE RNR DTE REJ Reset request DTE reset confirmation	DCE RR DCE RNR Reset indication DCE reset confirmation	Flow control
Restart request DTE restart confirmation	Restart indication DCE restart confirmation	Restart

FIGURE 7.9

PPDU types and their usage.

The last two of these parameters allow the two correspondent transport layer protocol entities to negotiate the use of the two optional services, which may be used during the subsequent data transfer phase. The network addresses are global network-wide addresses and the address extensions are the logical channel numbers associated with the call.

As can be deduced from Figure 7.5, the transport layer may have a number of network connections (calls) set up at one time, each call being associated with a particular NSAP. The packet layer thus performs a multiplexing function: all connections – virtual circuits (VCs) and permanent virtual circuits (PVCs) – are multiplexed on to the single data link controlled by the link layer. The flow of packets over each virtual circuit is then separately controlled by the packet layer protcol.

Protocol operation

Two packet layer protocol entities communicate with each other to implement the user services by exchanging **packet protocol data units (PPDUs)**. Each PPDU may contain either user (transport layer) data, PCI or, in some instances, both. The different PPDU types used to implement the user services listed earlier are shown in Figure 7.9. The use of each PPDU and its relationship with the various service requests will now be described.

(a)

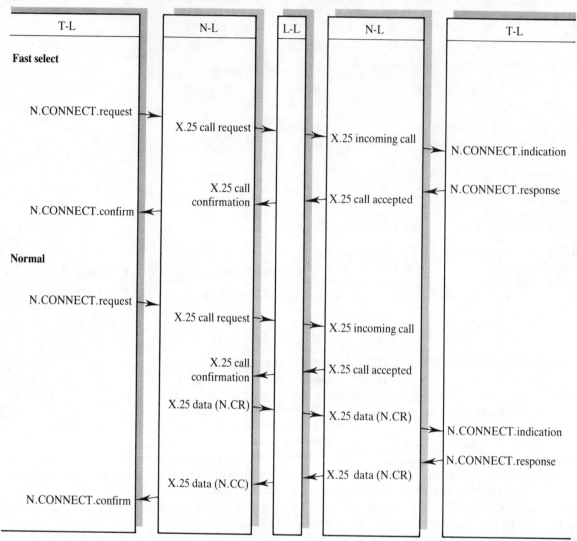

FIGURE 7.10

Network (packet) services:
(a) mapping alternatives;
(b) example use of LCIs.

Virtual call establishment and clearing A time sequence diagram illustrating the various phases of a virtual call is shown in Figure 7.10(a). A virtual circuit is established (set up) as a result of the user issuing an N.CONNECT.request primitive at a user service access point. The parameters associated with this primitive include the network address of the called DTE and also a limited amount of user data. As can be seen, two alternative procedures may be adopted to set up the network connection.

(b)

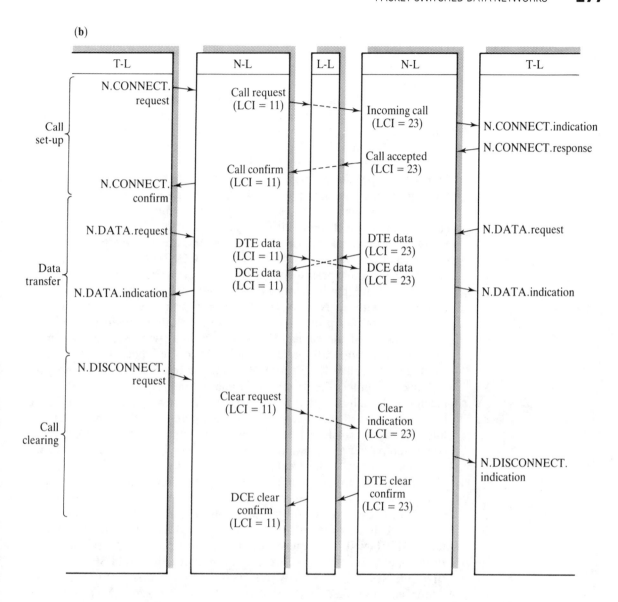

In the second (normal), an X.25 virtual circuit is established on receipt of the N.CONNECT.request primitive and the network connect request (N.CR) is then passed over this circuit using an X.25 data packet. The overheads associated with this method are high, however, and hence the alternative (**fast-select**) mode has been introduced. As can be seen, the network connect request is mapped directly into an X.25 call-request packet in this method and hence the call set-up overheads are reduced

FIGURE 7.10 (cont.)

Network (packet) services:
(a) mapping alternatives;
(b) example use of LCIs.

significantly. The reset and disconnect services are mapped in a similar way.

A time sequence diagram illustrating the use of the logical channels is shown in Figure 7.10(b), assuming the fast-select facility. On receipt of the N.CONNECT.request primitive, the source protocol entity first selects the next free LCI and creates a call-request packet (PPDU) containing the calling and called DTE addresses and the selected LCI. The packet is then passed to the link layer for forwarding to its local PSE.

On receipt of the packet, the local PSE notes the LCI selected and forwards the packet, according to the internal protocol of the network, to the appropriate destination PSE. The latter then selects the next free LCI for use on the link to the called DTE, writes this into the packet and changes the packet type into an incoming-call packet. This is then forwarded to the called DTE where its contents are used by the correspondent packet protocol entity to create an N.CONNECT.indication primitive, which is then passed to the correspondent user.

Assuming that the correspondent user is prepared to accept the call, it responds with an N.CONNECT.response primitive which, in turn, is used by the packet protocol entity to create a call-accepted packet. The latter is assigned the same LCI as the one that was used in the corresponding incoming-call packet. The call-accepted packet is then forwarded to the called DTE's local PSE and the reserved logical channel on this link then enters the data transfer phase. Similarly, the source PSE, on receipt of the call-accepted packet, inserts the previously reserved LCI for use on this part of the circuit into the packet and sets this logical channel into the data transfer state. It then converts the packet into a call-connected packet and forwards this to the calling DTE. Finally, on receipt of this packet, the calling-packet protocol entity issues an N.CONNECT.confirmation primitive to the user and enters the data transfer state.

If the correspondent user does not wish, or is not able, to accept an incoming call, it responds to the N.CONNECT.indication primitive with an N.DISCONNECT.request primitive. This results in the called packet protocol entity returning a clear-request packet to its local PSE. The latter first releases the previously reserved LCI and then returns a clear-confirmation packet to the called DTE. It then sends a clear-request packet to the source PSE which, in turn, passes the packet to the packet protocol entity in the calling DTE as a clear-indication packet. The DTE first releases the reserved LCI and then passes an N.DISCONNECT.indication primitive to the user. It then returns a clear-confirmation packet to its local PSE to complete the clearance of the virtual circuit. Similarly, either the user or the correspondent user can initiate the clearing of a call at any time by issuing an N.DISCONNECT.request primitive at the corresponding user interface.

Data transfer   After a virtual call (network logical connection) has been established, both the user and correspondent user may initiate the transfer of data independently of one another by issuing an N.DATA.request primitive at its network interface with the data to be transferred as a parameter. As has been mentioned, the maximum length of each data packet in a packet-switched network is limited, typically to 128 octets of data, to ensure a reliably fast response time. Hence, if a user wishes to transfer a message containing more than this number of octets, the message is first divided into an appropriate number of data packets and each packet sent separately. For the recipient user to know when each message is complete, therefore, each data packet sent through the network contains a single bit in its header known as the more-data bit, which is set whenever further data packets are required to complete a user-level (that is, transport layer) message.

Although the transport layer normally initiates the transfer of its own protocol control messages (TPDUs), to one or more peer transport layers, using an N.DATA.request primitive with the TPDU as a data parameter, the X.25 packet layer also allows the user to specify whether the associated parameter contains user-level control or data information. The type of the information is then embedded into the resulting data packet by the packet layer, which sets a special bit in the packet header known as the Qualifier or Q bit. Then, on receipt of each data packet, this information is passed with the associated data to the correspondent user.

Although the three protocol layers associated with the X.25 protocol set normally have only local significance, there is also a facility provided to allow acknowledgement information at the packet level to have end-to-end significance. This again is implemented by means of a special bit in each packet header known as the delivery confirmation or D bit. The D bit in the header of a data packet is set to 1 if the source DTE requires an end-to-end confirmation (acknowledgement) of correct receipt by the remote peer packet layer. As will be seen in Section 7.4, this information is carried in the header of a packet flowing in the reverse direction.

Flow control   All packet layer packets are transferred from a DTE to its local PSE using the services provided by the link layer. The use of the HDLC protocol at the link layer means that the basic packet transport facility supported is relatively reliable; hence, the emphasis at the packet layer is on flow control rather than error control. The flow control algorithm is based on a window mechanism similar to that introduced in Chapter 4. The flow of packets is controlled separately for each logical channel and for each direction of a call; that is, the flow of data packets relating to each call from DTE to PSE is controlled separately from the flow of packets from PSE to DTE.

To implement the window mechanism, all data packets contain a send sequence number, $P(S)$, and a receive sequence number, $P(R)$. As the sequence numbers are normally incremented modulo 8, they cycle repeatedly from 0 through to 7. The $P(R)$ contained in each data packet relates to the flow of data packets in the reverse direction. Alternatively, if there are no data packets awaiting transmission in the reverse direction, the $P(R)$ may be sent by the receiver in a special receiver-ready (RR) supervisory packet.

The first data packet in each direction (DTE to PSE and PSE to DTE) of a logical channel is given a $P(S)$ of 0 and each subsequent packet in the same direction carries the previous $P(S)$ incremented by 1. The number of packets relating to the same call that may be sent in each direction before a response is received is limited by the agreed window size, K, for the channel which, for reasons described in Chapter 4, has a maximum value of 7 if eight unique sequence numbers are being used. Thus, once the sender has initiated the transfer of a number of data packets up to the window size, it must then cease transmitting further packets until it receives either a data packet or a receiver-ready supervisory packet containing a $P(R)$ that indicates the willingness of the receiver to accept further packets on this channel.

To implement this scheme, the DTE and PSE each maintain three variables for each active logical channel (and hence virtual circuit):

- $V(S)$: This is known as the send sequence variable and indicates the $P(S)$ that will be assigned to the next data packet *sent* on this logical channel.

- $V(R)$: This is known as the receive sequence variable and indicates the $P(S)$ of the next in-sequence data packet that is expected to be *received* on this logical channel.

- $L(W)$: This is known as the lower window variable (edge) and is used to determine when the flow of data packets should be stopped.

All three variables are set to 0 when the virtual circuit is first set up or subsequently reset (see later). Then, as each data packet is prepared for sending, it is assigned a send sequence number, $P(S)$, equal to the current $V(S)$, which is then incremented (modulo 8). Similarly, on receipt of each data packet or receiver-ready flow control packet, the receive sequence number, $P(R)$, contained within it is used to update $L(W)$. The sender can continue sending data packets until either the window size is reached (that is, until the incremented $V(S)$ reaches $L(W) + K$) or a data or a receiver-ready packet is received containing a $P(R)$ that advances the current $L(W)$. Further data packets may then be sent until the window limit is again reached. A typical packet sequence illustrating this procedure for a window size of 3 is given in Figure 7.11(a). For clarity, just a single logical

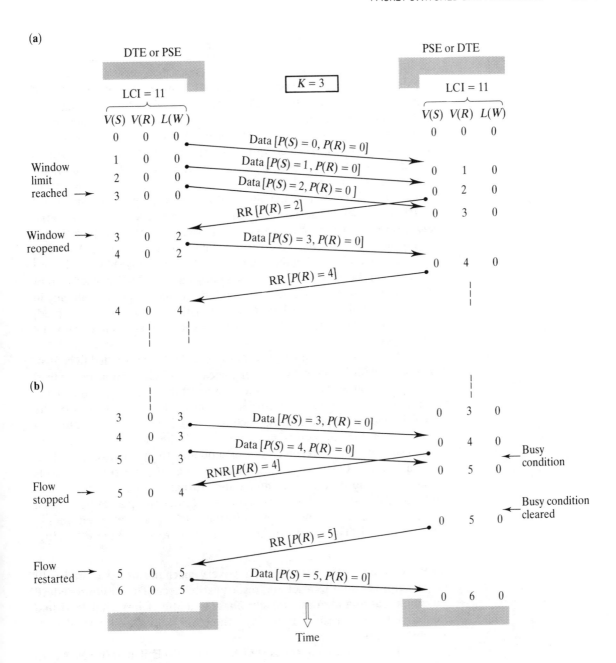

FIGURE 7.11

Flow control examples:
(a) window operation; (b) RNR
operation.

channel is assumed and only a unidirectional flow of data packets is shown.

The use of a window mechanism to control the flow of data packets means that the maximum number of packet buffers required to handle each call is readily determined. In practice, however, the total number of buffers provided to cater for all the calls that may be currently active is often less than the maximum number required. A facility is provided in the protocol, therefore, to allow the DTE (or PSE) to temporarily suspend the flow of data packets associated with a specific call (virtual circuit). This is achieved by the receiver returning a receiver-not-ready (RNR) packet for this logical channel, instead of a receiver-ready packet. Each RNR packet contains a $P(R)$ that defines the new $L(W)$ for this channel but, on receipt of an RNR, the sender must cease transmission of further packets until the receiver is ready to continue receiving data packets on this channel. This is normally achieved by the receiver returning an RR packet. A typical packet sequence illustrating the use of the RNR packet is shown in Figure 7.11(b). It can be deduced from this figure that the RNR packet cannot stop the flow of packets immediately, since there may be packets already in transit on the link. Any packets received in this way must be accepted, however, because of the lack of any error control associated with the packet layer.

Although the two mechanisms just described are provided to control the flow of data packets over each logical channel, as was mentioned earlier, provision is also made in the protocol for a DTE to send a single high-priority data packet to a correspondent DTE independently of the normal flow control procedures. Such a packet is known as an interrupt packet. Since this packet is not affected by the normal flow control mechanisms, it may be received out of sequence from other data packets over this circuit. On receipt of an interrupt packet, the receiving DTE (packet layer) must return an interrupt-confirmation packet, since there can be only one outstanding unacknowledged interrupt packet per virtual circuit at any time. This then allows a further such packet to be sent should this be required. This is shown in diagrammatic form in Figure 7.12(a).

Error recovery   The main error recovery mechanisms associated with the packet layer are the reset and restart procedures. The reset procedure is used only during the data transfer phase and affects just a single virtual call (circuit). The restart procedure, however, affects all virtual calls currently in progress.

A reset-request packet is sent by either DTE if it receives a data packet that is outside the current window limit. This indicates the two DTEs have become unsynchronized and hence the flow of data packets must be restarted. A typical packet sequence associated with the reset procedure is shown in Figure 7.12(b). Any data packets associated with the affected virtual circuit are discarded by the packet layer and the user is

(a)

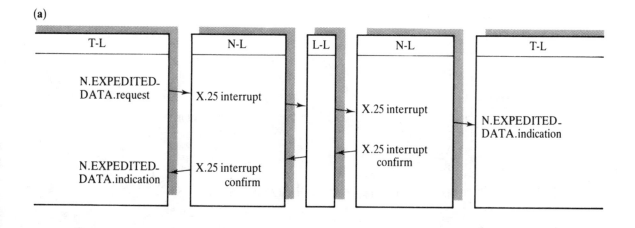

(b)

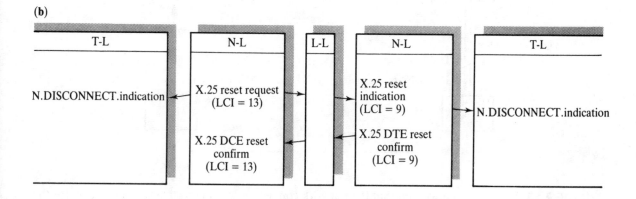

(c)

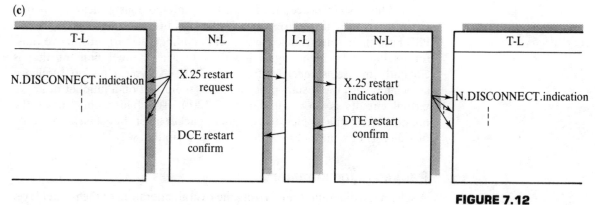

FIGURE 7.12

Additional services: (a) expedited data; (b) reset; (c) restart.

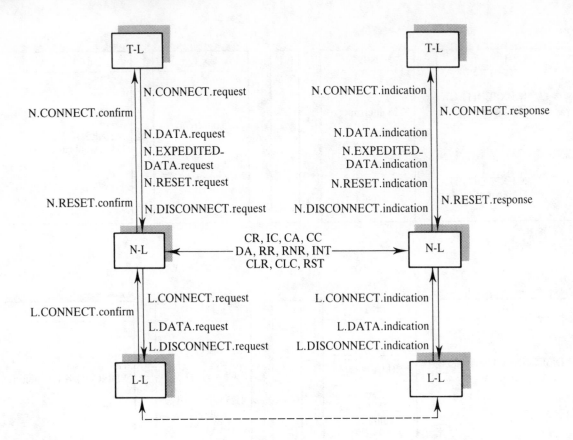

FIGURE 7.13

X.25 packet layer summary.

informed that the network connection has been cleared. The reason for the clearing is passed as a parameter and it is then up to the user (the transport layer, in practice) to recover from any possible loss of data.

The restart procedure is used to simultaneously clear all virtual circuits currently in progress at a DTE. It is utilized when the DTE and PSE become unsynchronized at a level that affects all currently active calls; for example, an incoming call with a logical channel number that is currently in use is received from the PSE. A typical packet sequence associated with the restart procedure and the effect on a number of active virtual circuits is shown in Figure 7.12(c). The figure only shows the possible effect at a single correspondent packet layer, but clearly a number of other DTEs may also be affected in a similar way.

Packet layer summary

A schematic diagram summarizing the overall operation of the packet layer is shown in Figure 7.13. The same form of presentation used for the link layer has been adopted. The three aspects of the operation of the layer can be clearly identified:

- the services it offers to the transport layer above it;
- the PDUs exchanged between two correspondent network (packet) layer protocol entities;
- the link layer services it uses to transport these PDUs.

Protocol specification

To give an insight into the specification of the packet layer protocol, the call establishment phase of the protocol will now be described. The time sequence diagram for this phase was shown earlier in Figure 7.10. For clarity, it is assumed that the fast-select facility is being used and also that a data link has already been set up.

In keeping with the style of presentation introduced in the last chapter, a list of all the incoming events, automaton states, outgoing events, predicates and specific actions related to the call establishment phase of the protocol are listed in Figure 7.14. To aid understanding, a state-transition diagram of the call establishment phase is shown in Figure 7.15(a). Note that the incoming event and associated outgoing event are shown alongside each transition arc. Figure 7.15(b) gives a more formal definition of the protocol in the form of an event-state table. It should be stressed, however, that the definitions given are not intended to be complete but rather serve as an introduction to understanding the formal specification of the X.25 packet layer protocol.

7.3.4 Terminal access

The preceding sections relating to the X.25 network access protocol have assumed that the DTE to be connected to the network has sufficient intelligence (or processing capability) to be able to implement the various protocol layers just described. In general, this is true, certainly if the DTE is a computer, for example. In some instances, however, the DTE may not operate in a packet mode nor have sufficient processing capability to implement a protocol like X.25. Hence, to interface this type of DTE to the network it is necessary to provide an additional piece of equipment, which implements the various protocol layers on its behalf and provides a much simpler user-level interface to the DTE. An example of a DTE in this category is a simple asynchronous character-mode terminal like a VDU. This normally has only a limited level of intelligence with a simple RS-232C/V.24 physical interface.

To meet this type of requirement, the user may, of course, choose to provide the additional equipment to perform the necessary assembly of character strings from the terminal into network packets and vice versa.

(a)

Name	Interface	Meaning
NCONreq	NS-user	N.CONNECT.request received
NCONresp	NS-user	N.CONNECT.response received
CALLconn	Link layer	Call connected packet received
INCcall	Link layer	Incoming call packet received
TCALLconn	Timer	Call connected timer expires

(b)

Name	Meaning
IDLE	No connection established
WFCC	Waiting for a call connected packet
WFNCR	Waiting for an N.CONNECT.response from NS-user
WFCLCF	Waiting for a clear confirm packet
DATA	Connection established and ready for data transfers

(c)

Name	Interface	Meaning
NCONind	NS-user	Send N.CONNECT.indication
NCONconf	NS-user	Send N.CONNECT.confirm
NDISind	NS-user	Send N.DISCONNECT.indication
CALLreq	Link layer	Send call request packet
CALLacc	Link layer	Send call accepted packet
CLRreq	Link layer	Send clear request packet

(d)

Name	Meaning
P0	N.CONNECT.request from NS-user unacceptable
P1	N.CONNECT.response from NS-user unacceptable

FIGURE 7.14

Abbreviated names for call establishment phase of network (packet) layer: (a) incoming events; (b) automaton states; (c) outgoing events; (d) predicates; (e) specific actions.

(e)

Name	Meaning
[1]	Start TCALLconn timer
[2]	Stop TCALLconn timer

(a)

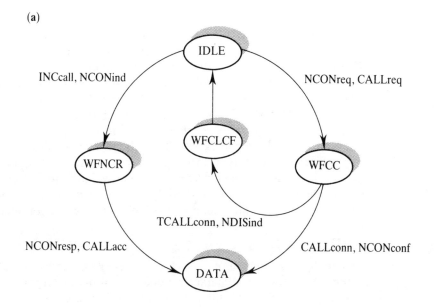

(b)

State Event	IDLE	WFCC	WFNCR	WFCLCF	DATA	- - -
NCONreq	1	0	0	0	0	
NCONresp	0	0	3	0	0	
CALLconn	0	2	0	0	0	
INCcall	4	0	0	0	0	
TCALLconn	0	5	0	0	0	
⋮						

0 = NDISind, CLRreq, WFCLCF   (Error condition)

1 = PO: NDISind, IDLE;
    NOT PO: CALLreq, [1], WFCC

2 = NCONconf, [2], DATA

3 = NOT P1: CALLacc, DATA

4 = NCONind, WFNCR

5 = NDISind, CLRreq, WFCLCF

FIGURE 7.15

Protocol specification for call
establishment: (a) state-
transition diagram; (b) event-
state table.

Alternatively, because this is not an uncommon requirement, the various PSDN authorities also offer users an alternative network access protocol which is intended for use with asynchronous character-mode terminals. This is known as X.28 and the additional equipment necessary to provide this type of interface is known as a **packet assembler–disassembler (PAD)**. Since the PAD is provided by the PSDN authority, it is normally located with the local PSE. A single PAD is used to support a number of character-mode DTEs. A schematic diagram showing the function and location of a PAD, together with the additional protocols that have been defined for use with it, is given in Figure 7.16. As can be seen, protocol X.3 defines the operation and facilities that are provided by the PAD, and X.29 defines the interface between the PAD and a remote packet-mode DTE. Selected aspects of this mode of working will now be considered.

PAD and X.3

Essentially, the function of a PAD is to assemble the individual characters entered by a user at a character-mode asynchronous terminal into meaningful packets that are suitable for transmission through an X.25 PSDN. Similarly, on receipt of such packets, the PAD disassembles them and passes the individual characters contained within them to the terminal a single character at a time. The PAD, therefore, must perform all the X.25 protocol functions on behalf of the terminal (such as call establishment, flow control, etc.) and in general make the packet mode of working of the network transparent to the user.

The function and facilities of a PAD are defined in recommendation X.3. In addition to the basic functions just outlined, each terminal connected to a PAD has a number of parameters associated with it, because character-mode terminals vary widely in their operation and characteristics. These are normally set from the commands entered at the terminal or, alternatively, from the remote packet-mode DTE being accessed. They relate to such features as:

- whether local echo checking is required;
- selection of **packet terminating (data forwarding)** characters, which allow the user of the terminal to signal to the PAD that the transmission of a (partly complete) packet should be initiated;
- specification of alternative control characters for such functions as line feed and carriage return.

To facilitate the use of the PAD, all the parameters associated with a terminal have a default value; hence, only those parameters that differ from these need be changed. The initial parameter settings are determined by the **standard profile** selected for use with the terminal. A number of alternative standard profiles have been defined for use with the more

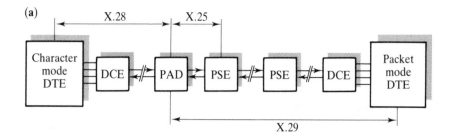

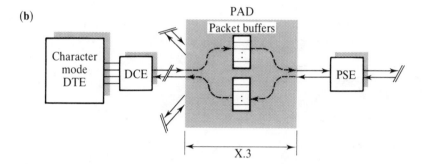

FIGURE 7.16

PAD and its protocols:
(a) interface protocols;
(b) internal protocol.

popular types of terminal. Both the standard profile to be used and any changes to be made from this are normally selected and entered when a communication link between the terminal and the PAD is first established. The procedure to do this is as defined in recommendation X.28.

Recommendation X.28

This recommendation specifies the protocol to be used between an asynchronous character-mode terminal and the PAD. It contains the procedures to be followed to:

- access the PAD;
- set the terminal parameters to the required values;
- establish a virtual call to a destination packet-mode DTE;
- control the exchange of user's data between the terminal and the PAD;
- clear an established call.

Access to the PAD may take several forms. It may be via a switched connection set up using the PSTN or it may be over a leased line. Clearly, if the PSTN uses analogue transmission, modems must be used at each end of the link. Alternatively, if digital data services are provided by the network,

(a)

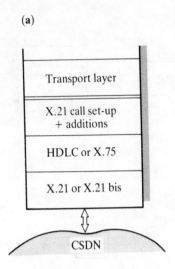

(b)

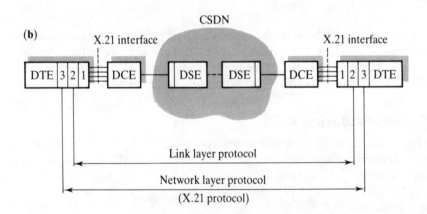

FIGURE 7.17

CSDNs: (a) network-dependent
protocols; (b) applicability.

a direct digital path can be either set up or leased, and hence a
conventional RS-232C/V.24 interface may be used.

Once the terminal has gained access to the PAD, the terminal sends
a service request character sequence. This enables the PAD to determine
the data rate being used by the terminal and the terminal to select an initial
standard profile. Procedures are then defined to allow the terminal user to
read the parameters associated with the profile and, if required, to change
them to other values. The PAD is then ready to establish a virtual call
through the PSDN to a remote packet-mode DTE.

To establish a virtual call, the user first indicates to the PAD the address of the required packet-mode terminal. The PAD then follows the virtual call establishment procedure outlined earlier. Once the call has been established, the PAD enters the data transfer phase.

When in the data transfer phase, the PAD performs the necessary packet assembly and disassembly functions. During the assembly process, the PAD initiates the transfer of a packet either when the user enters an agreed packet termination control character or after an agreed timeout period. Finally, after all information has been exchanged, the user may request the PAD to initiate the clearing of the call.

Recommendation X.29

This recommendation specifies the interaction between the PAD and the remote packet-mode DTE. The basic procedures associated with X.29 for call establishment and data transfer are essentially the same as those used in X.25. Additional procedures are also defined in the recommendation, however, that reflect the presence of the PAD between the terminal and remote packet-mode DTE. For example, during the call establishment phase, the PAD uses the first four octets of the optional user data field in a call-request packet as a so-called **protocol identifier** field. This allows different types of calling subscriber (terminal) to be identified so that the called packet-mode DTE can utilize alternative protocols should this be necessary.

Similarly, in the reverse direction, when in the data transfer phase, the packet-mode DTE is able to communicate with the PAD directly using the Q bit in the header of each data packet. When the Q bit is set, this indicates that the remaining information in the packet is intended for use by the PAD and should not therefore be disassembled and passed to the user terminal. This procedure allows, for example, the remote packet-mode DTE to read and, if necessary, set the current values of the parameters associated with the calling terminal.

7.4 CIRCUIT-SWITCHED DATA NETWORKS

The various protocols associated with the lowest three network-dependent layers in the ISO Reference Model for use with a CSDN are as shown in Figure 7.17(a). The operational characteristics of the physical interface to a circuit-switched network are defined in recommendation X.21. The aim is to provide the user with a full-duplex, synchronous, data transmission path, which is available for the duration of the call. The various inter-change circuits associated with X.21 were shown in Figure 7.6 and hence the remainder of this section will concentrate on the operation of the X.21 interface protocol.

7.4.1 X.21 interface protocol

With a circuit-switched network, once a call has been established, a physical communication path exists between the calling and called DTEs. The X.21 interface protocol is concerned, therefore, only with the set-up and clearing operations associated with each call. The control of the ensuing data transfer is the responsibility of the link layer which, because of the operation of a circuit-switched network, operates on an end-to-end basis. This is shown in diagrammatic form in Figure 7.17(b).

A typical interchange sequence to first set up a call, perform an exchange of data and then clear the call using the various interchange circuits associated with X.21 is shown in Figure 7.18. (a) shows the interchange sequence across the calling DTE/DCE interface and (b) shows the interchange sequence across the called DTE/DCE interface. Initially, the transmit (T) circuit from both the calling and called DTE are both at logical 1, indicating that they are both ready to either initiate a call or receive a call. Similarly, the receive (R) circuit from each DCE is also at logical 1, indicating their availability.

The calling DTE first indicates it wishes to make a call by setting its control (C) circuit to the on state and simultaneously setting its transmit circuit to the logical 0 state (Figure 7.18(a)). When the DCE is ready to accept the call, it responds by transmitting two (or more) SYN characters on the receive circuit followed by a series of '+' IA5 (ASCII) characters. On receipt of the '+' characters, the calling DTE proceeds by transmitting two (or more) SYN characters followed by the network address of the required destination DTE, again in the form of IA5 characters each with a single parity bit. The address is terminated by a single '+' character. The DTE then enters a wait state and the DCE responds by transmitting idle (call progress) characters while it attempts to set up the call.

When the call request reaches the required destination DCE, the latter informs the called DTE by first transmitting two SYN characters followed by a series of BEL characters (Figure 7.18(b)). The called DTE then accepts the call by setting its control circuit to on and the DCE, in turn, passes other call set-up information in the form of a series of IA5 characters on the receive circuit; this information includes reverse charging and other similar information. Finally, the call set-up phase is completed by both the calling and called DCEs setting their indication (I) control circuits to indicate a circuit has been set up and the network is ready for data.

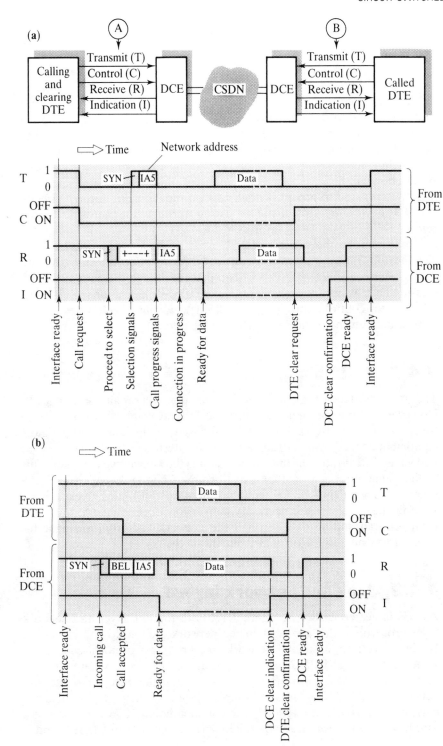

FIGURE 7.18

Successful call and clear
interchange sequences:
(a) calling DTE/DCE interface (A);
(b) called DTE/DCE interface (B).

After the connection has been established, a data transparent, full-duplex communication path is available to both the calling and called DTEs for the transfer of link layer data. (Typically, this involves the exchange of frames according to the HDLC protocol.) Each DTE initiates the transmission of a data frame on its transmit circuit. This is then sent through the network and passed to the recipient DTE on the incoming receive circuit from its local DCE. Finally, after one of the DTEs has finished transmitting all its data, it initiates the clearing of the call (circuit) by switching its control circuit to off (DTE clear-request) (Figure 7.18(a)). As can be seen, however, since the circuit is full-duplex, the clearing DTE must be prepared to accept further data on the incoming receive circuit.

The clear-request signal is passed through the network to the remote DCE and the latter informs its local DTE by setting the indication control circuit to the off state (DCE clear-indication) (Figure 7.18(b)). The local DTE then responds by setting its control circuit to the off state (DTE clear-confirmation). This is then passed through the network to the clearing DCE which informs the DTE by setting its indication circuit to off (DCE clear-confirmation) (Figure 7.18(a)). Finally, both sides of the connection return to the 'interface ready' state.

7.4.2   X.21 bis

The X.21 interface protocol is intended for use with an all-digital CSDN. However, before such networks become fully available, and to ease the transition from existing RS-232C/V.24-based equipment to the newer equipment needed with X.21, an alternative interface protocol was defined known as X.21 bis, the bis indicating that it is the alternative protocol. This is the same interface as that described in Chapter 2 for use with a synchronous modem – that is, one that supplies a bit-timing clock signal – since it must perform the necessary conversions from digital-to-analogue form for transmitting data through the network and from analogue-to-digital form on receipt of data from the network.

7.4.3   Link and network layers

As was indicated earlier in Figure 7.17, both the link layer and network layer protocols with a circuit-switched network are end-to-end protocols. However, with an all-digital network, the link layer protocol can be the same as that used in X.25 since a full-duplex circuit is set up; that is, HDLC with LAPB. But with the older analogue access circuits and networks, only a two-wire, half-duplex circuit is set up and hence a derivative of HDLC as defined in recommendation X.75 must be used. The link set-up procedure with X.75 is also a derivative of LAPB and is known as LAPX. This again is intended for the set up of a logical data link over a half-duplex physical circuit.

If no flow control functions are being supported, the network layer (level 3) with a CSDN can be relatively simple, since, after setting up the connection, each network data transfer service primitive issued by the transport layer can be mapped directly into a similar request to the intermediate link layer. The transport layer would then perform its own flow control functions. Alternatively, to ease interworking with other types of network, it is possible to have a network layer similar to that used with X.25. If this is done, however, the various logical channel identifiers discussed would have an end-to-end significance rather than local significance, as with an X.25 packet-switched network. Also, each call would, of course, be a separate circuit with a CSDN.

7.5 INTEGRATED SERVICES DIGITAL NETWORKS

As was indicated earlier, the PTT authorities in most countries are rapidly upgrading their existing PSTNs to be all-digital in operation. When this is complete, a high bit rate, all-digital interface will be available at each subscriber outlet. Also, since the new networks will employ all-digital transmission and switching, a very fast connection (call) set-up time will be provided both for local, national and international calls. It is intended that the new subscriber interface will have sufficient capacity not only to handle voice communications but also data communications directly, the two services operating concurrently if this is desired. These new networks are referred to therefore as **integrated services digital networks (ISDNs)**.

Because of the far-reaching consequences of such networks, the CCITT has already evolved a draft set of standards for interfacing equipment to such networks; these are referred to as the I-series recommendations. The remainder of this chapter gives an overview of the different types of user interface proposed for ISDNs and also the function of some of the I-series recommendations.

7.5.1 User interfaces

A limited set of standard, multi-purpose user (subscriber) interfaces have been proposed for ISDNs and these are summarized in Figure 7.19. As can be seen, the basic service offered will be for voice communications, as is the case for existing telephone networks. It should be noted, however, that since the subscriber outlet is digital, voice traffic will have to be digitized in the subscriber (telephone) handset prior to transmission and the reverse operation on reception. As the bit rate required to transmit digitized voice is 64 kbps, the user interface will offer multiples of this basic rate.

In the second example in the figure, the same outlet (but with a different user terminal of course) is used to provide a circuit-switched connection for data communications. The basic data rate will be 64 kbps. Also, because of the use of digital transmission and switching, a very fast call set-up time will be available. Then, in the third example, the user may be utilizing the outlet as an integrated voice and data facility, both operating concurrently.

The fourth example is intended to show that, with an appropriate terminal, the basic outlet may also be used to provide access to a packet-switching service. This, as will be seen, may be at 64 kbps or, optionally, at a lower bit rate of 16 kbps.

These four examples utilize the ISDN simply for providing a switched transmission path and are referred to as **bearer services**. However, it is intended that the PTT authorities will also provide additional, more sophisticated, equipment to allow the ISDN to be used as a fast Teletex, Facsimile or Videotex network. The latter are referred to as **teleservices** and are illustrated in Figure 7.19(b). Essentially, a **Teletex** network provides a general-purpose facility for messages (comprising alphanumeric and graphical characters) to be exchanged between similar terminals; a **Facsimile** network a general-purpose facility for transmitting scanned images of documents electronically between similar terminals; and a **Videotex** network a general-purpose facility for gaining access to a remote computer managed by the PTT authorities and containing, for example, a particular type of database such as stocks and share prices.

7.5.2 Network access points

To allow for this wide range of uses, the **network termination equipment (NTE)** provided by the PTT authorities will have a number of alternative access points associated with it. These are shown in diagrammatic form in Figure 7.20.

Clearly, by the time ISDN networks are fully operational, a high level of investment will have been made by users into equipment that adheres to existing standards, such as the V- and X-series. To cater for this, therefore, it is intended that the NTE associated with ISDNs will support not only the newer generation of equipment but also existing equipment and interfaces. This will be achieved by providing a range of **terminal adapters** which will perform the necessary mapping function.

The alternative access points (R, S or T) illustrated in the figure clearly imply a varying level of intelligence in the NTE. In relation to the ISO Reference Model, the various access points require a varying number

(a)

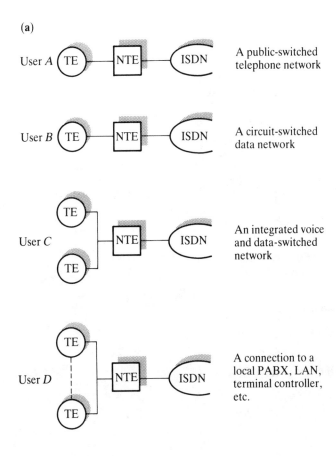

User A — TE — NTE — ISDN   A public-switched telephone network

User B — TE — NTE — ISDN   A circuit-switched data network

User C — TE / TE — NTE — ISDN   An integrated voice and data-switched network

User D — TE / TE — NTE — ISDN   A connection to a local PABX, LAN, terminal controller, etc.

(b)

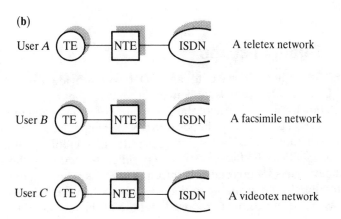

User A — TE — NTE — ISDN   A teletex network

User B — TE — NTE — ISDN   A facsimile network

User C — TE — NTE — ISDN   A videotex network

FIGURE 7.19

ISDN user services: (a) bearer services; (b) teleservices.

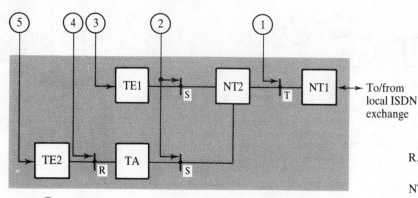

① = Access point for basic bearer (i.e., transmission only) services

② = Access point for supplementary bearer services (i.e., enhanced connection incorporating layers 1–3 of the ISO Reference Model)

③ = Access point for teleservices with full ISDN interface

④ = Access point supporting existing interface standards (X-series, V-series, etc.)

⑤ = Access point for teleservices through different TA-defined interfaces

R, S, T = Access reference points

NT1, 2 = Network terminator points

TA = Terminal adaptor

TE1, 2 = Terminal equipment

FIGURE 7.20

ISDN customer access points.

of protocol layers and Figure 7.21 summarizes the layers required to support each service. As can be seen, these range from layer 1 to support a basic transmission service, layers 1–3 to support such services as a switched voice and/or data terminal, to layers 1–7 to support the different types of teleservices.

7.5.3 Channel types

The basic subscriber interface to an ISDN will provide two 64 kbps channels, known as **B channels**, and an additional 16 kbps channel, known as the **D channel**. The basic use of the D channel is for signalling purposes; that is, for the NTE to inform the local ISDN exchange the address of the required destination NTE. The use of a separate channel for signalling will result in a significantly faster call set-up time. In addition, however, because a new call is set up relatively infrequently, it is proposed that the D channel should also be available to the subscriber when signalling is not in progress. Because of this, it is proposed that the D channel should be used

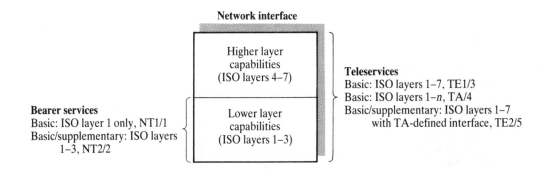

Network interface

Higher layer
capabilities
(ISO layers 4–7)

Teleservices
Basic: ISO layers 1–7, TE1/3
Basic: ISO layers 1–*n*, TA/4
Basic/supplementary: ISO layers 1–7
    with TA-defined interface, TE2/5

Bearer services
Basic: ISO layer 1 only, NT1/1
Basic/supplementary: ISO layers
    1–3, NT2/2

Lower layer
capabilities
(ISO layers 1–3)

FIGURE 7.21

Customer access summary.

for packet-switching purposes also. The total available bit rate to the subscriber at the basic interface is thus 144 kbps − (2B + D).

It is also proposed that higher bit rate channels should be available on request. These are referred to as **primary rate** or **H channels**. Currently, the bit rates associated with these channels are being discussed but include:

- H0 : 384 kbps,
- H11: 1536 kbps,
- H12: 1920 kbps.

The proposed uses of these channels include high bit rate dedicated communication channels (as are currently available) and also switched channels for high-speed teleservices. The various interfaces and the proposed range of alternative bit rates are summarized in Figure 7.22.

7.5.4 User interface protocols

As was indicated earlier in the context of the ISO Reference Model, the basic (bearer) services, such as a switched voice and/or data service, utilize layers 1–3 while the various teleservices utilize the full seven layer stack. The various I-series recommendations for use at layers 1–3 are shown in Figure 7.23.

Layer 1 (I430) defines the physical interface to the network. It includes, in addition to the definition of the proposed interface arrangement, the mechanisms to be used for bit, octet and channel synchronization, D channel access control and power feeding.

Layer 2 (I440/1) provides one or more data link (logical) connections using the (single) D channel. Identification of the data link connec-

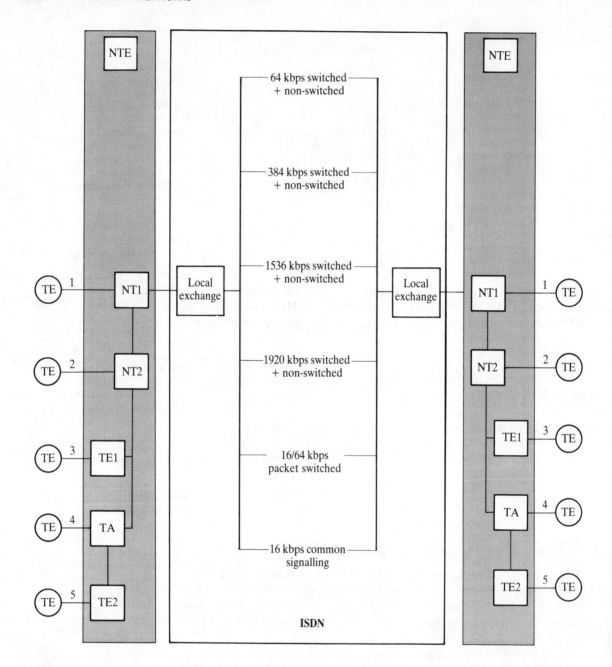

FIGURE 7.22

User network interface summary.

tion is by means of an identifier in each frame transmitted. In addition, it provides a defined set of services to layer 3 above it to establish and clear (release) a call (circuit switched and packet switched), and also to transfer packet data over the D channel.

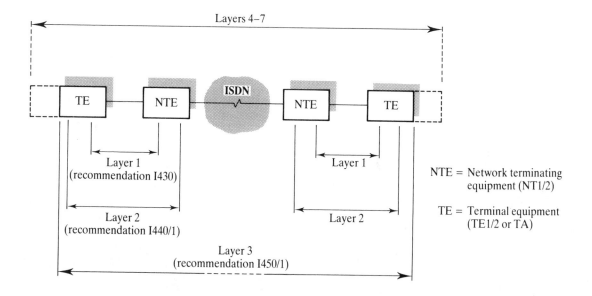

FIGURE 7.23

User network interface protocols.

Layer 3 (I450/1) controls the setting up of circuit-switched and packet-switched connections (calls) using the services provided by layer 2 over the D channel. In addition, it is responsible for the control of information transfer across an established connection.

I440/1

The layer 2 service definition and protocol specification is contained in recommendation I440 and I441, respectively. It is based on the HDLC protocol and is known as LAP D. A time sequence diagram showing the service primitives associated with LAP D is shown in Figure 7.24.

As can be seen from the figure, both unacknowledged and acknowledged information transfer is supported. To allow for this, an additional unnumbered frame known as UI (unnumbered information) is utilized with LAP D. Apart from this, however, the other frames are the same as those described earlier in Chapter 5, except that the address and control fields have each been extended to two octets. The frame format used with LAP D is shown in Figure 7.25(a).

The **extended control field** is provided to enable the send and receive sequence numbers ($N(S)$ and $N(R)$) to be extended to modulo 128, should this be necessary. The format of the two address octets is as shown in Figure 7.25(b) and a schematic diagram showing their use is given in Figure 7.26. Essentially, the **service access point identifier (SAPI)** identifies the layer 3 service access point to which the frame relates. Only two identifiers are used, however; SAPI = 0 means the frame is a call control (signalling)

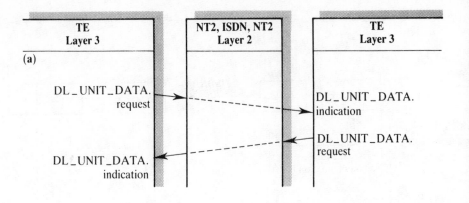

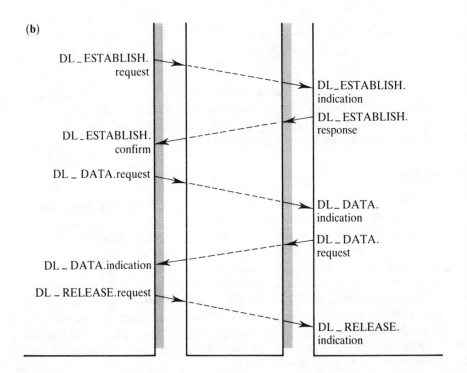

FIGURE 7.24

Layer 2 user service primitives:
(a) unacknowledged information
transfer; (b) acknowledged
information transfer.

frame and SAPI = 16 means the frame is a data packet. Also, a single
NTE may have more than one user device attached to it; hence, an
additional identifier, the **terminal endpoint identifier (TEI)**, is provided to
allow the terminal to relate frames to specific devices. An example is a
small private exchange.

(a)

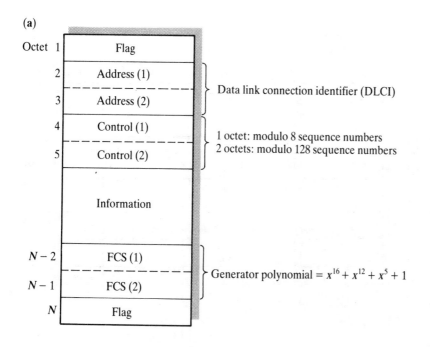

Octet 1 — Flag

2 — Address (1)
3 — Address (2)
} Data link connection identifier (DLCI)

4 — Control (1)
5 — Control (2)
} 1 octet: modulo 8 sequence numbers
2 octets: modulo 128 sequence numbers

Information

$N - 2$ — FCS (1)
$N - 1$ — FCS (2)
} Generator polynomial = $x^{16} + x^{12} + x^5 + 1$

N — Flag

(b)

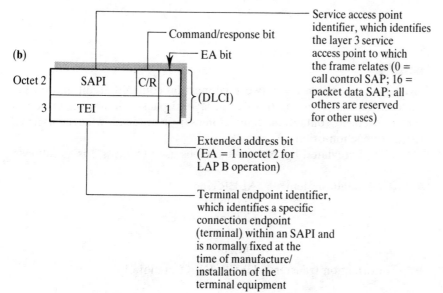

Octet 2 — SAPI | C/R | 0
3 — TEI | 1
} (DLCI)

Command/response bit

EA bit

Service access point identifier, which identifies the layer 3 service access point to which the frame relates (0 = call control SAP; 16 = packet data SAP; all others are reserved for other uses)

Extended address bit (EA = 1 inoctet 2 for LAP B operation)

Terminal endpoint identifier, which identifies a specific connection endpoint (terminal) within an SAPI and is normally fixed at the time of manufacture/ installation of the terminal equipment

FIGURE 7.25

LAP D: (a) frame format;
(b) address field usage.

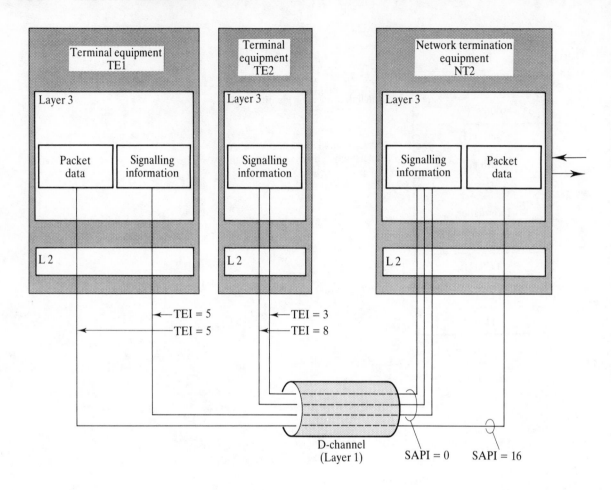

FIGURE 7.26

Example address field usage.

I450/1

Layer 3 is responsible for network connection control (circuit and packet switched) and also for the transfer of layer 3 packet data using either an unacknowledged (datagram/connectionless) or an acknowledged (virtual circuit/connection-oriented) service.

An abbreviated list of message types used by layer 3 is as follows:

- Call establishment: ALERTing
                        CONNECT
                        CONnect ACKnowledge
                        SETUP
                        Others

- Information transfer: USER INFOrmation
                          Others

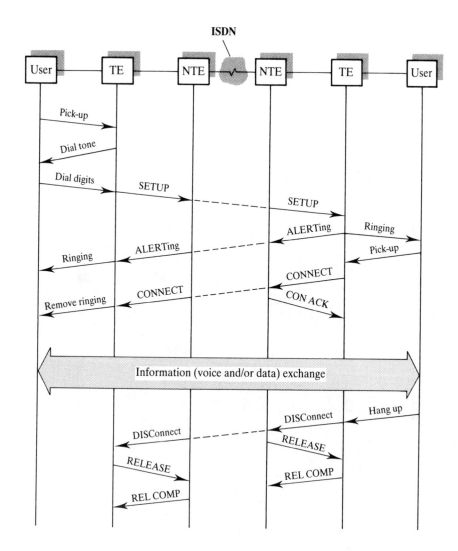

FIGURE 7.27

Example message sequence –
circuit-switched call.

- Call clearing: DISConnect
  RELEASE
  RELease COMPlete
  Others

Some of these messages have local significance (TE/NTE) while others
have end-to-end significance (TE/TE). All the messages, however, are
transferred within layer 2 I-frames. An example illustrating the use of
these messages is shown in Figure 7.27. The example assumes it is a circuit-
switched call that may be used for voice and/or data over the B channel(s).

CHAPTER SUMMARY

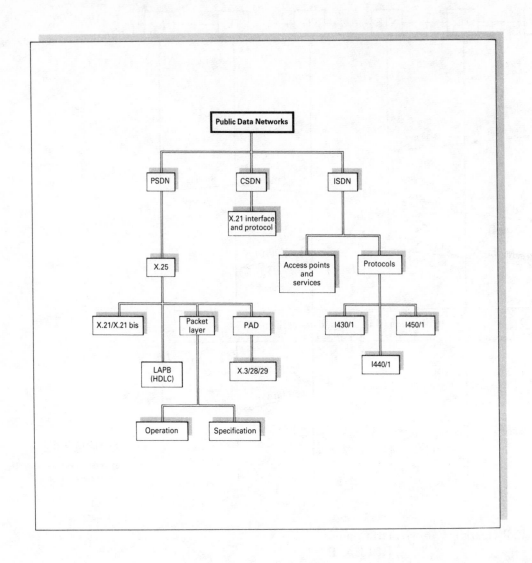

EXERCISES

7.1   (a)   Describe the differences between a circuit-switched data network and a packet-switched data network. Clearly identify the effects on the users of these networks.

   (b)   Explain what is understood by the following techniques used in packet-switched data networks:

   • datagram,
   • virtual call (circuit),
   • logical channel.

7.2   Sketch diagrams to illustrate the applicability and components of the X.25 network access protocol and write explanatory notes describing the function of each component.

7.3   (a)   Define the set of user service primitives associated with the packet (network) layer of the X.25 protocol. Explain the use of the following additional facilities:

   • more-data,
   • qualifier,
   • delivery confirmation.

   (b)   Tabulate the main PDUs (packet types) used by the packet layer protocol to perform the following operations:

   • establish a virtual call (circuit),
   • exchange a message unit over this circuit,
   • clear the call.

   Sketch a time sequence diagram to illustrate the sequence in which the PDUs are exchanged to implement these operations.

7.4   (a)   Describe the flow control method used by the packet layer protocol in the X.25 and list the packet layer PDUs (packet types) that are used to implement it.

   (b)   Sketch diagrams to illustrate how the flow of data packets relating to a single logical channel is controlled by:

   • the window mechanism,
   • the use of additional supervisory packets.

   Include in the diagrams the state of the send and receive variables ($V(S)$ and $V(R)$) and the window variable ($L(W)$) at both sides of the logical channel as each data packet is transmitted.

7.5   Discriminate between the reset and restart error recovery procedures used in the packet layer of the X.25 and explain their operation.

7.6 (a) Describe the function of a PAD as used in the X.25-based networks and identify on a diagram the various protocols that have been defined for use with it.

  (b) Outline the essential features of the following protocols used with PADs:

- X.3,
- X.28,
- X.29.

7.7 (a) Outline the function of the three lowest network-dependent protocol layers used with a circuit-switched data network.

  (b) Sketch a diagram showing the various interchange circuits associated with the X.21 and outline their function.

  (c) With the aid of a time sequence diagram, describe the operation of the X.21 interface protocol. Clearly show the transitions on each interchange circuit at both the calling DTE/DCE interface and also the called DTE/DCE interface. Identify on this diagram the call set-up, data transfer and call clearing phases.

7.8 (a) What is understood by the term ISDN?

  (b) Give examples of the following user services related to an ISDN:

- bearer services,
- teleservices.

  (c) Produce a sketch and associated descriptions of an NTE and indicate on the sketch the following customer access points:

- basic bearer services,
- supplementary bearer services,
- teleservices,
- existing X-series services.

LOCAL AREA
DATA
NETWORKS

8

CHAPTER CONTENTS

8

CHAPTER OBJECTIVES

When you have completed studying the material in this chapter you should be able to:

- describe the different topologies and transmission media commonly used in local area networks;

- know the difference between baseband and broadband working;

- describe the alternative medium access control methods used in local area networks;

- describe the major components and mode of operation of a CSMA/CD bus network;

- describe the major components and mode of operation of a token ring network;

- describe selected aspects of the operation of a token bus network;

- appreciate the function of the various network-dependent protocols used with local area networks and be able to describe the services and operation of the logical link control protocol layer;

- understand the function of an internetwork bridge and gateway and describe how two DTEs connected to two separate local area networks may communicate through an intermediate public data network.

8.1 INTRODUCTION

Local area data networks, normally referred to simply as local area networks or LANs, are concerned with the interconnection of distributed communities of computer-based DTEs whose physical separation is confined to a single building or localized group of buildings. For example, an LAN may be used to interconnect a community of computer-based workstations distributed around a block of offices within a single building or a group of buildings such as a university campus. Alternatively, it may be used to interconnect various computer-based pieces of equipment distributed around a factory or hospital complex. Since all the equipment is located within a single establishment, however, LANs are normally installed and maintained by the organization and hence they are also referred to as **private data networks**.

The main difference between a communication path established using an LAN and a connection made through a public data network is that with an LAN, because of the relatively short physical separation, much higher data transmission rates are normally available. In the context of the ISO Reference Model for OSI, however, this difference manifests itself only at the lower network-dependent layers and hence, as was indicated in Chapter 6, the higher protocol layers in the reference model are, in many instances, the same for both types of network. This chapter, therefore, is primarily concerned with a description of the different types of LAN and the function and operation of the associated network-dependent protocol layers.

8.2 SELECTION ISSUES

Before describing the structure and operation of the different types of LAN, it is perhaps helpful to first identify some of the different selection issues that must be considered. A summary of some of these issues is shown in Figure 8.1. It should be stressed, however, that this is intended only as a summary. There are, in addition, many possible links between the tips of the branches associated with the figure. Each of the issues identified will now be considered in some detail.

8.2.1 Topology

Most WANs, such as the PSTN, PSDN, etc., use a **mesh** (sometimes referred to as a **network**) **topology**. With LANs, however, the limited physical separation of the subscriber DTEs means simpler topologies may

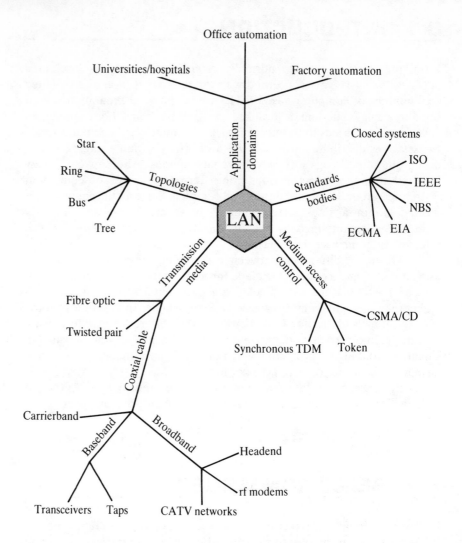

FIGURE 8.1

LAN selection issues.

be used. The three topologies in common use are star, bus and ring. These are shown in diagrammatic form in Figure 8.2.

Perhaps the best example of an LAN based on a **star topology** is the digital **private automatic branch exchange (PABX)**. A connection established through a traditional analogue PABX is in many ways similar to a connection made through an analogue PSTN in so much that all paths through the network are designed to carry limited-bandwidth analogue speech. To use such a facility to carry data, therefore, requires modems as discussed in Chapter 2. The more modern types of PABX, however, utilize digital-switching techniques within the exchange and for this reason they are also referred to as **private digital exchanges (PDX)**. Moreover, the

(a)

(b)

(c)

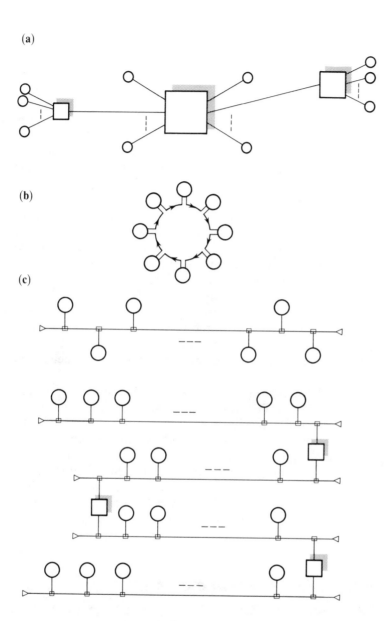

FIGURE 8.2

LAN topologies: (a) star; (b) ring; (c) bus/tree.

availability of inexpensive integrated circuits to perform the necessary analogue-to-digital and digital-to-analogue conversion functions means that it is rapidly becoming common practice to extend the digital mode of working right back to the subscriber outlets. This means that a switched 64 kbps path, which is the digitizing rate normally used for digital voice, is available at each subscriber outlet, which can therefore be used for both voice and data.

The main use of a PDX, however, is likely to be to provide a switched communication path between a localized community of integrated voice and data terminals (workstations) for the exchange of such information as electronic mail, electronic documents, etc., in addition, of course, to normal voice communications. Furthermore, the use of digital techniques within the PDX will mean that it can also be used to provide such services as voice store-and-forward (that is, a subscriber may leave (store) a voice message for another subscriber for later retrieval (forwarding)) and teleconferencing (multiple subscribers taking part in a single call).

The preferred topologies of LANs designed specifically to function as a data communication subnetwork for the interconnection of local communities of computer-based equipment are bus (linear) and ring. In practice, bus networks are normally extended into an interconnected set of buses with the resulting topology resembling an unrooted tree structure. Typically, with a **bus topology**, the single network cable is routed through those locations (offices, for example) that have a DTE to be connected to the network and a physical connection (tap) is made to the cable to allow the user DTE to gain access to the network services supported. Appropriate medium access control circuitry and algorithms are then used to share the use of the available transmission bandwidth between the attached community of DTEs.

With a **ring topology**, the network cable passes from one DTE to another until all the DTEs are interconnected in the form of a loop or ring. A feature of a ring topology is that there is a direct point-to-point link between each neighbouring DTE which is unidirectional in operation. Appropriate medium access control algorithms then ensure the use of the ring is shared between the community of users. The data transmission rates used with both ring and bus topologies (typically from 1 to 10 Mbps) mean that they are best suited for interconnecting local communities of computer-based pieces of equipment; for example, intelligent workstations in an office environment or intelligent controllers around a process plant.

8.2.2 Transmission media

Shielded twisted pair, coaxial cable and optical fibre are the three main types of transmission medium used for LANs. One of the main advantages of both twisted pair and coaxial cable is that it is straightforward to make a physical connection (tap) to the cable. This is necessary with a bus topology, for example, and hence bus networks mainly use these types of transmission media.

Optical fibre cable, as was mentioned in Chapter 2, is best suited to those applications demanding either high levels of immunity to electromagnetic interference or very high data rates. Also, it is not easy to make a number of physical taps to a single optical fibre cable. Optical fibre is best suited, therefore, for point-to-point communications as used with a ring network, for example.

The form of the electrical interface with the different types of transmission media were discussed in Chapter 2. Coaxial cable, when used for an LAN, is operated using both baseband and broadband techniques. As was described in Chapter 2, the latter, instead of transmitting information on to the cable in the form of, say, two voltage levels corresponding to the bit stream being transmitted (baseband), divides the total available bandwidth (frequency range) of the cable into a number of smaller subfrequency bands or channels. Each subfrequency band is then used, with the aid of a pair of special modems, to provide a separate data communication channel. This style of working is known as frequency-division multiplexing and, since the frequencies used are in the radio frequency band, the modems used are rf modems. This approach is known as broadband working and the same principle is currently in widespread use in the **community antenna television (CATV)** industry to multiplex a number of TV channels on to a single coaxial cable.

A schematic of a typical CATV system is shown in Figure 8.3(a). Each TV channel is allocated a particular frequency band, typically of 6 MHz bandwidth. Each received video signal (from the various antenna or aerials) is then used to modulate a carrier frequency in the selected frequency band. These modulated carrier signals are transmitted over the cable network and are thus available at each subscriber outlet. The subscriber selects a particular TV channel by tuning to the appropriate frequency band.

In a similar way, it is possible to derive a range of data transmission channels from a single cable by allocating each channel a portion of the total bandwidth, the amount of bandwidth for each channel being determined by the required data rate. For data communication, however, a two-way (duplex) capability is normally required. This may be achieved in one of two ways:

(1) **Single-cable system**: The transmit and receive paths are assigned two different frequency bands on the same cable.

(2) **Dual-cable system**: Two separate cables are used, one for the transmit path and the other for the receive path.

A schematic of each type of system is shown in Figure 8.3. The main difference between the two systems is that a dual-cable system requires twice the amount of cable and cable taps to install. Nevertheless, with a dual-cable system the total cable bandwidth (typically 5 to 450 MHz) is available in each direction. Moreover, the headend equipment is simply an amplifier, whereas with a single-cable system a frequency translator is

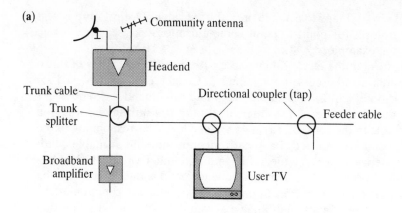

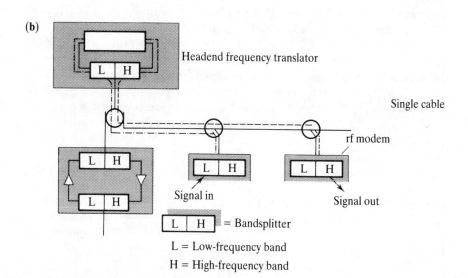

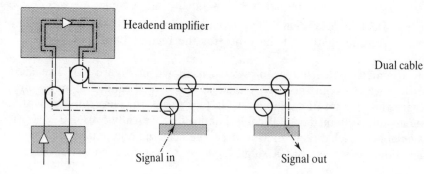

FIGURE 8.3

Broadband coaxial cable systems: (a) basic CATV system components; (b) data network alternatives; (c) frequency usage.

(c)

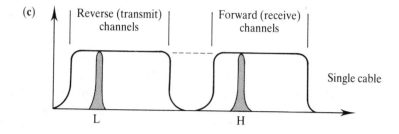

Reverse (transmit) channels | Forward (receive) channels

L H

Single cable

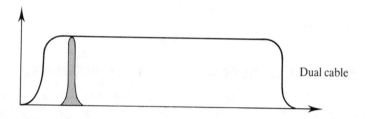

Dual cable

FIGURE 8.3 (cont.)

Broadband coaxial cable systems: (a) basic CATV system components; (b) data network alternatives; (c) frequency usage.

required to translate the incoming frequency signals associated with the various receive paths to the corresponding outgoing frequencies used for the transmit paths.

A sinusoidal signal in the selected frequency band in the reverse direction (that is, to the headend) is first modulated using the data to be transmitted by an rf modem and this signal is fed on to the cable using a special **directional coupler** or **tap**. The latter is designed so that most of the transmitted signal flows in the reverse direction to the cable **headend (HE)**. Another special device known as a **frequency translator** is then used to convert (translate) the signals received on the different receive frequency bands to a corresponding set of forward frequency bands. The received modulated signal is thus frequency translated by the headend and the rf modem associated with the receiving DTE tuned to receive the matching frequency translated signal frequency band. The transmitted data are then demodulated from the received signal by the receiving modem and passed on to the attached DTE.

It may be deduced from this that a single pair of frequencies provides just a simplex (unidirectional) data path between the two DTEs; hence, to support duplex communication, two separate pairs of frequencies must be used. Nevertheless, a 9.6 kbps simplex data channel only requires in the order of 20 kHz of the total available bandwidth and hence a pair of 6 MHz subfrequency bands, for example, can be used to provide 300 such channels or 150 full-duplex channels. Higher data rate channels then require progressively more of the available bandwidth; for example, two 6 MHz bands for a 5 Mbps full-duplex channel or three 6 MHz bands for a 10 Mbps full-duplex channel.

The price to pay for deriving this multiplicity of different data channels from a single cable is the relatively high cost of each pair of rf modems. But an added advantage of a broadband coaxial cable is that it can be used over longer distances than a baseband cable. The primary use of broadband coaxial cable, therefore, tends to be as a flexible transmission medium for use in manufacturing industry or in establishments comprising multiple buildings, especially when the physical separation of the buildings is quite large (up to tens of kilometres, for example). When used in this way, other services such as closed-circuit television and voice can be readily integrated on to the cable being used for data; hence, broadband is a viable alternative to baseband for networks providing a range of services.

8.2.3 Medium access control methods

When a communication path is established between two DTEs through a star network, the central controlling element (a PDX, for example) ensures that the transmission path between the two DTEs is reserved for the duration of the call. With both a ring and a bus topology, however, there is only a single logical transmission path linking all the pieces of equipment together. Consequently, a discipline must be imposed on all the items connected to the network to ensure that the transmission medium is accessed and used in a fair way. The two techniques that have been adopted for use in the various standards documents are **carrier-sense-multiple-access with collision detection (CSMA/CD)**, for use with bus network topologies, and **control token**, for use with either bus or ring networks. Both will now be described. In addition, an access method based on a **slotted ring** is also in widespread use with ring networks and hence this will also be described.

CSMA/CD

The CSMA/CD access method is used solely with bus networks. With this type of network topology, all DTEs are connected directly to the same cable, which is therefore used for transmitting all data between any pair of DTEs. The cable is thus said to operate in a **multiple access (MA) mode**. All data are transmitted by the sending DTE first encapsulating the data in a frame with the required destination DTE address at the head of the frame. The frame is then transmitted (or **broadcast**) on the cable. All DTEs connected to the cable detect whenever a frame is being transmitted and, when the required destination DTE detects that the frame currently being transmitted has its own address at the head of the frame, it continues reading the data contained within the frame and responds according to the defined link protocol. The source DTE address is also included as part of the frame header so that the recipient DTE can direct its response to the originating DTE.

With this style of operation, it is clearly possible for two DTEs to attempt to transmit a frame over the cable at the same time, with the effect that the data from each source would be corrupted. To reduce the possibility of this, before transmitting a frame, the source DTE first *listens* to the cable to detect if a frame is currently being transmitted. If a carrier signal is *sensed* (CS), the DTE *defers* its transmission until the passing frame has been transmitted, and only then does it attempt to send the frame. Even so, two DTEs wishing to transmit a frame may determine that there is no activity (transmission) currently taking place on the bus at the same instant of time and hence both start to transmit their frames simultaneously. A **collision** is then said to occur since the contents of both frames will collide and hence be corrupted. This is shown in diagrammatic form in Figure 8.4.

To allow for this possibility, a DTE simultaneously monitors the data signal actually present on the cable when transmitting the contents of a frame on to the cable. If the transmitted and monitored signals are different, a collision is assumed to have occurred – collision detected (CD). To ensure that the other DTE(s) involved in the collision is (are) aware that a collision has occurred, it first *enforces* the collision by continuing to send a random bit pattern for a short period. This is known as the **jam sequence**. The two (or more) DTEs involved then wait for a further short random time interval before trying to retransmit the affected frames again. It can be concluded from this that access to a CSMA/CD bus is probabilistic and clearly depends on the network (cable) loading. It should be stressed, however, that since the bit rate used on the cable is very high (up to 10 Mbps), the network loading tends to be low. Also, since the transmission of a frame is initiated only if the cable is inactive, the probability of a collision occurring is in practice quite low.

Control token

Another way of controlling access to a shared transmission medium is by the use of a control (permission) token. The control token is passed from one DTE to another according to a defined set of rules understood and adhered to by all DTEs connected to the medium. A DTE may only transmit a frame when it is in possession of the token and, after it has transmitted the frame, it passes the token on to allow another DTE to access the transmission medium. The sequence of operation is as follows:

- A logical ring is first established, which links all the DTEs connected to the physical medium, and a single control token is created.

- The token is passed from DTE to DTE around the logical ring until it is received by a DTE waiting to send a frame(s).

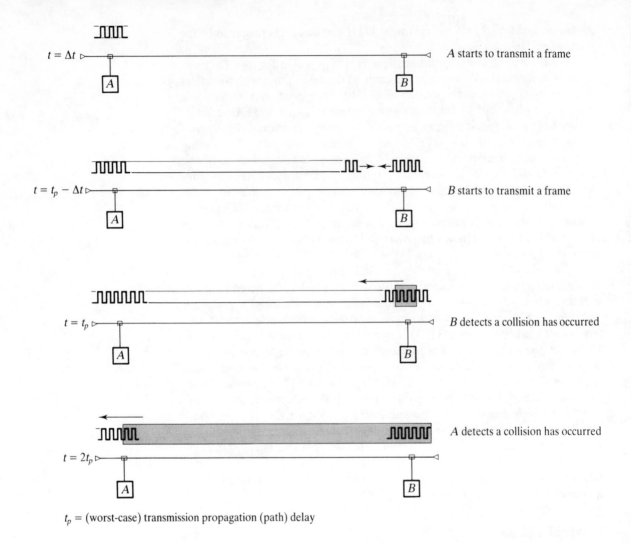

t_p = (worst-case) transmission propagation (path) delay

FIGURE 8.4

CSMA/CD collision schematic.

• The waiting DTE then sends the waiting frame(s) using the physical medium, after which it passes the control token to the next DTE in the logical ring.

Monitoring functions within the active DTEs connected to the physical medium provide a basis for initialization and recovery of both the connection of the logical ring and from the loss of the token. Although the monitoring functions are normally replicated among all the DTEs on the medium, only one DTE at a time carries the responsibility for recovery and re-initialization.

(a)

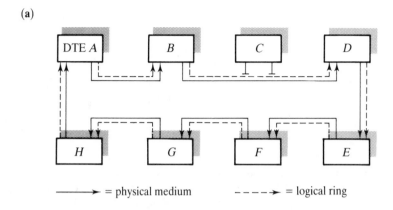

DTE *C* assumed switched off
and hence in bypass mode

———▶ = physical medium   - - - -▶ = logical ring

(b)

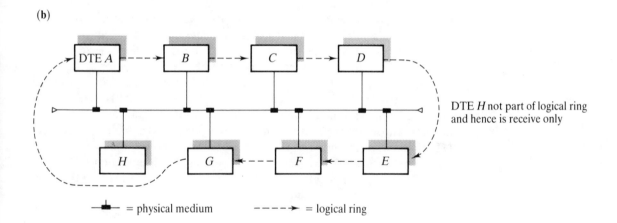

DTE *H* not part of logical ring
and hence is receive only

—■— = physical medium   - - - -▶ = logical ring

The physical medium need not necessarily be a ring topology; a token may also be used to control access to a bus network, for example. The establishment of a logical ring on the two types of network is shown in Figure 8.5.

With a physical ring (Figure 8.5(a)), the logical structure of the token-passing ring is the same as the structure of the physical ring, with the order of the token passing being the same as the physical ordering of the connected DTEs. With a bus network (Figure 8.5(b)), however, the ordering of the logical ring need not necessarily be the same as the physical ordering of the DTEs on the cable. Moreover, with a token access method on a bus network, all DTEs need not necessarily be connected in the

FIGURE 8.5

Control token medium access control: (a) token ring; (b) token bus.

logical ring; for example, DTE *H* is not part of the logical ring shown in Figure 8.5(b). This means that DTE *H* can only operate in a receive mode, since it will never own the control token. Another feature of the token access method is that it is possible to associate a priority with the token, thereby allowing higher priority frames to be transmitted first. This and other aspects will be expanded upon in later sections.

Slotted ring

Slotted rings are used solely for controlling the access to a ring network. With this approach, the ring is first initialized to contain a fixed number of binary digits by a special node in the ring known as a **monitor**. This stream of bits continuously circulates around the ring from one DTE to another. Then, as each bit is received by a DTE, the DTE interface examines (reads) the bit and passes (repeats) it on to the next DTE in the ring, and so on. The monitor ensures that there is always a constant number of bits circulating in the ring, irrespective of the number of DTEs making up the ring. The complete ring is arranged to contain a fixed number of **slots**, each made up of a set number of bits and capable of carrying a single, fixed-size frame of information. The format of a frame slot is shown in Figure 8.6(a).

Initially, all the slots are marked empty by the monitor setting the full/empty bit at the head of each slot to the empty state. When a DTE wishes to transmit a frame, it first waits until an empty slot is detected. It then marks the slot as full and proceeds to insert the frame contents into the slot with both the required destination DTE address and the source DTE address at the head of the frame and the response bits at the tail of the frame both set to 1. The slot containing this frame then circulates around the physical ring from one DTE to another. Each DTE in the ring examines the destination address at the head of any slot marked full and, if it detects its own address, and assuming it is willing to accept the frame, it reads the frame contents from the slot while at the same time repeating the unmodified frame contents around the ring. In addition, after reading the frame contents, it modifies the pair of response bits at the tail of the slot to indicate that it has read the frame contents or, alternatively, if the addressed DTE is either busy or inoperable, the response bits are marked accordingly or left unchanged (inoperable).

The source DTE, after initiating the transmission of a frame, waits until the frame has circulated the ring by counting the (fixed number) of slots that are repeated at the ring interface. Then, on receipt of the first bit of the slot used to transmit the frame, it marks the slot as empty once again and waits to read the response bits from the tail of the slot to determine what action to take next.

The monitor-passed bit is used by the monitor to detect if a DTE fails to release a slot after it has transmitted a frame. This bit is reset by the source DTE as it transmits a frame on to the ring. The monitor then

(a)

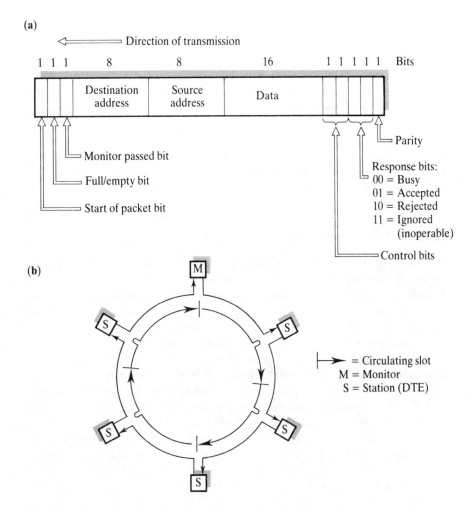

FIGURE 8.6

Slotted ring principles: (a) bit definitions of each slot; (b) outline topology.

subsequently sets the bit in each full slot as it is repeated at its ring interface. Hence, if the monitor detects that the monitor-passed bit is set when it repeats a full slot, it assumes the source DTE has failed to mark the slot as empty and hence resets the full/empty bit at the head of the slot. The two control bits at the tail of each slot are provided for use by the higher protocol software layers within each DTE and have no meaning at the medium access level.

It should be noted that, with a slotted ring medium access method, each DTE can only have a single frame in transit on the ring at a time, and also that it must release the slot used for transmitting a frame before trying to send another frame. In this way, access to the ring is fair and shared between the various interconnected DTEs. The main disadvantages of a slotted ring are that:

(1)   a special (and hence vulnerable) monitor node is required to maintain the basic ring structure; and

(2)   the transmission of each complete link-level frame normally requires multiple slots, since each slot can carry only 16 bits of useful information.

With a token ring, of course, once a DTE receives the control token it may transmit a complete frame containing multiple bytes of information as a single unit.

8.2.4   Standards

As LANs evolved in the late 1970s and early 1980s, a wide range of different network types were proposed and implemented. However, because of small differences between them, such networks could only be used, in general, to interconnect computers or workstations belonging to the supplier of the LAN. Such networks, of which there are still many in existence, are known, therefore, as closed systems.

To alleviate this situation, some major initiatives were launched by various national standards bodies with the aim of formulating an agreed set of standards for LANs. The major contributor to this activity was the IEEE which formulated the IEEE 802 series of standards and, as a result of this, these have now been adopted by the ISO as international standards. As can be concluded from the previous sections, however, there is not just a single type of LAN. Rather, there is a range of different types, each with its own topology, medium access control method and intended application domain. Some of the different types of LAN in the standards documents will now be described and the protocols associated with them are presented later in Section 8.4.

8.3   LOCAL AREA NETWORK TYPES

The two dominant types of LAN that have been developed specifically for interconnecting localized communities of computer-based equipment are bus and ring. Currently, there are many different varieties of both types, although many of these do not adhere to the international standards for LANs. The three types in the standards documents are CSMA/CD bus, token ring and token bus, and hence the descriptions that follow will be constrained to these three types.

8.3.1 CSMA/CD bus

CSMA/CD bus networks are used extensively in technical and office environments. For historical reasons, a CSMA/CD bus network is also known as **Ethernet**. Normally, it is implemented as a 10 Mbps baseband coaxial cable network, although other bit rates and cable media are supported in the standards documents. A typical CSMA/CD bus network is shown in Figure 8.7(a) and a schematic diagram showing the various components necessary to connect a DTE to this type of network is given in Figure 8.7(a) and (b).

The integrated **tap and transceiver unit** (also known as the **medium access control (MAC) unit**) includes a tap, which makes a non-intrusive physical connection to the coaxial cable, closely coupled to the transceiver itself. The transceiver contains the necessary electronics to:

- send and receive data to and from the cable;
- detect occurrences of collisions on the cable medium;
- provide electrical isolation between the coaxial cable and the cable interface electronics;
- protect the cable from any malfunctions in either the transceiver or the attached DTE.

The latter function is often referred to as **jabber control** since without the appropriate protection electronics, if a fault develops, it is possible for a faulty transceiver (or DTE) to continuously transmit random data on to the cable medium (jabber) and hence inhibit or corrupt all other transmissions. The jabber control essentially isolates the transmit data path from the cable if certain defined time limits are violated; for example, all frames transmitted on the cable have a defined maximum length and, if this is exceeded, the jabber control inhibits further output data from reaching the cable.

The transceiver unit is connected to its host DTE by means of a shielded cable containing five sets of twisted pair wires: one for carrying power to the transceiver from the DTE, two for data (one send and one receive) and two for control purposes (one to allow the transceiver to signal a collision to the DTE and the other for the DTE to initiate the isolation of the transmit data path from the cable). The four signal pairs are differentially driven, which means that the host DTE may be up to 50 m from the transceiver and hence from the cable tapping point.

The communication controller card contains:

- A medium access control (MAC) unit, which is responsible for such functions as the encapsulation and de-encapsulation of frames for transmission/reception on the cable, error detection and the imple-

(a)

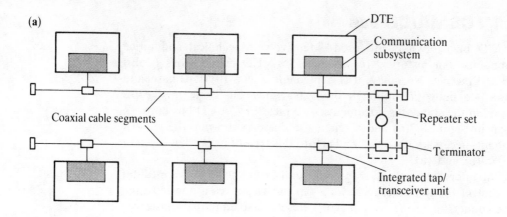

(b)

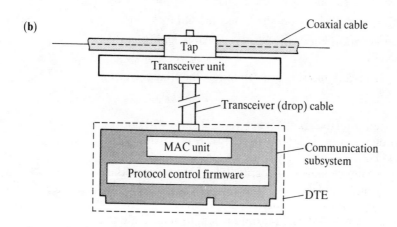

(c)

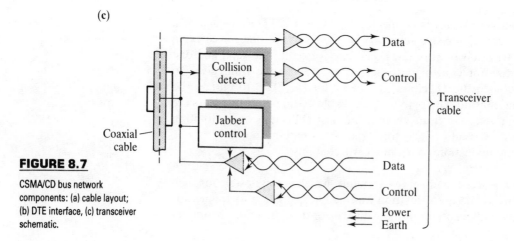

FIGURE 8.7

CSMA/CD bus network
components: (a) cable layout;
(b) DTE interface, (c) transceiver
schematic.

mentation of the medium access control algorithm.

- A separate microprocessor, which implements both the network-dependent protocols (to be described in a later section) and also the higher level protocols described earlier in Chapter 6.

In this way, the complete communication subsystem is normally self-contained on a single printed circuit card that slots into the host system bus and provides a defined set of network (application) services to the host software.

Frame format and operational parameters

The format of a frame and the operational parameters of a typical CSMA/CD bus network are shown in Figure 8.8. The meaning and use of the various parameters will be described as the operation of the MAC unit is presented.

Each frame transmitted on the cable has eight fields. All of these fields are of fixed length except the data and associated padding fields.

The preamble field is sent at the head of all frames and its function is to allow the receiving electronics in each MAC unit to reliably achieve bit synchronization before the actual frame contents are received. The preamble pattern is a sequence of seven octets, each equal to the binary pattern 10101010. All frames are transmitted on the cable using Manchester encoding and hence, as was described in Chapter 3, the preamble results in a periodic waveform being received by the receiver electronics. The start-of-frame delimiter (SFD) is a single octet comprising 10101011. This immediately follows the preamble and signals the start of a valid frame to the receiver.

The destination and source network addresses specify the identity of both the intended destination DTE(s) and the originating DTE, respectively. Each address field may be either 16 or 48 bits but for any particular LAN installation the size used must be the same for all DTEs. The first bit in the destination address field specifies whether the address is an individual address or a group address. If the former is specified, the transmitted frame is intended for a single destination DTE; if the latter is specified, the frame is intended either for a logically related group of DTEs (group address) or for all other DTEs connected to the network (broadcast or global address). In the latter case, the address field is set to all binary 1s.

The length indicator is a two-octet field whose value indicates the number of octets in the data field. If this value is less than the minimum number required for a valid frame (minimum frame size), a sequence of octets is added, known as **padding**. Finally, the FCS field contains a four-octet (32-bit) cyclic redundancy check value that is used for error-detection purposes.

(a)

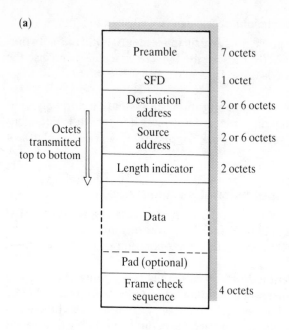

Preamble	7 octets
SFD	1 octet
Destination address	2 or 6 octets
Source address	2 or 6 octets
Length indicator	2 octets
Data	
Pad (optional)	
Frame check sequence	4 octets

Octets transmitted top to bottom

(b)

Cable medium	50Ω coaxial cable
Bit rate	10 Mbps (Manchester encoded)
Slot time	512 bit times
Interframe gap	9.6 μs
Attempt limit	16
Backoff limit	10
Jam size	32 bits
Maximun frame size	1518 octets
Minimum frame size	512 bits

FIGURE 8.8

CSMA/CD bus network characteristics: (a) frame format; (b) operational parameters.

Frame transmission

When a frame is to be transmitted, the frame contents are first encapsulated by the MAC unit into the format shown. To avoid contention with other transmissions on the medium, the medium access control section of the MAC unit first monitors the carrier sense signal and, if necessary, defers to any passing frame. Then, after a short additional time delay (known as the **interframe gap**), to allow the passing frame to be received and processed by the addressed DTE(s), transmission of the frame is initiated. The Manchester-encoded bit stream is first sent to the transceiver unit via the interconnecting cable and the latter converts this into the appropriate format for transmission on the cable.

As the bit stream is transmitted on the cable, the transceiver's electronics simultaneously monitor the cable signal to detect if a collision has occurred. Assuming a collision has not been detected, the complete frame is transmitted and, after the FCS field has been sent, the MAC unit awaits the arrival of a new frame, either from the cable or from the controlling microprocessor. If a collision is detected, the transceiver's electronics immediately turn on the collision detect signal. This, in turn, is detected by the MAC unit which first enforces the collision by transmitting the jam sequence to ensure that the collision is detected by all other DTEs involved in the collision. Then, after the jam sequence has been sent, the MAC unit terminates the transmission of the frame and schedules a retransmission attempt after a short randomly selected time interval.

In the event of a collision, retransmission of the frame is attempted up to a defined maximum number of tries known as the **attempt limit**. Since repeated collisions indicate a busy medium, the MAC unit attempts to adjust to the medium load by progressively increasing the time delay between repeated retransmission attempts. The scheduling of retransmissions is controlled by a process called **truncated binary exponential backoff** which works as follows. When transmission of the jam sequence is complete, and assuming the attempt limit has not been reached, the MAC unit delays (backsoff) a random integral number of **slot times** before attempting to retransmit the affected frame. A given DTE can experience a collision during the initial part of its transmission, the **collision window**, which is effectively twice the time interval for the first bit of the preamble to propagate to all parts of the cable medium (network). The slot time is thus the worst-case time delay a DTE must wait before it can reliably know a collision has occurred. It is defined as:

Slot time = 2 × (transmission path delay) + safety margin

where **transmission path delay** is the worst-case signal propagation delay going from any transmitter to any receiver on the cable network. This includes, therefore, any delays experienced in repeaters. The slot time is double this delay (to allow for the corrupted signal to propagate back to the transmitting DTE) plus a safety margin. The slot time used is made equal to this figure rounded up to be a multiple number of octets at the bit rate used. As an example, for a 10 Mbps baseband coaxial cable network with a maximum of 2.5 km between any transmitter and any receiver, it is equal to 512 bit times or 64 octets. The number of slot times before the Nth retransmission attempt is then chosen as a uniformly distributed random integer, R, in the range $0 \leqslant R \leqslant 2^K$, where $K = \text{Min}(N, \text{backoff limit})$.

Frame reception

At each active DTE connected to the cable, the receiving electronics within the MAC unit first detect the presence of an incoming signal from the transceiver and switch on the carrier sense signal to inhibit any new transmissions from this DTE. The incoming preamble is then used to achieve bit synchronization and, after synchronization has been achieved, the Manchester-encoded data stream is translated back into normal binary form. The incoming bit stream is then processed.

First, the remaining preamble bits are discarded together with the start-of-frame delimiter, when this is detected. The destination address field is then processed to determine whether the frame should be received by this DTE. If so, the frame contents comprising the destination and source addresses and the data field are loaded into a frame buffer to await further processing. The received FCS field is then compared with that computed by the MAC unit during reception of the frame and, if they are equal, the start address of the buffer containing the received frame is passed to the next higher protocol layer, in the form of a service primitive, for further processing. Other validation checks are also made on the frame before initiating further processing. These include checks to ensure that the frame contains an integral number of octets and that it is neither too short nor too long. If any of these checks fail, the frame is discarded and an error report is made to the network management sublayer. The latter will be expanded upon in Chapter 10.

Initially, the transmitted bit stream resulting from a collision is received by each active DTE in the same way as a valid frame. After the colliding DTEs have detected the collision and transmitted the jam sequence, however, they cease transmission. Fragmentary frames received in this way therefore violate the minimum frame size limit and hence are discarded by the receiving DTEs. Also, the adoption of a **maximum frame size** means that the length of the frame buffers used for transmission and reception purposes can be quantified. The FCS field is a 32-bit sequence generated using a polynomial code and a generator polynomial of degree 32.

8.3.2 Token ring

Token ring networks are also used primarily in technical and office environments. A schematic diagram illustrating the principle of operation of such networks is given in Figure 8.9. Whenever a DTE (node or station) wishes to send a frame, it first waits for the token. On receipt of the token, it initiates the transmission of the frame, which includes the address of the intended recipient at its head. The frame is repeated (that is, each bit is received and then retransmitted) by all DTEs in the ring until it circulates back to the initiating DTE, where it is removed. In addition to repeating

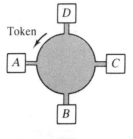

Assume DTE *A* wishes to send
a frame to DTE *C*

DTE *A* waits for receipt of
control token from its
upstream neighbour

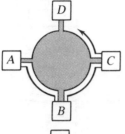

DTE *A* transmits frame on to
ring; DTE *C* copies frame
addressed to it; frame
continues around ring

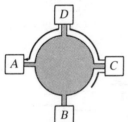

DTE *A* awaits receipt of
start of frame but does not
repeat the frame thereby
removing it

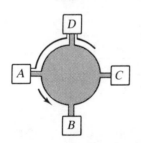

When last bits of frame have
been transmitted, DTE *A*
generates and passes on the
token; it then waits for the
response bits at the tail of
the frame

FIGURE 8.9

Token ring network: principle of
operation.

the frame, however, the intended recipient retains a copy of the frame and
indicates it has done this by setting the **response bits** at the tail of the frame.
After transmitting the last bits of the frame, the initiating DTE generates
and passes on the token and awaits receipt of the response bits.

A typical token ring network is shown in Figure 8.10(a) and a
schematic diagram showing the various components necessary to connect a
DTE to the cable medium is given in Figure 8.10(b) and (c). The (trunk)
cable medium is typically a screened twisted pair which, since each

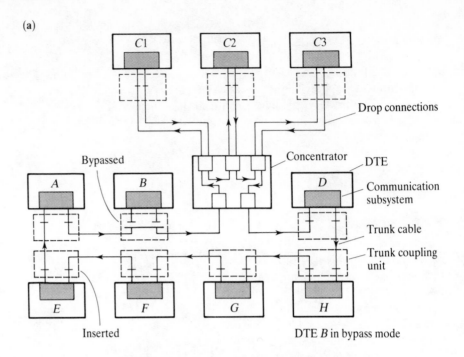

(a)

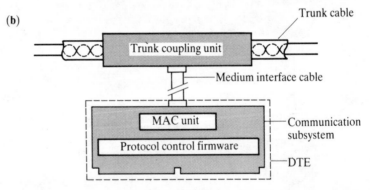

(b)

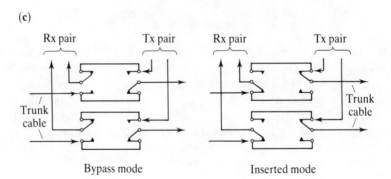

(c)

FIGURE 8.10

Token ring network components:
(a) ring configuration; (b) DTE
interface; (c) TCU schematic.

segment around the ring forms a point-to-point link, is differentially driven at a bit rate of between 1 and 4 Mbps.

As can be seen from Figure 8.10(b), a DTE may not necessarily be connected directly to the ring, but rather through a device known as a **concentrator**. The latter connects directly to the main trunk cable and, in turn, provides direct drop connections to a number of DTEs. A concentrator is often used to simplify the wiring within a building. Typically, it is located at the point where the trunk cable enters (and leaves) an office and direct drop connections are then used to connect each DTE in the office to the concentrator. It is also known, therefore, as a **wiring concentrator** and a typical installation may use many such devices.

Ring interface

The **trunk coupling unit** (**TCU**) forms the physical interface with the cable medium. It contains a set of relays and additional electronics to drive and receive signals to and from the cable. The relays are so arranged that whenever the DTE is switched off, the TCU is in the **bypass state** and a continuous transmission path through the TCU is maintained. The insertion of a DTE into the ring is controlled by the MAC unit on the communication controller card within the DTE. The MAC unit initiates the insertion of the DTE by activating both pairs of relays in the TCU and, as can be seen in Figure 8.10(c), when inserted, this causes all received signals to be routed through the MAC unit. The receive/transmit electronics in the latter then either simply read and relay (repeat) the received signal to the transmit side, if this DTE is not the originator of the frame, or remove the received signal from the ring, if it initiated the transmission.

The use of two pairs of relays connected in this way means that the MAC unit can detect certain open-circuit and short-circuit faults in either the transmit or receive pair of signal wires. Also, in the bypass state, the MAC unit can conduct self-test functions, since any data output on the transmit pair are looped back on the receive pair. The DTE is connected to the TCU by means of a shielded cable containing two twisted pair wires: one for transmission and the other for reception.

The MAC unit is responsible for such functions as frame encapsulation and de-encapsulation, FCS generation and error detection, and the implementation of the medium access control algorithm. Also, it supplies the master clock for the ring that is used for data encoding and decoding purposes, when the DTE is the active ring monitor (see later). Each circulating bit stream is Manchester encoded by the active ring monitor and all other DTEs on the ring then frequency and phase lock to this bit stream by means of a phase-locked loop (PLL) circuit. In addition, when the DTE is the active ring monitor, it ensures the ring has a **minimum latency time**; that is, the time, measured in bit times at the ring data transmission rate, for a signal to propagate once around the ring. The ring latency time thus includes the signal propagation delay through the ring transmission medium together with the sum of the propagation delays through each MAC unit. Hence, for the control token to circulate continuously around the ring when none of the DTEs require to use the ring (that is, all DTEs are simply in the repeat mode), the ring must have a minimum latency time of at least the number of bits in the token sequence. This ensures that the token is not corrupted.

As will be defined later, the token is 24 bits in length; hence, to allow for this, when a DTE is the active ring monitor, its MAC unit provides a fixed 24-bit buffer, which effectively becomes part of the ring to ensure its correct operation under all conditions. Although the mean data signalling rate around the ring is controlled by a single master clock in the active monitor, the use of a separate PLL circuit in each MAC unit means that the actual signalling rate may vary slightly around the ring. The worst-case variation is when the maximum number of DTEs (250) are all active which is equivalent to plus or minus three bits. Unless the latency of the ring remains constant, however, bits will be either corrupted as the latency of the ring decreases, or additional bits added as the latency increases. To maintain a constant ring latency, therefore, an additional **elastic (variable) buffer** with a length of six bits is added to the fixed 24-bit buffer. The resulting 30-bit buffer is first initialized to 27 bits, then, if the received signal at the master MAC unit is faster than the master oscillator, the buffer is expanded by a single bit. Alternatively, if the received signal is slower, the buffer is reduced by a single bit. In this way the ring always comprises sufficient bits to allow the token to circulate continuously around the ring in the quiescent (idle) state.

Frame formats

There are two basic formats used in token rings: one for the control token and the other for normal frames. The control token is the means by which the right to transmit (as opposed to the normal process of repeating) is passed from one DTE to another, whereas a normal frame is used by a DTE to send either data or medium access control information around the ring. The format of the two types of frame is given in Figure 8.11 together with the bit sequence used for each field.

The start delimiter (SD) and end delimiter (ED) fields are special bit sequences used to achieve data transparency. They exploit the symbol encoding method used on the cable medium: all information bits transmitted on the medium are Manchester encoded except for selected bits in the SD and ED fields. In contrast, the J and K symbols depart from the normal encoding rules, these symbols being used instead to represent constant levels for the complete bit cell period; the J symbol has the same polarity as the preceding symbol whereas a K symbol has the opposite polarity to the preceding symbol. In this way the receiver can reliably detect the start and end of each transmitted token or frame irrespective of its contents or length. It should be noted, however, that only the first six symbols (JK1JK1 in the figure) are used to indicate a valid end of frame. The other two bits, I and E, have other functions:

- In a token, both the I and E bits are 0.
- In a normal frame, the I bit is used to indicate whether the frame is the first (or an intermediate) frame in a sequence (I = 1) or the last (or only) frame (I = 0).
- The E bit is used for error-detection purposes. It is set to 0 by the originating DTE but, if any DTE detects an error while receiving or repeating the frame (FCS error, for example), it sets the E bit to 1 to signal to the originating DTE that an error has been detected.

The access control (AC) field comprises the priority bits, the token and monitor bits, and the reservation bits. As the name implies, it is used to control access to the ring. When it is part of the token, the priority bits (P) indicate the priority of the token and hence those frames a DTE may transmit on receipt of the token. The token bit (T) is used to discriminate between a token and an ordinary frame (a 0 indicates a token and a 1 a frame). The monitor bit (M) is used by the active monitor to prevent a frame from circulating around the ring continuously. Finally, the reservation bits (R) allow DTEs holding high-priority frames to request (in either repeated frames or tokens) that the next token to be issued should be of the requisite priority.

The frame control (FC) field defines the type of the frame (medium access control or information) and also certain control functions. If the frame type bits (F) indicate a MAC frame, all DTEs on the ring interpret and, if necessary, act on the control bits (Z); if it is an I-frame, the control bits are only interpreted by the DTEs identified in the destination address field.

The source address (SA) and destination address (DA) fields can be either 16 bits or 48 bits in length, but for any specific LAN they are the same for all DTEs. The DA field identifies the DTE(s) for which the frame is intended. The first bit of the field indicates whether the address is an individual address (0) or a group address (1); individual addresses identify a specific DTE on the ring while group addresses are used to send a frame to multiple destination DTEs. The SA is always an individual address and identifies the DTE originating the frame. In addition, a DA consisting of all 1s is known as a broadcast address and denotes that the frame is intended for all DTEs on the ring.

The information (INFO) field is used to carry either user data or additional control information when included in a MAC frame. Although there is no maximum length specified for the information field, it is limited in practice by the maximum time a DTE is allowed to transmit a frame when holding the control token. A typical maximum length is 132 octets.

The frame check sequence (FCS) field is a 32-bit CRC. Finally, the frame status (FS) field is made up of two fields: the address-recognized bits (A) and the frame-copied bits (C). Both the A and C bits are set to 0 by the DTE originating the frame. If the frame is recognized by one or more DTEs on the ring, the DTE(s) sets the A bits to 1; also, if it copies the frame, it sets the C bits to 1. In this way, the originating DTE can determine if the addressed DTE(s) is non-existent or switched off, is active but did not copy the frame, or is active and copied the frame.

Frame transmission

On receipt of a service request to transmit a piece of data (which includes the priority of the data as a parameter), the data are first encapsulated by the MAC unit into the standard format shown in Figure 8.11. The MAC unit then awaits the reception of a token with a priority less than or equal to the priority of the assembled frame. Clearly, in a system that employs multiple priorities, a procedure must be followed to ensure that all DTEs have an opportunity to transmit frames in the correct order of priority. This works as follows.

After formatting a frame and prior to receiving an appropriate token (that is, one with a priority less than or equal to the priority of the waiting frame), each time a frame or a token with a higher priority is repeated at the ring interface, the MAC unit reads the value of the reservation bits contained within the AC field. If this is higher than the priority of the waiting frame, the reservation bits are simply repeated unchanged. If it is lower, however, the MAC unit replaces the current value with the priority of the waiting frame. Then, assuming there are no other higher priority frames awaiting transmission on the ring, the token is passed on by the current owner (user) with this priority. The waiting MAC unit, on receipt of the token, detects that the priority of the token is equal to the priority of the frame it has waiting to be transmitted. It therefore accepts the token by changing the token bit in the AC field to 1, prior to repeating this bit, which effectively converts the token to a start-of-frame sequence for a normal frame. The MAC unit then stops repeating the incoming signal and follows the converted start-of-frame sequence with the preformatted frame contents. In addition, while the frame contents are being transmitted, the FCS is computed and subsequently appended after the frame contents, before transmitting the end-of-frame sequence.

Once the transmission of the waiting frame(s) has been started, the MAC unit stops repeating, thus removing the transmitted frame(s) after it has circulated the ring. In addition, it notes the state of the A and C bits in the FS field at the tail of the frame(s) to determine if the frame(s) has

(a)

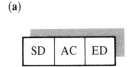

(b)

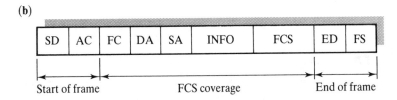

| SD | AC | FC | DA | SA | INFO | FCS | ED | FS |

Start of frame   FCS coverage   End of frame

(c)

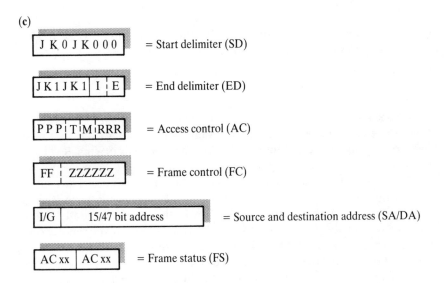

J K 0 J K 0 0 0   = Start delimiter (SD)

J K 1 J K 1 | I | E   = End delimiter (ED)

P P P | T | M | RRR   = Access control (AC)

FF | ZZZZZZ   = Frame control (FC)

I/G   15/47 bit address   = Source and destination address (SA/DA)

AC xx | AC xx   = Frame status (FS)

FIGURE 8.11

Token ring network frame formats and field descriptions: (a) token format; (b) frame format; (c) field descriptions.

(have) been copied or ignored. It then generates a new token and forwards this on the ring to allow another waiting DTE to gain access to the ring. (Note that it is possible to send more than one frame providing, firstly, that the priority of the other waiting frame(s) is (are) greater than or equal to the priority of the token and, secondly, that the total time taken to transmit the other frame(s) is within a defined limit known as the **token holding time**.)

Frame reception

In addition to repeating the incoming signal (bit) stream, the MAC unit within each active DTE on the ring detects the start of each frame by recognizing the special start-of-frame bit sequence. It then determines whether the frame should simply be repeated or copied: if the F bits indicate the frame is a MAC frame (see later section on ring management), the frame is copied and the C bits are interpreted and, if necessary, acted upon; if the frame is a normal data-carrying frame and the DA matches either the DTE's individual address or relevant group address, the frame contents are copied into a frame buffer and passed on for further processing. In either case, the A and C bits in the frame status field at the tail of the frame are set accordingly prior to being repeated.

Priority operation

The priority assigned to a token by a MAC unit after it has completed transmitting any waiting frame(s) is determined by a mechanism that endeavours to ensure that:

(1)   frames with a higher priority than the current ring service priority are always transmitted on the ring first, and

(2)   all DTEs holding frames with the same priority have equal access rights to the ring.

This is accomplished by combined use of the P and R bits in the AC field of each frame coupled with a mechanism that ensures that a DTE that raises the service priority level of the ring returns the ring to its original level after the higher priority frames have been transmitted.

To implement this scheme, each MAC unit maintains two sets of values: the first comprises three variables Pm, Pr and Rr. Pm specifies the highest priority value contained within any of the frames currently waiting transmission at the DTE. Pr and Rr are known as **priority registers** and contain, respectively, the priority and reservation values held within the AC field of the most recently repeated token or frame. The second set of values comprises two stacks known as the Sr and Sx stacks which are used as follows.

All frames transmitted by a DTE on receiving a usable token are assigned a priority value in the AC field equal to the present ring service priority Pr and a reservation value of zero. After all waiting frames at or greater than the current ring priority have been transmitted, or until the transmission of another frame would not be completed before the token holding time expires, the MAC unit generates a new token with:

(1)   P = Pr and R = the greater of Rr and Pm

if the DTE does not have any more waiting frames with a priority (as contained in register Pm) equal to or greater than the current ring service priority (as contained in register Pr), or does not have a reservation request (as contained in register Rr) greater than the current priority.

(2)   P = the greater of Rr and Pm   and   R = 0

if the DTE has another waiting frame(s) with a priority (as contained in Pm) greater than the current priority Pr, or if the current contents of Rr are greater than the current priority.

Since in the latter case the DTE effectively raises the service priority level of the ring, it becomes what is known as a **stacking station** (DTE) and, as such, stores the value of the old ring service priority (Pr) on stack Sr and the new ring service priority (P) on stack Sx. These values are saved as it is the responsibility of the DTE that becomes the stacking station to subsequently lower the ring service priority level when there are no further frames ready to transmit, at any point on the ring, with a priority equal to or greater than the P stacked on Sx. Also, a stack is used rather than a single register because a stacking station may need to raise the service priority of the ring more than once before the service priority is returned to a lower priority level. The different values assigned to the P and R bits of the token and the actions performed on the two stacks are summarized in Figure 8.12(a).

Having become a stacking station, the MAC unit claims every token that it receives with a priority equal to that stacked on Sx to examine the value in the R bits of the AC field to determine if the service priority of the ring should be raised, maintained or lowered. The new token is then transmitted with:

(1)   P = Rr   and   R = 0

if the value contained in the R bits (the current contents of register Rr) is greater than Sr. The new ring service priority (P) is stacked (PUSHed) on to Sx and the DTE continues its role as a stacking station.

(2)   P = Sr   and   R = Rr (unchanged)

if the value contained in the R bits is less than or equal to Sr. Both values currently on the top of stacks Sx and Sr are POPped from the stack and, if both stacks are then empty, the DTE discontinues its role as a stacking station. These two operations are summarized in Figure 8.12(b).

Ring management

The preceding sections were primarily concerned with the transmission of frames and tokens during normal operation of the ring. Before this can take place, however, the ring must first be set up. Also, if a DTE wishes to join an already operational ring, it is necessary for the DTE to first go through an initialization procedure to ensure that it does not interfere with the correct functioning of the already established ring. In addition, during

(a)

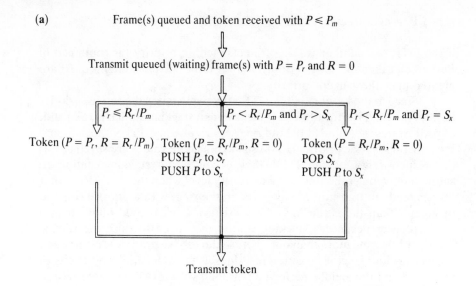

Frame(s) queued and token received with $P \leqslant P_m$

Transmit queued (waiting) frame(s) with $P = P_r$ and $R = 0$

$P_r \leqslant R_r/P_m$

Token $(P = P_r, R = R_r/P_m)$

$P_r < R_r/P_m$ and $P_r > S_x$

Token $(P = R_r/P_m, R = 0)$
PUSH P_r to S_r
PUSH P to S_x

$P_r < R_r/P_m$ and $P_r = S_x$

Token $(P = R_r/P_m, R = 0)$
POP S_x
PUSH P to S_x

Transmit token

(b)

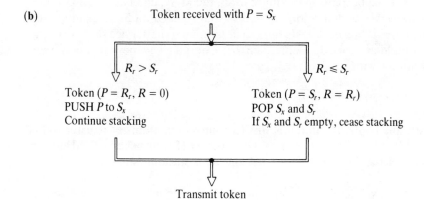

Token received with $P = S_x$

$R_r > S_r$

Token $(P = R_r, R = 0)$
PUSH P to S_x
Continue stacking

$R_r \leqslant S_r$

Token $(P = S_r, R = R_r)$
POP S_x and S_r
If S_x and S_r empty, cease stacking

Transmit token

FIGURE 8.12

Token generation and stack modifications: (a) token generation [*Note*: Sx = 0 if stack empty]; (b) stack modification.

normal operation, it is necessary for each active DTE on the ring to monitor continuously its correct operation and, if a fault develops, to take corrective action to try to re-establish a correctly functioning ring. Collectively, these functions are known as **ring management** and a list of the various MAC frame types associated with these functions is given in Figure 8.13. Selected aspects of each function will now be described.

Initialization When a DTE wishes to become part of the ring, after having been switched on or after it has been reset, an initialization sequence is entered, firstly, to ensure that no other DTEs present in the

Frame Type	Function
Duplicate address test (DAT)	This is used during the initialization procedure to enable a station to determine that no other stations in the ring are using its own address
Standby monitor present (SMP)	Again, this is used in the initialization procedure to enable a station to determine the address of its upstream neighbour (successor) in the ring
Active monitor present (AMP)	These types of frames are transmitted at regular intervals by the currently active monitor and each station monitors their passage
Claim token (CT)	This is used in the procedure to determine a new active monitor if the current one fails
Purge (PRG)	This is used by a new active monitor to initialize all stations into the idle state
Beacon (BCN)	This is used in the beaconing procedure

FIGURE 8.13

Token ring management of MAC frame types.

ring are using the same address and, secondly, to inform its immediate downstream neighbour that it has (re)entered the ring.

The initialization procedure starts with the transmission of a duplicate address test (DAT) MAC frame by the DTE with the A bits in the FS field set to 0. On receipt of a DAT frame, each active DTE in the ring inspects the DA field contained within it and, if it determines that it is the same as its own address, sets the A bits to 1. Hence, if the DAT frame returns to its originator with the A bits set to 1, the originator informs the network management sublayer and returns to the bypass state. The latter (as will be described in Chapter 10) then determines if it should try again to become inserted into the ring. Alternatively, if on return of the DAT frame the A bits are still set to 0, the DTE continues the initialization sequence by transmitting a standby monitor present (SMP) MAC frame.

A DTE that receives an SMP frame with the A and C bits set to 0 regards the frame as having originated from its immediate upstream neighbour and hence records the SA contained within the frame as the upstream neighbours address (UNA). This is required for fault detection and monitoring functions as will be described later. The initialization phase is then complete.

Standby monitor Upon completion of the initialization sequence, the DTE can start to transmit and receive normal frames and tokens. In addition, the DTE enters the standby monitor state to monitor continuously the correct operation of the ring. It does this by monitoring the passage of tokens and special active monitor present (AMP) MAC frames, which are periodically transmitted by the current active monitor, as they are repeated at the ring interface. Then, if tokens or AMP frames are not periodically detected, the standby monitor times out (it maintains two timers for this function) and enters the claim token state.

When in the claim token state, the DTE continuously transmits claim token (CT) MAC frames and also inspects the SA in any CT frames it receives. Each CT frame transmitted contains, in addition to the SA of the originating DTE, the latter's stored UNA. Consequently, if a CT frame is received with an SA that matches its own address and a UNA that matches its own stored UNA, this means that the CT frame has successfully circulated around the ring and hence the DTE becomes the new active ring monitor. Alternatively, if a CT frame is received with an SA greater than its own address, this means that another DTE has made an earlier bid to become the new monitor and hence the DTE effectively relinquishes its bid by returning to the standby monitor state.

Active monitor   If the DTE is successful in its bid to become the new active monitor, it first inserts its latency buffer into the ring and enables its own clock. (Note that there is only one active monitor in the ring at any point in time.) It then initiates the transmission of a purge (PRG) MAC frame to ensure that there are no other tokens or frames on the ring before it initiates the transmission of a new token. When the DTE receives a PRG frame containing an SA equal to its own address, this indicates that the ring has been successfully purged. The DTE then initiates the neighbour notification process by broadcasting an AMP MAC frame. After a short time delay, this is followed with the transmission of a new control token.

The DTE immediately downstream of the active monitor detects that the A bits in the AMP frame are 0 and hence reads the UNA from within the frame and updates its existing UNA variable. It then sets the A and C bits to 1 and repeats the frame. Subsequent DTEs around the ring detect that the A bits are non-zero and hence just record the passage of the AMP frame by resetting the AMP timer.

In addition, the DTE immediately downstream from the active monitor, after repeating the AMP frame, continues the neighbour notification process by broadcasting a similar SMP frame. The next DTE downstream then, in turn, detects that the A bits are set to 0 in this frame, updates its UNA variable, sets the A and C bits to 1 and repeats the frame. It continues the process by broadcasting a new SMP frame with the A bits again set to 0. This procedure is carried out by each DTE around the ring and is subsequently re-initiated by the active monitor transmitting a new AMP frame at regular intervals. In this way, each active DTE in the ring can detect such failures as a DTE jabbering (continuously sending tokens, for example): the absence of AMP frames flowing around the ring will mean that the AMP timer in all the other DTEs will expire, thus initiating the transmission of CT frames followed, if the fault is still present, by entering a failure diagnostic procedure known as beaconing.

Beaconing If a serious failure, such as a broken cable, arises in the ring, each DTE on the ring is informed that the token-passing protocol has been suspended (until the affected failure domain has been located and subsequently repaired) by means of a procedure known as **beaconing**. The failure domain consists of:

- the DTE reporting the failure, which is referred to as the **beaconing station;**
- the DTE upstream of the beaconing station; and
- the ring medium between them.

As an example, Figure 8.14(a) illustrates a failure domain assuming a break has occurred in the ring medium between DTEs F and G. In this example, G is the beaconing station and F its upstream neighbour. Normally, the beaconing state is entered if the timers associated with the AMP or token-passing procedures expire. When in this state, beacon (BCN) supervisory frames are continuously transmitted until either a beacon frame is received or a timer expires. If the latter occurs, the network management sublayer is notified and transmissions cease. Alternatively, if a beacon frame is received by a DTE with an SA equal to its own address, the failure is assumed to have cleared and the DTE enters the claim token state or, if a beacon frame is received with an SA different from the DTE address, the DTE enters the standby monitor state.

Clearly, if the network comprises just a single ring, then, in the event of a failure occurring, it is necessary to repair the faulty segment before any network transmissions can be resumed. An optional feature with the token ring, therefore, is to utilize a second, redundant ring whose direction of transmission is opposite to that of the first ring. A schematic of this type of network configuration is shown in Figure 8.14(b).

The TCU with such networks, in addition to supporting the functions outlined earlier, can also be used to bypass a faulty ring segment or DTE. As an example, Figure 8.14(c) shows how the faulty ring segment (failure domain) illustrated in Figure 8.14(a) is bypassed. Essentially, once the failure domain has been located and reported, the relays in the TCU of F and G are activated to (hopefully) re-establish a continuous ring. If isolating the suspected faulty segment does not remove the fault, however, the next step is to initiate the isolation of DTE G completely; this is shown in Figure 8.14(d). It should be noted from these figures that the redundant

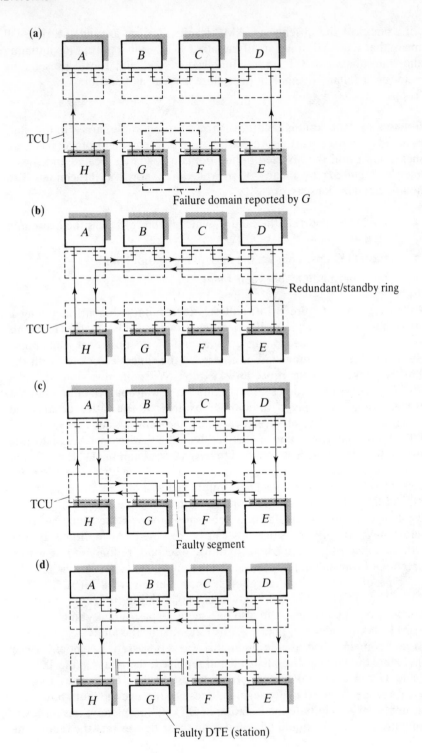

FIGURE 8.14

Ring fault detection and isolation:
(a) failure detection;
(b) redundant ring configuration;
(c) segment isolation; (d) DTE
(station) isolation.

ring does not have a direct path to the MAC unit and is used simply to provide a means of bypassing a section of the ring. In this way, the order of the DTEs on a re-established ring is the same as that in the original ring.

It can be concluded from the foregoing that the medium access control procedures used with a token ring network are quite complicated, certainly compared with a CSMA/CD bus, for example. It should be remembered, however, that most of the procedures described are implemented in special controller integrated circuits within the MAC unit and hence their operation is transparent to the user. Moreover, many of these ring management procedures are only invoked when faults develop and so the overheads associated with them are, on the whole, modest.

8.3.3   Fibre distributed data interface

The basic token ring network described in the previous section is intended for use primarily in office environments in which the total network traffic is *modest*. This is the case, for example, if the network is being used by, say, a distributed community of personal workstations to access such functions as electronic mail or shared devices, such as printers or backup file servers. As the level of sophistication of the workstations increases, however, there is a need for a network that can transmit large quantities of data at rates well in excess of 4 Mbps, the rate of the basic token ring; for example, to transfer large quantities of data from, say, a graphics server or from a file server to a number of diskless nodes. To meet such needs, an alternative type of token ring network, which operates at a data rate of 100 Mbps, has been introduced. This network uses an optical fibre as the transmission medium and is known as the **fibre distributed data interface** (**FDDI**). Although this type of network has many features in common with the basic token ring network – for example, it uses dual, counter-rotating rings to obtain enhanced reliability – it also has some differences. These are primarily in the transmit and receive electronics associated with the MAC unit and will now be described.

Physical interface

The physical interface to the fibre cable is shown in schematic form in Figure 8.15. In a basic token ring network, at any point in time, there is a single active ring monitor which, amongst other things, supplies the master clock for the ring. Each circulating bit stream is Manchester encoded by the active ring monitor and all the other DTEs (stations) in the ring then frequency and phase lock to the clock extracted from this bit stream. However, such an approach is not suitable at the data rates of an FDDI ring; instead, each ring interface has its own local clock. Outgoing data are

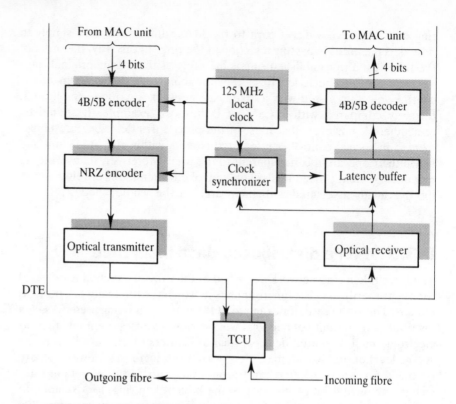

From MAC unit

To MAC unit

FIGURE 8.15

FDDI physical interface schematic.

then transmitted using this clock while incoming data are received using a clock that is frequency and phase locked to the transitions in the incoming bit stream. As will be seen, all data are encoded prior to transmission so that there is a guaranteed transition in the data stream at least every two bit cell periods, thereby ensuring that the received data are sampled (clocked) very near to the nominal bit cell centres.

All data to be transmitted are first encoded, prior to transmission, using a 4 of 5 group code. This means that for each four bits of data to be transmitted a corresponding five-bit **code word** or **symbol** is generated by the encoder. The latter is thus known as a **4B/5B encoder**. The five-bit symbols corresponding to each of the 16 possible four-bit data groups are shown in Figure 8.16(a) and, as can be seen, there is a maximum of two consecutive zero bits in each symbol. The latter are then shifted out through a further NRZI encoder which produces a signal transition whenever a 1 bit is being transmitted and no transition when a 0 bit is transmitted. In this way, there is a guaranteed signal transition at least every two bits.

The use of five bits to represent each of the 16 four-bit data groups means that there is a further 16 unused combinations of the five bits. Some of these combinations (symbols) are thus used for other (link) control functions, such as indicating the start and end of each transmitted frame or

(a)

Data symbols

4-bit data group   5-bit symbol

```
0000 — — — — — — 11110
0001 — — — — — — 01001
0010 — — — — — — 10100
0011 — — — — — — 10101
0100 — — — — — — 01010
0101 — — — — — — 01011
0110 — — — — — — 01110
0111 — — — — — — 01111
1000 — — — — — — 10010
1001 — — — — — — 10011
1010 — — — — — — 10110
1011 — — — — — — 10111
1100 — — — — — — 11010
1101 — — — — — — 11011
1110 — — — — — — 11100
1111 — — — — — — 11101
```

Control symbols

```
IDLE  — — — — — — 11111
 J    — — — — — — 11000
 K    — — — — — — 10001
 T    — — — — — — 01101
 R    — — — — — — 00111
 S    — — — — — — 11001
QUIET — — — — — — 00000
HALT  — — — — — — 00100
```

(b)

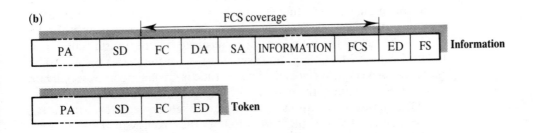

PA = Preamble (16 or more symbols)
SD = Start delimiter (2 symbols)
FC = Frame control (2 symbols)
DA = Destination address (4 or 12 symbols)
SA = Source address (4 or 12 symbols)
FCS = Frame check sequence (8 symbols)
ED = End delimiter (1 or 2 symbols)
FS = Frame status (3 symbols)

FIGURE 8.16

(a) 4B/5B codes; (b) frame formats.

token. A list of the link control symbols used is also shown in the figure, and Figure 8.16(b) shows the format used for frames and tokens. In general, the meaning and use of each field is the same as with the basic token ring but, because of the use of symbols rather than bits, there are some differences in the structure of each field. Some of these differences will now be explained.

The preamble (PA) field is comprised of 16 or more IDLE symbols which, since the latter are each comprised of five 1 bits, causes the line signal to change at the maximum frequency. This is thus used for establishing (and maintaining) clock synchronization at the receiver. The start delimiter (SD) field consists of two control symbols (J and K) which enable the receiver to interpret the following frame contents on the correct symbol boundaries. The FC, DA and SA fields have the same meaning as before but the (decoded) information field in the data frames can be up to 4500 octets with FDDI. The end delimiter (ED) field contains one or two control symbols (T). Finally, the frame status (FS) field, although it has a similar function to the FS field in the basic ring, consists of three symbols that are combinations of the two control symbols R and S.

The local clock used in the physical interface is 125 MHz which, because of the use of 4B/5B encoding, yields a data rate of 100 Mbps. Moreover, since all transmissions are encoded into five-bit symbols, each five-bit symbol must first be buffered at the receiver before it can be decoded. The use of two symbols (J and K) for the SD field to establish correct symbol boundaries, however, means that a 10-bit buffer is used at the receiver. This is known as the **latency** (or **elastic**) **buffer**.

Frame transmission and reception

The short latency time (and hence number of bits in circulation) of the basic token ring means that it is necessary for a DTE (station), after initiating the transmission of an information frame, to wait until the FS field at the tail of the frame has been received before transmitting a new token. With an FDDI ring, however, because of the presence of a 10-bit buffer in each ring interface, the latency time is much longer, especially for a large ring containing the maximum of 500 DTEs. With FDDI, therefore, a DTE initiates the transmission of a new token immediately after it has transmitted the FS symbol. It then follows the token with IDLE symbols until it receives the SD symbols indicating the start of a new frame or token.

As with the basic ring, it is the source DTE that removes a frame from the ring after it has circulated the ring. Because of the long latency of an FDDI ring, however, there may be more than one frame circulating around the ring at one time. The ring interface, therefore, must repeat the SD, FC and DA fields (symbols) of any received frames before it can determine if its own address is in the SA field. But this can result in one or more frame fragments – comprising SD, FC and DA fields – circulating around the ring. This means that a DTE, on receipt of a usable token, starts to transmit a frame and concurrently receives and discards any frame fragments that may be circulating around the ring.

Priority operation

Unlike the basic ring, which is based on the use of priority and reservation bits, the priority operation of an FDDI ring uses the same principle as that used with a token bus network. This, as will be expanded upon in the next section, is based on a parameter known as the token rotation time (TRT). The TRT is the time that has expired since a DTE *last received* the token. It thus includes the time taken to transmit any waiting frames by this DTE and also the time taken by all other DTEs in the ring for this rotation of the token. Clearly, therefore, if the ring is lightly loaded, then the TRT is short. As the loading of the ring increases, however, so the TRT measured by each DTE increases. The TRT is thus a measure of the total ring loading. The priority control algorithm then works by only allowing lower priority frames to be transmitted if the measured TRT is lower than a preset maximum limit for each priority class.

8.3.4   Token bus

The third type of LAN supported in the standards documents is the **token bus** network. Because of the deterministic nature of a token medium access control method and the ability to prioritize the transmission of frames, token bus networks are used in the manufacturing industry (for factory automation) and other related domains, such as the process control industry. Under normal (error-free) conditions, the operation of this type of network is similar to that of the token ring network. However, due to the differences in the two medium access methods (broadcast for bus, sequential for ring), the various procedures used for handling the management of the logical ring, such as initialization and lost token, are inevitably different. To avoid repetition, therefore, this section will concentrate mainly on the management procedures associated with token bus networks.

Various aspects of the operation and components associated with token bus networks are shown in Figure 8.17. Token bus networks normally utilize coaxial cable as the transmission medium and operate in either a broadband mode or a modified baseband mode known as **carrierband**. The modulation and interface control circuitry, as illustrated in Figure 8.17(a), performs such functions as:

- transmit data encoding (modulation),

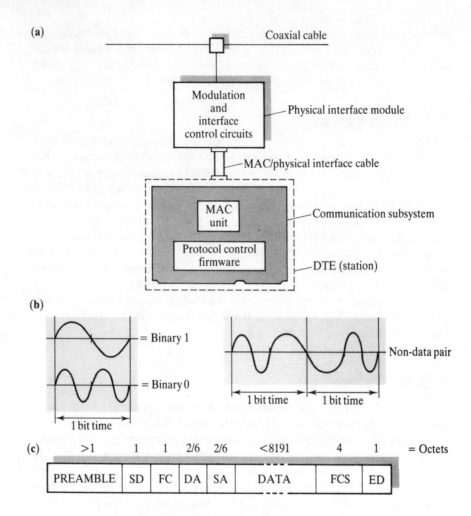

FIGURE 8.17

Token bus network principles:
(a) DTE interface schematic;
(b) carrierband encoding;
(c) frame format.

- receive data decoding (demodulation), and
- clock generation.

There is a standard interface between the physical interface module (PIM) and the attached DTE and, in some instances, the PIM is integrated on to the communication board in the DTE.

The principle of operation of the carrierband mode is shown in Figure 8.17(b). Although the carrierband mode is the same as baseband in so much that each transmission occupies the complete cable bandwidth, in carrierband mode all data are first modulated before transmission using phase-coherent, frequency-shift keying. As can be seen, a binary 1 is transmitted as a single cycle of a sinusoidal signal of frequency equal to the bit rate, normally between 1 and 5 Mbps, while a binary 0 is transmitted as two cycles of a signal of twice the bit rate frequency. Notice also that there

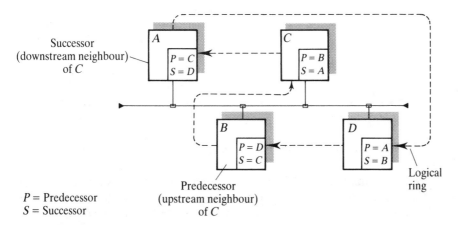

Successor
(downstream neighbour)
of C

Predecessor
(upstream neighbour)
of C

P = Predecessor
S = Successor

Logical
ring

FIGURE 8.18

Token bus network: (a) principle
of operation.

is no change of phase at the bit cell boundaries, hence, the term phase coherent.

It may be recalled from Chapter 2 that any extraneous noise signals picked up in the cable are comprised of an infinite number of frequency components. Furthermore, a basic baseband signal (waveform) is also made up of a possibly infinite number of frequency components. In contrast, a carrierband waveform has only two frequency components. This means that with the latter it is possible to use a filter at the receiver which only passes these two frequencies, thereby effectively blocking most of the noise signal. This significantly improves the noise immunity of the system. Clearly, this cannot be done with baseband since the filter would also affect the data signal.

The frame format used with token bus networks is as shown in Figure 8.17(c) and, as can be seen, it is almost identical to that used with a token ring network. However, the J and K non-data bits, which are used in the SD and ED fields of a token ring to achieve data transparency, are replaced in carrierband mode by pairs of special non-data symbols.

Basic operation

A schematic diagram illustrating the basic operation of a token bus network is shown in Figure 8.18. There is a single control token and only the possessor of the token can transmit a frame. All DTEs that can initiate the transmission of a frame are linked in the form of a **logical ring**. The token is passed physically using the bus around the logical ring. Thus, on receipt of the token from its *predecessor* (upstream neighbour) on the ring, a DTE may transmit any waiting frames up to a defined maximum. It then passes the token on to its known *successor* (downstream neighbour) on the ring.

Before describing the various ring management procedures, it is perhaps helpful to restate two basic properties of bus networks. Firstly, with a bus network all DTEs are connected directly to the transmission medium and hence, when a DTE transmits (broadcasts) a frame on the medium, it is received (or heard) by all active DTEs in the network. Secondly, there is a maximum time a DTE need wait for a response to a transmitted frame before it can assume that either the transmitted frame is corrupted or the specified destination DTE is inoperable. This time is known as the slot time (not the same as that used with a CSMA/CD bus) and can be defined as:

$$\text{Slot time} = 2 \times (\text{transmission path delay} + \text{processing delay})$$

where transmission path delay is the worst-case transmission propagation delay going from any transmitter to any receiver in the network and processing delay is the maximum time for the MAC unit within a DTE to process a received frame and generate an appropriate response. A safety margin is then added and the slot time value is expressed in bit times rounded up to a multiple number of octets.

Under normal operation, the token is passed from one DTE in the logical ring to another using a short token frame. Each DTE need only know, therefore, the address of the next (downstream neighbour or successor) DTE in the logical ring. If a DTE fails to accept the token, however, the sending DTE uses a series of recovery procedures to find a new successor; these procedures get progressively more drastic if the DTE fails to evoke a response from a neighbouring DTE. Other procedures are concerned with the initialization of the ring and maintaining the correct operation of the ring as DTEs enter and leave the ring. Although it is possible to prioritize the token, as with a token ring, only a single priority ring will be considered initially. The MAC frame types used with the various ring management procedures to be described, together with a brief explanation of their use, are shown in Figure 8.19. More detailed explanations will be given as the different procedures are discussed.

Token passing

On receipt of a valid token frame, a DTE may transmit any frames it has waiting. It then passes the token to its known successor. After sending the token, the DTE listens to any subsequent activity on the bus to make sure that its successor is active and has received the token. If it hears a valid frame being transmitted, it assumes that all is well and that its successor received the token correctly. However, if it does not hear a valid frame being transmitted after the slot time interval, it must take corrective action.

If, after sending the token, the DTE hears a noise burst or frame with an incorrect FCS, it continues to listen for up to four more slot times. Then, if nothing more is heard, the DTE assumes that the token itself has become corrupted during transmission and repeats the token transmission. Alternatively, if a valid frame is heard during the delay of four slot times, it

Frame Type	Function
Claim token	This is used during the initialization sequence of the (logical) ring
Solicit successor	This is used during both the recovery procedure when a station leaves the ring and also during the procedure that allows a station to (re)enter the ring
Who follows me	This is used during the procedure that enables a station to determine the address of the station that is its successor in the ring
Resolve contention	This is used during the procedure that allows a new station to enter the ring
Set successor	This is used to allow a new station entering the ring to inform its new predecessor that it has joined the ring
Token	This is the control token frame

FIGURE 8.19

Token bus ring management of MAC frame types.

again assumes that its successor has the token. Also, if a second noise burst is heard during this interval, the DTE treats this as a valid frame being transmitted by its successor and hence assumes the token has been passed.

If, after repeating the token-passing operation and the monitoring procedures just outlined, the successor does not respond to the second token frame, the DTE assumes that its successor has failed and hence proceeds to establish a new successor. The sender first broadcasts a who-follows-me frame with its current successor's address in the data field of the frame. On receipt of this type of frame, all DTEs compare the address in the data field of the frame with its own predecessor address; that is, the address of the DTE that normally sends it the token. Then, the DTE whose predecessor is the same as the successor contained within the frame, responds by sending its own address in a set-successor frame. The DTE holding the token has thus established a new successor and in so doing has bridged around the failed DTE.

If the sending DTE does not receive a response to a who-follows-me frame, it repeats the frame a second time. If there is still no response, the DTE takes more drastic action by sending a solicit-successor frame with its own address in the DA field. This effectively asks any DTE in the network to respond to it; hence, if there are any operational DTEs that hear the frame, they respond and the logical ring is re-established using a procedure known as **response window**. Alternatively, if no response is received, the DTE assumes that a catastrophe has occurred; for example, all other DTEs have failed, the medium has broken, or the DTE's own receiver section has failed (and hence cannot hear the response(s) from other DTEs to its own requests). Under such conditions, the DTE becomes silent but continues to listen for another DTE's transmissions.

Response window

This procedure is followed at random time intervals to allow new DTEs to enter an operational logical ring. The response window is in fact a length of time that a DTE needs to wait for a response after transmitting a frame, and hence is the same as the network slot time. Each solicit-successor frame transmitted by a DTE specifies an SA and a DA, and the frame is responded to by a DTE that wishes to enter the ring and has an address between the two addresses specified. Each DTE sends a solicit-successor frame at random intervals whenever it is the owner of the token.

When a DTE sends a solicit-successor frame, it is said to have *opened* a response window since, after sending this type of frame, the sending DTE waits for a response within the response window period. Then, if a DTE whose address lies within the range specified in the solicit-successor frame is waiting to enter the ring, it responds by sending a request to the sender of the frame to become its new successor in the logical ring. If the sender hears the response, called a set-successor frame, it allows the new DTE to enter the ring by making it its new successor and, in turn, passes it the token. Clearly, the address range specified may contain multiple DTEs all waiting to enter the ring and hence the response frames returned by each DTE will be corrupted. If this happens, the soliciting DTE must try to identify a single responder. This is accomplished by the soliciting DTE entering an arbitration procedure, which works as follows.

Having ascertained that more than one DTE in the specified address range is waiting to enter the ring, the soliciting DTE starts to sequence through the possible DTEs by sending a resolve-contention frame. This procedure continues until it receives a positive reply. In addition, the DTEs that responded to the earlier solicit-successor frame but which did not subsequently receive the token, each choose a value in the range 0 to 3 and listen for any further activity on the bus for this number of slot times. Then, if a DTE hears a transmission during its selected time, it delays its request and waits for another opportunity to become part of the ring; that is, when the next response window is opened. Alternatively, if it does not hear a transmission during its selected time, it continues to wait for the possible receipt of a resolve-contention frame. In this way, the worst-case delay the soliciting DTE need spend resolving the contention is limited.

Initialization

The initialization procedure is in fact built on top of the response window procedure. Each DTE in the network monitors all transmissions on the bus and, whenever a transmission is heard, it resets a timer, known as the **inactivity timer**, to a preset value. If a DTE loses the token during normal operation, this inactivity timer expires and the DTE enters the initialization phase, at which point it sends a claim-token frame. Clearly, as before, a number of DTEs may try to send a claim-token frame simultaneously and hence the following procedure is followed to ensure that only a single token is generated.

Each potential initializer sends a claim-token frame with an information field length that is a multiple number of slot times. The multiple chosen is either 0, 2, 4 or 6, the number chosen being derived from the first two bits in the DTE's network address. After sending its particular claim-token frame, the DTE waits a further slot time before listening to the transmission medium. If it hears a transmission while listening, it knows that another DTE(s) has sent a longer claim-token frame and so the DTE simply eliminates itself from trying to become the first owner of the token. If a transmission is not heard, however, the DTE repeats the above process using the next two bits from its address field. Again, if no transmission is detected, it uses the next pair of bits and so on until all address bits have been used. Then, if the medium is still quiet, the DTE has successfully become the first owner of the token. The unique owner of the token then continues the initialization process by using the response window procedure to allow the other waiting DTEs to enter the logical ring.

Although a DTE may remove itself from the logical ring at any time by simply not responding when the token is passed to it, a cleaner method is for the DTE to first wait until it receives the token and then to send a set-successor frame to its predecessor with the address of its own successor in the information field. The DTE then sends the token to its own successor, as usual, in the knowledge that it is no longer part of the (logical) ring.

Priority operation

As with a token ring network, it is also possible to implement a priority mechanism with a token bus network. However, the access method used with a token bus only distinguishes four levels of priority, called **access classes**. These are named 0, 2, 4 and 6 with 6 being the highest priority. As was mentioned earlier, token bus networks are used primarily in application domains such as manufacturing automation and process control and hence typical usage of the four access classes may be:

- Class 6: Urgent messages such as those relating to critical alarm conditions and associated control functions.
- Class 4: Messages relating to normal control actions and ring management functions.
- Class 2: Messages relating to routine data gathering for data logging purposes.
- Class 0: Messages relating to program downloading and general file transfers; that is, low-priority long messages.

The transmission of waiting frames with the highest priority is controlled to ensure that the available ring capacity (bandwidth) is shared between all DTEs. On receipt of the token, a DTE may send any waiting high-priority frames up to a maximum governed by a time interval known as the **high-priority token-hold time**. Then, when this time expires, it must pass on the token to its successor. Thus, when a DTE receives the token, it first sends any high-priority frames it has waiting; then, assuming the DTE is using the priority mechanism and providing the token-hold time has not expired, the DTE begins to transmit any waiting lower priority frames using the following control algorithm.

Each DTE in the logical ring keeps a timer that indicates the time that has expired since the DTE *last received* the token. This is held in a variable known as the **token rotation timer** (**TRT**). When the DTE next receives the token, it first transmits any waiting high-priority frames, thus increasing the TRT value, and then it computes the difference between a fixed time known as the **target token rotation time** (**TTRT**) and its current TRT. If the difference is positive, the DTE can send any waiting lower priority frames until the TTRT is reached; if the difference is zero or negative, the DTE cannot send any lower priority frames on this pass of the token. Each DTE using the priority mechanism maintains a separate TRT for the three lowest priority access classes and transmits waiting frames working from higher to lower access class until the TTRT is reached.

To illustrate the operation of this mechanism, consider the example shown in Figure 8.20. For clarity, the example assumes only two access classes, the highest and one lower class. Also, all frames transmitted are assumed to be of a fixed length and hence the various times are directly proportional to the number of frames. The example assumes DTEs 9 and 1 each send only high-priority frames each time they receive the token whereas DTEs 7 and 5 send only lower priority frames whenever possible. Note that the logical ring is built such that the physical DTE addresses are in descending numerical order. Also, the TTRT for the lower priority frames is fixed at a value equivalent to eight frames. The values in the left-hand column under each DTE labelled TRT are the token rotation times measured by that DTE for the previous rotation of the token. The values in the right-hand column labelled XMIT are the number of frames transmitted by the DTE each time it receives the token. Each row represents one rotation of the token.

All transmissions are assumed to begin after a period of inactivity and hence after the token has been rotating as rapidly as possible. The TRT in DTE 9 is therefore shown as zero to begin with. This assumes that the token passing and propagation delays are negligible compared with the time taken to transmit a normal frame. Also, it is assumed that the high-priority token-hold time is such that a DTE can send up to three high-priority frames on receipt of the token.

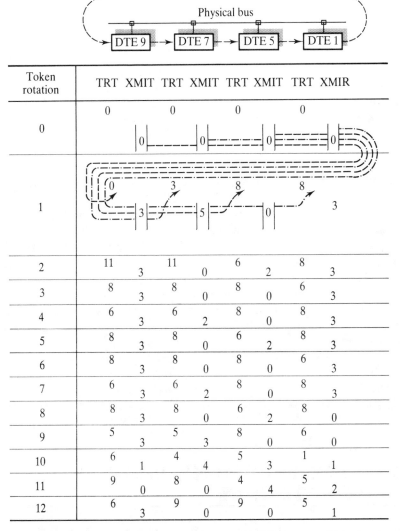

Token rotation	TRT	XMIT	TRT	XMIT	TRT	XMIT	TRT	XMIR
2	11	3	11	0	6	2	8	3
3	8	3	8	0	8	0	6	3
4	6	3	6	2	8	0	8	3
5	8	3	8	0	6	2	8	3
6	8	3	8	0	8	0	6	3
7	6	3	6	2	8	0	8	3
8	8	3	8	0	6	2	8	0
9	5	3	5	3	8	0	6	0
10	6	1	4	4	5	3	1	1
11	9	0	8	0	4	4	5	2
12	6	3	9	0	9	0	5	1

FIGURE 8.20

Prioritorized ring example.

During the first rotation of the token, DTE 9 receives the token and sends its maximum of three high-priority frames before passing on the token. When DTE 7 receives the token from DTE 9, therefore, its TRT will have incremented to 3, since three frames have been transmitted since it last received the token. This means that DTE 7 can transmit five (TTRT − TRT) lower priority frames before passing on the token. On receipt of the token, the TRT held by DTE 5 will now be 8, as a total of eight frames have been transmitted since it last received the token. It cannot therefore transmit any lower priority frames on this pass of the token. DTE 1 then transmits three high-priority frames unconstrained by its computed TRT.

During the second rotation of the token, both DTE 9 and DTE 1 send three high-priority frames unaffected by their computed TRT, but this time DTE 7 is blocked from transmitting any lower priority frames (since its computed TRT exceeds 8 on receipt of the token) and DTE 5 is able to transmit two lower priority frames (TTRT − TRT = 2).

During the third rotation of the token, again both DTE 9 and DTE 1 each send three high-priority frames but this time both DTE 7 and DTE 5 are blocked from sending any lower priority frames, since both their computed TRTs have reached the TTRT limit (8).

During the fourth rotation of the token, a situation similar to that in the second rotation prevails, but notice this time that the computed TRTs are such that DTE 7 has an opportunity to send two lower priority frames instead of DTE 5, which this time cannot send any frames. Similarly, during the fifth rotation of the token, DTE 5 is able to transmit two lower priority frames but DTE 7 is inhibited from sending any lower priority frames. The cycle then repeats itself and it can be readily deduced that, over any three rotations, DTEs 9 and 1 use 18/22nds (82%) of the available capacity and DTEs 7 and 5 share the remaining 4/22nds (18%) equally.

During the eighth rotation of the token, it is assumed that DTE 1 temporarily runs out of high-priority frames to transmit and hence DTEs 7 and 5 are able to transmit more of their waiting lower priority frames. Similarly, during the tenth rotation, DTE 9 runs out of high-priority frames and so on.

Although this is a simple example, it nevertheless shows how the priority mechanism allows, firstly, high-priority frames to be transmitted relatively unconstrained and, secondly, lower priority frames to be transmitted in a fair manner whenever there is spare capacity available.

8.4 LOCAL AREA NETWORK PROTOCOLS

The various protocol standards for LANs, which deal with the physical and link layers in the context of the ISO Reference Model, are those defined in IEEE Standard 802. This standard defines a family of protocols, each relating to a particular type of medium access control method. The various IEEE standards and their relationship to the ISO Reference Model are shown in Figure 8.21.

The three medium access control (MAC) standards together with their associated physical media specifications are contained in the following IEEE standards documents:

- IEEE 802.3: CSMA/CD bus,

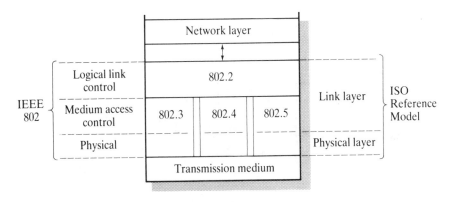

802.2 = Logical link control protocol
802.3 = CSMA/CD ⎫
802.4 = Token bus ⎬ Medium access control protocols
802.5 = Token ring ⎭

FIGURE 8.21

IEEE 802 protocol set.

- IEEE 802.4: Token bus,
- IEEE 802.5: Token ring.

The relevant ISO standards are the same except an additional 8 is used: ISO 8802.3, etc.

The descriptions that have been presented so far in this chapter have been concerned with the MAC control and physical layers of these three standards. Although each is different in its internal operation, they all present a standard set of services to the logical link control (LLC) layer, which is intended therefore to be used in conjunction with any of the underlying MAC standards. In general, as has been mentioned earlier, the various MAC control and physical layers are normally implemented in firmware in special-purpose integrated circuits. This section, therefore, will concentrate only on the LLC layer and simply define the interface between the LLC and MAC layers. It should be noted that with an LAN the LLC and MAC layers are peer (end-to-end) protocols, since there are no intermediate switching nodes within the network itself similar, for example, to a packet-switching exchange in a PSDN.

8.4.1 Logical link control layer

The description of the LLC layer will be presented in the form used with the higher protocol layers described in Chapter 6; that is, first the user (network layer) services provided by the layer will be described, then the operation of the LLC protocol entity itself and finally the services used by the LLC layer to transfer LLC-PDUs to a peer LLC layer. In general, the primitives used in the ISO/IEEE standards for LANs for layers 1 and 2 are

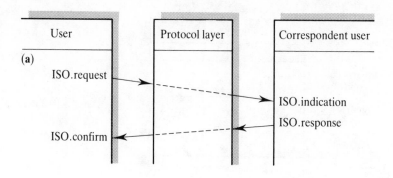

(a)

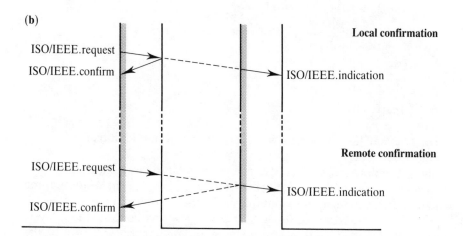

(b)

FIGURE 8.22

LAN protocol service primitives: (a) higher layers (3–7); (b) lower layers (1–2).

similar to those used in the ISO standards for layers 3 through 7 except that with the IEEE standards there are no response primitives. This means that when a confirmation primitive is associated with the user service, it is generated either by the local protocol entity directly or by the remote peer protocol entity; that is, it is not generated as a result of a response primitive being received at the remote user interface. The two alternatives are shown in Figure 8.22(b). Figure 8.22(a) illustrates the sequence of primitives used with the higher protocol layers.

In the case of local confirmation, the confirmation primitive simply indicates to the user whether the local protocol entity has been successful (or unsuccessful) in sending the associated request to the remote peer protocol entity; that is, it does not imply that the latter received it correctly. Similarly, in the case of remote confirmation, the confirmation primitive indicates that the remote peer protocol entity successfully passed the associated indication primitive to the correspondent user; that is, it has not been generated as a result of a response from the correspondent user as is the case in the ISO documents for higher layers.

User services

Two types of user service are provided by the LLC layer: an unacknowledged connectionless service and a set of connection-oriented services. The unacknowledged connectionless service provides the user with the means of initiating the transfer of service data units with a minimum of protocol overheads. Typically, this service is used when such functions as error recovery and sequencing are being provided in a higher protocol layer and hence need not be replicated in the LLC layer. Alternatively, the connection-oriented services provide the user with the means to first establish a link-level logical connection before initiating the transfer of any service data units and, should it be required, to then implement error recovery and sequencing of the flow of these units across an established connection.

In certain real-time applications of LANs, such as in the process control industry for interconnecting items of computer-based instrumentation equipment distributed around, say, a chemical plant, the time overheads of setting up a logical connection prior to sending data is often unacceptable. Nevertheless, some acknowledgement of correct receipt of a transmitted item of data is often needed and hence the basic unacknowledged connectionless service is not acceptable. To cater for this type of requirement, therefore, an additional service known as the acknowledged connectionless service is provided. Similarly, a service is also provided to allow an item of data to be requested from a remote user without a connection first being established. This is known as the obtain reply service.

The various primitives associated with the two sets of services are shown in diagrammatic form in the time sequence diagram of Figure 8.23. Each of the primitives illustrated has parameters associated with it. These include a specification of the source (local) and destination (remote) addresses and other parameters where appropriate. The source and destination addresses are present in all primitives. They specify, at a minimum, the physical addresses to be used on the network medium, and hence the destination address can be either an individual or a group address. Normally, however, both addresses are a concatenation of the addresses as used on the physical medium and the local service access point identifier (LLC-SAP).

With the unacknowledged connectionless service, on receipt of a data transfer request primitive (L.DATA.request), the LLC protocol entity makes a best attempt to send the accompanying data using the MAC sublayer; there is no confirmation that the transfer has been successful or indeed unsuccessful. With the acknowledged connectionless service, however, the user is notified of the success or failure of the passing of the L.DATA_ACKNOWLEDGE.indication to the remote user by means of the L.DATA_ACKNOWLEDGE_STATUS.indication primitive.

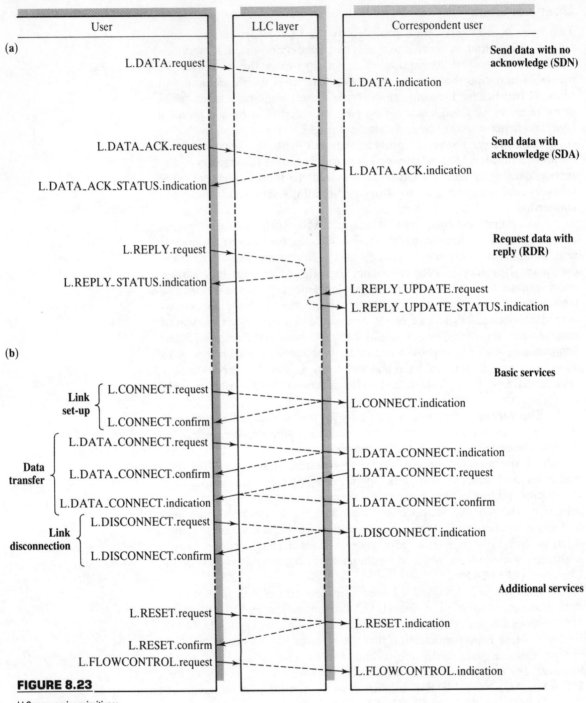

FIGURE 8.23

LLC user service primitives:
(a) connectionless;
(b) connection oriented.

The various primitives associated with the obtain reply service allow a user:

(1) To request the contents of a message buffer maintained by a remote LLC entity – L.REPLY.request/indication.

(2) To update the contents of a message buffer that is maintained by its local LLC entity – L.REPLY_UPDATE.request and L.REPLY_UPDATE_STATUS.indication.

With the connection-oriented service, prior to any data transfers, a logical connection must first be established using the L.CONNECT primitives. Similarly, after all data transfers have taken place over this connection, the connection must be cleared using the L.DISCONNECT primitives. Also, during the data transfer phase, the receipt of each error-free data unit is acknowledged by the remote LLC entity and this is then converted by the local entity into an L.DATA_CONNECT.confirm primitive and passed to the user.

The RESET and FLOWCONTROL service primitives are provided to allow the user to control the flow of service data units across an established connection. The RESET service has an abortive action as it results in any unacknowledged data being discarded. It is used, therefore, only if the network layer protocol entity loses track of the sequence of data units being transferred.

The two flow control primitives have only local significance: the L.FLOWCONTROL.request primitive specifies the amount of data the user is prepared to accept from its local LLC protocol entity and the L.FLOWCONTROL.indication primitive the amount of data the LLC protocol entity is prepared to accept from the user, both related to a specific connection. If the amount is specified as zero, then the flow of data is stopped; if the amount is infinite, no flow control is to be applied on the connection. The amount of data allowed is dynamically updated by each request.

Protocol operation

The format of each LLC-PDU is shown in Figure 8.24(a). The source and destination address fields both refer to the LLC service access point only, they do not contain the addresses to be used on the network medium. Also, there is no FCS field. Essentially, the complete LLC-PDU is passed to the MAC layer, as a service data unit, in the form of a primitive that includes the LLC-PDU and the address to be used on the network medium as parameters. It is thus the MAC layer that handles the network addressing and error-detection functions. If is for this reason that, in the context of the ISO Reference Model, the link layer is equivalent to a combination of the LLC layer and a portion of the MAC layer.

The control field in each LLC-PDU is a single octet. It defines the

(a)

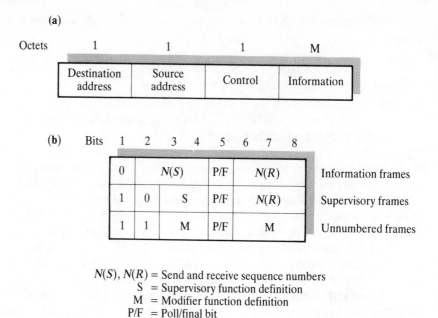

(b)

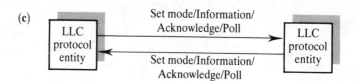

$N(S)$, $N(R)$ = Send and receive sequence numbers
S = Supervisory function definition
M = Modifier function definition
P/F = Poll/final bit

FIGURE 8.24

Aspects of LLC protocol: (a) LLC-PDU format; (b) control field bit definitions; (c) data link control functions (type 2).

type of the PDU and, where appropriate, the send and receive sequence numbers for error and sequence control purposes. The use of the various bits in this field are shown in more detail in Figure 8.24(b).

The LLC protocol entity supports two types of operation: type 1 to support the unacknowledged connectionless service and type 2 to support the connection-oriented service. Type 2 is in practice very similar to the HDLC protocol except that the framing and error-detection functions are provided by the MAC layer.

The data link control functions for type 2 operation are shown in schematic form in Figure 8.24(c). A description of HDLC was presented in Chapter 5 and hence this will not be repeated here. The major difference between the LLC protocol and HDLC is the provision of the unacknowledged connectionless (type 1) service. The set of commands and responses supported in type 1 are:

Commands	Responses
UI	–
XID	XID
TEST	TEST

The UI command PDU is used to send a block of data (information) to one or more LLCs. Since there is no acknowledgement or sequence control associated with type 1 operation, however, the UI PDU does not contain an $N(S)$ or $N(R)$ field. Also, there is no response to a UI PDU.

The exchange identification (XID) and TEST command PDUs are optional. However, if they are sent, the recipient LLC(s) is (are) obliged to respond. The uses of these commands are not fully defined but include:

- The XID command PDU used with a group address is used to determine the current membership of the group. Each member of the group responds to the command by returning an XID response PDU addressed specifically to the originating LLC entity.
- An LLC entity may use an XID command PDU with a broadcast (global) destination address to announce its presence on the network medium.
- The TEST comand PDU is used to provide a loopback test facility on each LLC to LLC transmission path.

MAC services

Irrespective of the mode of operation of the underlying MAC layer – CSMA/CD, token ring, token bus – a standard set of user services are defined for use by the LLC layer to transfer LLC-PDUs to a correspondent layer. The user service primitives supported are:

- MA.DATA.request,
- MA.DATA.indication,
- MA.DATA.confirmation.

A time sequence diagram illustrating their use is shown in Figure 8.25. For a CSMA/CD LAN, the confirm primitive indicates that the request has been successfully (or not) transmitted while for a token LAN it indicates that the request has been successfully (or not) delivered.

Each service primitive has parameters associated with it. The MA.DATA.request primitive includes: the required destination address (this may be an individual, group or broadcast address), a service data unit (containing the LLC-PDU) and the required class of service associated

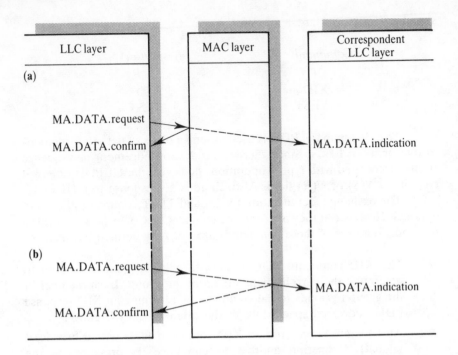

FIGURE 8.25

MAC user service primitives:
(a) CSMA/CD; (b) token ring/bus.

with the PDU. The latter is used with token ring and token bus networks, for example, when a prioritorized medium access control protocol is being used.

The MA.DATA.confirm primitive includes a parameter that specifies the success or failure of the associated MA.DATA.request primitive. As can be seen from the figure, however, the confirmation primitive is not generated as a result of a response from the remote LLC layer but rather by the local MAC entity. If the parameter is successful, this simply indicates that the MAC protocol entity (layer) was successful in transmitting the service data unit on to the network medium; if unsuccessful, the parameter indicates why the transmission attempt failed. As an example, if the network is a CSMA/CD bus, 'excessive collisions' may be a typical failure parameter.

Layer interactions A summary of the various services associated with the LLC and MAC layers is given in Figure 8.26 together with a list of the various LLC-PDU types that are exchanged between two LLC protocol entities. As can be seen, apart from the UI, XID and TEST PDUs, these are the same as those used with HDLC.

To illustrate how the two layers interact, a time sequence diagram showing the various interlayer primitives and the associated PDUs, generated with both a connectionless and a connection-oriented service, is

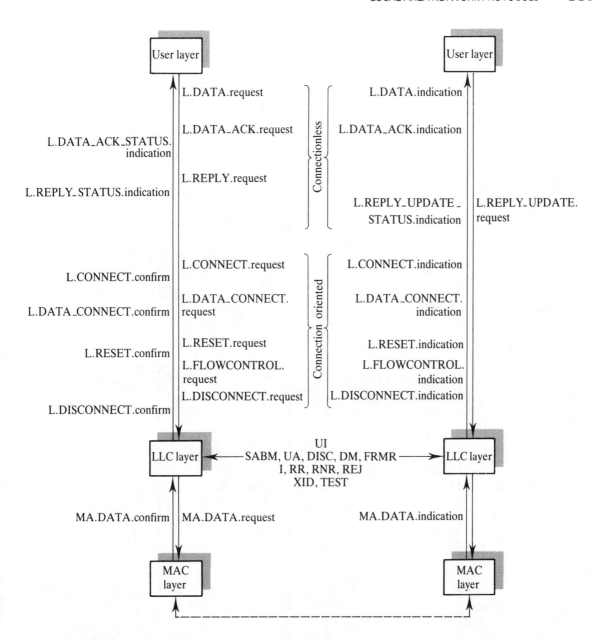

FIGURE 8.26

LLC sublayer summary.

given in Figure 8.27. The added overheads associated with the connection-oriented service are readily apparent.

In addition to understanding how the various layer services are used to transfer the different PDU types, it is also necessary to understand how each layer interprets and uses the parameters associated with each primitive. To illustrate this, an example showing how the parameters

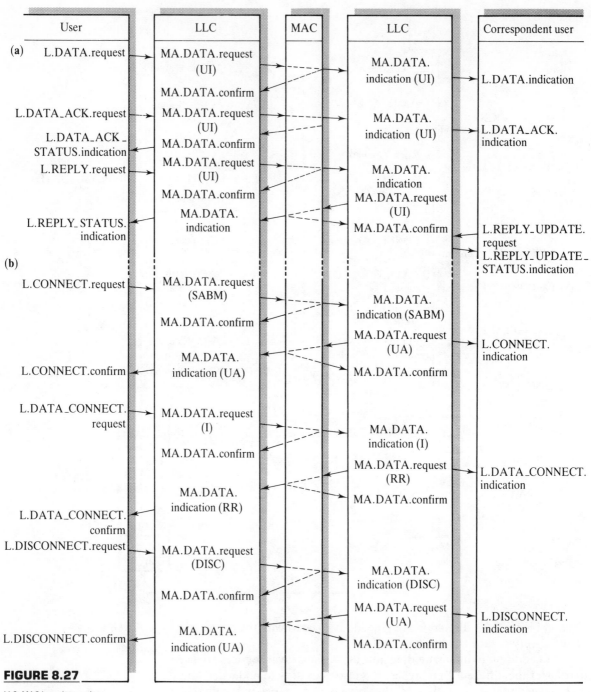

FIGURE 8.27

LLC–MAC layer interactions:
(a) type 1; (b) type 2.

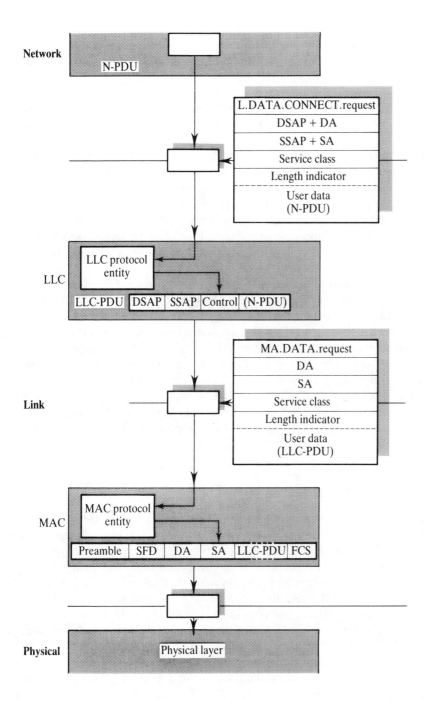

FIGURE 8.28

Interlayer primitives and parameters.

associated with an L.DATA_CONNECT.request primitive are used is shown in Figure 8.28.

As can be seen, the LLC layer, which is a sublayer in the context of the ISO link layer, reads the destination and source (LLC) service access point addresses (DSAP and SSAPs) from the two address parameters associated with the service primitive and inserts these into the corresponding address fields of an information (I) PDU. In addition, it creates the control field octet, containing the appropriate $N(S)$ and $N(R)$, and inserts this into the PDU together with the user data parameter in the I-field. Typically, the latter contains a network layer PDU with the number of octets in the PDU (the length indicator) at its head.

The created LLC-PDU is then passed down to the MAC layer in the user data parameter field of a MA.DATA.request primitive together with the physical destination and source addresses (DA and SA) and the desired service class as additional parameters. Typically, the latter is used by the MAC layer protocol entity to determine the priority to be associated with the frame if a token network is being used.

On receipt of the request, the MAC protocol entity creates a frame ready for transmission on the link. Thus, in the case of a CSMA/CD bus network, it creates a frame containing the preamble and SFD fields, the DA and SA fields, an I-field and the appropriate FCS field. The complete frame is then transmitted bit serially on to the cable medium.

A similar procedure is followed in the destination DTE except that the corresponding fields in each PDU are read and interpreted by each layer. The user data field in each PDU is then passed up to the next layer together with the appropriate address parameters. A further description of layer interactions will be presented in Chapter 10, after the application-oriented protocols have been discussed.

8.4.2 Network layer

It should be remembered that the primary aim of the ISO Reference Model is to achieve true open systems interconnection so that pieces of equipment from different manufacturers can freely communicate with each other, irrespective of whether the physical communication path is through a public WAN or a private LAN. As was indicated in Chapter 6, however, in the context of the ISO Reference Model, the transport layer is the first true end-to-end (peer) protocol layer and its aim is to shield the higher protocol layers from the different types of underlying network. Providing the LAN is only being used to provide a communication facility between a localized community of equipments, therefore, the network layer can contain only a minimum protocol entity supporting, for example, a basic datagram (connectionless) service. The main requirement of the network layer would then be to provide a standard set of user services to the transport layer above it and to transform these requests into the standard LLC form.

When the network layer is operating in a connectionless mode, only a single service type is necessary to initiate a transfer. To discriminate between data transfers using both modes, the connectionless mode service is known as N.UNIT_DATA. As it is connectionless, the two primitives associated with this service are:

- N.UNIT_DATA.request,
- N.UNIT_DATA.indication.

To support this service, the network protocol entity requires just two PDU types:

- data (DT),
- error (ER).

The latter is used by a network entity to inform a correspondent entity of the occurrence of a network error.

In many instances, and certainly in the context of larger open systems environments, a DTE connected to one LAN may also need to communicate with a DTE that is connected to another LAN, which may be in the same establishment or in another remote establishment. Clearly, to meet these requirements it is necessary to provide some form of link between the two (or more) LANs through, if necessary, one or more public data networks. Two different types of device have been designed to meet these requirements:

- An internetwork **bridge** or **router**: This is used for interconnecting two (or more) LANs within the same establishment.
- An internetwork **gateway**: This is used for interconnecting two (or more) LANs through an intermediate public data network.

A schematic diagram showing the application domain of both types of device is given in Figure 8.29.

To perform the necessary functions associated with the two types of device, an **internetwork protocol** (IP) comprising four major functional units or sublayers is used:

- internetwork (sublayer 3.1),
- harmonizing (sublayer 3.2),
- intranetwork (sublayer 3.3),
- link access (sublayer 3.4).

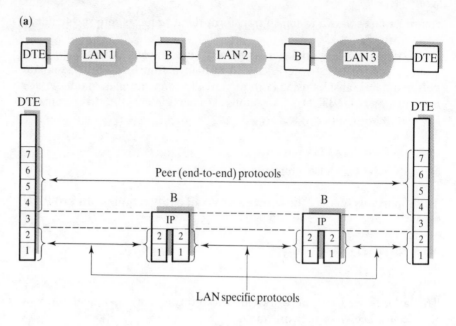

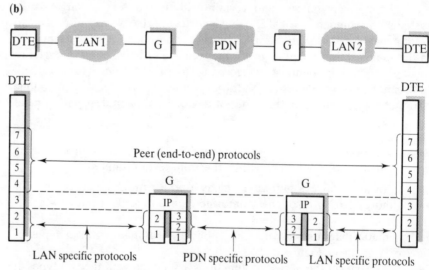

FIGURE 8.29

Internetwork schematics:
(a) bridge (router); (b) gateway.

For a bridge, only the last two functional units are necessary while for a gateway all four functional units are utilized.

The **link access functional unit** is responsible for interfacing with the underlying link layer. It thus receives service primitives from the link layer and, after processing, passes them on to the appropriate functional unit for further processing. It also performs the reverse function.

The **intranetwork functional unit** is concerned with maintaining routing tables and for routing each incoming primitive to its proper outgoing path. It thus recognizes any incoming message primitives addressed to a DTE on a different network and relays these to the appropriate outgoing path.

The **harmonizing functional unit** is concerned with the handling of any differences between the two interconnected network types. Thus, if one network is an LAN and the other is a PSDN, for example, it performs such functions as opening and closing logical (X.25) network connections and the segmentation (and reassembly) of data units received from the LAN ready for transmission through the PSDN.

The **internetwork functional unit** is concerned with the maintenance of the complete global routing tables and with interpreting global addresses. It thus routes incoming messages to and from the appropriate outgoing path and provides complete address information, to allow messages to be routed through a national (and international) public data network(s). A complete global network address is thus made up of a number of fields:

- Authority identifier and address: Identity of the type of public data network (if any) being used and the global address of the internetwork gateway that is connected to it.

- Subnetwork identity: Address of the subnetwork in relation to the global address of the gateway.

- LAN-specific identity: This includes the physical address of a DTE on the identified LAN and also the LSAP or NSAP suffixes associated with the correspondent application process.

A more detailed description of the addressing schemes used with LANs will be presented in Chapter 10.

8.5 PERFORMANCE ISSUES

In general, the user of an LAN is concerned only with three things:

(1) Has the system (office workstation, for example) got the necessary hardware to allow it to be physically connected to the network.

(2) Does the system have the appropriate software to allow the services supported by the network (electronic mail, file archiving, etc.) to be accessed.

(3) Is the access time to these services within acceptable limits.

Provided these conditions are met, the user is not concerned with the type of underlying LAN being used to access these services. Moreover, as can be concluded from the previous section and the earlier discussions in Chapter 6, the overall end-to-end (application layer-to-application layer) performance of any computer communication network is likely to be dominated by the delays experienced in the higher protocol layers rather than any small variations that may be caused by the different LAN topologies and MAC methods. Nevertheless, since the different types of LAN clearly have varying operational characteristics, it is important, certainly for the network designer, to have a knowledge of these characteristics so that it is possible to determine whether a particular LAN design will meet the expectations of the users under, for example, various offered load conditions.

Although some detailed comparison figures for the three types of LAN considered have been published by the IEEE, the aim of this section is simply to outline how some informative estimates of overall network performance can be made by applying some basic requirements analysis. It is left to the reader to refer to the references at the end of the book for a more detailed analysis.

Assume, for example, that an LAN is to be installed to provide a range of network-wide services for a defined number of user workstations. The first estimate the network designer must make is the frequency with which each user will generate a network service request, in addition to the likely length (in bits) of the messages that are exchanged to implement each request. Then, from these estimates, coupled with an estimation of the additional messages that will be required to implement the overheads associated with the various protocol layers, it is possible to derive an estimate of the aggregate mean offered load to the network. The latter can then be used to define the minimum cable bandwidth (network capacity) that is required to ensure that any delays introduced at the network interface will be within acceptable limits.

For example, assume that the network to be installed is to support up to 100 workstations and that each user is anticipated to generate a network transaction once every five minutes. It is further estimated that each transaction will involve, on average, the exchange of six 1000-bit data frames. Also, the additional frames associated with the overheads of the intermediate protocol layers are estimated to be, say, twelve 500-bit frames. A simple calculation then shows that this is equivalent to a mean offered load per user of 40 bps. Clearly, therefore, even allowing for up to, say, 10 or more users being active concurrently, the total mean offered load will be in the order of 400 bps, which is of course only a small fraction of the bandwidth of the cables used in the three types of network considered. This means that irrespective of the type of LAN selected, the delays introduced by the network will, on average, be very small.

In general, it is good design practice to ensure that the capacity (bandwidth) of an installed LAN is more than adequate to handle the aggregate mean offered load of its users. Conversely, it is bad practice to try to operate a network close to its total capacity since, under these conditions, predictably long delays at the network interface are inevitable with the effect that the end-to-end response time rapidly rises above the maximum level acceptable to its users. This is especially the case with a CSMA/CD protocol since, because it is a contention protocol, its performance under heavy offered loads is relatively unstable: as the offered load increases to the point at which the network utilization starts to become a significant proportion of its maximum capacity, so the probability of collisions also increases. This has the effect that in some instances, even with a backoff mechanism, some frames fail to be transmitted. Of course, with heavy offered loads, this is also the case with a token-based protocol since, as the transmission medium approaches saturation, only high-priority frames are transmitted and lower priority frames are queued indefinitely.

It should be stressed that, even with a small mean offered load and a cable bandwidth of, say, 10 Mbps, the maximum end-to-end data transfer rate associated with a particular user transaction is likely to be nearer to tens of kilobits (rather than megabits) because of the processing delays associated with the higher protocol layers. Providing the aggregate mean offered load remains only a modest fraction of the cable bandwidth, however, many user transactions at this rate can be in progress concurrently.

CHAPTER SUMMARY

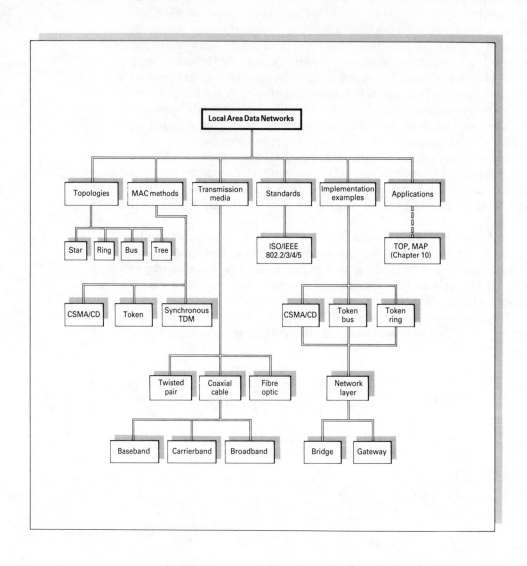

EXERCISES

8.1 (a) List the three main types of network topology currently in widespread use for LANs and explain their major differences.

(b) What is understood by broadband working in the context of a coaxial cable LAN? Sketch a typical broadband LAN showing the main networking components required and explain their function. Describe the overall operation of such a network and how multiple data transmission services are derived from a single cable.

8.2 (a) Describe the principle of operation of the following medium access control methods as used in LANs:

- CSMA/CD,
- control token,
- slotted ring.

(b) Explain the meaning of the following terms associated with a CSMA/CD bus network:

- slot time,
- jam sequence,
- random backoff.

8.3 (a) Describe the principle of operation of the control token medium access control method and, with the aid of diagrams, explain how it may be used with both a bus and a ring network topology.

(b) Define the structure and contents of a typical frame as used in a slotted ring. Describe the meaning of each field within a frame and the operation of the associated ring protocol. Clearly explain how access to the ring is shared between the stations (DTEs) making up the ring.

8.4 Produce a sketch showing the components necessary to attach a DTE (station) to a CSMA/CD bus network. Give an outline of the function of each component in the context of the overall operation of such a network. Define the structure and contents of each frame transmitted and the meaning of each field.

8.5 (a) Produce a schematic diagram showing the components necessary to attach a DTE (station) to a token ring network and give an outline of the function of each component. Include sufficient detail to show how a DTE, once attached to the network, may operate in either the inserted or bypassed mode.

(b)   Explain what is understood by the following terms as used in a token ring network:

- minimum latency time,
- token-holding time,
- modified Manchester encoding.

8.6   Describe the operation of the priority control scheme used with token ring networks to control the order of transmission of frames of varying priority on to the ring. Include in this description the function of:

(a)   the priority and reservation bits contained within each frame,

(b)   the priority registers and stacks held in each station,

(c)   a stacking station.

8.7   State the aims of the following ring management procedures used with a token ring network and explain their operation:

(a)   initialization,

(b)   standby monitor,

(c)   active monitor,

(d)   beaconing.

8.8   Define the meaning of the term slot time as used with a token bus network and explain the token-passing procedure used with such networks during both normal and abnormal operation. Include in these descriptions references to the procedures followed:

(a)   to bridge around a faulty DTE,

(b)   to allow new DTEs to enter an operational logical ring,

(c)   to create a new token when a ring is first established.

8.9   Explain the function of the following variables held by each DTE to control the order of transmission of frames that have varying priority on a token bus network:

(a)   high-priority token-hold time,

(b)   token rotation timer,

(c)   target token rotation time.

Produce a sketch, with an accompanying description of an example, to illustrate how the token rotation timer varies as frames are transmitted and the token rotates around the ring. Assume just two priority levels and deduce, from the example, the percentage of the available transmission capacity used by each level.

8.10 (a) Outline the function of the LLC and MAC protocol layers as defined in the IEEE 802 standards documents and indicate their relationship with the lower protocol layers in the ISO Reference Model. Define a typical set of user service primitives for both the LLC and MAC layers and produce a time sequence diagram to illustrate how each LLC primitive is implemented using the defined MAC services.

(b) Explain the function of an internetwork bridge and an internetwork gateway and hence outline how two DTEs, each connected to a different LAN, can communicate with one another through an intermediate network using two such devices.

PART THREE

OSI – OPEN SYSTEMS INTERCONNECTION

Part Three of this book is concerned with the various application-oriented protocols relating to the ISO Reference Model for OSI. Collectively, these provide the means for an application process to exchange information with another (remote) application process to achieve a common distributed information processing goal.

Chapter 9 first describes the function and structure of the various application-oriented protocols. These include the session and presentation protocols in addition to the various protocol entities associated with the application layer of the reference model.

Chapter 10 then concentrates on how the various network- and application-oriented layers act together to implement a specific distributed information processing task. Additional issues relating to network-wide addressing and system management are also considered.

APPLICATION-ORIENTED PROTOCOLS

9

9

CHAPTER OBJECTIVES

When you have completed studying the material in this chapter you should be able to:

- describe the function and services associated with the session layer and how the session protocol entity (machine) is specified;

- describe the function and services associated with the presentation layer and how the presentation protocol entity is specified;

- understand the various data types and encoding rules associated with the Abstract Syntax Notation Number One;

- describe the function and services associated with the common application service element;

- appreciate the benefits of adopting a virtual device approach within the open systems interconnection environment;

- describe the services and operation of the file transfer access and management protocol;

- understand the function of other selected specific application service elements including MHS, MMS, JTM and DS.

9.1 INTRODUCTION

The three highest layers in the ISO Reference Model for open systems interconnection (OSI) – session, presentation and application – build on the basic network-independent message interchange service of the transport layer to provide a user application process with the means of exchanging information with another (remote) user application process (AP) to achieve a common distributed information processing goal. For example, one of the APs may be a client process that wishes to access a remote file system managed by a remote (server) AP.

Collectively, the three layers are referred to as application-oriented layers. Briefly, the function of each layer is as follows:

- Session layer: This provides the means for two application layer protocol entities (through the services provided by the intermediate presentation layer) to manage and synchronize their dialogue (message exchange).

- Presentation layer: This provides the means for two APs to exchange messages that are in an abstract (as opposed to a fixed) syntax.

- Application layer: This provides a user AP with the means of accessing and providing a range of distributed information processing services.

In practice, the application layer is comprised of a number of separate entities known as service elements. Some of these elements are common to a number of applications and are thus referred to as **common application service elements** (CASEs). There are also a number of other elements, each of which has been developed to allow user APs to access and provide specific services. These are referred to, therefore, as **specific application service elements** (SASEs). The general structure of the three application-oriented layers is shown in Figure 9.1.

The **user element** (UE), which is also known as the **user interface** (UI) or **user agent** (UA), provides the user interface to the various distributed information processing services supported by the application layer. Typically, it is implemented in the form of a set of library procedures or functions, which are linked to the user AP requiring access to the distributed information services supported. As will be seen, the interface primitives between a user AP and the UE need not be the same as the (standard) service primitives provided by the particular application entity being used. In this way, existing manufacturer (and hence operating system) dependent user interface primitives can be used. The UE then performs the necessary mapping function between the two; that is, between the real systems environment and the open systems environment. This will be expanded upon later.

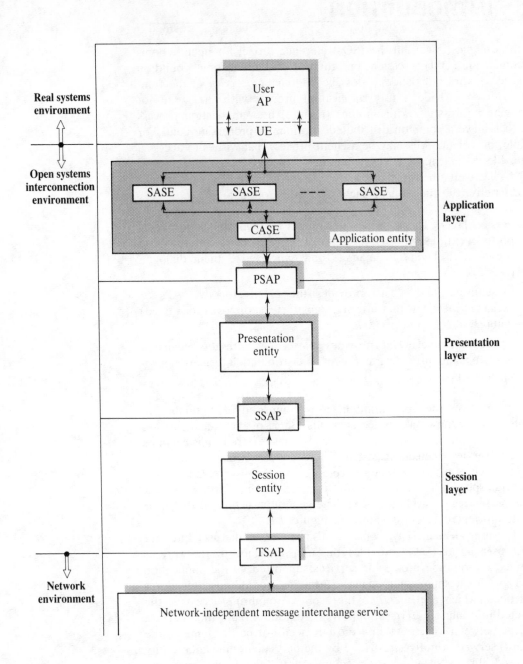

FIGURE 9.1

Application-oriented layers.

Normally, a single application entity (layer) supports a range of distributed information processing services, each of which is provided by an SASE. These include:

- FTAM (File transfer, access and management): This provides a facility for a user AP (through its UE) to access a remote file system managed by another AP.

- JTM (Job transfer and manipulation): This provides a facility for a user AP to submit a job (work specification) to a remote AP for processing and to subsequently monitor its execution.

- VT (Virtual terminal): This provides a facility for an AP, which is managing a dialogue with a local terminal, to communicate with a remote AP in a standardized way (that is, independent of the manufacturer and hence characteristics of the terminal).

- MHS (Message handling service): This provides a generalized facility for two APs to exchange (electronic) messages.

- MMS (Manufacturing message service): This provides a generalized facility for an AP in, say, a supervisory computer associated with an automated manufacturing plant, to send messages to a distributed community of other APs each controlling, say, an intelligent instrument or a programmable controller such as a robot.

- DS (Directory services): User APs identify correspondent user APs using symbolic names and the DS provides a facility whereby the UE may obtain the corresponding (fully qualified) network addresses of the two correspondents.

These are just some examples of SASEs that have been defined but, as the applications of OSI expand, so the number and range of such protocols will also expand.

As already mentioned, the application entity also contains a set of protocol entities (CASE) that provide some general supporting services, such as establishing a network-wide logical connection (association) between two SASEs prior to them carrying out their specific application function. Before describing the operation of these various application service elements in more detail, the function and services of the session and presentation layers will be described. It should be stressed, however, that although the three application-oriented layers can be treated separately for description purposes, they should be considered collectively as providing a particular application service on behalf of a user AP. Thus, there is a single connection identifier common to all three layers; that is, the presentation and session addresses are one and the same. Also, many of the parameters associated with the service primitives exchanged between the three layers map directly from one layer to the other without change.

9.2 SESSION LAYER

The session layer provides the means for an application protocol entity, through the services offered by the presentation layer, to:

- establish a logical communication path (session connection) with another application entity, to use it to exchange data (**dialogue units**) and to release the connection in an orderly way;
- establish synchronization points during a dialogue and, in the event of errors, to resume the dialogue from an agreed synchronization point;
- interrupt (suspend) a dialogue and resume it later at a prearranged point;
- be informed of certain exceptions that may arise from the underlying network during a session.

9.2.1 Token concept

For two application entities to manage a dialogue over an established (session) connection, a set of tokens are defined:

- the data token,
- the release token,
- the synchronization-minor token, and
- the major/activity token.

Each of these tokens is assigned dynamically to one session-service (SS) user (that is, application entity through its related presentation entity) at a time to allow that user to carry out the corresponding service. The current owner of a token gives that user the exclusive use of the related service. Thus, the data token, for example, is used to enforce a half-duplex data exchange between the two users and the release token to negotiate the release (termination) of a connection in a controlled way, and so on.

The synchronization-minor and the major/activity tokens are associated with the synchronization process that may be used during a session. When two SS-users are exchanging large quantities of data, it is advisable to structure the data into a number of identifiable units so that, should a (network) fault develop during the session, only the most recent data transferred are affected. To allow a user to perform this function, a number of

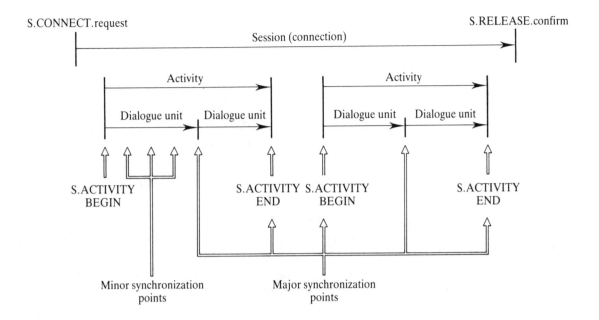

S.CONNECT.request

S.RELEASE.confirm

FIGURE 9.2

Activity and dialogue unit concepts.

synchronization points may be inserted into sequential blocks of data before transmission. Each synchronization point is identified by a serial number which is maintained by the session protocol entity. Two types of synchronization points are provided:

- Major: Normally, these are associated with complete units of data (dialogue units) being exchanged between two users.
- Minor: Normally, these are associated with portions of a dialogue unit.

These two types of synchronization token are provided to allow two users to implement the associated synchronization process. Typical synchronization points established during a complete session connection are shown in Figure 9.2.

The concept of an *activity* is used to allow two SS-users to distinguish between different logical pieces of work associated with a session. Although a complete session may comprise a number of activities, only one activity may be in progress at a time. In this way, an activity can be interrupted and then resumed either on the same session connection (SC) or on a different connection. Each activity is therefore made up of a number of dialogue units.

9.2.2 User services

The services offered by the session layer to its users are extremely varied and hence are grouped into a number of **functional units** to allow two SS-users to negotiate the precise services required when the SC is first established. The functional units available include:

- Kernel: This provides the basic (and minimal) functions of connection management and duplex data transfer.

- Negotiated release: This provides an orderly release service.

- Half-duplex: This provides for one-way alternate data exchange.

- Synchronization: This provides for (re)synchronization during a session connection.

- Activity management: This provides for identifying, starting, ending, suspending and restarting activities.

- Exception reporting: This provides for reporting an exception during a session connection.

To avoid the user having to specify each required functional unit when a SC is first established, a number of subsets, comprising different combinations of units, have been defined. These are:

- Basic combined subset: This includes the kernel and half-duplex units.

- Basic synchronized subset: This includes the synchronization units.

- Basic activity subset: This includes the activity management and exception reporting units.

There are also user service primitives available to implement all the foregoing functions. As an example, the services provided to implement the basic combined subset (BCS) are shown in the time sequence diagram in Figure 9.3(a).

In addition, there are parameters associated with each service. For example, the parameters associated with the S.CONNECT primitives allow the two SS-users to negotiate such things as: the services (functional units) to be used during the SC, initial token ownership and (when selected) sync-point serial number settings. These are in addition, of course, to the normal calling and called addresses and a (session) connection identifier to be used during the subsequent data exchange phase. The parameters associated with the two TOKEN primitives include the type of the token – data, release etc. The S.TOKEN_PLEASE service is used to request the specified token(s) and the S.TOKEN_GIVE service to transfer the specified token(s).

(a)

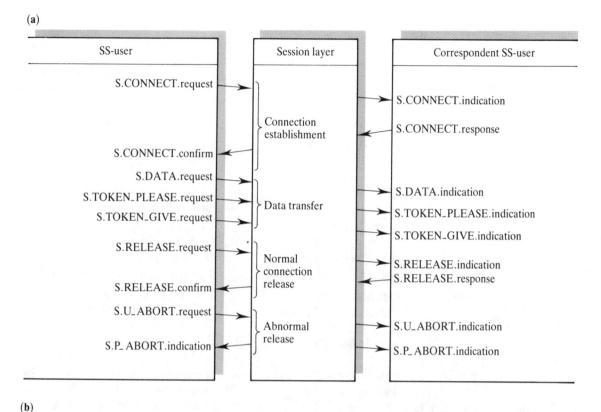

(b)

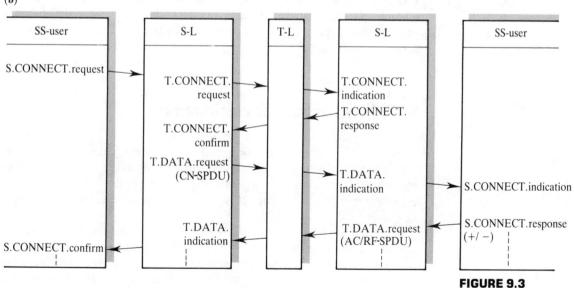

FIGURE 9.3

Session services: (a) user services; (b) used services.

9.2.3 SPDU types and layer summary

Most of the service primitives previously described result in a corresponding session protocol data unit (SPDU) being created and sent by the session protocol entity. For example, the SPDUs associated with the BCS service primitives are:

SPDU	*Sent in response to:*
CONNECT, CN	S.CONNECT.request
ACCEPT, AC	S.CONNECT.response (successful)
REFUSE, RF	S.CONNECT.response (unsuccessful)
DATA, DT	S.DATA.request
GIVE TOKEN, GT	S.GIVE_TOKEN.request
GIVE TOKEN ACK, GTA	GT received
PLEASE TOKEN, PT	S.PLEASE_TOKEN.request
FINISH, FN	S.RELEASE.request
DISCONNECT, DN	S.RELEASE.response
ABORT, AB	S.U_ABORT.request
ABORT ACCEPT, AA	AB received

Before any SPDUs can be sent, a transport connection (TC) must be established over which all the SPDUs can be transferred using the T.DATA.service. This is shown in diagrammatic form in Figure 9.3(b). A summary of the various SS-user services, together with the SPDUs exchanged and the used services, associated with the BCS is given in Figure 9.4.

9.2.4 Protocol specification

The formal specification of the session protocol entity is presented in the standards documents in the form outlined earlier in Chapter 6. The aim here, therefore, is to present just an introduction; the reader is referred to the relevant standard for a more complete description. The connection establishment phase for the BCS subset has been selected for example purposes.

First, a list of the various incoming events, automaton states, outgoing events, predicates and specific actions are given, which are shown in Figure 9.5. The abbreviated names used for each incoming and outgoing event, together with the layer interface to which they relate, are presented and the same names are then used in the event-state table, shown in Figure 9.6.

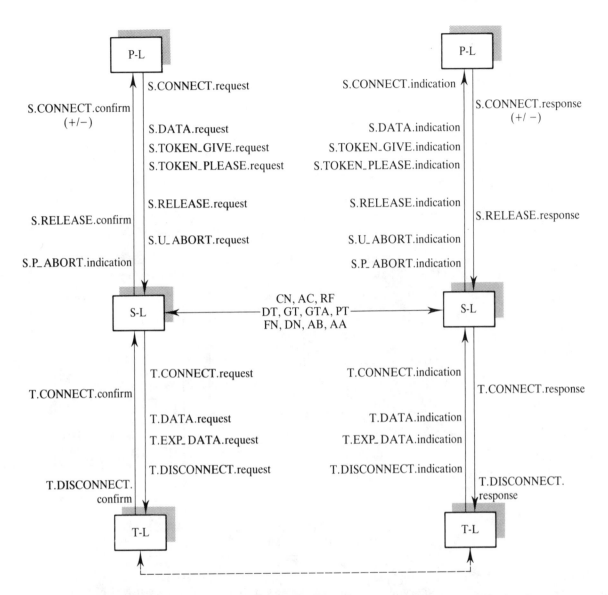

FIGURE 9.4

Session layer summary (BCS only).

As can be deduced, the underlying TC to be used can be initiated by either session entity. The latter is normally referred to as the **session protocol machine (SPM)**. Also, a timeout mechanism is associated with the RF-(REFUSE) SPDU; if the timer (STIM) expires before a T.DISCONNECT.indication is received (signalling that the TC has been disconnected), then the RF-SPDU is retransmitted. In practice, if a different subset is used, there are a number of additional state variables associated with the SPM for retaining such information as the type of tokens in use with the SC, the current assignment of the tokens, the current

(a)

Name	Interface	Meaning
SCONreq	SS-user	S.CONNECT.request received
SCONresp(+)	SS-user	S.CONNECT.response (accept) received
SCONresp(−)	SS-user	S.CONNECT.response (reject) received
TCONind	TS-provider	T.CONNECT.indication received
TCONconf	TS-provider	T.CONNECT.confirm received
CN	TS-provider	Connect SPDU received
AC	TS-provider	Accept SPDU received
RF	TS-provider	Refuse SPDU received
⋮	⋮	
STIM	Timer	Timer STIM expires

(b)

Name	Meaning
STA 01	Idle, no transport connection
STA 01B	Wait for T.CONNECT.confirm
STA 01C	Idle, transport connection in place
STA 02	Wait for AC-SPDU
STA 08	Wait for S.CONNECT.response
STA 16	Wait for T.DISCONNECT.indication
⋮	⋮
STA 713	Data transfer

(d)

Name	Meaning
P1	This SPM initiated TC
⋮	⋮

(e)

Name	Meaning
[1]	Set P1 false
[2]	Set P1 true
[3]	Stop timer STIM
[4]	Start timer STIM
⋮	⋮

(c)

Name	Interface	Meaning
SCONind	SS-user	S.CONNECT.indication issued
SCONconf(+)	SS-user	S.CONNECT.confirm (accept) issued
SCONconf(−)	SS-user	S.CONNECT.confirm (reject) issued
SPABTind	SS-user	S.P_ABORT.indication issued
TCONreq	TS-provider	T.CONNECT.request issued
TCONresp	TS-provider	T.CONNECT.response issued
TDISreq	TS-provider	T.DISCONNECT.request issued
CN	TS-provider	Connect SPDU sent
AC	TS-provider	Accept SPDU sent
RF	TS-provider	Refuse SPDU sent
AB	TS-provider	Abort SPDU sent
⋮		

FIGURE 9.5

Abbreviated names for session protocol specification: (a) incoming events; (b) automaton states; (c) outgoing events; (d) predicates; (e) specific actions.

State \\ Event	STA 01	STA 01B	STA 01C	STA 02	STA 08	STA 16	---	STA 713
SCONreq	1	0	2	0	0	0		
SCONresp (+)	0	0	0	0	3	0		
SCONresp (−)	0	0	0	0	4	0		
TCONind	5	0	0	0	0	0		
TCONconf	0	6	0	0	0	0		
CN	0	0	8	0	0	7		
AC	0	0	7	9	0	12		
RF	0	0	7	10	0	12		
⋮								
STIM	0	0	0	0	0	11		

0 = SPABTind, AB, STA 01

1 = TCONreq, [2], STA 01B

2 = P1: CN, STA 02A

3 = AC, STA 713

4 = RF, [4], STA 16

5 = TCONresp, [1], STA 01C

6 = CN, STA 02A

7 = TDISreq, [3], STA 01

8 = P1: TDISreq, STA 01;
    NOT P1: SCONind, STA 08

9 = SCONconf(+), STA 713

10 = SCONconf(−), TDISreq, STA 01

11 = RF, [4], STA 16

12 = STA 16

FIGURE 9.6

SPM event-state table.

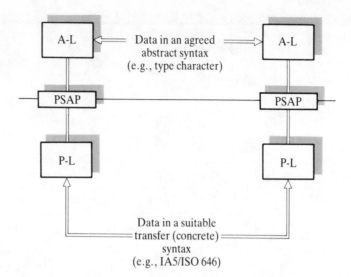

FIGURE 9.7

Presentation services schematic.

synchronization point serial number, and so on. Nevertheless, the specification follows exactly the form presented earlier in Chapter 6 and hence the same procedure can be used for its implementation.

9.3 PRESENTATION LAYER

The design of an open systems interconnection environment means that the application entities involved in providing a particular distributed information service may be resident in different computer systems from different manufacturers. Although a data value stored in each system may be of the same (abstract) type, therefore, the value may be represented in different ways in each system. For example, a value of type integer may be represented in a 16-bit, 24-bit or 32-bit form depending on the system. Clearly, therefore, when two application layer protocol entities communicate with each other, it is essential that the messages exchanged have a common meaning (**shared semantics**) to both entities. To achieve this, as will be expanded upon in Section 9.4, all messages exchanged between two application entities are in a mutually agreed abstract syntax, such as type character or type integer. Then, since the actual form of representation of such types may be different in the two systems, an agreed fixed **transfer** or **concrete syntax** is used for the transfer of each data value between the two systems. This is shown in diagrammatic form in Figure 9.7.

The association of an abstract syntax with a compatible transfer syntax constitutes a **presentation context** and one of the functions associated with the presentation layer is to negotiate a suitable presentation context for use with this SC. Also, since an application entity must use many of the services provided by the session layer through the services provided by the presentation layer, another function of the presentation layer is to map such services directly into the corresponding service provided by the session layer. The functions performed by the presentation layer can be summarized, therefore, as:

- negotiation of an appropriate transfer syntax(es) which is (are) suitable for conveying the type of (presentation) PS-user data messages to be exchanged;
- transformation of PS-user data from its specified abstract syntax form into the selected transfer syntax form;
- transformation of received message data in its transfer syntax form into the specified abstract syntax form for use by the PS-user;
- mapping application layer service requests for such functions as dialogue control (token management) and synchronization control into the corresponding session service primitives.

It can be deduced from the foregoing that, if the PS-user data to be exchanged during an application session are of a variety of abstract types, then a number of different presentation contexts may be selected. The proposed presentation context(s) to be used during a session is (are) negotiated during the connection establishment phase and such contexts are collectively referred to as the **presentation context set**. Alternatively, the two PS-users may adopt an existing **default context** for the transfer, such as IA5/ISO 646.

The PS-user data, and hence application layer user data, are passed to the presentation layer in the form of **tagged data elements**, where the tag or name associated with an element identifies the presentation context associated with it. The presentation entity then applies, if necessary, the corresponding transformation on each element prior to forwarding it to the session layer.

9.3.1 Presentation services

A time sequence diagram showing the basic (kernel) services supported by the presentation layer is given in Figure 9.8(a). As can be seen, each primitive has parameters associated with it. For example, the P.CONNECT parameters include the called and calling presentation (session) addresses, the session connection (SC) identifier and other session-related parameters such as token requirements. Because the presentation and session layers form an integrated function on behalf of the application layer, most of the presentation service primitives shown result in a corresponding presentation protocol data unit (PPDU) being generated using the parameters associated with the primitives. Thus:

Service Primitive	*Generates PPDU*
P.CONNECT.request	Connect presentation, CP
P.CONNECT.response(+)	Connect presentation accept, CPA
P.CONNECT.response(−)	Connect presentation reject, CPR
P.DATA.request	Presentation data transfer, TD
P.U_ABORT.request	Abnormal release (user), ARU
P.P_ABORT.indication	Abnormal release (provider), ARP

This is shown in diagrammatic form in Figure 9.8(b).

In addition, there are a number of presentation service primitives that map directly into a corresponding SS primitive without modification; that is, without a PPDU being generated. Normally, the parameters associated with such primitives are passed in the user data field of the associated SS primitive. These include the P.RELEASE service primitives and also the primitives provided for the (optional) functions of:

- synchronization control,
- token control,
- exception reporting,
- activity management.

Finally, although there is always an agreed default presentation context for a connection, there are also service primitives to allow two PS-users to negotiate a presentation context set for use with a connection. A summary of the various presentation services associated with the basic subset, together with the PPDUs and the used session services, is given in Figure 9.9.

9.3.2 Protocol specification

To re-inforce understanding of the various functions and the interrelationships between the presentation services and associated PPDUs, the connection establishment phase of the specification of the presentation protocol is summarized in Figures 9.10 and 9.11. As in the previous examples, the abbreviated names used in the event-state table for the **presentation protocol machine (PPM)** are given first (Figure 9.10) followed by the event-state table (Figure 9.11). The procedure outlined in Chapter 6 can then be followed for its subsequent implementation.

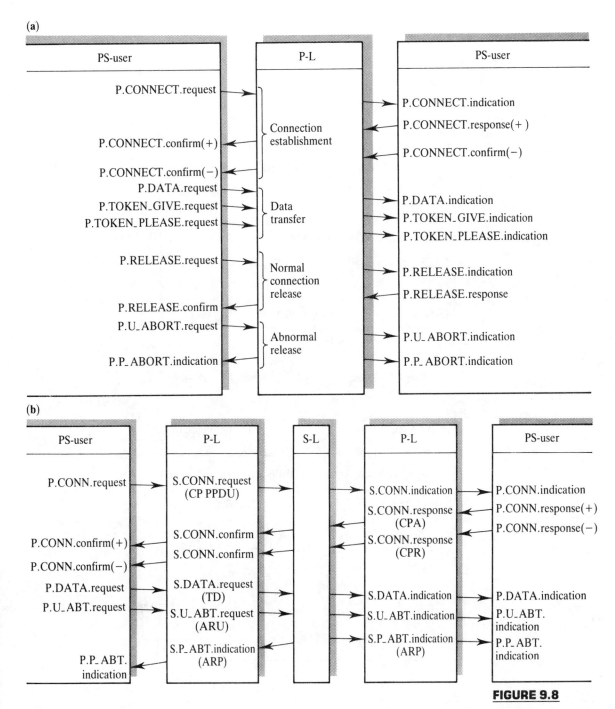

FIGURE 9.8

Presentation services: (a) basic services; (b) related session services.

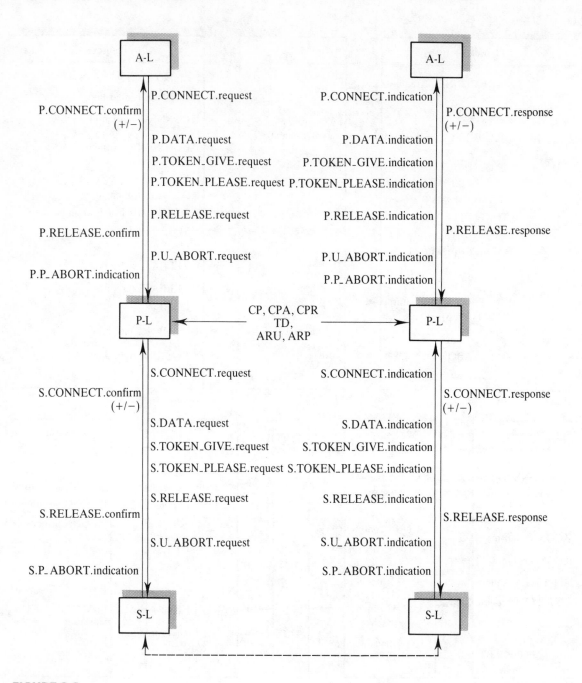

FIGURE 9.9

Presentation layer summary
(basic services only).

(a)

Name	Interface	Meaning
PCONreq	PS-user	P.CONNECT.request received
PCONresp(+)	PS-user	P.CONNECT.response (accept) received
PCONresp(−)	PS-user	P.CONNECT.response (reject) received
CP	SS-provider	CONNECT PRESENTATION PPDU received
CPA	SS-provider	CONN.PRESENT.ACCEPT PPDU received
CPR	SS-provider	CONN.PRESENT.REJECT PPDU received
¦		
¦		

(b)

Name	Meaning
STA 10	Idle, no presentation connection (PC)
STA 11	Wait for CPA-PPDU
STA 12	Wait for P.CONNECT.response
¦	¦
¦	¦
STA CO	Data transfer

(c)

Name	Interface	Meaning
PCONind	PS-user	P.CONNECT.indication issued
PCONconf(+)	PS-user	P.CONNECT.confirm (accept) issued
PCONconf(−)	PS-user	P.CONNECT.confirm (reject) issued
PPABTind	PS-user	P.P_ABORT.indication issued
CP	SS-provider	CONNECT PRESENTATION PPDU sent
CPA	SS-provider	CONN.PRESENT.ACCEPT PPDU sent
CPR	SS-provider	CONN.PRESENT.REJECT PPDU sent
¦		
¦		

(d)

Name	Meaning
P1	CN-PPDU acceptable
P5	Presentation contexts acceptable
¦	
¦	

(e)

Name	Meaning
[1]	Record abstract and transfer syntaxes for the defined and default context sets
[2]	Select a transfer syntax for each context set
[3]	Propose a transfer syntax for each context set
¦	
¦	

FIGURE 9.10

Abbreviated names for presentation protocol specification: (a) incoming events; (b) automaton states; (c) outgoing events; (d) predicates; (e) specific actions.

State Event	STA 10	STA 11	STA 12	---	STA CO
PCONrequest	1	0	0		
PCONresp(+)	0	0	2		
PCONresp(−)	0	0	3		
CP	4	0	0		
CPA	0	5	0		
CPR	0	6	0		
⋮					

0 = PPABTind, ARU, STA 10

1 = P5: CP, [3], STA 11

2 = CPA, [1], [2], STA CO

3 = CPR, STA 10

4 = P1: PCONDind, STA 12;

    NOT P1: CPR, STA 10

5 = PCONconf(+), [1], STA CO

6 = PCONconf(−), STA 10

FIGURE 9.11

PPM event-state table.

9.4 APPLICATION LAYER

Normally, as was indicated earlier in the chapter, the application layer (also referred to as the application entity or AE) is comprised of a number of SASEs, each providing a specific application service, in addition to one or more CASEs, which provide a common set of services – for example, for establishing and terminating a logical connection (association) between two correspondent SASEs.

The presentation layer, as has just been outlined, is concerned solely with the means of transferring messages (information) between two AEs (or SASEs in practice) so that their structure (syntax) is maintained. That is, the presentation layer is not concerned with the meaning (semantics) of the information being exchanged. Clearly, however, the information being exchanged must have a common meaning to both user APs in the case of user data and SASE protocol entities in the case of protocol control information (PDUs).

In the case of user data, one approach is to define a network-wide application (concrete) syntax for all data associated with a particular distributed information service; for example, a message service based on IA5/ISO 646. Then, providing all systems adhere to this syntax, all data exchanged will have a common meaning to all systems. Clearly, however, since the goal of open systems interconnection is to allow APs running in different computers to communicate in an open (transparent) way, it is necessary first to define an agreed network-wide transfer (concrete) syntax and then for the presentation layer associated with each AP to perform a suitable transformation function to and from this syntax if this is different from the internal (local) syntax.

In the case of protocol control information (PDUs) being exchanged between two SASE protocol entities, the approach adopted is first to utilize an abstract syntax known as **Abstract Syntax Notation Number One** or **ASN.1** for the definition of each PDU and then an associated encoding method to produce the PDU in a standard concrete syntax form. However, since each PDU will have a different structure (unknown by the presentation entity), the encoding of PDUs must be carried out within the SASE protocol entity rather than by the presentation entity. A brief description of ASN.1 and its associated encoding rules will now be given.

9.4.1 ASN.1

ASN.1 has been defined for use both as an application syntax (for example, for electronic mail) and as a means of defining the structure of PDUs associated with a particular protocol entity. Although it is not possible to give a complete definition of ASN.1 in a book of this type, what follows should be sufficient to give the reader the ability to interpret the meaning of a set of PDUs relating to a particular protocol entity defined in ASN.1. The principle is the same as that adopted with most high-level programming languages for defining the data types associated with the variables used in a program: as each variable is declared, the data type associated with it is also defined. Then, when a value is assigned to the variable, its syntax is of the defined type.

ASN.1 supports a number of type identifiers, which may be members of four classes:

- *UNIVERSAL*: These are the generalized types such as integer.
- *CONTEXT_SPECIFIC*: These are related to the specific context in which they are used.
- *APPLICATION*: These are common to a complete application entity.
- *PRIVATE*: These are user definable.

The data types associated with the *UNIVERSAL* class may be either primitive (simple) or constructed (structured). A primitive type is either a basic data type that cannot be decomposed – for example, a *BOOLEAN* or an *INTEGER* – or, in selected cases, a string of one or more basic data elements all of the same type – for example, a string of one or more bits, octets or IA5/graphical characters. The keywords used with ASN.1 are always in uppercase letters and the primitive types available include:

UNIVERSAL (primitive): *BOOLEAN*
INTEGER
BITSTRING
OCTETSTRING
IA5String/GraphString
NULL
ANY

The *NULL* type relates to a single variable and is commonly used when a component variable associated with a constructed type has no type assignment. Similarly, the *ANY* type is used to indicate that the type of the variable is defined elsewhere.

A constructed type is a type defined by reference to one or more other types, which may be primitive or constructed. The constructed types used with ASN.1 include:

UNIVERSAL (constructed): *SEQUENCE* – This is a fixed (bounded), ordered list of types some of which may be declared optional; that is, the associated typed value may be omitted by the entity constructing the sequence.

: *SEQUENCEOF* – This is a fixed or unbounded, ordered list of elements, all of the same type.

: *SET* – This is a fixed, unordered list of types, some of which may be declared optional.

: *SETOF* – This is a fixed or unbounded, unordered list of elements, all of the same type.

: *CHOICE* – This is a fixed, unordered list of types, selected from a previously specified set of types.

In addition, ASN.1 supports the concept of assigning a **tag** or **identifier** to a single existing type. The latter may be a primitive or constructed type and the new type, although it has the same structure as the existing type, is distinguishable from it. Tagging is used, therefore, when a particular data type must be distinguishable from other similar data types. For example, if a *SET* type is used to declare a collection of variables whose order is insignificant, each variable may be identified by assigning a tag to it. When a variable is tagged, the tag number is inserted in square brackets after the variable name. Also, if the new type is not context specific, the appropriate keyword – *UNIVERSAL, APPLICATION* or *PRIVATE* – precedes the tag number.

Another facility supported in ASN.1 is the ability to declare a variable to be of an *implied type*. This is done by means of the keyword *IMPLICIT*, which is written after the variable name, and tag field should one be present, written before the type identifier. Normally, the type of a variable is explicitly defined but, if a variable has been declared to be of an *IMPLICIT* type, this means that the type associated with a variable is implicit (implied). This facility is usually used with tagged types since, if a tagged variable is declared to be of an *IMPLICIT* type, then the type of the variable can be implied from the tag field. The benefit of this will become more apparent when the encoding and decoding rules associated with ASN.1 are described later.

The operation of the protocol entity FTAM will also be described later but, as an example of the use of ASN.1, the definition of a PDU relating to it is given in Figure 9.12 – this is the same as that initially given in Figure 6.11(b).

The complete set of PDUs relating to a particular protocol entity is defined as a **module**. The name of a module is known as the **module definition** and, in the example of Figure 9.12, this is given as *ISOFTAM-FTAM DEFINITIONS*. This is followed by the assignment symbol (::=) and the module body is then defined between the *BEGIN* and *END* keywords. As with a program listing, comments may be inserted in an ASN.1 definition at any point; the comment starts with a pair of adjacent hyphens and ends either with another pair of hyphens or the end of a line.

Following *BEGIN*, the *CHOICE* type is used to indicate that the PDUs used with FTAM belong to one of three types: *InitializePDU, FilePDU* and *BulkdataPDU*. A further *CHOICE* type is then used to indicate that there are six different types of PDU associated with the *InitializePDU* type: *FINITIALIZErequest, FINITIALIZEresponse*, and so on. Note that each of these is tagged so that they can be subsequently distinguished from one another. Also, since the tags are followed by *IMPLICIT*, this means that the type of PDU can be implied from the tag field; that is, no further definition is needed, such as a PDU type. Note also that since the *FINITIALIZErequest* PDU will always be the first PDU received in relation to FTAM, it is assigned an application-specific tag

```
ISO8571-FTAM DEFINITIONS ::=

BEGIN

PDU ::= CHOICE {
                InitializePDU,
                FilePDU,
                BulkdataPDU
                }

InitializePDU ::= CHOICE {
                [APPLICATION 1]    IMPLICIT FINITIALIZErequest,
                [1]                IMPLICIT FINITIALIZEresponse,
                [2]                IMPLICIT FTERMINATErequest,
                [3]                IMPLICIT FTERMINATEresponse,
                [4]                IMPLICIT FUABORTrequest,
                [5]                IMPLICIT FPABORTresponse
                }


FINITIALIZErequest  ::= SEQUENCE {
                protocolId [0] INTEGER { isoFTAM (0) },
                versionNumber [1] IMPLICIT
                                SEQUENCE { major INTEGER,
                                           minor INTEGER},
                                -- initially { major 0, minor 0}
                serviceType [2] INTEGER { reliable (0),
                                          user correctable (1)}
                serviceClass [3] INTEGER { transfer (0),
                                           access (1),
                                           management (2)}
                functionalUnits [4] BITSTRING    {read (0),
                                                  write (1),
                                                  fileAccess (2),
                                                  limitedFileManagement (3),
                                                  enhancedFileManagement (4),
                                                  grouping (5),
                                                  recovery (6),
                                                  restartDataTransfer (7) }
                attributeGroups [5] BITSTRING  { storage (0),
                                                 security (1)   }

                rollbackAvailability [6] BOOLEAN DEFAULT FALSE,
                presentationContextName [7] IMPLICIT ISO646String {"ISO8822"},
                identityOfInitiator [8] ISO646String OPTIONAL,
                currentAccount [9] ISO646String OPTIONAL,
                filestorePassword [10] OCTETSTRING OPTIONAL,
                checkpointWindow [11] INTEGER OPTIONAL}


FINITIALIZEresponse ::= SEQUENCE {

                                |
                                |

END
```

FIGURE 9.12

ASN.1 PDU definition example.

number of 1. The remaining PDU types then have a context-specific tag; note that the word *CONTEXT* is not needed as they will have meaning in the context of FTAM. The definition of each PDU is then given and, in the example, the *FINITIALIZErequest* PDU is defined.

The *SEQUENCE* structured type (similar to the **record** type in Pascal) is used firstly in this definition to indicate that the PDU is comprised of a number of typed data elements, which may be primitive or constructed. Although with the *SEQUENCE* type the list of variable types are in a set order, normally the individual elements are (context specifically) tagged since, as will be seen later, this can result in a more efficient encoded version of the PDU. The first element, *protocolId*, is of type *INTEGER* and is set to zero, which indicates it is ISO FTAM (*isoFTAM*). The second element, *versionNumber*, is then defined as a *SEQUENCE* of two *INTEGER* types – *major* and *minor*. As before, the use of the word *IMPLICIT* means that the type (*SEQUENCE*) can be implied from the preceding tag field, and so it need not be encoded. A comment field is used to indicate the initial setting of the two variables. The next two elements are both of type *INTEGER* and the possible values of each are shown in the curly brackets.

The next element, *functionalUnits*, is of type *BITSTRING* and the eight bits in the string are set to 1 or 0 depending on whether the particular unit is (1) or is not (0) required. Finally, some of the later elements in the sequence are declared *OPTIONAL*, which means that they may or may not be present in an encoded PDU. Since the individual elements in the PDU have been tagged, however, the receiver of the PDU can determine if the element is present or not. The keyword *DEFAULT* has a similar meaning except that if the element is not present in a PDU, then the default value is assigned to it.

Encoding

It should be stressed that ASN.1 is an abstract syntax, which means that although a data element is defined to be of a specified type, this does not imply that it has a fixed syntax. For example, a variable of type *INTEGER* in one computer may have a different syntax, in terms of the number of bits and position of the sign bit, for example, from an *INTEGER* type in another computer. This means that even though the various data elements making up a PDU are of the same (abstract) type, their structure (syntax) may be different. Associated with ASN.1, therefore, is an associated encoding method that converts each field in a PDU, which has been defined in ASN.1 form, into a corresponding concrete syntax form. It is then the latter that is transferred between two application entities so that the exchanged PDU has a common meaning to both entities.

The standard representation for a value of each type is a data element comprising three fields:

- Identifier, which defines the ASN.1 type.
- Length, which defines the number of octets in the contents field.
- Contents, which defines the contents (which may be other data elements for a structured type).

Each field comprises one or more octets and the structure of the identifier octet is as shown in Figure 9.13. Some example encodings of different typed values are given in Figure 9.14. To help readability, the content of each octet is represented as two hexadecimal digits and the final encoded value (as a string of octets) is given at the end of each example. If the number of octets in the contents field exceeds 127, the most significant bit of the first length octet is set to 1 and the length is then defined in two (or more) octets.

In the first example, the identifier 01 (hex) indicates that the class is *UNIVERSAL* (bits 8 and 7 = 00), it is a primitive type (bit 6 = 0) and the tag (bits 1 through 5) is 1, indicating it is Universal 1 and hence *BOOLEAN*. The length is 01 (hex) indicating the content is a single octet. *TRUE* is then encoded as FF (hex) and *FALSE* as 00 (hex).

Integer values are encoded in two's complement form with the most significant bit used as the sign bit. Thus, a single octet can be used to represent a value in the range −128 to +127. For values greater than these, progressively more octets must be used. It should be stressed, however, that only sufficient octets are used to represent the actual value, irrespective of the number of bits used in the original form. That is, even if the value 29 shown in the example is represented as a 16-bit or 32-bit integer locally, only a single octet would be used to represent it in its encoded form. Similarly, if the type is *BITSTRING*, the individual bits are assigned starting at the most significant bit with any unused bits set to zero.

With a variable of type *SEQUENCE* (or *SEQUENCEOF*), the identifier is 30 (= 0011 0000 binary). This indicates that the class is *UNIVERSAL* (bits 8 and 7 = 00), it is a constructed type (bit 6 = 1) and the tag equals 16 (bit 5 = 1 and bits 4 through 1 = 0). Similarly, the identifier with a *SET* (or *SETOF*) type is 31, indicating it is *UNIVERSAL*, constructed, with tag 17.

Note also that the two fields in the type *UserName* have been context specifically tagged – [0] and [1]. The two identifiers associated with these fields are 80 (= 1000 0000 binary) and A1 (= 1010 0001 binary), respectively. The first indicates that the class is context specific (bits 8 and 7 = 10), it is a simple type (bit 6 = 0) and the tag is 0. The second, however, is context specific, constructed and the tag is 1. This is the case because the first context specific tag has been declared *IMPLICIT*, in which case the type field can be implied from the tag. With the second,

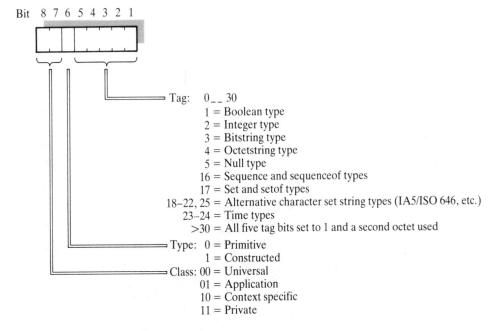

Bit 8 7 6 5 4 3 2 1

Tag: 0 _ _ 30
       1 = Boolean type
       2 = Integer type
       3 = Bitstring type
       4 = Octetstring type
       5 = Null type
       16 = Sequence and sequenceof types
       17 = Set and setof types
18–22, 25 = Alternative character set string types (IA5/ISO 646, etc.)
       23–24 = Time types
       >30 = All five tag bits set to 1 and a second octet used
Type: 0 = Primitive
       1 = Constructed
Class: 00 = Universal
       01 = Application
       10 = Context specific
       11 = Private

Note

The null type is used to indicate the absence of
an element in a sequence.

The two time types are used to specify time in a standardized
way as a string of IA5/ISO 646 characters. For example:
YY MM DD hh mm ss
88 09 30 20 45 58   = current time

FIGURE 9.13

ASN.1 identifier bit definitions.

however, the type field must also be defined and hence two additional octets are required.

An example FTAM PDU encoding is given in Figure 9.15. The PDU selected is *FINITIALIZErequest*, as defined earlier in its ASN.1 form in Figure 9.12. The actual values associated with the PDU are defined in Figure 9.15(a) while Figure 9.15(b) shows how the selected values are encoded. Typically, as will be expanded upon in Chapter 10, the various fields in the PDU are abstract data types associated with a data structure in a program. After the encoding operation, however, the PDU is comprised of a precisely defined string of octets which, for readability, are shown in hexadecimal form. The complete octet string is then transferred to the correspondent (peer) FTAM protocol entity where it is decoded back into its (local) abstract form.

(a) BOOLEAN – UNIVERSAL 1

e.g., *Employed* ::= *BOOLEAN*
– – assume true

Identifier = 01 (Hex)   – – Universal 1
Length   = 01
Contents   = FF

i.e., 01   01   FF

INTEGER – UNIVERSAL 2

e.g., *RetxCount* ::= *INTEGER*
– – assume = 29 (decimal)

Identifier = 02   – – Universal 2
Length   = 01
Contents   = 1D   – – 29 decimal

i.e., 02   01   1D

BITSTRING – UNIVERSAL 3

e.g., *FunctionalUnits* ::= *BITSTRING* {*read* (*0*), *write* (*1*), *fileAccess* (*2*)}
– – assume read only is required

Identifier = 03
Length   = 01
Contents   = 80   – – read only = 1000   0000

i.e., 03   01   80

UTCTime – UNIVERSAL 23

e.g., *UCTTime* ::= [*UNIVERSAL 23*] *IMPLICIT ISO646String*
– – assume 2.58 p.m. on 5th November 1989 = 89   11   05   14   58

Identifier = 17 (Hex)   – – Universal 23
Length   = 0A
Contents   = 38   39   31   31   30   35   31   34   35   38

i.e., 17   0A   38   39   31   31   30   35   31   34   35   38

FIGURE 9.14

ASN.1 encoding examples:
(a) primitive; (b) constructed.

(b) SEQUENCE/SEQUENCEOF – UNIVERSAL 16

e.g., *File ::= SEQUENCE {userName IA5String, contents OCTETSTRING}*
– – assume userName = "FRED" and contents = 0F   27   E4   Hex

Identifier = 30 (Hex)   – – Constructed, Universal 16
Length   = 0B   – – Decimal 11
Contents = Identifier = 16   – – Universal 22
       Length   = 04
       Contents = 46   52   45   44
       Identifier = 04   – – Universal 4
       Length   = 03
       Contents = 0F   27   E4

i.e., 30   0B   16   04   46   52   45   44   04   03   0F   27   E4

Tagging/IMPLICIT

e.g., *UserName ::= SET {surname [0] IMPLICIT ISO646String, password [1] ISO646String }*
– – assume surname = "BULL" and password = "KING"

Identifier = 31   – – Constructed, Universal 17
Length   = 0E   – – Decimal 14
Contents = Identifier = 80   – – Context-specific 0 = surname
       Length   = 04
       Contents = 42   55   4D   4D
       Identifier = A1   – – Context-specific 1 = password
       Length   = 06
       Contents = Identifier = 16   – – Universal 22
          Length   = 04
          Contents = 4B   4A   4E   47

i.e., 31   0E   80   04   42   55   4D   4D   A1   06   16   04   4B   4A   4E   47

Decoding

On receipt of the encoded string, the correspondent entity performs an associated decoding operation. For example, the leading octet in the string is first used to determine the type of PDU received – Application-specific 1 = *FINITIALIZErequest*. Clearly, since each PDU has a unique structure, it is necessary to have a separate decode procedure for each PDU type. Hence, on determining the type of PDU received, the corresponding decode procedure is invoked. Once this has been done, the various fields (data elements) making up the PDU will be in their local (abstract) syntax form and hence the processing of the PDU may take place.

FIGURE 9.14 (cont.)

ASN.1 encoding examples:
(a) primitive; (b) constructed.

(a) *FINITIALIZErequest* = {*protocolId = 0,*
                    versionNumber {major = 0, minor = 0}
                    serviceType = 1,
                    serviceClass = 1,
                    functionalUnits {read = 1, write = 1, fileAccess = 1,
                            limitedFileManagement = 0,
                            enhancedFileManagement = 0,
                            grouping = 0, recovery = 0,
                            restartDataTransfer = 0}
                    attributeGroups {storage = 0, security = 1}
                    rollbackAvailability = T,
                    PresentationContextName = "ISO8822"}

(b)

Identifier = 61	– – Application-specific 1 = *FINITIALIZErequest*
Length = 2D	– – Decimal 45
Contents = Identifier = A0	– – Context-specific 0 = *protocolId*
Length = 03	
Contents = Identifier = 02	– – Universal 2 – *INTEGER*
Length = 01	
Contents = 00	– – *isoFTAM*
Identifier = A1	– – Context-specific 1 = *versionNumber*
Length = 06	
Contents = Identifier = 02	– – Universal 2
Length = 01	
Contents = 00	– – *major*
Identifier = 02	– – Universal 2
Length = 01	
Contents = 00	– – *minor*
Identifier = 02	
Length = 01	
Contents = 01	– – *serviceType* = user correctable
Identifier = 02	
Length = 01	
Contents = 01	– – *serviceClass* = access
Identifier = A4	– – Context-specific 4 = *functionalUnits*
Length = 03	
Contents = Identifier = 03	– – Universal 3 = *BITSTRING*
Length = 01	
Contents = E0	– – *read, write, fileAccess* = 1110 000
Identifier = A5	– – Context-specific 5 = *attributeGroups*
Length = 03	
Contents = Identifier = 03	
Length = 01	
Contents = 40	– – *security* = 0100 000
Identifier = A6	– – Context-specific 6 = *rollbackAvailability*
Length = 03	
Contents = Identifier = 01	– – Universal 1 = *BOOLEAN*
Length = 01	
Contents = FF	– – *true*
Identifier = A7	– – Context-specific 7 = *PresentationContextName*
Length = 07	
Contents = 49 53 4F 38 38 32 32	– – "ISO8822"

FIGURE 9.15

Example FTAM PDU encoding:
(a) PDU contents; (b) encoded
form.

Concrete syntax of the above PDU is thus:

```
61  2B  A0  03  02  01  00  A1  06  02  01  00  02  01  00  02
01  01  02  01  01  A4  03  03  01  E0  A5  03  03  01  40  A6
03  01  01  FF  A7  07  49  53  4F  38  38  32  32
```

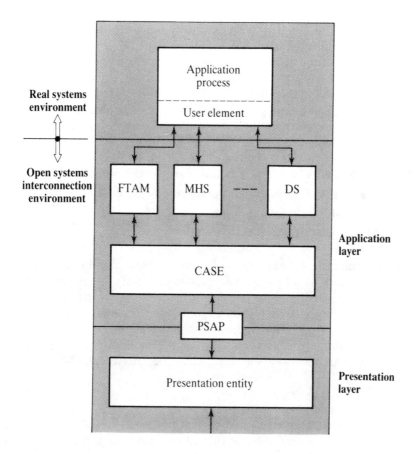

FIGURE 9.16

Logical position of CASE in the application entity.

9.4.2 CASE

A schematic diagram showing the relationship of CASE to the other protocol entities is given in Figure 9.16. CASE is itself comprised of one or more protocol elements. For example, the **association control service element (ACSE)** is concerned solely with the establishment and release of a logical association (connection) between two SASEs; the **remote operations service element (ROSE)** is concerned with initiating operations and receiving results from a remote SASE; and the **commitment, concurrency and recovery (CCR)** element is concerned with the implementation of atomic actions. The latter will be expanded upon in Chapter 10.

Normally, an association is established in response to a request from a user AP (UE in practice) for a particular application service, such as FTAM. Typically, the latter, on receipt of the request, first creates its own initialize (connect-request) PDU and then uses the services provided by the ACSE of CASE to establish an association with the correspondent (called) SASE. The initialize PDU, together with other information such as the address of the calling and called SASE, are passed as parameters with the ACSE associate request service primitive.

Once an association has been established, ACSE does not feature in the subsequent SASE dialogue until the latter requests that the association be released (disconnected). The service primitives associated with ACSE are thus:

- A.ASSOCIATE.request/indication/response/confirm,
- A.RELEASE.request/indication/response/confirm,
- A.ABORT.request/indication,
- A.P_ABORT.indication.

A time sequence diagram showing the interrelationship between the various application and presentation service primitives is shown in Figure 9.17. As can be seen, each service primitive maps directly from one layer to another including (but not shown) from the presentation layer to the session layer. Also, as was indicated in the previous section, there is a single connection identifier common to all the application-oriented layers.

The parameters associated with the A.ASSOCIATE service include:

- Calling and called application entity titles: These are the unique (system-wide) names used to identify each user AP (and hence application entity (AE) to which the user AP is attached) in the OSI environment.
- Calling and called presentation addresses: These are the corresponding fully qualified addresses (P/SAP + TSAP + NSAP, which includes the LSAP and NSAP address extensions and also the physical network adddress) associated with each AE.
- Application context name: FTAM, JTM, etc.
- Presentation context information.
- Communication quality of service (QOS).
- Connection identifier.
- Session requirements: Subset, token assignment, etc.
- User data: Typically, the SASE initialize-PDU.

On receipt of each service primitive from the SASE, the ACSE protocol machine (entity) creates a corresponding PDU. This, together with other parameters from the service primitive, is then passed to the correspondent ACSE entity in the user data parameter of the corre-

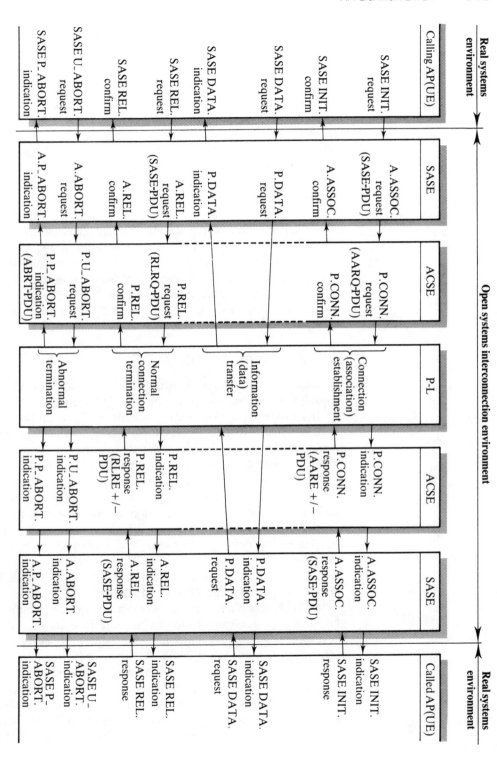

FIGURE 9.17

Interrelationship of service primitives.

sponding presentation service primitive. The PDUs associated with the ACSE protocol machine, together with the appropriate presentation service primitives, are also shown in Figure 9.17.

As was described in Chapter 6, user APs communicate using names or titles. Consequently, prior to initiating a particular service, the UE must first obtain the corresponding fully qualified addresses of the two correspondent AEs (to which the user APs are attached). These are obtained from the local directory server (DS) SASE (using an appropriate service primitive). Subsequent service calls to other SASEs then normally have both the names and corresponding addresses of the two AEs as parameters.

Finally, to re-inforce understanding of the operation of ACSE, the formal specification of the ACSE protocol machine for the association establishment phase is given in Figures 9.18 and 9.19. As in the previous examples, a list of the abbreviated names and meanings of the incoming events, states, outgoing events and predicates is given first (Figure 9.18) followed by the event-state table (Figure 9.19). The same procedure as outlined in Chapter 6 can then be used for its implementation.

9.4.3 User element

Before describing aspects of the operation of selected SASEs, it is perhaps helpful first to consider the interface between the OSI environment (OSIE) and the real systems environment (RSE) in a little more detail. As there is much investment in existing (manufacturer-dependent) applications software (and their associated operating systems), it is clearly important that the approach adopted allows such software to be used whenever possible, if an easy migration path from a closed to an open system is to be achieved. The approach adopted by the ISO attempts to achieve this goal by, essentially, decoupling the OSIE from the RSE.

First, for each application service, a **virtual device** is defined, together with a defined set of user service primitives for use with it. All user requests and responses at the OSIE interface then relate to this virtual device. An additional, implementation-dependent software layer is then introduced between the OSIE and the user AP (that is, the RSE) to perform the necessary mapping between the service primitives relating to the virtual device (and hence at the interface to the OSIE) and the corresponding primitives relating to the real device, should these be different. The approach is shown in diagrammatic form in Figure 9.20(a).

In practice, the UE is a set of library procedures or functions linked to the user AP. Normally, there is an initiator AP (and hence AE to which it is attached) and a responder AP. The former normally acts as the initiator (or originator) of virtual device requests while the latter acts as the responder (or recipient) to virtual device requests. Thus, the role of the

(a)

Name	Interface	Meaning
AASCreq	CS-user	A.ASSOCIATE.request received
AASCresp(+)	CS-user	A.ASSOCIATE.response (accept) received
AASCresp(−)	CS-user	A.ASSOCIATE.response (reject) received
AARQ	PS-provider	AARQ-PDU received
AARE(+)	PS-provider	AARE + PDU received
AARE(−)	PS-provider	AARE − PDU received
PCONconf(−)	PS-provider	P.CONNECT.confirm (reject) received

(b)

Name	Meaning
STA 0	Idle (unassociated)
STA 1	Awaiting AARE-APDU
STA 2	Awaiting A.ASSOCIATE.response
STA 5	Associated

(c)

Name	Meaning
P1	CPM can support connection

(d)

Name	Interface	Meaning
AASCind	CS-user	A.ASSOCIATE.indication issued
AASCconf(+)	CS-user	A.ASSOCIATE.confirm (accept) issued
AASCconf(−)	CS-user	A.ASSOCIATE.confirm (reject) issued
AARQ	PS-provider	AARQ-PDU sent
AARE(+)	PS-provider	AARE + PDU sent
AARE(−)	PS-provider	AARE − PDU sent
AABRind	CS-user	A.ABORT.indication issued
ABRT	PS-provider	ABRT-PDU sent

FIGURE 9.18

Abbreviated names for ACSE protocol machine: (a) incoming events; (b) automaton states, (c) outgoing events; (d) predicates.

State Event	STA 0	STA 1	STA 2	
AASCreq	1	0	0	
AASCresp(+)	0	0	2	
AASCresp(−)	0	0	3	
AARQ	4	0	0	
AARE(+)	0	5	0	
AARE(−)	0	6	0	
PCONconf(−)	0	6	0	

0 = AABRind, ABRT, STA 0

1 = P1: AARQ, STA 1

2 = AARE(+), STA 5

3 = AARE(−), STA 0

4 = P1: AASCind, STA 2;
   NOT P1: AARE(−), STA 0

5 = AASCconf(+), STA 5

6 = AASCconf(−), STA 0

FIGURE 9.19

Event-state table for ACSE protocol machine.

UE linked to the initiator AP is to perform the necessary mapping between the service primitives as provided to the user and those defined for use with the initiating AE. Similarly, the role of the UE linked to the responder AP is to perform the necessary mapping between the (standard) requests as produced by the responder AE and the corresponding requests associated with the real device being used. In this way, all communications, both at the user interface to the OSIE and also between AEs within the OSIE, are of a defined (and hence standard) form while within the RSE, existing software and associated operating system primitives can be used. Also, as was described earlier, if the syntax of the data being exchanged between two user APs is different, then the presentation entity performs the necessary mapping from the agreed transfer (concrete) syntax to the local syntax as appropriate; the particular presentation context(s) to be used being negotiated when the association (connection) is first established.

9.4.4 FTAM

It should be stressed that the various SASE protocol elements are not concerned with *providing* a specific application service but rather with creating the means by which a related service provided by a user AP in the RSE can be accessed and used in an open way. Thus, the **file transfer, access and management (FTAM)** SASE, for example, provides the means whereby a distributed community of client processes (APs) can access and manage a remote (server) file store implemented as a user AP running, possibly, on a computer from a different manufacturer from the client

(a)

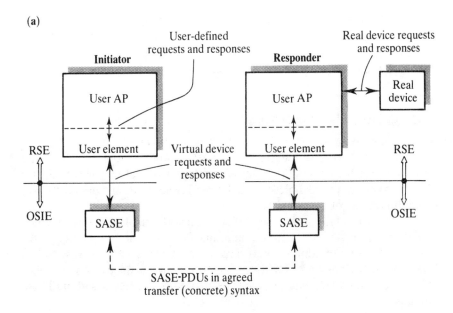

(b)

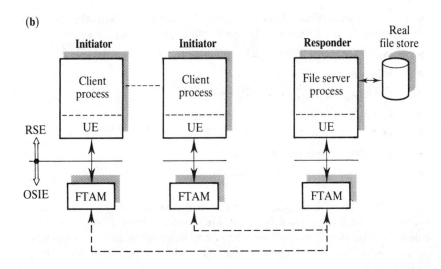

FIGURE 9.20

Virtual device approach:
(a) schematic; (b) virtual file
store.

system. Each client process (and hence the AE to which it is attached) is referred to as an initiator AP and the server process the responder AP. This is shown in diagrammatic form in Figure 9.20(b).

The primitives used by the client APs to access and manage the remote file store, in addition to the primitives used to access and manage the real file store, are local (that is, machine-dependent) matters. In this way, existing file systems and associated access software can be used, and the user need only provide (assuming the OSI software is in place) the associated UE to perform the necessary mapping functions.

The virtual file store model

Before describing the user service primitives associated with FTAM, it is first necessary to describe the (virtual) file store model to which the primitives relate. Clearly, the aim is to adopt a model that is sufficiently flexible to allow any real file store to be readily accessed and managed with a minimum set of mapping functions.

The virtual file store is modelled as an addressable entity with which a remote user (initiator) may communicate (have an association). An arbitrary number of initiators may have an association with the (responder) file store at any one time. The file store may comprise an arbitrary number of files, each of which has a number of attributes associated with it. These include:

- A filename: This allows the file to be referenced in an unambiguous way.
- Permitted actions: These indicate the range of actions (read, insert, replace, etc.) that can be performed on the file
- Access control: Read-only, read-write, etc.
- File size.
- Presentation context of file contents.
- Identity of creator.
- Date and time of creation.
- Identity of last modifier/reader.
- Data and time of last access.

Selection of a file takes place in two phases: first an association is established with the parent file store and then the identity of the required file within the file store is given. The access structure within the file store is as shown in Figure 9.21 and, as can be seen, it is based on an ordered, rooted tree.

The structure of the tree consists of a single **root node** with **internal nodes** and **leaves** connected by directed **arcs**. A node can belong to only one level. Each node, in turn, gives access to its **subtree**, which is known as a **file access data unit** (**FADU**). The contents of a file in the file store are held in one or more **data units** (**DUs**). At most, there can be only one DU assigned to a node, which means that a DU may be accessed by the

(a)

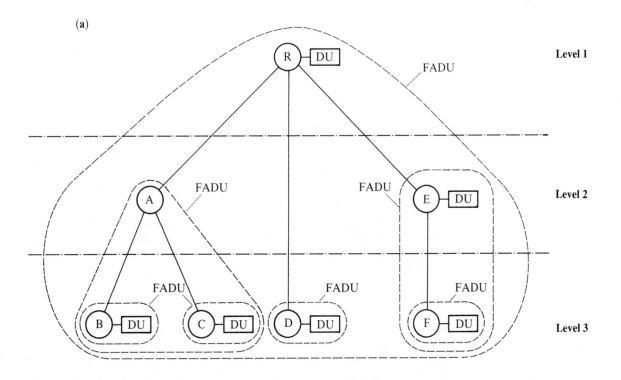

(b)

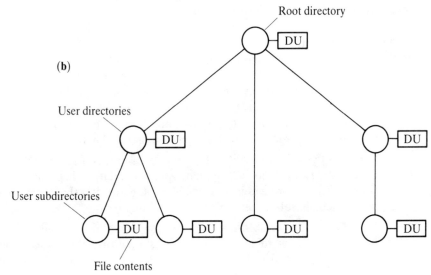

FIGURE 9.21

Virtual file store access structure:
(a) FTAM; (b) typical real file
store.

identification of the node FADU. Access to each node within the FADU is in the assumed order: R, A, B, C, D, E, F.

A DU is a typed data object (scalar, vector, set) and contains elements of atomic data called **data elements**. Associated with each data element is an abstract syntax (character, octet, integer, etc.) and all the elements within a DU are related. The normal relationship of elements is in the form of a tree although alternative relationships, such as a single data element or a vector, may be used. The tree is traversed in the order just outlined and the accessed DUs are passed to the presentation entity in this sequence. The latter then treats each element as independent and uses the corresponding (negotiated) transfer syntax to transfer the elements while at the same time maintaining their relative order.

The actions relating to the file store are invoked by corresponding service primitives. These include create, open, close and delete on complete files and locate, read, insert, replace, extend and erase on the DUs within a file.

Service primitives

Having given a brief overview of the virtual file store model, it is now possible to define the user service primitives associated with FTAM. These services are grouped into the form of a nested set of **regimes**, as shown in Figure 9.22(a). As can be seen, as progressively more contextual detail is established, a corresponding regime is entered.

Associated with each regime is a defined set of service primitives, as shown in the simplified event-state diagram in Figure 9.22(b). A summary of the services associated with each regime is as follows:

- Application connection (association): This is not specific to FTAM but rather relates to CASE (ACSE). In relation to FTAM, however, it establishes the authorization and accounting information necessary for the ensuing operations on the file store.

- File selection: This identifies (or creates) a unique file (FADU) to which operations in subsequent phases relate. The selection (identification) process is in terms of a file name and the operations performed in subsequent phases relate to this file.

- File access: This establishes a regime in which file data transfer can take place. This includes the establishment of the capabilities required for the transfer and of a suitable access context.

- Data transfer: This includes commands (read, write, etc.) that relate to actions on the DU within the accessed (identified) FADU. Smaller data elements may be identified for presentation purposes but they cannot be acted upon alone.

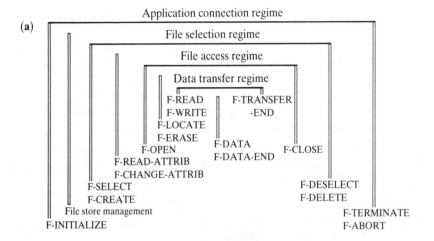

(a)

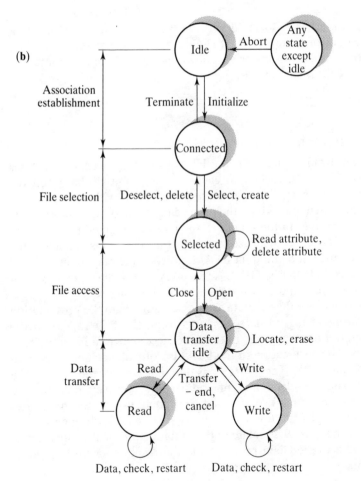

(b)

FIGURE 9.22

FTAM service primitives:
(a) service regimes; (b) simplified
event-state diagram.

As with some of the other protocol layers, the service primitives associated with FTAM are grouped into a number of functional units (FUs). The FUs required during a specific (dialogue) session are specified during the association establishment phase. The FUs supported include:

- Kernel: This provides facilities for application association and termination, file selection (deselection) and file opening (closing).
- Read: This provides facilities for reading files (bulk data) and individual DUs.
- Write: This provides facilities for writing files (bulk data) and individual DUs.
- File access: This provides facilities for locating and erasing FADUs.
- Limited file management: This provides facilities for file creation and deletion and for reading attributes.

Some of the primitives associated with each FU are shown in the time sequence diagram of Figure 9.23. It should be noted that for reasons of clarity only the request primitives are shown in Figure 9.23(c). In practice, they are each confirmed services.

Protocol machine

As can be seen from Figure 9.22, the FTAM protocol machine creates a corresponding PDU, on receipt of each service primitive, based on the service primitive type and the parameters associated with the primitive. The PDUs are then passed in the user data field of the appropriate presentation primitive. In the sequence shown, it is assumed that the data token is used; hence, in this case, prior to the data transfer phase, the token is passed from the initiating FTAM entity to the responding FTAM entity using the P.TOKEN_GIVE service. Also, in the data phase, it should be noted that there is no PDU corresponding to the F.DATA service. This is because the file data are passed directly to the presentation entity as a string of tagged data elements using the P.DATA service.

Finally, to formalize some of the sequences shown in Figure 9.23, a part of the formal specification of the FTAM protocol machine is given in Figures 9.24 and 9.25. The parts considered relate to the association establishment and file selection regimes. First, the abbreviated names and meanings of the incoming events, states, outgoing events and predicates are given in Figure 9.24 followed by the event-state tables in Figure 9.25. The two tables in Figure 9.25 relate to the initiating protocol entity (that is, the entity linked to the client process) and the responding entity (that is, the entity linked to the server process).

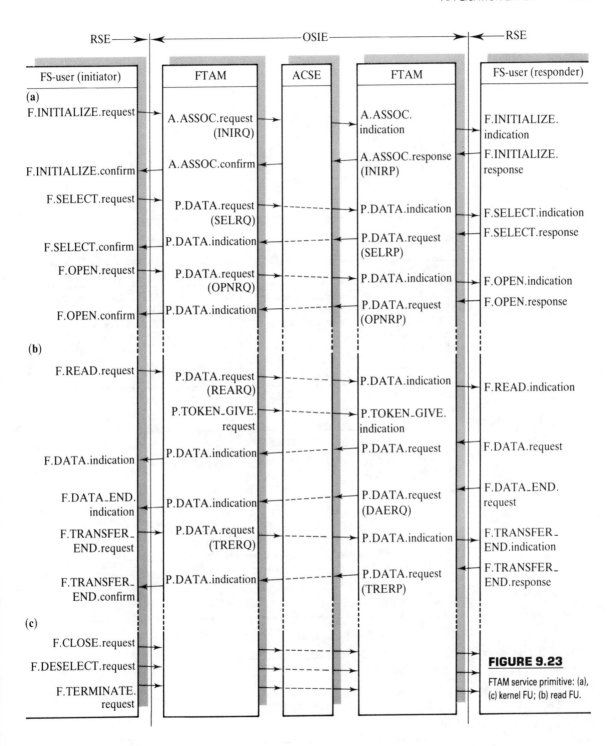

FIGURE 9.23

FTAM service primitive: (a), (c) kernel FU; (b) read FU.

(a)

Name	Interface	Meaning
F_INIRQ	FS-user	F.INITIALIZE.request received
F_INIRP	FS-user	F.INITIALIZE.response received
F_SELRQ	FS-user	F.SELECT.request received
F_SELRP	FS-user	F.SELECT.response received
INIRQ	CS-provider	Initialize request PDU received
INIRP	CS-provider	Initialize response PDU received
SELRQ	PS-provider	Select request PDU received
SELRP	PS-provider	Select response PDU received

(b)

Name	Meaning
STA 0	Application connection closed
STA 1	Association pending
STA 2	Application connection open
STA 3	Select pending
STA 4	Selected

(d)

Name	Meaning
P1	F.INITIALIZE.request acceptable
P2	INIRP-PDU acceptable
P3	INIRQ-PDU acceptable
P4	SELRP-PDU acceptable
P5	F.SELECT.response acceptable

(c)

Name	Interface	Meaning
F_INIIN	FS-user	F.INITIALIZE.indication issued
F_INICF	FS-user	F.INITIALIZE.confirm issued
F_SELIN	FS-user	F.SELECT.indication issued
F_SELCF	FS-user	F.SELECT.confirm issued
INIRQ	CS-provider	Initialize request PDU issued
INIRP	CS-provider	Initialize response PDU received
SELRQ	PS-provider	Select request PDU issued
SELRP	PS-provider	Select response PDU issued
F_ABTIN	FS-user	F.ABORT.indication issued
ABTRQ	CS-provider	Abort request PDU issued

FIGURE 9.24

Abbreviated names for FTAM protocol machine: (a) incoming events; (b) automaton states; (c) outgoing events; (d) predicates; (e) specific actions.

(e)

Name	Meaning
[1]	Initialize all state variables
[2]	Set rejection parameter accordingly

(a)

State / Event	STA 0	STA 1	STA 2	STA 3	---
F_INIRQ	1	0	0	0	
INIRP	0	2	0	0	
F_SELRQ	0	0	3	0	
SELRP	0	0	0	4	

0 = F_ABTIN, ABTRQ, STA 0

1 = P1: INIRQ, [1], STA 1;
    NOT P1: F_INICF, [2], STA 0

2 = P2: F_INICF, STA 2;
    NOT P2: F_INICF, [2], STA 0

3 = SELRQ, STA 3

4 = P4: F_SELCF, STA 4;
    NOT P4: F_SELCF, [2], STA 2

(b)

State / Event	STA 0	STA 1	STA 2	STA 3	---
INIRQ	1	0	0	0	
F_INIRP	0	2	0	0	
SELRQ	0	0	3	0	
F_SELRP	0	0	0	4	

0 = F_ABTIN, ABTRQ, STA 0

1 = P3: F_INIIN, [1], STA 1;
    NOT P3: INIRP, [2], STA 0

2 = INIRP, STA 2

3 = F_SELIN, STA 3

4 = P5: SELRP, STA 4;
    NOT P5: SELRP, [2], STA 2

9.4.5 MHS

The MHS is a collection of like SASEs that provide a facility for a distributed community of user APs, through their linked UEs, to exchange electronic messages. It is also referred to, therefore, as an electronic mail service and is based on the PTT-supported public message handling service known as X400, which has been defined by the CCITT.

A functional model of an MHS is shown in Figure 9.26. Typically, user APs are the mail programs present in most modern networked computer systems. In such systems, a user AP (and hence its linked UE) is referred to either as an originator, when it is sending a message, or a recipient, when it is receiving a message. To send a message, a user first prepares the message in an agreed structure and syntax using the service

FIGURE 9.25

Event-state table for FTAM protocol machine: (a) initiating entity; (b) responder entity.

(a)

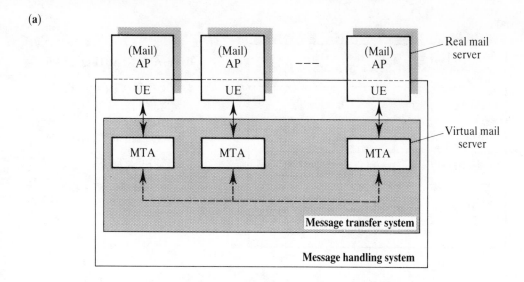

(b)

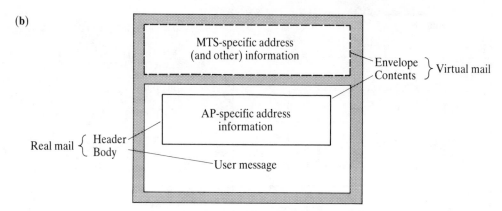

FIGURE 9.26

MHS: (a) functional model; (b) mail format.

primitives of its local (mail) AP. Then, on receipt of the message, the latter submits the message to its attached **message transfer agent** (**MTA**) using the standard service primitives. The MTA can be considered, therefore, as a **virtual mail server**. The linked set of MTA protocol entities then operate together, according to the defined protocol, to relay the submitted message to the specified recipient MTA(s). The latter then deliver the message to the recipient UE(s) and hence to the recipient user AP(s). Typically, the latter will store the received message in the mailbox of the intended recipient until the latter requests it. Collectively, the MTAs are referred to as the **message transfer system** (**MTS**) and the collection of UEs and MTAs the **message handling system** (**MHS**).

The basic structure of the messages exchanged within the (open) MTS comprises an **envelope**, which is the address information used for transferring the message within the MTS, and the **contents**, which is the actual message the originating AP (UE) wishes to be delivered to the recipient APs (UEs). Normally, the type of information in an envelope (the contents) is in an agreed syntax such as IA5/ISO 646. In some instances, however, certain syntax conversions may be selected; hence, the UE, should it be necessary, performs the conversion from the local to the agreed transfer syntax form. Similarly, on receipt of a message, the recipient UE performs any necessary conversion from the agreed transfer syntax to the local syntax form.

As with any postal system, the envelope is used simply to route a message to the intended recipient(s) within the MTS. In a similar way, the contents may also contain a secondary header field such as the sender's address or, if a memo, information such as subject: , from: to: , copies to: etc. The latter, however, is transparent to the MTS and so has only local significance; that is, only has meaning to its local mail service.

When a message is submitted with a basic MHS, the originating MTA transfers the message to the required recipient MTA directly and the latter then delivers it to the recipient UE. It is also possible, however, to implement a form of **central mailbox** or **repository service**. Essentially, a single AP/UE is designated as the mailbox manager and all messages submitted are sent to it. Similarly, all message requests by recipient UEs are forwarded to the mailbox manager which, in turn, responds by sending any waiting messages.

Service primitives

There is a range of different service primitives associated with an MHS. Although most of these are confirmed services, the confirmation primitives normally have only local significance; that is, the confirm primitive is generated by the local MTA protocol entity rather than by a response from the remote entity. A selection of some of the primitives is shown in the time sequence diagram of Figure 9.27.

Prior to submitting a message for delivery, the originating UE must first be logged on; this is analogous to logging on to a multi-access computer. Hence, if necessary, the user AP (through its UE) first initiates the sending of a LOGON.request primitive to its local MTA with the user AP name and password as parameters. The MTA then responds with a LOGON.confirm primitive with parameters that indicate the reason for rejection, if the logon request was unacceptable. Once logged on, the user AP (UE) can submit messages for delivery at any time by using the SUBMIT.request primitive. The parameters associated with the latter include the following:

- recipient AP (UE) address,

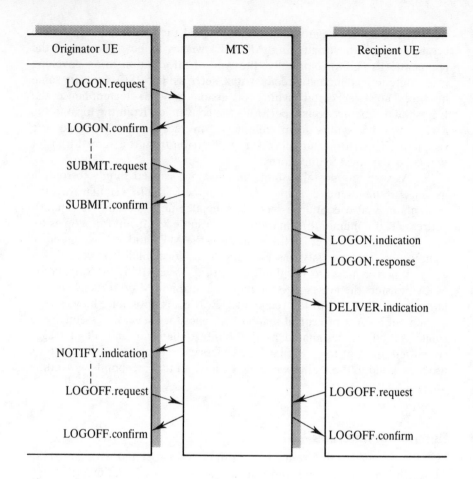

FIGURE 9.27

MHS service primitives.

- originator AP (UE) address,
- contents,
- content type, and
- priority (normal, urgent).

The matching SUBMIT.confirm primitive has only local significance and indicates the willingness (or otherwise) of the MTA to accept the message. With a basic MHS, the message is transferred by the originating MTA to the intended recipient MTA in the form of a PDU. The latter, on receipt of the message and assuming the user is currently logged on, then initiates the delivery of the message using the DELIVER.indication primitive with similar parameters to the original SUBMIT.request primitive. Alternatively, if the user is not logged on, the recipient MTA first issues a LOGON.indication primitive and, assuming the recipient UE is available and able to receive a message, it responds with a

LOGON.response primitive. The message is then delivered as before. Finally, the recipient MTA informs the originating MTA of the success (or failure) of the delivery attempt and the latter then informs the originating UE using the NOTIFY.indication primitive with, if necessary, the reason for non-delivery as a parameter.

Additional service primitives are provided for such functions as:

- LOGOFF.request/confirm,
- CHANGE_PASSWORD.request/confirm,
- REGISTER.request/confirm – this is used by a UE to stipulate any restrictions on messages it is prepared to accept.
- CONTROL.request/confirm – this is used to allow a UE to change any restrictions on messages the MTA can send to it.

9.4.6 MMS

The **manufacturing message service (MMS)** is an SASE that has been developed for use in fully automated manufacturing environments. Within such environments, there is a requirement for a facility to enable the various items of computer-based equipment to exchange messages in an open way. Normally, each manufacturing cell has an associated cell controller (control computer) which, in addition to communicating on a factory-wide basis with other systems using, say, FTAM, controls the various items of computer-based equipment associated with the cell. Typically, these include robot controllers (RCs), numerical machine tool controllers (NCs), automatic guided vehicle controllers (AGVs), program-mable logic controllers (PLCs), and so on. MMS has been defined to allow the cell controller to exchange messages with these various pieces of automated equipment in an open way.

A typical sequence of events might be as follows. First, at a factory-wide level, the FTAM is used to pass information about a part or component to a cell controller. The latter then uses MMS to send appropriate commands to the various items of automation equipment associated with the cell to cause the part (component) to be manufactured and/or assembled. Typically, commands such as:

- select and load a specific set of tools in an NC,
- request an RC to select an item of raw material and place on an AGV,
- instruct the AGV to transport the material to the NC,

would be issued by the cell controller (CC). Also, status messages would be returned to the CC as tasks are completed.

Service primitives

As the specific MMS primitives associated with each device (CC, RC, NC, etc.) vary, there are subsets of the total services intended for use with each type of device. For example, the services associated with a CC include:

- establish an association with a specific controller (context management);

- cause a controller to read a data file from the CC containing, say, tool data or operating instructions (obtain file);

- download a program to a controller (program load) from the CC;

- remotely control the operation of a controller (job control);

- read and change (write) selected variables associated with a controller program (variable access);

- request a controller to identify the MMS services that it supports (identify).

As with FTAM, the service primitives are grouped into a number of functional units (FUs) and a list of some of the primitives associated with each FU are as follows:

Functional Unit	Service Primitive	Confirmed
Context management	Initiate	Yes
	Release (Conclude)	Yes
	Abort	No
Obtain file	ObtainFile	Yes
File transfer	FileOpen	Yes
	FileClose	Yes
	FileRead	Yes
Program load	LoadFromFile	No
	StoreToFile	No
Job control	Start	No
	Stop	No
Variable access	Read	Yes
	Write	Yes
Device status	Status	No
	UnsolicitedStatus	No
General services	Reject	No
	Cancel	Yes
	Identify	No

It should be stressed that these are only examples and, of course, there are parameters associated with each primitive. As can be seen, MMS also supports a limited file service for local use within a cell; for example, to transfer a file containing the parts list associated with a controlled device. Of necessity, therefore, it is far less sophisticated than FTAM.

9.4.7 Job transfer and manipulation

The **job transfer and manipulation (JTM)** service is a collection of JTM SASEs located on different open systems. Collectively, the JTM elements (entities) form what is referred to as the **JTM service provider**. In the same way that FTAM does not actually implement a file service (that is, it only provides an environment whereby a real file system may be accessed and managed in an open way), so JTM provides an environment whereby documents relating to jobs, referred to as **job specifications**, may be transferred between real (open) systems and the jobs executed by them. Indeed, the type of job transferred is transparent to the JTM service provider.

The AP that submits a specification of an OSI job, through an associated UE, is known as the **initiating agency**. A job specification completely specifies the job to be carried out. For example, with a simple application of JTM, it may relate to a specification of a program together with the data to be run by an AP on a remote computer system, or a document to be printed by a remote print server application process. With a more sophisticated application, it may relate to, say, an order for an item of equipment from a remote suppliers computer, or to an invoice or statement relating to an order. Clearly, the type of processing associated with a job may vary: in its simplest form it may involve the processing of the document, resulting from the job specification, directly while in others the initial job specification may spawn other associated job specifications (subjobs).

The AP that actually executes a job is known as the **execution agency** while the AP that receives requests from the JTM service provider for information/data relating to a job is known as the **source agency** – for example, a local file store. Also, as the time between submitting a job specification and the job being completed may be long in some instances, the initiating agency may specify an AP to follow the progress of the job when it submits a job specification. This AP is known as the **job monitor**. Thus, whenever a significant event occurs in the lifetime of the job, the JTM service provider creates a **report document** and sends this to the associated job monitor. The initiating agency may then make enquiries as to the current status of the job. Finally, after an execution agency has completed all the work associated with a job specification, the JTM service provider submits a document to a nominated AP – the **sink agency**.

It may be concluded from the foregoing that JTM is concerned mainly with the movement of documents (which relate to jobs) between

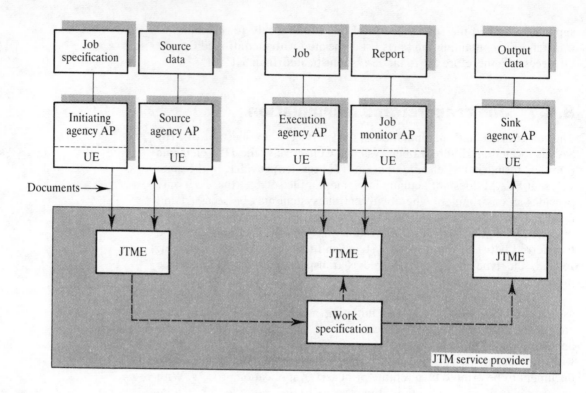

FIGURE 9.28

Model of JTM service.

APs. The latter are known as agencies to the JTM service provider and the various agencies associated with JTM are shown in Figure 9.28. Although each AP (agency) is shown as a separate entity, one or more of the APs may be associated with the same system in practice. For example, the initiating and sink agencies may be in the same system, or the sink and monitor agencies, and so on.

JTM services

The full range of services associated with JTM are too extensive to describe here; hence, only the user services associated with what is known as the **basic class** will be described. This supports only a restricted form of job specification – a single job; that is, it does not result in any subjobs being spawned. Also, as there is no secondary monitor agency, the only events reported are those related to an abnormal operation.

The user service primitives associated with the basic class are shown in the time sequence diagram of Figure 9.29. The initiating agency (AP) is known as the **JTM service requestor** and the various agencies (APs) that receive requests from the JTM service provider are known as **JTM service**

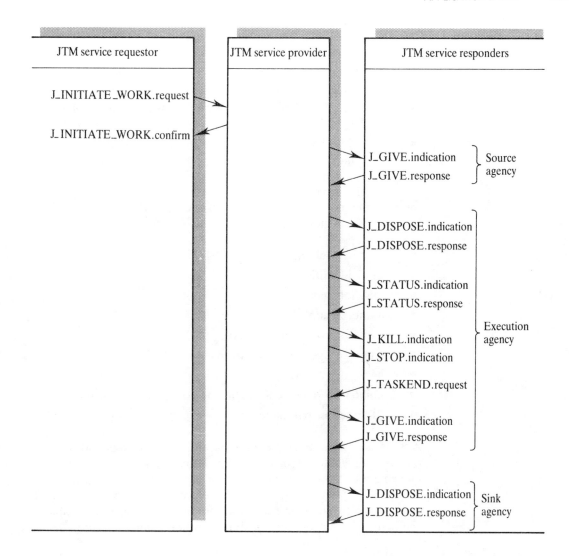

FIGURE 9.29

JTM basic class service primitives.

responders. The use of the various services shown are as follows:

- J_INITIATE_WORK: This allows an initiation agency to submit an OSI job specification document to its local JTM entity.

- J_GIVE: This allows a JTM entity associated with the JTM service provider to request a document from a source or an execution agency.

- J_DISPOSE: This allows a JTM entity to pass a document to an execution or sink agency.

- J_TASKEND: This allows an execution agency to signal completion of an activity associated with a job to its local JTM entity.

- J_STATUS: This allows a JTM entity to obtain information about the progress of an activity associated with a job.

- J_KILL: This allows a JTM entity to abruptly terminate all activity associated with a job.

- J_STOP: This allows a JTM entity to temporarily stop all activity associated with a job.

Again, parameters are associated with each primitive. For example, the parameters associated with the J_INITIATE_WORK.request primitive include the following:

- name of initiating agency AP,

- local identifier,

- OSI job name,

- authorization,

- name of source agency AP,

- name of execution agency AP,

- name of sink agency AP,

- pointer to document containing job specification, and

- JTM action parameter.

A JTM action parameter is present with all primitives and indicates the type of action associated with this primitive. This may be either document movement or work manipulation; the latter would be associated with a J_DISPOSE primitive passed to an execution agency, for example. In general, the response and confirm primitives only have the local identifier used with the corresponding indication and request primitives.

9.4.8 Directory services

The need for a **directory service (DS)** SASE arises from the fact that user APs utilize symbolic names (or identifiers) for identification purposes when corresponding with other APs. Hence, prior to initiating a request for a specific application service, the UE linked with an AP must first ascertain the fully qualified address within the OSIE of the named correspondent AP. A minimal function of the DS, therefore, is to provide what is referred to as an **address resolution service** to a UE; that is, a means of acquiring the fully qualified address corresponding to a specified (symbolic) name.

One of the main reasons for utilizing names is to isolate the user from any knowledge of the configuration of the network being used. Clearly, the latter may change as, for example, a new subnetwork (LAN) is added or removed or perhaps a different public data service is used to interconnect subnetworks. Also, in some applications, a user AP may migrate from one location on a network to another without, ideally, other APs being aware of this. To allow for such eventualities, the DS must provide, in addition to an address resolution service, additional services to allow the contents of the **directory**, containing the list of symbolic names and their corresponding fully qualified addresses, to be changed and updated in a controlled way.

The names associated with each user AP must of course be unique and any request to enter a name into the directory must be verified to ensure that the name supplied is not already in use. Clearly, with a large network comprising, say, a number of country-wide subnetworks, this can be a difficult task; hence, normally, names are managed in a distributed way. For example, in a large international network a name might have a number of components (attributes) of the form:

Country. Subnetwork. System. User Name.

Thus, providing a user name is unique within the associated system, then it is guaranteed to be unique within the OSIE.

Essentially, there are two ways of implementing a DS: either each system (station or node) on the network has a local copy of the directory or there is a single central directory associated with the network. The advantage of the former is that each address resolution request can be carried out locally, thereby reducing the speed of response to requests and the amount of network traffic associated with the DS function relative to the centralized approach. The disadvantage of this approach is that each copy of the directory must be updated whenever a change or addition is made. But as this situation is relatively infrequent, the multiple directory approach is the one most frequently adopted.

To implement such a scheme, each DS element has an associated **directory service agent (DSA)** which, on receipt of a resolution request, accesses its local copy of the directory (the **local directory information base** or **LDIB**) and returns the fully qualified network address corresponding to the supplied entity symbolic name. In addition, for each subnetwork, there is normally a centralized DSA that is responsible, firstly, for maintaining an up-to-date copy of the complete system-wide directory (the **directory information base** or **DIB**) and, secondly, for responding to requests from a local DSA if the latter cannot resolve a request. This is shown in diagrammatic form in Figure 9.30.

Changes to the DIB (and hence LDIBs) normally result from a user AP (hence UE) initiating a change through its attached DSA. Each DSA,

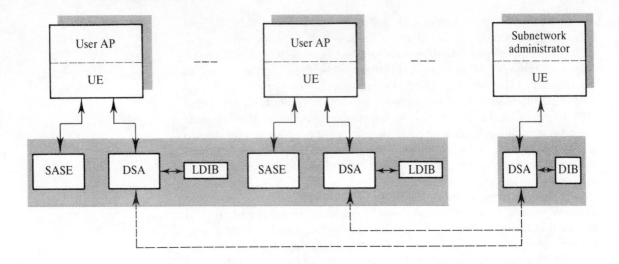

FIGURE 9.30

Directory services schematic.

therefore, must support, firstly, a set of user service primitives to allow directory requests to be resolved or updates to be made and, secondly, a protocol for communications within the OSIE with other DSAs to allow update information to be exchanged. Both of these aspects will now be considered, but it should be noted that this area of OSI is still evolving and so what follows is intended only as a guide to the type of services provided.

Service primitives

The services associated with each DSA can be extensive depending on the level of sophistication of the DS being used. Nevertheless, the basic elements associated with any DS must include:

- Access control: The DSA must be able to determine if a user has the right to perform the specific request.
- Address resolution: This is concerned with the basic name-to-address mapping.
- Name handling: This includes verification that the name supplied by a user is unique within that system.

The address associated with a given name is then the fully qualified address of the AE to which the DSA (and hence the attached UE) belongs.

A suitable set of service primitives to perform these functions, together with a list of parameters associated with each primitive, is given in

Service Primitive	Parameters	Function
ResolveAddress.request	*RequestId* *SymbolicName*	This service provides a UE with the means of obtaining the fully qualified address associated with a specified symbolic name.
ResolveAddress.response	*RequestId* *DIBAddress* *ErrorCode*	The *RequestId* allows the UE to distinguish between multiple outstanding requests. The *ErrorCode* allows for such cases as undefined entry.
AddDIBEntry.request	*AuthenticatorId* *RequestId* *SymbolicName*	This service allows a user to initiate the addition of a new entry into the DIB and hence LDIBs.
AddDIBEntry.confirm	*RequestId* *ErrorCode*	The *AuthenticatorId* is a means of establishing that the user can initiate changes to the DIB. The CSA itself will, of course, provide the local fully qualified address to be passed to the DSA (in a PDU).
DeleteDIBEntry.request	*AuthenticatorId* *RequestId* *SymbolicName*	This service allows a user to initiate the deletion of an existing entry in the DIB.
DeleteDIBEntry.confirm	*RequestId* *ErrorCode*	The *ErrorCode* indicates the success or failure of the request.
ChangeDIBEntry.request	*AuthenticatorId* *RequestId* *SymbolicName*	This service allows a user to initiate the change of an entry in the DIB; for example, to allow a user to migrate around a network.
ChangeDIBEntry.confirm	*RequestId* *ErrorCode*	

FIGURE 9.31

DS service primitives and parameters.

Figure 9.31. The primitives shown all relate to a single symbolic name. In some instances, however, it may be advantageous for the add, delete and change primitives to relate to, say, a complete node. In this way, if all the user APs are affected by a change (for example, if a node is relocated to a different part of the network), then a single primitive could be used to initiate the change.

Protocol operation

Associated with each of the add, delete and change primitives is a corresponding PDU, which is sent by the DSA protocol machine to the central DSA protocol machine to initiate the appropriate change to the DIB. Normally, the latter then responds either with an acknowledgement PDU, to indicate the change has been carried out, or with an error PDU (which includes the reason), if the change could not take place. On receipt of the response PDU, the local DSA then issues an appropriate confirm primitive to the user.

Since each DSA maintains a local copy of the DIB, after performing (and acknowledging) a change request, the central DSA must inform all the local DSAs of the change. For a relatively small network comprising, say, a number of interconnected LANs located in a single establishment, this is readily achieved by simply broadcasting the change, embedded in a PDU and passed through the lower protocol layers in the normal way, over the complete network. As was described in Chapter 8, most LANs support this means of addressing and communication mode. For larger networks, however, comprising, say, a set of subnetworks (interconnected LANs) interconnected by means of a public data network, this is more difficult to implement and administer. In such cases, therefore, there is normally a separate DSA per establishment and hence, in addition to broadcasting changes over its local subnetwork, the DSA informs all other DSAs in the network of any changes as they occur.

To facilitate operations of this type, the second CASE entity ROSE has been defined. This, like the ACSE part of CASE, performs some generalized functions on behalf of other SASEs. The user services associated with ROSE include:

- RO_INVOKE: This is used to initiate a remote operation.
- RO_RESULT: This is used to request (remotely) a value or parameter.
- RO_REJECT: This is used to reject a remote request.
- RO_ERROR: This is used to signal an error condition.

CHAPTER SUMMARY

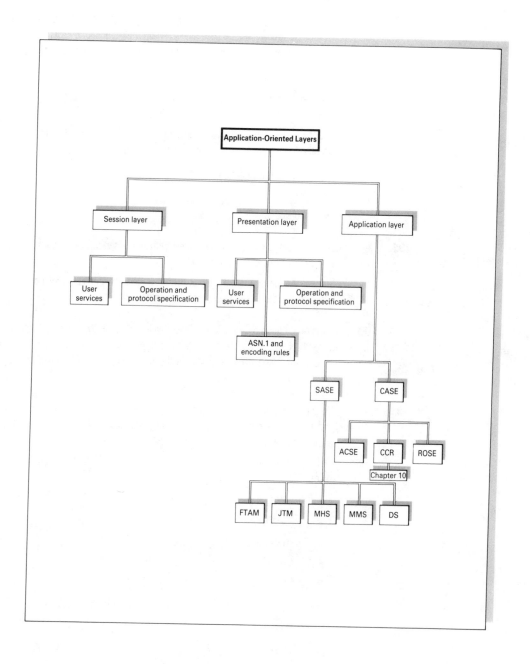

EXERCISES

9.1 Produce a sketch showing the position of the various application-oriented protocol entities in relation to the ISO Reference Model and explain their function. Describe in outline how they function collectively to perform a specific distributed information service such as FTAM.

9.2 (a) Describe the function of the session layer in the context of the ISO seven-layer model.

(b) Produce a sketch showing the following parts of a session and identify where the various tokens associated with the session service might be used:

- session connection,
- activity,
- dialogue unit.

9.3 (a) List the service primitives associated with the basic combined subset of the session service and explain their function.

(b) Produce a time sequence diagram to show how the services provided by the transport layer are used to establish a session connection.

9.4 Using the implementation methodology introduced in Chapter 6, outline the structure of a pseudo-Pascal program module to implement the SPM event- state table given in Figure 9.6. Use the same variable names in the program as used in the SPM event-state table.

9.5 (a) Discriminate between an abstract data type and a concrete (transfer) data type and hence describe the function of the presentation layer in relation to the application layer.

(b) Define a set of variables in ASN.1 to illustrate the meaning of the following data types:

- BOOLEAN,
- BITSTRING,
- ISO646String,
- CHOICE,
- SEQUENCE.

(c) Define a variable of type SET to illustrate the use of the following keywords:

- IMPLICIT,
- OPTIONAL,
- DEFAULT,
- NULL.

9.6   Use the variable type definitions declared in Exercise 9.5 to show how a specific declared value associated with each variable would be encoded.

9.7   With reference to the encoding example given in Figure 9.15(b), show how the PDU would be encoded if all the tagged variables associated with the PDU had been declared *IMPLICIT*.

9.8   (a)   Explain the function and services associated with the ACSE component of CASE.

(b)   Produce a time sequence diagram to show the interrelationships between the service primitives used by a calling AP, an SASE, an ACSE and the presentation layer.

9.9   With the aid of a sketch, explain what is meant by the term virtual device. Hence show how the virtual device concept may be used to implement a virtual file store. Clearly identify a client (initiator) and a server (responder) AP and the real file store.

9.10   (a)   Produce a simplified state-transition diagram to show how the various file service regimes associated with FTAM are related.

(b)   Produce a time sequence diagram to show the relationship between the user service primitives associated with FTAM and the used services provided by ACSE and the presentation layer.

9.11   Give a brief explanation of the services provided by the following SASE protocol entities:

- MHS,
- MMS,
- JTM,
- DS.

SYSTEM ASPECTS

10

CHAPTER OBJECTIVES

When you have completed studying the material in this chapter you should be able to:

- describe the protocols used in selected open systems interconnection environments;

- understand how the seven protocol layers making up the ISO Reference Model function collectively to perform a specific application function;

- describe the interactions that occur between each layer (and their interrelationships) when performing such functions;

- describe a strategy for the implementation of a complete communication subsystem;

- understand the overall structure of the software relating to a complete communication subsystem and how it interfaces to the host system software;

- explain aspects of the function of the management sublayer part of a communication subsystem;

- describe the application and operation of a two-phase commit protocol with error recovery.

10.1 INTRODUCTION

The previous chapters have been concerned primarily with descriptions of the function, operation and specification of the different protocol entities that have been defined to enable open systems to be established in a range of application environments. The aim of this chapter is, firstly, to give some examples of open systems environments that utilize the ISO protocols and then to consider aspects relating to the operation and implementation of a complete communication subsystem.

10.2 EXAMPLE OSI ENVIRONMENTS

As was described in Chapter 9, there is not just a single protocol associated with the application layer. Rather, there are a number of alternative protocols (SASEs), each of which provides a means of achieving a specific distributed information processing function in an open way. Also, as was described in Chapters 6, 7 and 8, the transport layer and the lower network-dependent protocol layers offer a number of different classes of service and operational modes. Within a specific open systems interconnection environment (OSIE), therefore, the administrative authority responsible for the environment must select the specific application services to be supported, and also the different modes of operation and classes of service to be provided by the lower network-dependent layers.

A number of OSIEs based on the ISO seven-layer reference model are currently being established by PTTs for use in the public domain. These include Teletex, Videotex and Facsimile networks. Essentially, the various pieces of equipment used to provide access to such networks operate using international standard protocols defined by the CCITT. Collectively, such networks are referred to by the PTTs as teleservices, whose functions were outlined earlier in Chapter 7 when public data networks were discussed.

In the private sector, two examples of OSIEs are MAP and TOP. In the manufacturing industry, an initiative by General Motors of the United States has resulted in a set of protocols, all based on ISO standards, being selected to achieve open systems interconnection within an automated manufacturing plant. The resulting set of protocols selected are known as **manufacturing automation protocols** (MAPs). A schematic of a typical MAP network, together with the protocols selected for use with it, is shown in Figure 10.1.

As can be seen from the figure, MAP is based on a factory-wide, backbone cable distribution network. This is coaxial cable and operates at 10 Mbps. Because of the wide range of communication requirements

(a)

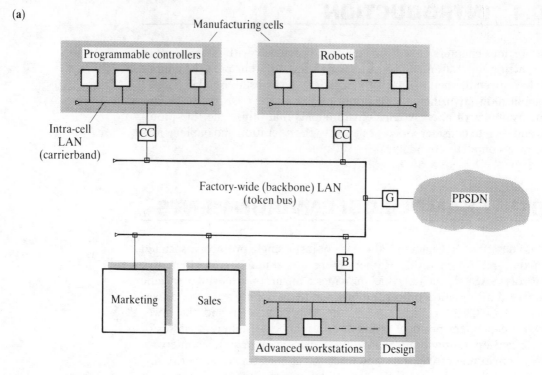

Manufacturing cells

Programmable controllers

Robots

Intra-cell
LAN
(carrierband)

CC

CC

Factory-wide (backbone) LAN
(token bus)

G

PPSDN

Marketing

Sales

B

Advanced workstations

Design

(b)   **Full MAP**

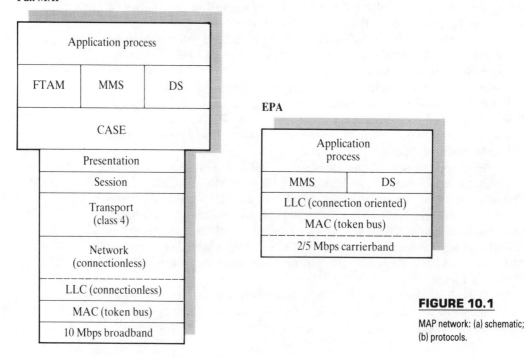

Application process		
FTAM	MMS	DS
CASE		

| Presentation |
| Session |
| Transport (class 4) |
| Network (connectionless) |
| LLC (connectionless) |
| MAC (token bus) |
| 10 Mbps broadband |

EPA

Application process	
MMS	DS
LLC (connection oriented)	
MAC (token bus)	
2/5 Mbps carrierband	

FIGURE 10.1

MAP network: (a) schematic;
(b) protocols.

within a factory, the broadband mode of working has been selected. The MAC sublayer is ISO 8802.4, the token bus standard, which has been selected because of its deterministic access time. Both the network layer and the LLC sublayer operate in a connectionless mode and the transport layer operates using the class 4 connection-oriented protocol. The distributed information services currently selected include FTAM and MMS, each of which operates through the ACSE component of CASE.

For communications within a manufacturing cell (that is, for exchanging messages between, say, a cell controller and a distributed set of robots and other computer-controlled machines), the simpler and less costly carrierband transmission method is used. Since most communications within a cell are local, a reduced set of protocols has been selected. Clearly, the time overheads associated with the full seven-layer model are significant and, in some instances, unacceptable for communications between the cell controller and the various pieces of automated equipment. The reduced set of protocols selected, therefore, comprises MMS (which also includes a basic file service) interfaced directly to the LLC sublayer, which then operates in a connection-oriented mode. In this way, the time overheads associated with intra-cell communications are much reduced. The resulting system is then known as the **enhanced performance architecture (EPA)**. Normally, a cell controller supports both the full seven-layer MAP architecture and the EPA; hence, in addition to performing a local supervisory or control function, the cell controller can also communicate on a factory-wide basis over the backbone network.

In a similar way, an initiative by the Boeing Corporation (also from the United States) has resulted in a set of ISO standards being selected to achieve open systems interconnection in a technical and office environment. The selected set of protocols is known as **technical and office protocols (TOPs)**. A schematic of a typical establishment-wide TOP network, together with the protocols selected for use with it, is shown in Figure 10.2.

The transmission medium used with a TOP network is also coaxial cable operating at 10 Mbps. In general, the communication requirements in such environments are limited to voice (which normally is already provided by the existing telephone system) and data, the latter being primarily concerned with communications between a distributed community of advanced workstations (performing computer-aided design, for example). The cable, therefore, is operated in a baseband mode and the MAC protocol is ISO 8802.3 (CSMA/CD). As with MAP, the network layer and LLC sublayer operate in a connectionless mode and the transport layer operates using the class 4 service. The distributed information services selected include FTAM, MHS, JTM and VT.

These are just some examples of currently established OSIEs. As the administrative authorities in other application domains move towards open systems, however, many others will evolve.

(a)

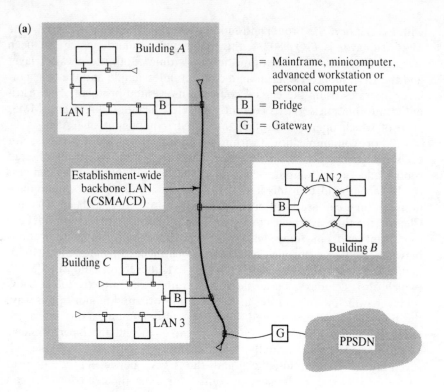

Building *A*

LAN 1

B

☐ = Mainframe, minicomputer,
     advanced workstation or
     personal computer

B = Bridge

G = Gateway

Establishment-wide
backbone LAN
(CSMA/CD)

LAN 2

B

Building *B*

Building *C*

B

LAN 3

G

PPSDN

(b)

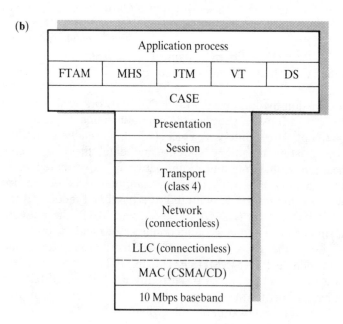

Application process				
FTAM	MHS	JTM	VT	DS
CASE				

Presentation

Session

Transport
(class 4)

Network
(connectionless)

LLC (connectionless)

MAC (CSMA/CD)

10 Mbps baseband

FIGURE 10.2

TOP network: (a) schematic;
(b) protocols.

10.3 LAYER INTERACTIONS

To gain an understanding of the operation of a complete communication subsystem, it is first necessary to understand how the various protocol entities making up the subsystem interact to perform a particular application function. To achieve this, consider an application domain comprising a community of advanced workstations (each with an integral communication subsystem) with the following properties:

- the selected OSIE is based on TOP;
- the LAN is CSMA/CD;
- one workstation is functioning as a central file server to which user APs running in the other workstations require access;
- the SASE being used is FTAM;
- the network-dependent protocol layers (network, LLC, MAC) all operate using the connectionless mode;
- the transport layer provides a class 4 connection-oriented service.

A typical sequence of frame transmissions on the LAN cable medium between a client (initiator) AP and the server (responder) AP, together with the layer interactions that take place relating to each transmission, is given in Figure 10.3. For clarity, it is assumed that all service primitives and associated PDUs are of the correct structure (and hence accepted) and also that no transmission errors occur.

To initiate a file access, transfer or management operation, the client user AP (through its linked UE) first issues a F.INITIALIZE.request primitive. This results in the layer interactions depicted in Figure 10.3(a), where the numbers in parentheses indicate the sequence in which the interactions occur. Thus, as can be seen, on receipt of the request primitive (1), the initiator FTAM entity generates an INIRQ-PDU, using the parameters associated with the service request, and writes the ASN.1 encoded version of the PDU into a memory buffer, the user data buffer (UDB). The latter, as was described in Chapter 6, is simply an array of octets (bytes) and it is the contents of the UDB that are eventually transmitted on the cable medium.

The address pointer of the UDB is then passed to the ACSE component of CASE in the user data parameter of an A.ASSOCIATE.request primitive (2) together with additional parameters as defined for use with this primitive. The ACSE entity, in turn, generates its own protocol control information (PCI) and adds this at the tail of the existing INIRQ-PDU in the UDB. Collectively, the two parts form an AARQ-PDU. The address pointer of the UDB is then passed in the user data parameter of a P.CONNECT.request primitive, again with additional

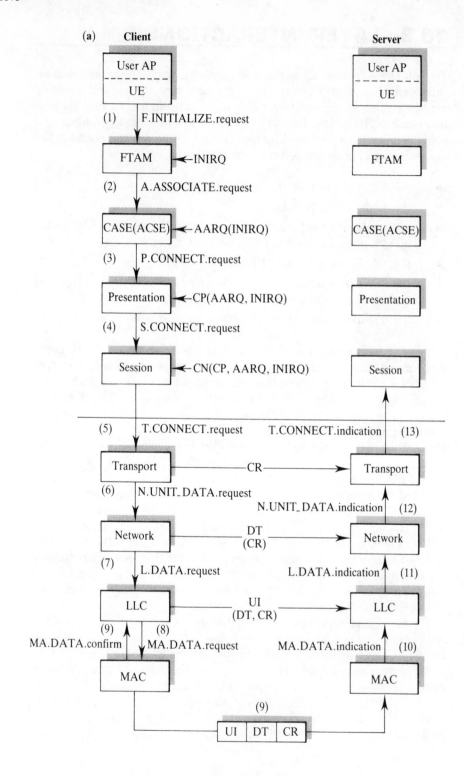

FIGURE 10.3

Layer interactions.

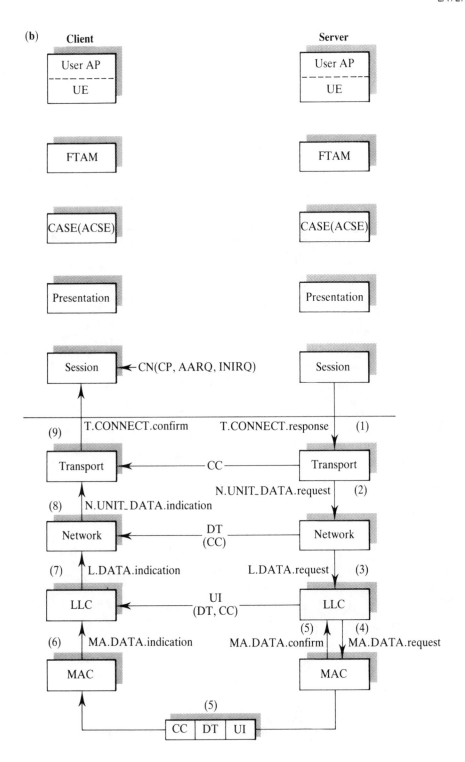

FIGURE 10.3 (cont.)

Layer interactions.

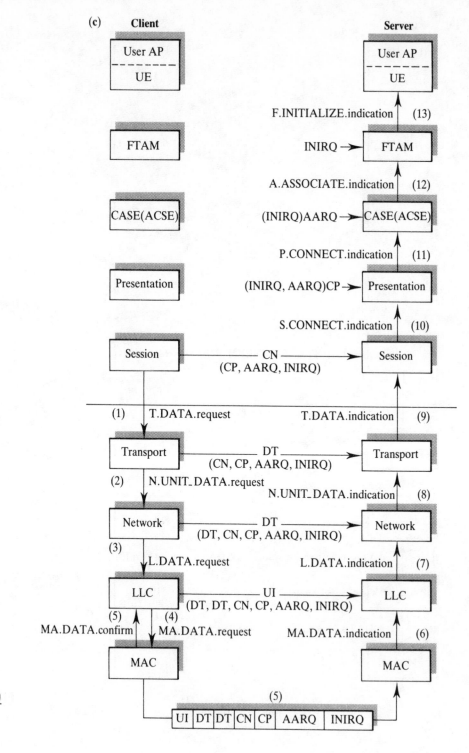

FIGURE 10.3 (cont.)

Layer interactions.

(d)

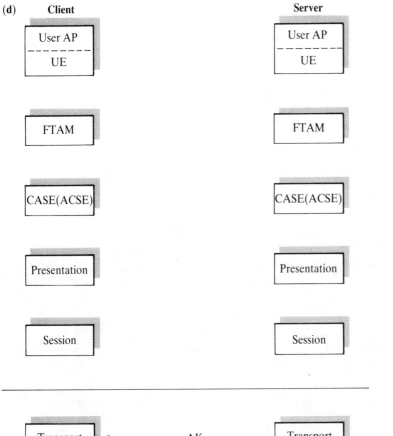

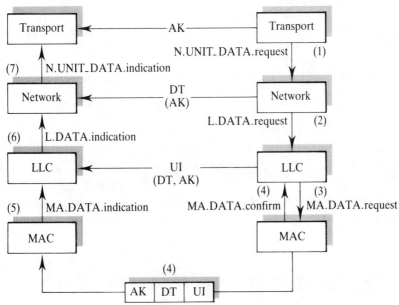

FIGURE 10.3 (cont.)

Layer interactions.

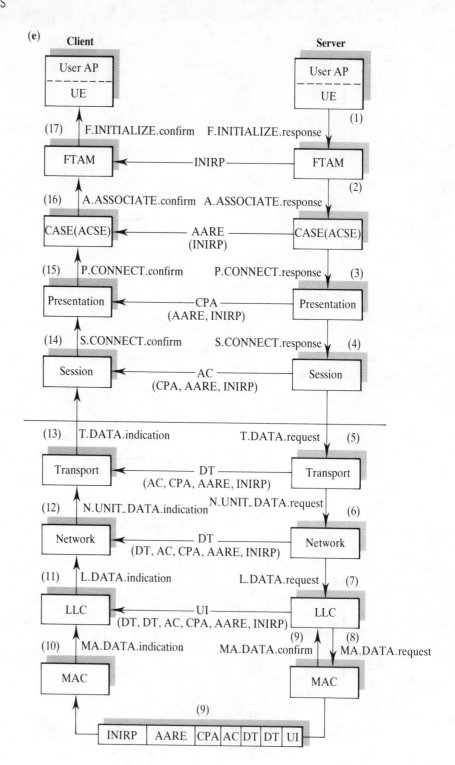

FIGURE 10.3 (cont.)

Layer interactions.

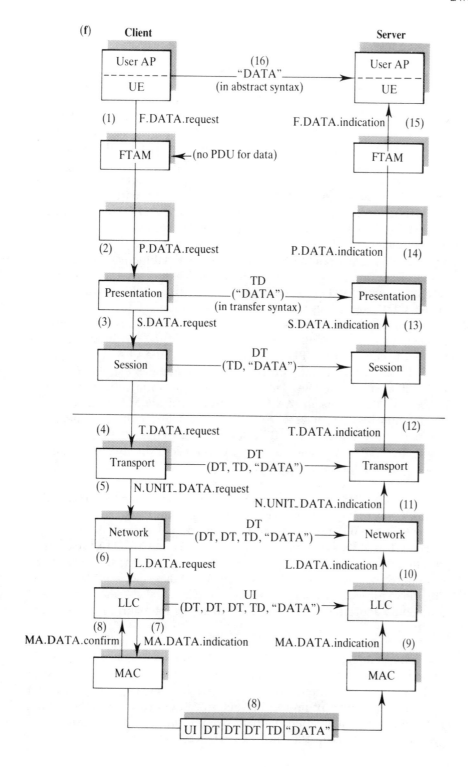

FIGURE 10.3 (cont.)

Layer interactions.

parameters as defined for use with this primitive (3).

The same procedure is then followed by the presentation entity: it first generates its own PCI, adds this to the UDB (to form, collectively, a CP-PDU) and finally issues an S.CONNECT.request primitive (4). Similarly, the session entity generates its own PCI and adds this to the UDB to form, collectively, a CN-PDU. At this point, however, it is assumed that a transport connection (TC) is not currently established with the remote system and hence, before the session entity can transfer the composite PDU to the peer session entity, it must establish a TC.

The session entity thus uses the address information (and the specified communication QOS) associated with the parameters of the S.CONNECT.request primitive and issues a T.CONNECT.request primitive (5). On receipt of this, the transport entity creates a CR-PDU, using the parameters associated with the service request, and writes this into a new UDB. As has been indicated, it is assumed that the network and link layers operate in a connectionless mode and hence the transport entity then issues an N.UNIT_DATA.request primitive with the address pointer of the UDB containing the CR-PDU as a parameter (6).

On receipt of this, the network entity uses the parameters to generate its own PCI and adds this at the tail of the CR in the UDB to form, collectively, a DT-PDU. It then issues an L.DATA.request primitive with the address pointer of the UDB as a parameter (7). Similarly, the LLC sublayer adds its own PCI to the UDB, to form collectively a UI-PDU, and then issues an MA.DATA.request to the MAC sublayer (8). Finally, the MAC sublayer first adds its own PCI (which includes the destination and source LAN addresses) and adds this to the UDB. At this point, the UDB thus contains the PCI relating to the four layers in the order transport, network, LLC and MAC.

The MAC sublayer now initiates the transmission of the complete UDB contents. It first gains access to the shared cable medium (according to the CSMA/CD medium access control method) and, as the preassembled frame contents are being transmitted, it generates the FCS field and adds this at the tail of the frame. It then issues an MA.DATA.confirm primitive to the LLC sublayer to inform the latter that the frame has been transmitted successfully (9). It should be noted that since the MAC PCI is the same for each frame transmitted – that is, the same source and destination addresses – it is not shown in any of the figures for reasons of clarity.

On receipt of the frame, the MAC sublayer in the server station stores the complete frame in a UDB so that the UDB contents are in the same order as they were transmitted. It should be stressed at this point that, although the frame (and hence UDB contents) comprises PCI relating to a number of protocol layers, since the PCI for each layer (and hence PDU) is in a precisely defined (fixed) format, each layer can readily access and interpret just its own PCI. Hence, on receipt of the complete frame, the MAC sublayer first interprets its own PCI and then passes the address pointer of the UDB up to the LLC sublayer using an MA.DATA.indication primitive (10).

In practice, as will be described later, the UDB also contains an address offset that indicates the start address of the next PCI to be processed. Thus, on receipt of the UDB pointer, the LLC sublayer uses the address offset to determine the start address of its own PCI. Having established the type of PDU received (UI), it then processes the remaining PCI pertaining to it according to the standard format and issues an L.DATA.indication primitive, with appropriate parameters, to the network layer (11). The latter, in turn, processes its own PCI in the UDB and issues an N.UNIT_DATA.indication primitive to the transport layer (12). Finally, the transport entity processes its own PCI and issues an T.CONNECT.indication primitive to the session layer (13).

The recipient session entity, assuming it is prepared to establish a TC, responds by issuing a T.CONNECT.response primitive. The resulting layer interactions are shown in Figure 10.3(b). On receipt of the T.CONNECT.response primitive (1), the transport entity first creates a CC-PDU, writes this into a (new) UDB and then issues an N.UNIT_DATA.request primitive to the network layer (2). The same procedure is then followed as in the previous example and finishes when the transport entity issues a T.CONNECT.confirm to the originating session layer to confirm that a TC has been established (9).

The originating session entity is now able to transfer the waiting CN-PDU (which includes the CP-, AARQ- and INIRQ-PCI in its user data field) across the TC. It does this by issuing a T.DATA.request primitive with the address pointer of the UDB containing the waiting CN-PDU as a parameter. The resulting interlayer interactions are as shown in Figure 10.3(c). As can be seen, a similar sequence ensues as in the earlier examples except that this time the lower network-dependent layers simply add their own PCI after the CN-PDU in the UDB.

On receipt of the UDB at the server station (5), each protocol layer proceeds to process its own PCI and passes the remaining contents up to the next higher protocol layer. Finally, on receipt of the UDB by the FTAM entity (12), the latter issues a F.INITIALIZE.indication primitive to the responder UE with parameters constructed from the INIRQ-PDU (13). In addition, however, since the PCI relating to the application-oriented layers is passed as user data in a DT-TPDU by the calling transport entity, the called transport entity, after passing the UDB to the session layer (containing the CN-PDU), initiates the sending of an acknowledgement for the DT-TPDU. The sequence shown in Figure 3.10(d) traces the interactions resulting from this. As can be seen, the interactions are similar to those shown in Figure 10.3(b) except that in this case the TPDU is an AK.

On receipt of the F.INITIALIZE.indication primitive, the server

AP (through its linked UE) responds by issuing a F.INITIALIZE.response primitive to its attached FTAM entity. The interactions that follow are outlined in Figure 10.3(e). As can be seen, since a TC has now been established, the UDB contents eventually transmitted (9) contain PCI relating to all the protocol layers. Hence, as the received UDB is passed up through the layers in the client system, each layer reads and interprets the PCI relating to it. Finally, the initiating FTAM entity issues a F.INITIALIZE.confirm primitive to the client UE (17).

As was described in the previous chapter, the normal sequence with FTAM would then involve the required file being selected and opened before any specific action was carried out on the file. Each of these steps would result in a sequence similar to that just followed. The sequence shown in Figure 10.3(f), however, traces the layer interactions that occur when the client AP is sending data to the server. Clearly, therefore, this would have been preceded by an additional F.WRITE.request primitive. As can be seen, the data being transferred may be in an abstract syntax but the data transferred between the two presentation entities – that is, the TD-PDU – must be in an agreed transfer (concrete) syntax. Also, the ACSE entity is shown blanked out since it does not feature in the data transfer phase.

10.3.1 UDB decoding

To enforce understanding of the layer interactions shown in Figure 10.3, the contents of a typical transmitted frame are shown in Figure 10.4(a). This frame is intended to correspond to that shown earlier in Figure 10.3(a). The contents of the frame, and hence the UDB, are shown as a string of octets with each octet represented as two hexadecimal digits. The frame is also assumed to contain a destination and a source MAC address.

To illustrate how the received frame is interpreted by the various protocol layers, the decoded version of the frame is shown in Figure 10.4(b). In the example, it is assumed that 16-bit MAC addresses are used; hence, the MAC protocol entity first reads and interprets the first four octets in the UDB – the destination and source addresses. The UDB pointer is then passed to the LLC sublayer as the user data parameter of an MA.DATA.indication primitive with an address offset of 4.

On receipt of the UDB pointer, the LLC protocol entity reads and interprets its own PCI from the UDB; first the DSAP and SSAP octets and then the control field octet. From the latter, it determines that the frame is an UI (unnumbered information) frame and hence interprets this as the end of its own PCI. Thus, it increments the address offset to 7 and then passes the UDB pointer to the network layer as the user data parameter of an L.DATA.indication primitive.

A similar procedure is then followed by the network and transport

(a) 00 2E 36 39 FE 0E 03 81 21 01 09 1C 00 21 00 00 0B

    49 00 02 02 00 00 00 00 2E FE 00 0B 49 00 03 08 00

    00 00 36 39 0E 00 08 E0 00 00 70 00 40 97 B7

(b) MAC PCI

    00 2E = Destination address
    36 39 = Source address

    LLC PCI

    FE = DSAP
    0E = SSAP
    03 = UI (unnumbered information)

    Network PCI

    81   = Network protocol identifier
    21   = Header length
    01   = Version number
    09   = PDU life time
    1C   = 0001 1100 = no segmentation, DT PDU
    00 21 = PDU segment length
    00 00 = Check sum (ignored)
    0B   = Destination address length
    49 00 02 02 00 00 00 00 2E FE 00 = Destination address
                49 = Local
                00 02 02 00 00 = IDI
                00 = PSI
                00 2E = MAC SAP
                FE = LSAP
                00 = NSAP
    0B   = Source address length
    49 00 03 08 00 00 00 36 39 0E 00 = Source address

    Transport PCI

    08   = Length indicator
    E0   = 1110 = CR TPDU, 0000 = CDT
    00 00 = Destination reference
    70 00 = Source reference
    40   = Class 4 service
    70 00 = Check sum

FIGURE 10.4

Example UDB decoding: (a) UDB (frame) contents; (b) decoded fields.

layers. First, the network protocol entity reads and interprets the appropriate number of octets, according to the network protocol. It then passes the UDB pointer to the transport layer, with the address offset suitably incremented, as the user data parameter of an N.UNIT_DATA.indication primitive. Similarly, the transport protocol entity reads and interprets its own PCI. At this point, however, the UDB would be exhausted, so the transport entity simply issues a T.CONNECT.indication primitive to the session layer using some of the fields from the received UDB to form the necessary parameters.

10.3.2   Address parameters

The parameters associated with each service primitive include address information. For example, the calling and called addresses associated with the F.INITIALIZE.request primitive are fully qualified addresses obtained from, say, the local directory server. They include, therefore, the P/SSAP, TSAP and NSAP, with the latter including the NSAP and LSAP extensions (or suffixes) relating to the interlayer interfaces, and also the physical network address. As the service primitives resulting from the F.INITIALIZE.request pass down through the protocol layers, each protocol entity reads and embeds its own SAP into the PCI associated with that layer. Hence, as the primitives pass down through the layers, the size of the address parameters diminishes until, at the MAC sublayer, only the physical network address remains. Similarly, as the service primitives pass up through the protocol layers at the server, the address parameters are reconstructed as each protocol entity reads its SAP from the PCI and adds this to the existing addresses. This is shown in diagrammatic form in Figure 10.5(a).

Session and transport connection identifiers are assigned to the application association and transport connections as they are established. Subsequent service primitives then include only the relevant connection identifier as a parameter. When implementing each protocol entity, therefore, it is necessary to retain a record of the calling and called addresses in addition to the protocol state information relating to each connection. This is shown in diagrammatic form in Figure 10.5(b).

Once each TPDU associated with a connection is passed to the network layer, the network entity can access the corresponding stored NSAPs, which include the physical network address and the NSAP and LSAP extensions. In this way, the complete address information will have been inserted when the complete PDU is transmitted by the MAC layer. In the example chosen here, the network-oriented layers are assumed to operate in the connectionless mode. However, if a connection-oriented mode is used, it would also be necessary to utilize a separate network connection identifier.

10.3.3 Address structure

Clearly, in many OSIEs, there is a need to provide the capability for a DTE (advanced workstation, for example) connected to one subnetwork (LAN) to communicate with a DTE connected to a different subnetwork. Typically, the latter may be located within the same establishment or in a different establishment which, in turn, may be located either in the same country or in a different country. In such cases, therefore, it is essential that the network addresses used (that is, the NSAPs) are of the necessary length and structure to enable this to be achieved.

To meet this requirement, the ISO have proposed a structure for network addresses, which is shown in Figure 10.6(a). As can be seen, in keeping with most addressing schemes, each network address is hierarchical in so much that the lower level subaddresses have significance only within the domain of the next higher level subaddress. Each address is comprised of two parts: the **initial domain part** (IDP) and the **domain-specific part** (DSP). If an OSIE involving a purely private network (or set of networks) is used, then the IDP field can be a local matter; but, if public networks are to be involved, it is essential, firstly, to identify the type of public network to be used and, secondly, the structure and format of the addressing information to be used with it.

Clearly, as has been described in earlier chapters, there are a number of alternative means of achieving interworking between subnetworks (the PSTN, ISDN and PPSDN are just some examples), each of which has its own addressing scheme. To reflect this, therefore, the IDP is itself comprised of two parts: the **authority and format identifier** (AFI) and the **initial domain identifier** (IDI). Essentially, the AFI specifies both the type of internetworking facility to be used and the format of the IDI address information associated with it. For example, if the internetworking method is to be through the international public PSDN, the IDI typically relates to the address of the local internetwork gateway to which the subnetwork is connected. The IDI thus comprises a sequence of up to 14 digits which are allocated according to the CCITT recommendation X.121. The AFI value is then equal to 36 decimal, stored as two BCD digits in a single octet, if the INI address is represented in BCD form, or 37 decimal if it is in binary form. Other AFI values have been assigned for use with the PSTN and ISDN, for example, and some of these are shown in Figure 10.6(b). With all these networks, the IDI address itself is comprised of a number of hierarchical subaddresses representing the country code and the national network code.

The DSP is also comprised of a number of hierarchical subaddresses, including:

- Subnetwork identifier (SI): This identifies the particular subnetwork (LAN) to which the DTE is connected.

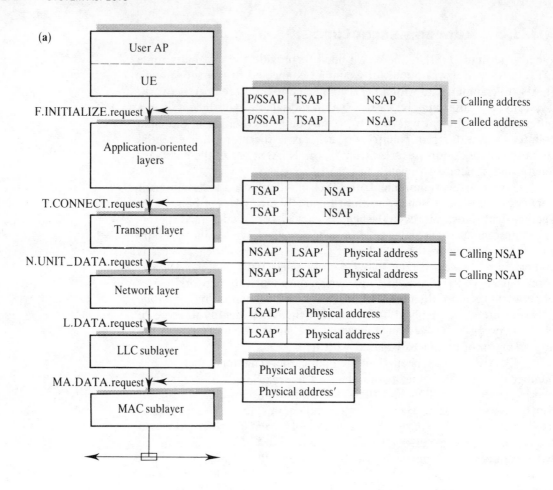

(a)

| | P/SSAP | TSAP | NSAP | = Calling address |
| F.INITIALIZE.request | P/SSAP | TSAP | NSAP | = Called address |

| | TSAP | NSAP |
| T.CONNECT.request | TSAP | NSAP |

| | NSAP' | LSAP' | Physical address | = Calling NSAP |
| N.UNIT_DATA.request | NSAP' | LSAP' | Physical address | = Calling NSAP |

| | LSAP' | Physical address |
| L.DATA.request | LSAP' | Physical address' |

| | Physical address |
| MA.DATA.request | Physical address' |

FIGURE 10.5

Address parameters:
(a) connection request; (b) data transfer.

- Physical address (PA): This is the physical address on the subnetwork identified in the SI field.
- NSAP' and LSAP': These are the address extensions for use at the appropriate interlayer interfaces.

The full NSAP addresses of both the called and the calling network entities are carried in the relevant network PDU – CONREQ (connection oriented) or DT (connectionless). Hence, to allow for the (possibly) different number of digits associated with the different network types, the called and the calling addresses in each PDU are both prefixed with an address length octet. An example can be seen in the UDB decoding example given earlier in Figure 10.4.

(**b**)

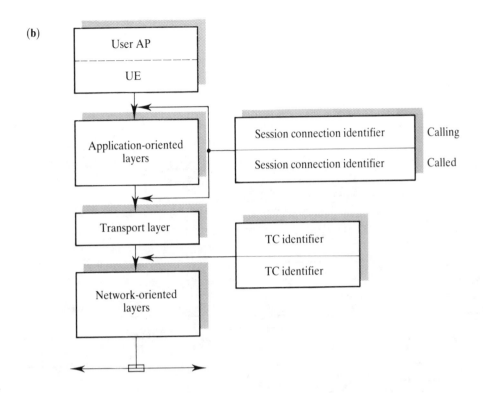

FIGURE 10.5 (cont.)

Address parameters:
(a) connection request; (b) data transfer.

10.4 IMPLEMENTATION METHODOLOGY

A basic methodology for implementing a protocol entity in the context of the seven-layer model was introduced in Chapter 6 when the OSI protocols were first discussed. However, a number of additional factors must be considered when implementing a complete communication sub-system, to allow for such issues as interlayer messages associated with service primitives and the means of passing user data between layers. As will be seen, both these factors are strongly influenced by the basic hardware and software architecture adopted; hence what follows is only intended to serve as an example of an implementation methodology.

(a)

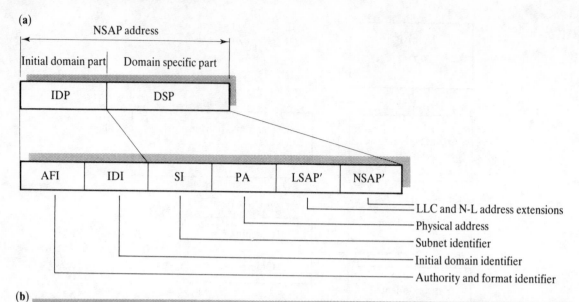

(b)

IDI Format	AFI Value		IDI Length (digits)	DSP Length (decimal digits)
	Decimal	Binary		
International PSDN – X.121	36	37	14	24
International Telex – F.69	40	41	8	30
International PSTN – E.163	42	43	12	26
International ISDN – E.164	44	45	15	23
Local	48	49	Null	38

FIGURE 10.6

NSAP addresses: (a) structure; (b) contents.

10.4.1 Overall architecture

An important issue relating to the implementation of a communication subsystem is the way it is interfaced (both in terms of hardware and software) to the host computer system. It may be concluded from the earlier descriptions of the various protocol layers in the ISO model that the processing overheads associated with their implementation are not insignificant. Hence, if just a single processor is used to perform both the communication processing functions and the normal (application) processing functions of the system, the amount of processing time available to perform the latter would be reduced considerably, especially during periods of high network activity.

The approach adopted, therefore, is to utilize a separate processing subsystem to perform most of the communication processing functions. The overall (hardware) architecture of a typical system is as shown in

Figure 10.7(a). Typically, the complete communication subsystem is implemented on a separate printed circuit board that plugs into the internal bus – interconnection mechanism – of the host system. This board contains, in addition to the local (communication) processor, an amount of memory for the protocol software, additional memory for holding protocol state information relating to each layer (local) and message buffers being passed between layers (shared), and also the circuitry that is required to perform the physical interface to the communication network. As has been mentioned, the latter may be a public WAN or an LAN, the only differences being the type of interface circuitry required and, as was described in Chapters 7 and 8, slightly different network protocol software.

Normally, the shared memory is multi-ported; that is, it may be accessed directly by the network interface unit, the local processor and, via the system bus, the host processor. In this way, all memory buffers (containing both interlayer messages and user data) are directly accessible to each device. Hence, when information is passed between the buffers (and between layers), only the address pointer to the buffer is utilized, thereby avoiding the added overheads associated with physically trans-ferring blocks of data from one layer or device (and hence part of memory) to another.

An associated software structure for use with this architecture is shown in Figure 10.7(b). It has been stressed in earlier chapters that when describing the operation of a communication subsystem structured according to the ISO Reference Model, it is essential to treat each protocol layer as an autonomous entity which provides a defined set of user services to the layer above it and, in turn, uses the services provided by the layer below it to transport the PDUs generated by the layer to a similar peer layer in a remote system. In the same way, when implementing the various protocol layers in software, it is essential to retain the same approach otherwise the benefits gained by the adoption of a layered architecture will, of course, be lost.

The communication subsystem, therefore, is implemented as a suite of task (process) modules; one per protocol entity with additional tasks for management (see later) and timer functions. Tasks communicate with each other through a set of FIFO queues or mailboxes as shown in Figure 10.8. Intertask communication is managed by the local real-time kernel which is also responsible for such functions as task scheduling and interrupt handling – for the timer task, for example, and for managing data transfer to and from the network interface unit. Communication between the subsystem and the host is through the interprocessor communication software, a copy of which is in both systems. Typically, the latter is interrupt driven to ensure a synchronized transfer of information between the two systems. Thus, whenever the host processor wishes to transfer information to the communication processor, it first writes the information into a free memory buffer associated with the application entity and then

(a)

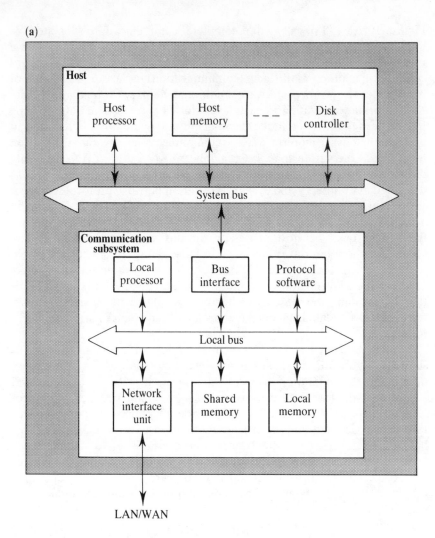

FIGURE 10.7

Overall architecture:
(a) hardware; (b) software.

generates an interrupt to the communication processor. The interrupt service routine in the latter first reads the address pointer of the buffer, determines the SASE involved and then places the pointer at the tail of the appropriate input queue to await processing. A similar procedure is followed for passing information in the reverse direction.

10.4.2 Interlayer communication

A user AP (task) gains access to the distributed information services supported by the communication subsystem through the defined set of primitives associated with its linked UE. As was described in Chapter 9,

(b)

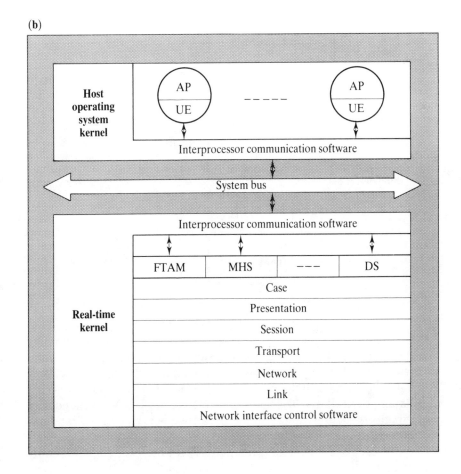

FIGURE 10.7 (cont.)

Overall architecture:
(a) hardware; (b) software.

the latter is a set of library procedures (or functions) which is linked to the user AP prior to running. Also, as was described in Section 6.7.6, inter-layer primitives and their associated parameters are passed between layers using a typed data structure known as an event control block (ECB). Since the number and type of the parameters associated with the primitives for each layer are usually different, there is a separate ECB data structure for each layer, which is used for passing all service primitives from a higher layer to that layer; that is, for all request, indication, response and confirm primitives received and issued by the layer from and to the higher layer. As as example, a typical ECB relating to the transport layer was shown earlier in Figure 6.28.

Thus, to communicate with an SASE, the UE first obtains a free

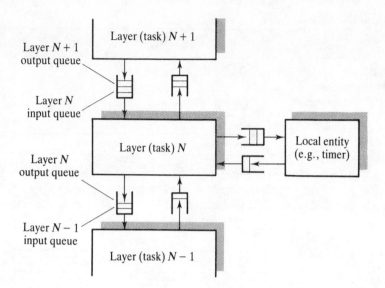

Layer N + 1
output queue

Layer N
input queue

Layer N
output queue

Layer N − 1
input queue

Layer (task) N + 1

Layer (task) N

Local entity
(e.g., timer)

Layer (task) N − 1

FIGURE 10.8

Interlayer communication
schematic.

ECB relating to it (in practice, the address pointer to a buffer in shared memory), writes the necessary parameters associated with the primitive into the ECB and then initiates the transfer of the address pointer of the ECB to the SASE using the interprocessor communication software. Any user data associated with the primitive is written into a separate buffer, the user data buffer (UDB). The address pointer of the UDB associated with the primitive is then written into the ECB together with an indication of the amount of data it contains.

On receipt of the service primitive (ECB), the selected SASE entity uses the parameters associated with the primitive, together with any protocol state information associated with the connection (association), to create the PCI for the layer. This is then added to any user data already in the UDB to form, collectively, an SASE-APDU. The SASE then obtains a free ECB associated with the presentation entity (task), writes the appropriate primitive type and parameter information into it (including the address pointer of the UDB containing the APDU and the updated length of its contents) and issues a send message request to the local real-time kernel. The latter, in turn, transfers the ECB address pointer to the input queue of the presentation task and, if it is idle (waiting for an incoming event), schedules the task to be run.

Each layer task then performs a similar function, first adding its own PCI to the UDB and then passing an appropriate primitive and associated parameters to the next lower layer using a free ECB of that layer. This is shown in diagrammatic form in Figure 10.9(a). It should be remembered that the PCI associated with each layer is in a concrete syntax comprising a string of octets. Thus, each UDB is simply an array of octets and it is the

(a)

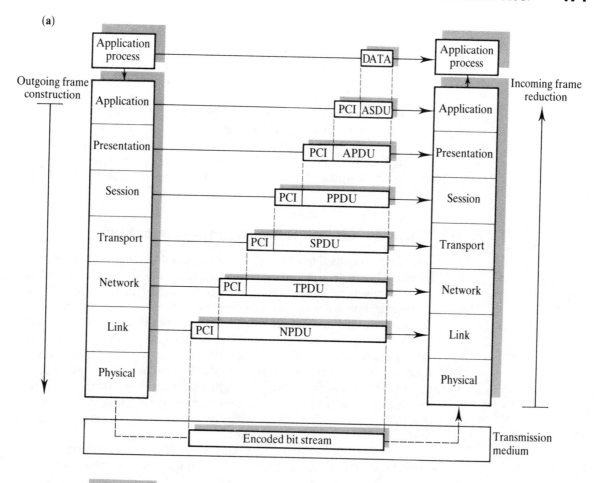

Outgoing frame construction

Incoming frame reduction

(b)

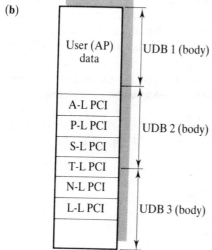

FIGURE 10.9

Layer interactions: (a) schematic; (b) UDB structure and contents.

contents of the UDB that are eventually transmitted under control of the network interface hardware and software.

Clearly, the amount of user data contained within a UDB, after it has passed through all the protocol layers, will vary from, say, a few hundred octets if only PCI is involved to, possibly, several thousand octets if, say, the contents of a file are being transferred. To allow for this, therefore, each UDB is of a fixed length and a linked-list strategy is used to handle composite dialogue units (PDUs) exceeding this length. Thus, if a UDB becomes full, a new UDB pointer is obtained, from the free list, and this is then linked to it. This is shown in a schematic form in Figure 10.9(b).

10.4.3 User element implementation

It may be concluded from the previous section that the primitives received by the UE are from two sources: those received from the user AP and those received from the interface with an SASE via the interprocessor communication software. Clearly, the primitives in each case may be of different types. For example, the primitives from the user AP may relate either to a confirmed service (that is, a request primitive that will subsequently generate a confirm primitive) or to an unconfirmed service (that is, a request primitive with no confirm). Similarly, the primitives from the SASE interface may also be of different types. For example, they may be either a confirm primitive returned in response to an earlier request primitive, an indication primitive that requires no response or an indication primitive that requires a response.

Hence, for the UE to respond to each incoming primitive in the correct way, it is necessary for the UE to retain a record of the last received primitive relating to this SASE transaction. In practice, this is best accomplished by using an event-state table similar to that defined for each protocol machine. Then, as with the implementation strategy for each protocol machine, the UE retains a state variable for each active transaction, which indicates the current status of the interface; that is, the previous primitive received. Then, on receipt of an incoming primitive (event), this is used to determine the processing to be carried out, from the event-state table.

As an example, assume that a user AP is accessing a remote file server AP through an OSIE-supporting FTAM and that the set of user primitives provided is:

- f_open (input_file, status),
- f_read (input_file, message_buffer, status),
- f_write (input_file, message_buffer, status),
- f_close (input_file, status).

input_file is the full path name (title) of the file to be manipulated; thus it includes the unique OSIE-wide name of the server system together with the name of the FTAM entity within that system and the name of the file to be operated on. status is an indication of the success or failure of the network request and, in the event of a failure, the reason for the failure. message_buffer is a pointer that indicates where the data relating to the transfer request (read or write) are to be put or found.

As has been outlined, each of these primitives has an associated library procedure, and the complete set of procedures – the FTAM UE – is linked to the user AP. A suitable event-state table for the UE is thus as shown in Figure 10.10.

It can be readily deduced from the short list of user primitives provided that each primitive results in multiple FTAM primitives. For example, the library procedure f_open generates a sequence of FTAM primitives associated with the services: F.INITIALIZE, F.SELECT and F.OPEN. Similarly, the f_read procedure generates a sequence related to the services: F.READ, F.DATA and F.TRANSER_END. Thus, the f_open procedure, after first obtaining the fully qualified address of the remote (called) FTAM entity from the directory service, creates an F.INITIALIZE.request primitive and initiates the transfer of this, together with its associated parameters, to its local FTAM entity in an FTAM ECB. Typically, as will be expanded upon in Section 10.5.2, this is accomplished using an appropriate interprocess communication primitive through the ICP software. The user AP, through the linked f_open procedure, is then suspended while waiting for an F.INITIALIZE.confirm primitive (ECB). The interface thus enters the WTINICF state.

The F.INITIALIZE.confirm primitive, together with its associated parameters, is now transferred by the local FTAM entity (in an FTAM ECB), again using an interprocess communication primitive and the ICP software. The user AP is then rescheduled at the point of suspension in the f_open procedure. The latter, as can be deduced from the event-state table, then issues an F.SELECT.request primitive, again with parameters deduced from the initial call, and enters the WTSELCF state. Similarly, on receipt of the F.SELECT.confirm primitive, it issues an F.OPEN.request. Finally, on receipt of the F.OPEN.confirm primitive, the interface enters the OPEN state and returns to the initiating user AP at the statement immediately following the f_open procedure call, the status parameter indicating the success or failure of the call.

Assuming that the f_open procedure was successful, this is typically followed by an f_read or f_write call, and again each results in a sequence of FTAM primitives. Finally, when all transfers are complete, the user AP initiates the termination of the association – and hence FTAM transaction – using the f_close procedure.

It may be deduced from the foregoing that, if a piece of software already exists with these same user primitives, then to change to an open

(a)

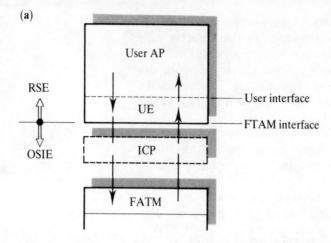

(b)

State \ Primitive	CLOSED	WTINICF	WTSELCF	WTOPNCF	OPEN	---
f_open	1					
f_read					5	
f_write						
f_close						
F_INICF		2				
F_SELCF			3			
F_OPNCF				4		
⋮						

From user interface

From FTAM interface

1: F_INIRQ,
   WTINICF

2: F_SELRQ,
   WTSELCF

3: F_OPNRQ,
   WTOPNCF

4: OPEN (return)

F_INIRQ/CF = F_INITIALIZE.request/confirm
F_SELRQ/CF = F_SELECT.request/confirm
F_OPNRQ/CF = F_OPEN.request/confirm
WTINICF   = Wait for F_INITIALIZE.confirm
WTSELCF   = Wait for F_SELECT.confirm
WTOPNCF   = Wait for F_OPEN.confirm

FIGURE 10.10

FTAM UE structure:
(a) interfaces; (b) event-state table.

system it is only necessary to change or rewrite the existing library procedures required to interface with the FTAM. It should be remembered, however, that, in addition to generating the appropriate FTAM primitives, it may be necessary to convert the file contents into or from the agreed transfer syntax. Also, the UE at the server converts the incoming FTAM primitives into those used by the particular server (file system) being used, if necessary.

10.5 SYSTEM AND LAYER MANAGEMENT

In addition to the tasks (protocol entities) associated with each layer, a complete communication subsystem has two other tasks: a timer task, which performs the necessary timeout functions associated with the various protocol entities (state machines), and a system management task which, as its name implies, is responsible for both layer and system management functions. These include such functions as the gathering of protocol error statistics and the setting of operational parameters associated with each protocol layer (entity). A schematic of a complete communication subsystem is thus as shown in Figure 10.11.

10.5.1 Timer task

As was first indicated in Chapter 6, to ensure that the incoming events associated with each protocol machine are atomic, the interface between the timer task and each of the protocol entities (tasks) using its services is through a separate intertask mailbox or queue. Since there is just a single timer task for the complete subsystem, there is normally only a single input queue associated with it. Also, as with other intertask communication, there is a single type of ECB associated with the timer task, which is then used for all communications with it.

A suitable set of user service primitives associated with the timer task are:

- TIMER.start (layer ID, timer ID, time),
- TIMER.cancel (layer ID, timer ID),
- TIMER.expired (timer ID).

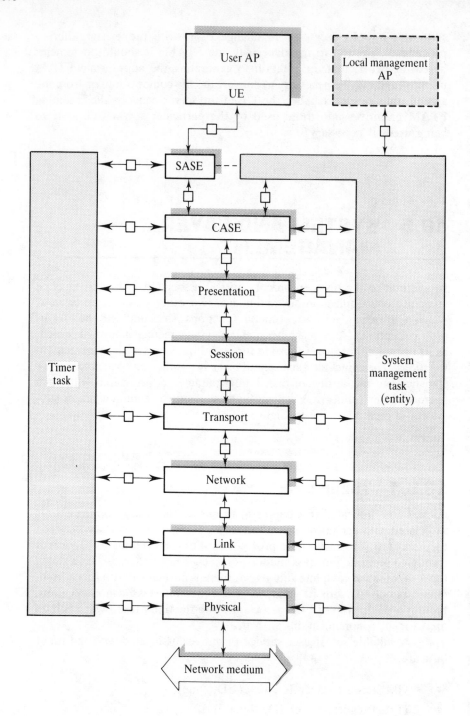

FIGURE 10.11

Complete communication
subsystem schematic.

Since there is a single input queue associated with the timer task, the two input primitives (start and cancel) each have a layer ID parameter associated with them to identify the protocol layer issuing the primitive. Also, since with each layer a number of timers may be running (active) concurrently, the timer ID parameter is used to identify which timer the primitive is associated with. Typically, the connection identifier is used for this purpose. The time parameter then indicates the time interval, in terms of system clock ticks, that must elapse before the timer task informs the appropriate protocol entity that the named timer has expired.

To initiate a timeout operation (for example, to limit the time a protocol entity will wait for a suitable response to an outgoing event), the protocol entity first obtains a free (timer) ECB and writes the layer and timer identities together with the required time interval as parameters within it. It then initiates the transfer of the ECB pointer to the timer task input queue (mailbox) by issuing a suitable intertask communication primitive – send message, for example – to the local real-time kernel. On receipt of the request, the timer task then creates an entry in a table indicating the identity of the timer and the time duration associated with it. The latter is simply a counter variable.

Normally, the timer task is interrupt driven from a system clock source. This means that a signal (the interrupt) is generated at preprogrammed time intervals, equal to the minimum clock tick time of, say, one second, and the timer task is then scheduled to run. First, it determines whether there are any ECBs in its input queue awaiting processing and, if so, these are processed. The outstanding time interval associated with any timers currently active are each decremented by one (tick). Then, if any of the timers become zero, indicating that the timeout interval for the timer has expired, a TIMER.expired primitive is generated (in an ECB) and the ECB pointer is transferred to the appropriate layer (timer) input queue using an intertask communication primitive. Thus, when the layer task is next scheduled to run, it examines not only its input queues with the layers (protocol entities) above and below it but also its input queue from the timer task. Any entries in each queue are then processed in an atomic way, including any actions resulting from a timeout occurring if the entry is from the input queue with the timer task.

If, after initiating a timer for a particular outgoing event, the protocol entity receives a suitable response (incoming event), it initiates the cancellation of the timer by passing a suitable TIMER.cancel primitive (in an ECB) to the timer task input queue, again using an intertask primitive supported by the real-time kernel. Then, when the timer task is next scheduled to run, it in turn removes the named timer from the timer table.

10.5.2 System management task

The issues of system and layer management in OSI are still evolving and hence what follows is intended only as a guide to their operation. The functions of the **system management task (SMT)** in each system are two-fold:

(1)   It is concerned with the management of its own local environment (system).

(2)   It is concerned, with other such tasks, in the management of the complete communication subnetwork to which the system is connected.

To perform the first function, it must exchange management information with the various protocol entities (tasks) within its own system using, for example, intertask queues similar to those described for the timer task. Execution of the second function necessitates the exchange of management information with a similar task (management entity) in a remote system.

Normally, there is a separate system associated with each component subnetwork of a complete OSIE which is devoted to the task of managing the subnetwork. A (human) network manager then controls the subnetwork through this system. The interaction between the network manager and the management system is through an application-level process known as the **network manager application process (NMAP)**. This, in turn, is interfaced to the SMT in the network manager system, which exchanges information with the SMTs in the other systems in that subnetwork to perform the overall management of the subnetwork. The SMT in the network management system is referred to therefore as the **manager system management entity (MSME)** and the SMT in the other systems the **agent SME (ASME)**.

Clearly, if management information is to be exchanged over the network between the MSME and the distributed community of ASMEs, a protocol must be employed. Hence, as can be seen in Figure 10.11, the ASME in each system has a number of interfaces: firstly, it has an interface with each protocol entity for the exchange of management information relating specifically to that layer and, secondly, it has an interface with the CASE entity for exchanging PDUs with a remote MSME. Also, as can be seen, in some instances there may be a local (that is, system or machine dependent) management AP used for purely local functions, such as system initialization.

A schematic diagram showing the various components associated with the management of a subnetwork is given in Figure 10.12. As can be seen in Figure 10.12(b), the NMAP is comprised of a number of functional

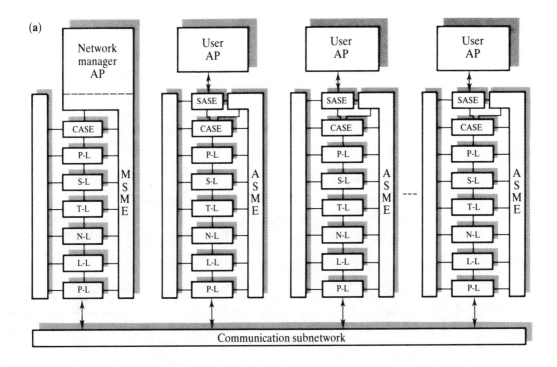

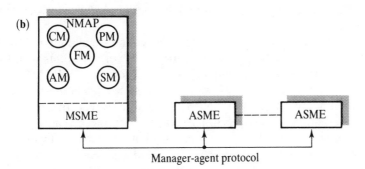

FIGURE 10.12

Network management components: (a) SMT components; (b) NMAP components.

components. These include the following:

- Configuration management (CM): This is a set of activities that collectively are concerned with monitoring and controlling the configuration of the various attached systems and their associated protocol layers.

- Performance management (PM): This is a set of activities that collectively are concerned with gathering and analyzing network performance statistics.

- Fault management (FM): This is a set of activities that collectively are concerned with detecting and, if possible, correcting faults in the network or its attached systems.

- Accounting management (AM): This is a set of activities that are concerned with the accumulation and analysis of statistics relating to the usage of various network resources.

- Security management (SM): This is concerned with controlling access to the various management operations to ensure the subnetwork is secure.

Associated with these functions is a set of actions (directives) that enable the NMAP to carry out remotely specific management operations on selected variables (pertaining to the status and statistics of the system) maintained by each layer and hence accessible through an attached systems ASME. For example, at a system level, the NMAP may wish to request an ASME to reset each layer protocol entity (machine) following a reconfiguration operation. Similarly, at a layer level, the NMAP may request a specific statistic maintained by a layer from an ASME, such as the number of abort PDUs received relating to that layer or the number of unsuccessful transmission attempts.

Clearly, the transfers relating to such actions are all initiated by the NMAP. In addition, however, the occurrence of certain events within an attached system may cause an ASME to inform the NMAP of its occurrence immediately. An example is if a statistic relating to a layer reaches a predefined threshold limit. In general, however, the bulk of the intelligence (and hence processing) associated with the management of a subnetwork is in the NMAP and only a minimum set of functions are associated with each layer, and hence the ASMEs in each system. In this way, the processing overheads in each system associated with network management are kept to a minimum.

10.5.3 Layer management

Each layer, in addition to maintaining state information (variables) relating to the current operational state of the protocol machine, maintains a set of variables relating to various operational statistics for layer management purposes. Some examples of the statistical information gathered by each layer task are as follows:

- ACSE (CASE): The number of negative A.ASSOCIATE.response primitives received; the number of ABORT APDUs received and sent.

- Presentation: The number of unsuccessful CPR (connect presentation response) PPDUs received and sent, with the reason codes; the number of unrecognized PPDUs received.

- Session: The number of RF (refuse) SPDUs received and sent; the number of AB (abort) SPDUs received and sent.

- Transport: The number of protocol errors that have occurred; the number of times a timeout expires on a transmitted TPDU; the number of TPDUs that have a bad check sum.

- Network: The number of NPDUs received and sent; the number of NPDUs discarded because of an unknown NSAP.

- LLC: The number of test LPDUs received and sent; the number of protocol errors.

- MAC: The number of collisions and retransmission attempts (CSMA/CD); the number of token pass failures (token bus).

Normally, most of the information is maintained by simple counters whose current contents may be requested by the ASME task in response to a request from the NMAP. However, if a particular event occurs in a layer, indicating a possible fault (for example, a predefined threshold limit for a variable being reached), the layer (task) may inform the ASME directly.

The ASME must also have a facility to inform a layer of specific operational parameters (characteristics) to be used, such as:

- window limit (T-L),
- timeout interval (all layers),
- routing table contents (N-L),
- maximum retransmission limit (CSMA/CD),
- target token rotation time (token bus).

As with the timer task, a set of service primitives must be defined (together with an associated ECB type and intertask queue structure) to enable these functions to be carried out in an atomic way. A typical set of primitives for the ASME layer interactions include:

- LM.GET_VALUE.request/confirm (parameter value): This is used by the ASME to obtain a statistic from a specific layer.

- LM.SET_VALUE.request/confirm (parameter ID, parameter

value): This is used by the ASME to set an operational parameter for a specific layer.

- LM.ACTION.request/confirm (action ID, action value): This is used by the ASME to, say, add one or more entries to a routing table.

- LM.EVENT.indication (layer ID, event identifier, event value): This is used by a layer entity to inform the ASME of, say, a threshold limit being reached.

10.5.4 Manager–agent protocol

As has been mentioned, a protocol is required for manager–agent (NMAP–ASME) communication, since most system management operations are carried out remotely via the network. Also, as was shown in Figure 10.11, the PDUs associated with the manager–agent protocol are exchanged in the same way as the PDUs relating to other SASEs using CASE.

The user services associated with the manager–agent protocol can be grouped into four categories and include:

- Association control: SM.INITIALIZE
  SM.TERMINATE
  SM.ABORT
- Information exchange: SM.GET_VALUE
- Control: SM.SET_VALUE
  SM.ACTION
- Event notification: SM.EVENT

Each of these service primitives has parameters associated with it. Also, some of the services are confirmed and others are unconfirmed. The association control group interacts directly with CASE and collectively provides the means whereby the manager (or, in the case of events, slave) system management protocol entity (task) can establish (and terminate) a logical connection with a remote management protocol entity.

The information exchange service is used by the MSME to request statistical data from an ASME. The control group of services are used by the MSME to initiate selected actions by an ASME; for example, to add one or more entries to the routing table associated with the network protocol entity or to, say, reset the collision counter associated with a CSMA/CD MAC sublayer. Finally, the event notification services are used by an ASME to initiate the transfer of event data to the MSME.

In general, a PDU is generated on receipt of each service primitive.

The PDUs associated with the association control group are then passed in the user data field of the corresponding ACSE service primitive whereas the PDUs associated with the information exchange, control and event notification groups are passed in the user data field of a ROSE service primitive. The latter, as was mentioned in Chapter 9, is a CASE protocol entity.

10.6 DISTRIBUTED PROCESSING

The various SASE protocol entities described in Chapter 9 provide the means whereby user APs may provide or gain access to a range of (open) distributed information processing services. As was indicated, for many distributed processing tasks, the use of a single SASE, together with DS and the ACSE component of CASE, is sufficient to provide the relevant service. For example, FTAM may be used to provide and gain access to a central (networked) file system whereby a number of client APs running on, say, a distributed community of advanced workstations may use the central file system to archive files. Clearly, in such an application, the client APs are effectively using the central file system as an extension of their own system and hence the files on the central system are private to a particular user (AP).

In a more sophisticated application of FTAM, however, the central file system may be used to hold a set of (shared) files which all users require to access and modify concurrently. For example, in an airline reservation system, the central file system may be used to hold information relating to the availability of seats on the scheduled flights of an airline, and in such a system all the client APs (handling booking enquiries at local or remote sites) will require to access and modify the contents of files concurrently. An important issue in such applications, therefore, is controlling access to the central file system or, more generally, the central resource, to ensure that the file contents are always consistent; that is, a client AP cannot access an item of data that is concurrently being processed, and hence possibly modified, by another AP.

Another related problem in some applications is that of error control. For example, assume that a banking system holds two copies of each customer's account: one at a local branch, say, and the other at a central site. Clearly, it is essential that both copies remain consistent; that is, if certain operations are performed on one copy, then exactly the same operations must be performed on the other. This is known as **multiple copy update**. Thus, if during a transaction a communication (or other) failure occurs, then it is necessary for both systems to recover to their original (consistent) state before a new attempt at updating the account takes place. Many other examples that demand control of access to shared resources, or concurrency control, coupled with error recovery can be identified in other application environments.

Since this is a common requirement in many areas of distributed information processing, the CASE part of the application layer has a protocol entity specifically designed for this purpose. It is known as the **commitment, concurrency and recovery (CCR)** service and a description of its function and operation will now be presented.

10.6.1 CCR

CCR is a component of CASE whose services are available to APs either directly or as pass-through services of a related SASE. The user services of JTM, for example, include additional primitives that are mapped directly into CCR primitives of the same name.

CCR is based on the concept of an atomic action with a two-phase commit protocol and rollback error recovery. Essentially, an **atomic action** is a sequence of operations that are performed by two or more co-operating APs such that:

- the sequence of operations is carried out without interference from an AP that is not part of the atomic action;
- the operations being carried out by each AP involved in the atomic action are either all completed successfully or are all terminated and any data modified during the preceding operations restored to the state they had prior to the commencement of the atomic action.

The AP initiating an atomic action is referred to as the *master* or *superior*, since it directly or indirectly controls the entire activity associated with the atomic action. Similarly, all other APs involved in the atomic action are known as *slaves* or *subordinates*, since they are all controlled (using the CCR protocol) by the single master who initiated the atomic action.

All data affected by the operations within an atomic action are known as **bound data**. The values of all bound data at the commencement of an atomic action are known as their *initial state* and their values after the atomic action their *final state*. After completion of an atomic action, the bound data associated with it is either *committed* to its final state, if all operations have been carried out successfully, or is *recovered* to its initial state, if one or more of the operations fail. This is accomplished using a form of **handshake procedure**: after all the operations associated with an atomic action have been carried out, the superior first requests all subordinates if they have successfully completed their processing; hence they are said to be 'prepared to commit'. Then, if all subordinates involved in the atomic action respond positively, the order to commit all bound data to its final state is given. Alternatively, if one or more of the subordinates responds negatively (or fails to respond), then the order to recover all bound data to its initial state is given. The various terms are shown in diagrammatic form in Figure 10.13.

It should be stressed that the nature of the atomic action being controlled is determined by the APs, and associated SASEs, which manipulate the bound data involved, and that the CCR protocol provides only the means whereby an AP may initiate and control the atomic action. That is, it is a purely local matter for the APs involved in the atomic action to take steps to ensure that the rules of an atomic action are adhered to. Thus, once an AP has indicated its willingness to take part in an atomic action, then it is a local matter for the AP to ensure that another AP not involved in this atomic action is not allowed to access or manipulate any of the bound data associated with the atomic action. Normally, this is accomplished using a form of **locking mechanism** such as a **semaphore**. The latter is a form of token since, once a semaphore has been set, then all other accesses to the data controlled by the semaphore is excluded until the semaphore has been reset. This is similar to the various forms of mutual exclusion mechanisms associated with concurrent programming languages such as Modula and Ada.

User services

The service primitives provided with CCR have been designed so that the atomic action being controlled by it is subjected to the following constraints:

- After the order to commit has been given by a superior, then the bound data held by the superior and the subordinate(s) will be in its final (permanent) state, and no recovery capability is supported to allow any data to be returned to its initial (or an intermediate) state.

- A superior may order rollback to the initial state at any time prior to ordering commitment.

- A superior may not order a subordinate to commit unless it has received an offer to commit from it.

- Once a subordinate has returned an offer to commit to the superior, it may not then refuse an order to commit.

- Prior to returning an offer to commit, a subordinate may abort the atomic action (and hence return all bound data to its initial state) at any time.

- The superior may order rollback if any of the subordinates refuse the offer to commit.

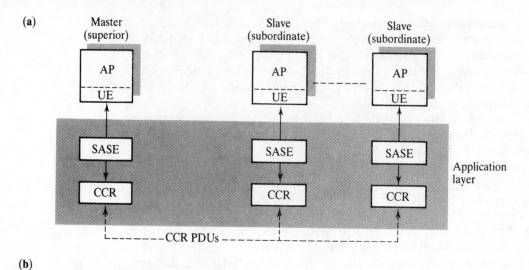

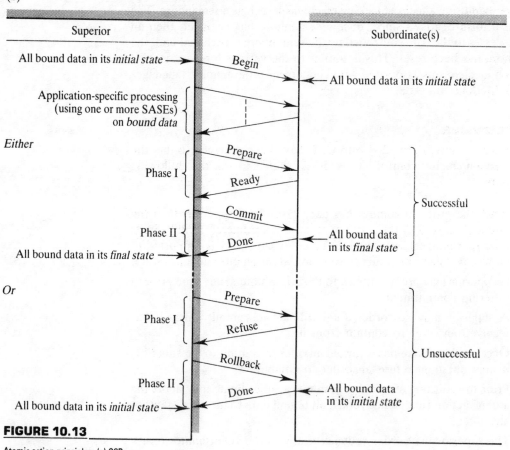

FIGURE 10.13

Atomic action principles: (a) CCR
schematic; (b) two-phase
commit sequence.

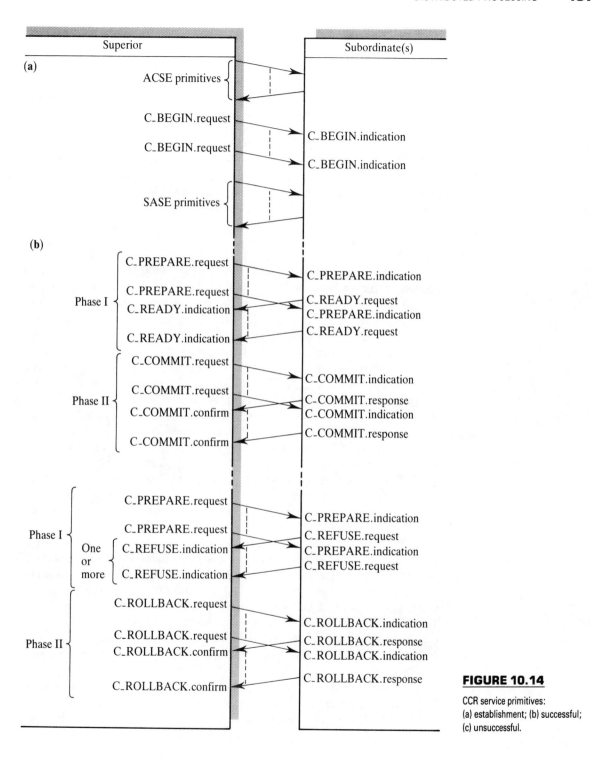

FIGURE 10.14

CCR service primitives:
(a) establishment; (b) successful;
(c) unsuccessful.

The service primitives associated with CCR are shown in the time sequence diagram of Figure 10.14. As can be seen, there can be more than one subordinate involved in an atomic action and, before an atomic action may be initiated, there must already be an association between the superior AP (and hence SASE) and each of the subordinate APs. Normally, these are established using the ACSE component of CASE. An atomic action is then started by the superior AP, informing each of the subordinates using the C_BEGIN service. Thus, on receipt of the C_BEGIN.indication primitive, each subordinate must create a new instance (working copy) of all the bound data values to be involved – for example, to read a copy of a file from disk – and initiate the locking mechanism being used. In practice, the C_BEGIN primitives have the effect of establishing a session layer major synchronization point for this association.

The application-specific processing associated with the atomic action, using SASE primitives, is then carried out. Figure 10.14 shows the two possible termination phases. In the first, all subordinates return a positive offer to commit, using the C_READY service, while in the second, one or more of the subordinates return a negative reply using the C_REFUSE service. In practice, the C_PREPARE service is an optional service and, if it is not used, the subordinate(s) indicate their readiness (or otherwise) to commit, with a C_READY or C_REFUSE, immediately after the relevant application processing has finished. In addition, there is a confirmed service, the C_RESTART service, which may be used by either a superior or a subordinate if it becomes necessary to return all bound data involved in an atomic action to an earlier known state. It can only be used by a subordinate, however, provided it has not signalled its readiness to commit. Typically, it is used by a superior if a response from a subordinate times out, indicating a possible application or communication failure.

Some of the occasions when the RESTART service may be used are best illustrated by considering several possible failures that may occur during an atomic action. Some examples are shown in the time sequence diagrams in Figure 10.15. Although the failure in the examples relates to the COMMIT service, it may equally arise with a failure with the ROLLBACK service. It can be deduced from these examples, however, that after a failure has occurred, the precise state of a subordinate may not be known; for example, in Figure 10.15(a), did the communication failure occur before the C_COMMIT request was received or after? The RESTART service is provided to allow a superior, for whatever reason, to return the state of an atomic action to an earlier known state. It is a confirmed service and may be used at any time, provided the atomic action is intact.

A superior determines the current state of a subordinate by issuing a C_RESTART.request primitive with a defined **resumption point** as a parameter. The resumption point in the request (and hence indication)

(a)

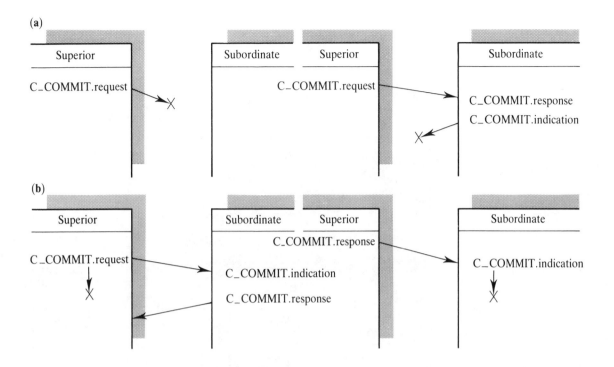

(b)

FIGURE 10.15

Some example failures:
(a) communications;
(b) applications.

primitive is one of the following:

- ACTION: This is used to request the subordinate to restart the atomic action at the beginning.
- COMMIT: This is used to request the subordinate to restart the atomic action after the last COMMIT point.
- ROLLBACK: This is used to request the subordinate to restart the atomic action after the last ROLLBACK point.

Similarly, the resumption point in the response (and hence confirmation) primitive is one of the following:

- DONE: This indicates that the subordinate has in fact done the last commit or rollback request.
- REFUSE: This indicates that the subordinate has not done the last commit request and hence the superior should issue a rollback request.
- ACTION: This indicates that the superior should restart the atomic action from the beginning.

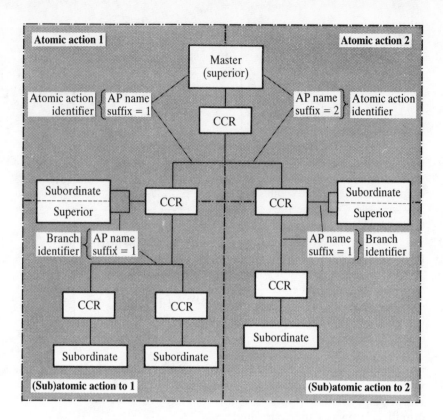

FIGURE 10.16

Example CCR atomic action tree.

- RETRY-LATER: This indicates that the subordinate cannot pro-
  ceed with a restart at this time and the superior should retry at a
  later time.

When an order to commit is received (C_COMMIT.indication), it is
necessary for the subordinate(s) to update the bound data from its initial to
its final state; that is, with the contents of the current working copy.
Typically, this involves writing the latter to disk; hence a check is often
carried out to ensure the final write operation is successful before returning
a positive C_COMMIT.response. The data are then said to be *secure* or
stable. One way of achieving this is first to write two copies of the data to
disk and then to read and compare them; only if the two copies are equal is
the data said to be secure.

Parameters are associated with the various CCR primitives. For
example, the parameters associated with the two C_BEGIN primitives
include:

- Atomic action identifier: This includes the name (title) of the master

AP and a suffix to allow for the possibility of more than one atomic action being in progress concurrently.

• Atomic action timer: This (if present) indicates the time interval the master waits before issuing a rollback request.

It is also possible with the CCR protocol for a subordinate of one atomic action to act as a superior for another atomic action, thus creating a form of tree structure. A further parameter, branch identifier, is then used to identify a specific branch in the hierarchy, and hence atomic action, in relation to the atomic action identifier assigned by the (single) master. The branch identifier is the name of the superior, for a particular (sub)atomic action in the tree, together with a branch suffix. An example of a typical CCR tree is shown in Figure 10.16.

When creating atomic action trees of the type shown, care must be taken to avoid the possibility of **deadlock** occurring. This occurs when an AP forms an atomic action with several other APs and makes a request to one of them. If, however, it is waiting for a response from another AP that cannot respond because it in turn is waiting for a response from an AP that itself is locked into the first atomic action, then a deadlock has occurred. A simple example is as follows.

Three APs (A, B and C) are involved in a particular distributed information processing task. First assume that A creates an atomic action with B and C as subordinates and requests data from B. Before B can respond to a request from A, however, assume that B must first form an atomic action with C to request data from it. The system is now deadlocked since A is waiting on B and B is waiting on C, whose resources are locked (bound) to A. Although it will not overcome the deadlock, the timer parameter associated with an atomic action is useful in such circumstances since it will ensure that an AP does not wait indefinitely for a response from another AP.

10.6.2 User primitives

As was mentioned in Chapter 9, although the service primitives and associated parameters for use with the various SASE protocol entities are in a well-defined (abstract syntax) form, the actual primitives (and associated parameters) provided to a user AP to access (or manage) a particular distributed information service may be quite different. In general, the service primitives provided to the user are much simpler so that it is the function of the linked UE to convert between those used by the user (in the RSE) and those defined for use with a particular SASE in the OSIE.

Clearly, therefore, the primitives provided to user APs vary for different SASEs and for different implementations. In general, however, the primitives provided to a client AP are of three types:

- Send message (SM),
- Send-message-with-acknowledge (SMA),
- Send-message-with-reply (SMR).

Each of these has defined parameters associated with it to enable the linked UE to create the corresponding SASE primitive(s). Also, each primitive has a status parameter to enable the UE to indicate to the AP the success or failure of the request and, if the latter, the reason for the failure. Normally, since each primitive involves communication with the communication (peripheral) subsystem, the user AP is suspended when the primitive is executed by the host operating system, the three alternatives indicating when the AP is rescheduled to run.

With a send message primitive, the user AP is rescheduled to run immediately a status message relating to the request is returned by the communication subsystem. This indicates either that the message has been sent successfully or that it was unable to send the message for the reason indicated. This implies that with a basic send message there is no indication that the intended recipient received the message. Normally, therefore, the send message is used with the various unconfirmed services associated with an SASE over a previously established association.

With the send-message-with-acknowledge, the user AP is rescheduled only when the message has been passed to the specified remote AP and a suitable acknowledgement of correct delivery received. Normally, therefore, it is used when the user primitive relates directly to an SASE confirmed service.

With the send-message-with-reply, the user AP is rescheduled only when the message has been delivered to the specified AP and the latter has returned a reply message back to the sending AP. Normally, therefore, it is used when the user primitive embraces a number of SASE primitives. Furthermore, the AP is rescheduled only when the reply associated with the send message is received. Because the parameters associated with this primitive may be used to pass data in both directions, it is also known as a **remote procedure call (RPC)**.

In general, the primitives associated with a server (responder) AP are of three types:

- Receive message (RM),
- Receive any (RA),
- Receive-message-with-reply (RMR).

Again, each of these has defined parameters associated with it to enable

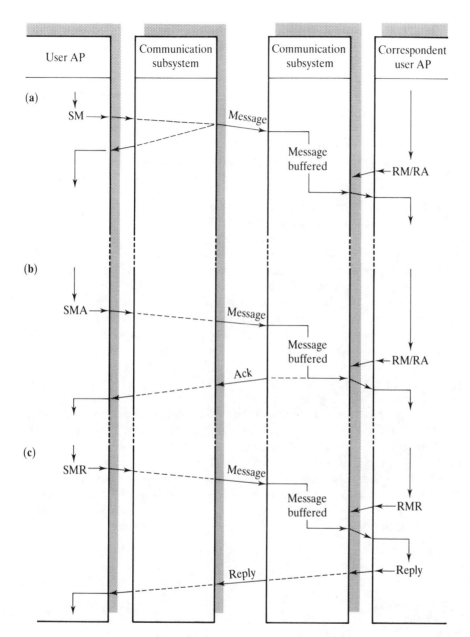

FIGURE 10.17

Interprocess communication primitives: (a) send message; (b) send-message-with-acknowledge; (c) send-message-with-reply.

the AP executing the call to pass information to the UE and also for the UE to return a received message (address pointer).

With the receive message, the issuing AP specifies a specific AP to which the primitive relates. Then, when the primitive is executed, the AP is either suspended until a message is received from the specified AP or, if one is already waiting, it is rescheduled to run immediately. Normally, this is associated with an unconfirmed or a confirmed service associated with a specific SASE after an association has been established.

The receive any primitive is similar to the basic receive message primitive except that with the former, the AP does not specify a specific AP; rather, it is prepared to accept a message from any AP. Normally, therefore, this is used by a server AP when it is prepared to establish an association with a new client AP. After the primitive is executed, the AP is either suspended until a message arrives or it is rescheduled to run immediately if a message is already waiting. With both primitives it is sometimes possible to specify a *condition* or *guard* with the primitive to indicate certain conditions that must be met.

The receive-message-with-reply is used with the send-message-with-reply to achieve bidirectional communication between two APs – RPC. Thus, after the primitive has been executed (and assuming a message is waiting), the AP is rescheduled. However, no response is returned to the source until a reply primitive is executed. The three alternative sequences are shown in the time sequence diagram of Figure 10.17.

It may be concluded from the foregoing that some form of message buffering is needed between the two communicating processes. Normally, as was described earlier, the communication subsystem has a quantity of memory (RAM) that is directly addressable by both the host processor and the communication processor, and this is used for all communications between the two. It is used, therefore, both for control messages (ECBs) and for actual data (UDBs). Clearly, the amount of memory is limited (bounded) and hence it is usual when first configuring the communication subsystem to specify the maximum number of concurrent sessions (associations) that should be allowed. Then, should this limit be reached, an AP may be suspended waiting for an association to be established due to lack of memory resources. Once an association is established, however, there is normally sufficient memory to handle all transactions involved in the association with minimal delays waiting for memory.

CHAPTER SUMMARY

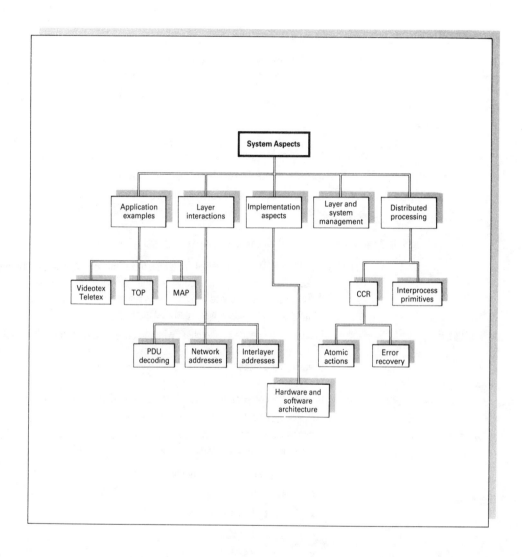

EXERCISES

10.1 (a) Produce a sketch of a typical MAP network including a token bus backbone, a number of carrierband subnetworks and a gateway to a WAN. Explain the function and operation of these various components.

(b) List the protocols associated with a MAP network and identify whether they operate in a connectionless or a connection-oriented mode.

(c) Explain the role of an EPA subnetwork in relation to MAP and list the protocols associated with such subnetworks.

10.2 (a) Produce a sketch of a typical TOP network including a CSMA/CD backbone, a number of different subnetworks and an internetwork gateway. Explain the principle of operation of each component identified.

(b) List the protocols associated with a TOP network and identify whether they operate in a connectionless or a connection-oriented mode.

10.3 Assume a client AP is communicating with a server AP using FTAM.

(a) List the service primitives that are generated at the various interlayer interfaces to establish an association between the two APs in response to an F_ INITIALIZE.request service primitive being issued by the client AP. Assume that a transport connection is not already established.

(b) Produce a sequence of sketches, with the seven layers of the ISO Reference Model including FTAM and ACSE, to show the sequence the primitives identified in (a) are issued.

10.4 (a) Identify the component subaddresses of the address parameters associated with each service primitive used in Exercise 10.4.

(b) With respect to the address used at the interface to the network layer, explain the meaning of the following:

- authority and format identifier,
- initial domain identifier,
- subnet identifier,
- physical address,
- LLC and NL address extensions.

Hence give an example of a typical network layer address of a system that is connected to an LAN with an internetwork gateway to the international PSDN. Assume that the gateway supports three separate subnetworks.

10.5 (a) Produce a sketch showing the major hardware components making up a communication subsystem (board) and show how the subsystem is interfaced to the host computer system.

(b) Describe a typical software structure associated with the hardware configuration produced in (a) and explain its operation. Include in the description how the host and the communication subsystem communicate with one another.

10.6 (a) Produce a sketch that shows the timer task in relation to the other protocol tasks, as used in a communication subsystem. Describe the role of the timer task and list a typical set of service primitives associated with it.

(b) Explain how the various tasks associated with each protocol entity operate in an atomic way in relation to the timer task.

10.7 With the aid of a sketch, explain the meaning of the following terms associated with network management:

- manager system management entity,
- agent system management entity,
- network manager process.

10.8 With the aid of a sketch, explain the principle of operation of a two-phase commit protocol with error recovery. Include in the description the meaning of the following terms:

- master (superior) and slave (subordinate),
- bound and secure data,
- initial and final state,
- two-phase commit sequence,
- rollback recovery sequence.

10.9 (a) Produce a sketch showing the position of the CCR entity in relation to the other protocol entities in the seven-layer ISO Reference Model and list the user service primitives associated with it.

(b) Assume an AP wishes to establish an atomic action involving two subordinate APs. Derive a time sequence diagram showing the sequence of the CCR service primitives associated with a successful and an unsuccessful atomic action.

10.10 Explain the meaning of the following interprocess communication primitives:

- send message,
- send-message-with-acknowledge,
- send-message-with-reply,
- receive message,
- receive any,
- receive-message-with-reply.

APPENDIX A

FORWARD ERROR CONTROL

A1.1 INTRODUCTION

With an automatic repeat request (ARQ) error control scheme, additional check digits are appended to each transmitted message (frame) to enable the receiver to detect when an error is present in a received message, assuming certain types of error. If an error is detected, additional control procedures are then used to request another copy of the message to be sent. With forward error control (FEC), however, sufficient additional check digits are added to each transmitted message to enable the receiver not only to detect the presence of one or more errors in a received message but also to locate the position of the error(s). Furthermore, since the message is in a binary form, correction is achieved simply by inverting the identified erroneous bit(s).

In practice, the number of additional check digits required to achieve error correction is much larger than that needed for just error detection. In most applications involving terrestrial (land-based) links, therefore, ARQ methods similar to those described in Chapter 4 are more efficient than FEC methods, and hence are the most frequently used. Such methods rely, of course, on a return path for acknowledgement purposes but, in certain applications, it may be that a return path is simply not available or the round-trip delay associated with it is very long compared with the data transmission rate of the link. For example, it is often the case that only a unidirectional link is utilized when transmitting information back from a space probe. Similarly, with many satellite links, the propagation delay may be such that several hundred messages may be transmitted by the sending station before a message, and hence an acknowledgement, is received in the reverse direction. In such applications, therefore, FEC methods are often utilized, normally in conjunction with ARQ methods, to reduce the number of retransmissions. The aim of this appendix is to give the reader an introduction to the techniques most widely used with FEC methods.

A1.2 HAMMING SINGLE-BIT CODE

In practice, this type of FEC method has only limited usefulness for data transmission purposes. Nevertheless, it will be briefly described to give an introduction, firstly, to the subject and, secondly, to some of the terms associated with coding theory. Clearly, a comprehensive description of the subject of coding theory is beyond the scope of this book and hence the aim here is simply to give the reader a brief introduction to the subject. For those who have an interest in coding theory and would like to gain a more extensive coverage, the references at the end of the book should be consulted.

The term used in coding theory to describe the combined message unit, comprising the useful data bits and the additional check bits, is **codeword**. The minimum number of bit positions in which two valid codewords differ is known as the **Hamming distance** of the code. As an example, consider a coding scheme that has seven data bits and a single parity bit per codeword. Assuming even parity is being used, consecutive codewords in this scheme will be:

```
0000000  0
0000001  1
0000010  1
0000011  0
```

It can be deduced from this list that such a scheme has a Hamming distance of 2, as each valid codeword differs in at least two bit positions. This means that it will not detect two-bit errors since the resulting (corrupted) bit pattern will be a different but valid codeword. It will, however, detect all single-bit errors since, if a single bit in a codeword is corrupted, an invalid codeword will result.

In general, the error-detecting and error-correcting properties of a coding scheme are both related to its Hamming distance. It can be shown that to detect n errors, a coding scheme with a Hamming distance of $n + 1$ must be used, while to correct for n errors a code with a Hamming distance of $2n + 1$ must be used.

The simplest error-correcting coding scheme is the Hamming single-bit code. Such a code not only detects when a single-bit error is present in a received codeword but also the position of the error. The corrected codeword is then derived by inverting the identified erroneous bit. This type of code is known as a **block code**, since the original message to be transmitted is treated as a single block (frame) during the encoding and subsequent decoding processes. In general, with a block code, each block of k source digits is encoded to produce an n-digit block (n greater than k) of output digits. The encoder is then said to produce an (n, k)

code. The ratio k/n is known as the **code rate** or **code efficiency** while the difference $1 - k/n$ is known as the **redundancy**.

To illustrate this, consider a Hamming code to detect and correct for single-bit errors assuming each codeword contains a seven-bit data field – an ASCII character, for example. Such a coding scheme requires four check bits since, with this scheme, the check bits occupy all bit positions that are powers of 2. Such a code is thus known as an (11, 7) block code with a rate of 7/11 and a redundancy of $1 - 7/11$. For example, the bit positions of the value 1001101 are:

```
11  10  9  8  7  6  5  4  3  2  1
 1   0  0  x  1  1  0  x  1  x  x
```

The four bit positions marked with x are used for the check bits, which are derived as follows. The four-bit binary numbers corresponding to those bit positions having a binary 1 are added together using modulo 2 arithmetic and the four check bits are then the four-bit sum:

$$
\begin{aligned}
11 &= 1\ 0\ 1\ 1 \\
7 &= 0\ 1\ 1\ 1 \\
6 &= 0\ 1\ 1\ 0 \\
3 &= \underline{0\ 0\ 1\ 1} \\
&= \underline{1\ 0\ 0\ 1}
\end{aligned}
$$

The transmitted codeword is thus:

```
11  10  9  8  7  6  5  4  3  2  1
 1   0  0 [1] 1  1  0 [0] 1 [0][1]
```

Similarly, at the receiver, the four-bit binary numbers corresponding to those bit positions having a binary 1, including the check bits, are again added together and, if no errors have occurred, the modulo 2 sum should be zero:

$$
\begin{aligned}
11 &= 1\ 0\ 1\ 1 \\
8 &= 1\ 0\ 0\ 0 \\
7 &= 0\ 1\ 1\ 1 \\
6 &= 0\ 1\ 1\ 0 \\
3 &= 0\ 0\ 1\ 1 \\
1 &= \underline{0\ 0\ 0\ 1} \\
& \quad\ \underline{0\ 0\ 0\ 0}
\end{aligned}
$$

Now consider a single-bit error; say bit 11 is corrupted from 1 to 0.

The new modulo 2 sum would now be:

$$
\begin{array}{r}
8 = 1\ 0\ 0\ 0 \\
7 = 0\ 1\ 1\ 1 \\
6 = 0\ 1\ 1\ 0 \\
3 = 0\ 0\ 1\ 1 \\
1 = \underline{0\ 0\ 0\ 1} \\
\underline{1\ 0\ 1\ 1}
\end{array}
$$

Firstly, the sum is non-zero, which indicates an error, and secondly the modulo 2 sum, equivalent to decimal 11, indicates that bit 11 is the erroneous bit. The latter would therefore be inverted to obtain the corrected codeword and hence data bits.

It can also be shown that if two bit errors occur, the modulo 2 sum will be non-zero, thus indicating an error, but the positions of the errors cannot be determined from the sum. The Hamming single-bit code can thus correct for single-bit errors and detect two-bit errors but other multiple-bit errors cannot be detected.

As was mentioned in Chapter 2, the main types of error occurring in many data communication networks are error bursts rather than, say, isolated single- or double-bit errors. Hence, although the Hamming coding scheme in its basic form would appear to be inappropriate for use with such networks, a simple technique is often used to extend the application of such a scheme.

Consider, for example, a requirement to transmit a block of data, comprising a string of, say, eight ASCII characters, over a simplex channel that has a high probability of an error burst (of, say, seven bits) occurring. The approach in such a case would be for the controlling device to first convert each ASCII character into its 11-bit codeword form, to give a block of eight 11-bit codewords. Then, instead of transmitting each codeword separately, the controlling device would transmit the contents of the block of codewords a column at a time. Thus the eight, say, most significant bits would be transmitted first, then the eight next most significant bits and so on, finishing with the eight least significant bits. The controlling device at the receiver then performs the reverse operation, reassembling the transmitted block in memory, prior to performing the detection and, if necessary, correction operation on each codeword.

The effect of this approach is, firstly, that a standard USRT device can be used as the transmission interface circuit and, secondly, and more importantly, that if an error burst of up to seven bits does occur, it will affect only a single bit in each codeword rather than a string of bits in one or two codewords. This means that, assuming just a single error burst in the 88 bits transmitted, the receiver can determine a correct copy of the transmitted block of characters.

Although the approach just outlined provides a way of extending the usefulness of this type of encoding scheme, Hamming codes are in general used mainly in applications that have isolated single-bit errors; an example is in error-correcting semiconductor memory systems. The preferred method of achieving FEC in data communication systems is based on **convolutional codes** and hence an introduction to this type of encoding process will now be presented.

A1.3   CONVOLUTIONAL CODES

Block codes are *memoryless* codes as each output codeword depends only on the current k-bit message block being encoded. In contrast, with a convolutional code, the continuous stream of source bits is operated upon to produce a continuous stream of output (encoded) bits. Because of the nature of the encoding process, the sequence of source bits is said to be convolved (by applying a specific binary operation on them) to produce the output bit sequence. Also, each bit in the output sequence is dependent not only on the current bit being encoded but also on the previous sequence of source bits, thus implying some form of memory. In practice, as will be seen, this takes the form of a shift register of a finite length, known as the **constraint length**, and the convolution (binary) operation is performed using one or more modulo 2 adders (exclusive-OR gates).

Encoding

An example of a convolutional encoder is shown in Figure A1.1(a). With this encoder, the three-bit shift register provides the memory and the two modulo 2 adders the convolution operation. For each bit in the input sequence, two bits are output, one from each of the two modulo 2 adders. The encoder shown is thus known as a rate 1/2 (k/n) convolutional encoder with a constraint length of 3.

Because of the memory associated with a convolutional encoder, it is necessary to have a convenient means of determining the specific output bit sequence generated for a given input sequence. There are three techniques that may be used to achieve this, each based on a form of diagrammatic representation: a tree diagram, a state diagram and a trellis diagram. In practice, the latter is the most frequently used method because it is the most useful one for demonstrating the decoding operation; hence, the discussion here will be restricted to this method.

As an example, Figure A1.1(b) shows the trellis diagram for the encoder shown in Figure A1.1(a). The branching points in the trellis are known as nodes and the trellis shows the two possible branches at each node; the upper of the two branches corresponds to a 0 input bit and the

(a)

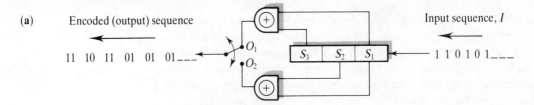

Encoded (output) sequence

$\longleftarrow$

11 10 11 01 01 01 _ _ _ $\longleftarrow$

O_1

O_2

S_3 | S_2 | S_1 $\longleftarrow$ 1 1 0 1 0 1 _ _ _

Input sequence, I $\longleftarrow$

Input sequence I	Shift register contents S_1		S_2		S_3	Output sequence O_1	O_2
1	1		0		0	1	1
1	1		1		0	1	0
0	0		1		1	1	1
1	1		0		1	0	1
0	0		1		0	0	1
1	1		0		1	0	1

(b)

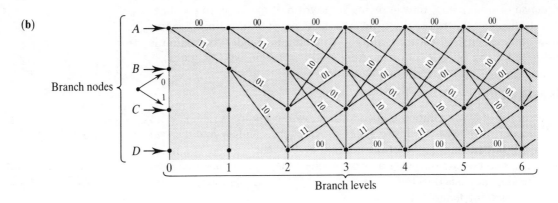

Branch nodes

A

B

C

D

0

1

Branch levels

(c)

Input sequence: 1   1   0   1   0   1
Encoded sequence: 11   10   11   01   01   01

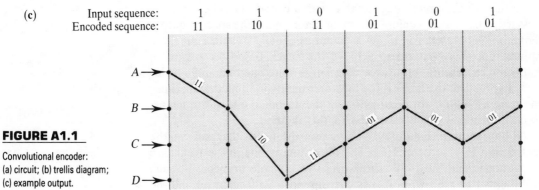

A

B

C

D

FIGURE A1.1

Convolutional encoder:
(a) circuit; (b) trellis diagram;
(c) example output.

lower branch a 1 bit. The pair of output bits corresponding to the two possible branches at each node are shown by the side of each branch line. Thus, for a particular input sequence, a specific path through the trellis results. As an example, Figure 1.1(c) shows the path through the trellis, and hence the output sequence, corresponding to the input sequence 110101 ... .

Initially, the shift register is assumed to be cleared; that is, it is set to all 0s. After the first bit in the input sequence has been shifted (entered) into the shift register, its contents are 001. The outputs from the two modulo 2 adders are then $0 + 1 = 1$ (adder 1) and $0 + 1 = 1$ (adder 2). Thus, the first two output bits are 11 and these are output before the next input bit is entered into the shift register. Since the input bit was a 1, the lower branch path on the trellis diagram is followed and the output is 11, as derived.

After the second input bit has been entered, the shift register contains 011. The two adder outputs are $0 + 1 = 1$ (adder 1) and $1 + 1 = 0$ (adder 2). Thus, the two output bits are 10 and again these are output before the next input bit is processed. Again, since the input bit was a 1, the lower branch on the trellis diagram is followed and the output is 10, as derived. Continuing, the third input bit makes the shift register contents 110 and hence the two output bits are 11; $1 + 0 = 1$ (adder 1) and $1 + 0 = 1$ (adder 2). Also, since the input bit was a 0, the upper branch path on the trellis diagram is followed. This process then continues.

A number of observations may be made by considering the trellis diagram in Figure A1.1(b). Firstly, after the first two input bits, the trellis is repetitive and the encoder always branches back to one of the four nodes labelled A, B, C and D. Secondly, and less obvious, once at one of these nodes the output for a specific succeeding input sequence is always the same and independent of the branch level; that is, once the encoder reaches a particular node (say A), irrespective of the start point in the trellis, the same output is always generated for the same input sequence. It is for this reason that the four nodes are also known as the four states of the encoder. In general, the number of states associated with an encoder is given by $2^{k(K-1)}$ where K is the constraint length.

Decoding

The aim of the decoder is to determine the *most likely* output sequence, given a received bit stream (that may have errors) and knowledge of the encoder used at the source. The decoding procedure is equivalent to comparing the received sequence with all the possible sequences that may be obtained with the respective encoder and then selecting the sequence that is closest to the received sequence. As was mentioned earlier, the Hamming distance between two codewords is the number of bits that differ between them. Therefore, when selecting the sequence that is closest to the received sequence, the Hamming distance between the received sequence and each of the possible sequences is computed, and the one with the least distance is selected. Clearly, in the limit, this would necessitate the complete received sequence being compared with all the possible sequences, and hence paths through the trellis. This is impractical in most cases and hence a compromise must be made.

Essentially, a running count is maintained of the distance between the actual received sequence and each possible sequence but, at each node in the trellis, only a single path is retained. There are always two paths merging at each node and the path selected is the one with the minimum Hamming distance, the other being simply terminated. The retained paths are known as **survivor paths** and the final path selected is then the one with a continuous path through the trellis with a minimum aggregate Hamming distance. This procedure is known as the **Viterbi algorithm**. The decoder, which aims to find the most likely path corresponding to the received sequence, is known as a **maximum-likelihood decoder**. The Viterbi algorithm will now be described by means of an example.

EXAMPLE

Assume that a message sequence of 1001110... is to be sent using the encoder shown in Figure A1.1(a). From the trellis diagram for this encoder, it can be deduced that this will yield a transmitted (output) sequence of:

    11 01 10 11 10 00 11...

Now assume a burst error occurs so that two bits of this encoded sequence are corrupted during transmission. The received sequence is then:

    11 01 00 11 11 00 11...
            ↑   ↑

Use the Veterbi algorithm to determine from this the most likely transmitted sequence.

The various steps associated with the encoding and decoding procedures are shown in Figure A1.2. Figure A1.2(a) shows the path through the trellis corresponding to the original output from the encoder and Figure A1.2(b) shows how the survivor paths are chosen. The number shown by each path merging at a node in Figure A1.2(b) is the accumulated Hamming distance between the path followed to get to that node and the actual received sequence.

If the path chosen is that starting at the route node (branch level 0), the received sequence is 11 and the Hamming distances for the two paths are 2 for path 00 and 0 for path 11. These two distance values are then added to the paths emanating from these nodes. Thus, at branch level 1, the received sequence is 01 and the two paths from node A have Hamming distances of 1 for path 00 and 1 for path 11. The accumulated distances are

(a)

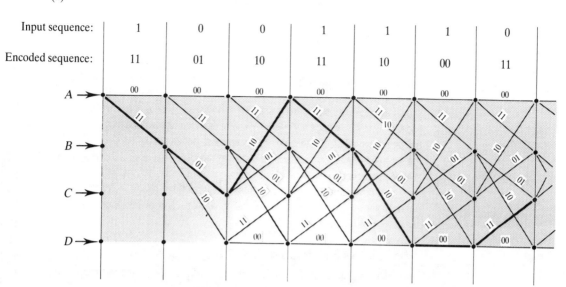

(b)

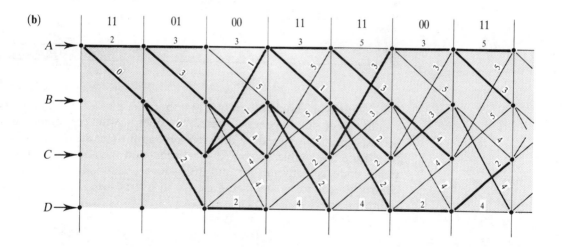

Continuous paths: A B C A B C B D
A B C A B D D C
A B C B C A A A
A B C B C A A B

FIGURE A1.2

Convolutional decoder:
(a) encoder output; (b) survivor
paths.

thus $2 + 1 = 3$ for each path. Similarly, the two paths emanating from node B have Hamming distances of 0 for path 01 and 2 for path 10, and hence the accumulated distances are $0 + 0 = 0$ and $0 + 2 = 2$, respectively. A similar procedure is then repeated at branch level 2.

At branch level 3 and onwards, however, the selection process starts. Thus, in the example, the two paths merging at node A (at branch level 3) have accumulated distances of 3 and 1, of which the latter is selected to be the survivor path for this node – this is shown as a bold line on the trellis diagram. A similar selection process is then followed at nodes B, C and D. At node C, however, it can be seen that the two merging paths both have the same accumulated distance of 4. In such cases, the upper path is selected. Also, after the selection process, all subsequent distances are calculated relative to the accumulated distance associated with the selected path.

It now remains to select the most likely path and hence the output sequence. Although the decoding procedure continues, by inspection of the portion of the trellis shown, it can be seen that:

- only four paths have a continuous path through the trellis, and
- the distance corresponding to the path $ABCABDDC$ is the minimum.

Thus, this is the path that is selected, the corresponding output sequence being 11 01 10 11 10 00 11 . . ., which corresponds to the original encoded (and hence transmitted) sequence.

Finally, it should be stressed that there are no FEC methods that can identify all errors. In general, therefore, codes like the convolutional code are used primarily to reduce the error probability (bit error rate) of a link to a more acceptable level. A typical reduction with a rate 1/2 convolutional code is between 10^2 and 10^3. Hence, assuming an ARQ error control procedure is also being used, the overall link efficiency is much improved.

APPENDIX B

DATA ENCRYPTION

B1.1   INTRODUCTION

In many applications, both the data stored within the computer and the messages that are transmitted over the computer communication network are of a highly confidential nature; for example, the details of a person's bank account and transactions involving it. In such cases, it is usual for the computer to perform some form of coding operation both on the data stored within its memory and on each message, prior to its transmission, so that if the data are accidentally or deliberately intercepted, the received data will be incomprehensible to the recipient. This assumes, of course, that both the sender and intended recipient know the type of coding operation used and also, ideally, that their code is unique.

Coding operations of this type are known as **encryption** (or **encipherment**); the corresponding decoding operation is referred to as **decryption** (or **decipherment**). The message data prior to being encrypted is known as **plaintext** and the message data after encryption is termed the **ciphertext**. Normally, as will be seen, the encryption and decryption processes are the same for all message transfers across a network and a **key**, known only by each pair of correspondents and featuring in both the encryption and decryption processes, is used to make each message transfer between a particular pair of correspondents unique.

B1.2   THE DATA ENCRYPTION STANDARD

The most widely used encryption method is that defined by the US National Bureau of Standards and is known simply as the **data encryption standard** (**DES**). As an introduction to the subject of data encryption, therefore, this appendix gives a brief description of the DES algorithm.

Fuller descriptions of DES are, of course, readily available and a reference to one of these is given at the end of the book.

The DES algorithm is a **block cipher**, which means that it works on fixed-sized blocks of data. Thus, a complete message is first split (segmented) into blocks of plaintext, each comprising 64 bits. A (hopefully) unique 56-bit key is then used to encrypt each block of plaintext into a 64-bit block of ciphertext, and it is this that is subsequently transmitted through the network. The receiver uses the same key to perform the inverse (decryption) operation on each 64-bit data block it receives and, in turn, reassembles the blocks into complete messages.

The larger the number of bits used for the key, the more likely it is that the key will be unique. Also, the larger the key, the more difficult it is for someone to decipher it. The use of a 56-bit key in the DES means that there are in the order of 10^{17} possible keys to choose from; hence, DES is regarded as providing sufficient security for most commercial applications.

The DES is a **product cipher**, which means that it is a combination of a number of different transposition and substitution operations. Essentially, a **transposition operation** takes a fixed block of bits and transposes the bits into a different order. A **substitution operation**, however, substitutes the complete set of bits by a different set of bits, the new set being determined by performing some processing operation on the old set.

A diagrammatic representation of the DES algorithm is shown in Figure B1.1. The 56-bit key selected by the two correspondents is first used to derive 16 different subkeys, each of 48 bits, and it is these that are used in the subsequent substitution operations. The algorithm comprises 19 distinct steps. The first step is a simple transposition of the 64-bit block of plaintext using a fixed transposition rule. The resulting 64 bits of transposed text then go through 16 identical iterations of substitution processing, except that at each iteration a different subkey is used in the substitution operation. The most significant 32 bits of the 64-bit output of the last iteration are then exchanged with the least significant 32 bits. Finally, the same transposition as was performed at step 1 is repeated to produce the 64-bit block of ciphertext to be transmitted. The DES algorithm is designed so that the received block is deciphered by the receiver in the same steps as are used for encryption, but in the reverse order.

The 16 subkeys used at each substitution step are produced as follows. First, a fixed transposition is performed on the 56-bit key. The resulting transposed key is then split into two separate 28-bit halves. Next, these two halves are rotated left independently and the combined 56 bits are then transposed once again. Each subkey comprises 48 bits which are chosen according to a set selection process on the final 56 bits of transposed data. The other subkeys are produced in a similar way except that the number of rotations performed is determined by the number of the subkey.

(a)

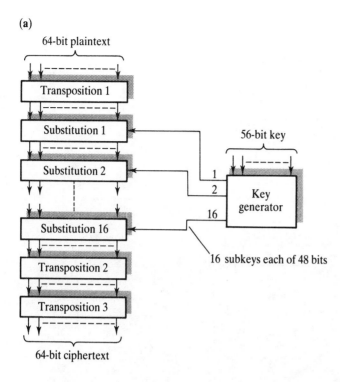

64-bit plaintext

Transposition 1

Substitution 1

Substitution 2

Substitution 16

Transposition 2

Transposition 3

64-bit ciphertext

56-bit key

Key generator

1
2
16

16 subkeys each of 48 bits

(b)

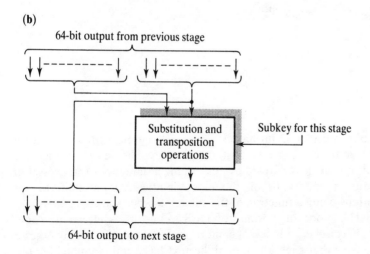

64-bit output from previous stage

Substitution and transposition operations

Subkey for this stage

64-bit output to next stage

FIGURE B1.1

The DES algorithm: (a) overall operation; (b) substitution processing.

The processing performed at each of the 16 intermediate steps in the encryption process is relatively complex as it is this that forms the effectiveness of the DES algorithm. The processing performed is shown in outline in Figure B1.1(b). The 64-bit output from the previous iteration is

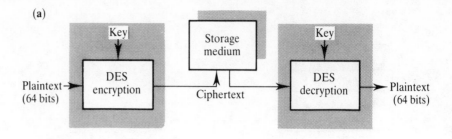

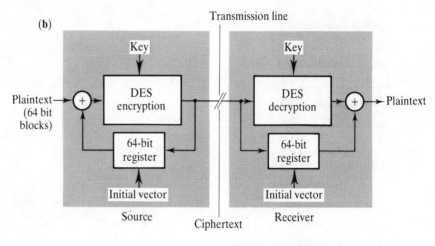

FIGURE B1.2

DES operating modes: (a) ECB mode; (b) CBC mode.

$\bigoplus$ = 64 exclusive–OR gates

first split into two 32-bit halves. The least significant half then forms the most significant 32-bit half of the output. The least significant 32-bit output, however, is derived by performing a sequence of transposition and substitution operations on the most significant input half, the precise operations being a function of the subkey for this stage.

The mode of working of DES is known as **electronic code book (ECB)** because each block of ciphertext is independent of any other block. This means that each block of ciphertext has a unique matching block of plaintext, which is analogous with entries in a code book. Because of this, the ECB mode is mostly used for the coding of data prior to its storage on, say, a disk system within the computer memory. An alternative mode, known as chaining, is preferable for data communication purposes. The ECB mode of working is shown in diagrammatic form in Figure B1.2.

B1.3 CHAINING

Although the ECB mode of operation of DES gives good protection against errors or changes that may occur in a single block of enciphered text, it does not protect against errors arising in a stream of blocks. Since each block is treated separately in the ECB mode, the insertion of an additional correctly enciphered block into a transmitted stream of blocks would not be detected by the receiver; it would simply decipher the inserted block and treat it as a valid block. This means that the stream of enciphered blocks could be intercepted and altered by someone who knows the key without the recipient being aware that any modifications had occurred. Also, this mode of operation has the weakness that repetitive blocks of plaintext generate a string of identical blocks of ciphertext, a factor that can be of great benefit to someone trying to break the code (key). Hence, an alternative mode of operation is to use the notion of **chaining**. This mode of operation of DES is known as **chain block cipher**, or simply **CBC**.

Although the chaining mode uses the same block encryption method previously described, each 64-bit block of plaintext is first exclusive-ORed with the enciphered output of the previous block before it is enciphered. This is shown in diagrammatic form in Figure B1.2(b). The first 64-bit block of plaintext is exclusive-ORed with a 64-bit random number called the **initial vector**, after which subsequent blocks operate in a chained sequence as shown. Thus, since the output of a block is a function both of the block contents and the output of the previous block, any alterations to the transmitted sequence can be detected by the receiver. Also, identical blocks of plaintext yield different blocks of ciphertext. For these reasons, this is the mode of operation normally used for data communication purposes.

B1.4 PUBLIC KEYS

Both of the methods described rely, of course, on the same key being used for the dual purpose of encryption and decryption. An obvious disadvantage of this is that some form of key notification must be used prior to the transfer of any encrypted data between two correspondents. This is perfectly acceptable providing the key does not change very often but, in some instances, this is not the case; it is in fact common practice to change the key on a daily, if not more frequent, basis. This gives rise to a problem known as the **key distribution problem**. In such situations, therefore, an alternative mode of operation, based on the use of a public rather than a private key, is often used.

(a)

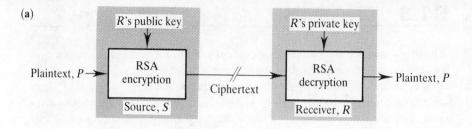

(b)

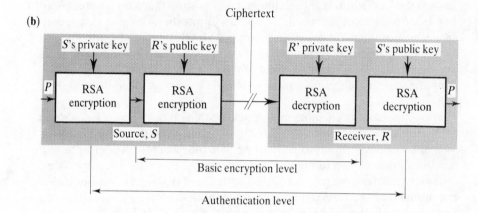

FIGURE B1.3

Public key systems: (a) without authentication (b) with authentication.

The principle of a public key system is that, instead of both the sender and receiver using the same (private) keys, any potential recipient of a message first generates a matched pair of keys: one is known as its **public key**, since it is made available to any system that may wish to communicate with it, and the other is known as its **private key**, since this is known only by itself. The two keys are generated in such a way that, firstly, it is not possible to derive the private key from the public key and, secondly, any data enciphered using a receiver's public key can only be deciphered by the receiver using its own matching private key.

An example of a public key system is the RSA algorithm which gets its name from the initials of the three researchers who invented it. To send a message using this method of encryption, the sender first uses the public key of the intended recipient to encipher the message – normally this is retained in a **key library**. On receipt of the message, the recipient deciphers it using its own matching private key. Of course, the message will be incomprehensible to any other recipient. The principle of operation of the RSA public key method is shown in Figure B1.3(a).

B1.5   MESSAGE AUTHENTICATION

Another important issue related to data encryption is concerned with **message authentication**. Essentially, the foregoing methods are concerned only with ensuring the reliable transfer of message data between two correspondents. In addition to this, however, there is also a requirement in some applications to provide some means of authenticating or verifying that each message received from a particular source was in fact sent by that source and not another system impersonating it. For example, since it is possible with a public key method for any system to initiate the sending of a message to any other system simply by using the intended receiver's public key, it is necessary to have some means of authenticating the identity of the sender of a message.

To meet this requirement, public key systems of the type already described provide such a capability. Essentially, the two keys used in this method have the dual property that not only is a receiver able to decipher all messages it receives (which have been encrypted with its own public key) using its own private key, but any receiver can decipher a message encrypted with the sender's private key, using the sender's public key.

A schematic diagram showing how this property may be exploited to achieve message authentication is shown in Figure B1.3(b). The encryption and decryption operations are performed at two levels. The inner level of encryption and decryption is the same as already described. At the outer level, however, the sender uses its own private key to encrypt the original (plaintext) message. Thus, if the receiver is able to decrypt this message using that sender's public key, this is treated as proof that that sender did in fact initiate the sending of the message.

As was mentioned at the beginning, this appendix is only intended to introduce the reader to the fascinating subject of cryptography. The more interested reader is referred to the reference section at the end of the book for further reading. As the uses of computer communication networks expand, however, so the various topics that have been introduced in this appendix will become increasingly important.

APPENDIX C
PROPRIETARY PROTOCOL ARCHITECTURES

C1.1 INTRODUCTION

The adoption worldwide of OSI by all the major computer manufacturers and procurement agencies means that, in the near future, most new communication subsystems will be based on the ISO Reference Model and associated CCITT or ISO-approved protocols. The major part of this book, therefore, is concerned with such protocols. Prior to the definition of the ISO Reference Model, however, a number of proprietary protocol architectures were developed and indeed many of these are still in widespread use. This appendix describes three such protocol architectures: the US Department of Defense's protocol architecture, IBM's systems network architecture and DEC's distributed network architecture. It should be stressed, however, that the descriptions presented do not attempt to describe these protocols in detail, rather they relate the architecture adopted to the seven layers of the ISO Reference Model.

C1.2 DARPA PROTOCOL ARCHITECTURE

The US Department of Defense (DOD) is one of the biggest procurement agencies of computers (and associated software) in the world and hence the potential benefits of adopting an open systems protocol architecture are considerable. The Defense Advanced Research Project Agency (DARPA) protocol architecture has been specified by the DOD, therefore, to achieve this goal. Although its aims are similar to OSI, however, it predates much of the ISO work and hence it does not have the same level of functionality as the latter. Thus, in the DARPA protocol architecture, all end user and application-specific software is considered as a process and the aim is to provide a means whereby such processes can interact with one another. The architecture adopted by the DOD is shown in Figure C1.1(a).

The network access layer embraces those protocols that are necessary to interface to the network being used; for example, the X.25 protocol set if the network is a packet-switched network, or the IEEE 802.2/3 protocol set if it is an LAN. From the outset, the DOD architecture was defined to allow processes to communicate over multiple networks, and it is the internet layer that makes this possible. The main function of the **internet protocol (IP)** is that of network routing, being essentially the same as the internet sublayer of the ISO network layer.

The transmission control layer builds on the services provided by the internet layer to provide the means whereby two processes can carry out a dialogue. The **transmission control protocol (TCP)** supports both a connectionless (datagram) and a connection-oriented service. The logical connections associated with the latter are known as sessions but, in relation to the ISO Reference Model, they are nearer to the logical connections associated with the transport layer. A logical connection provides a reliable (error free and in sequence) message interchange service between user and application processes.

Normally, the services provided by the TCP layer are accessed through a layer of software known as the **application program interface (API)**. Since, in the DARPA architecture, the TCP forms the interface with end user application processes, this is analogous to the user element (UE) associated with an application process in the ISO architecture. The API software thus varies for different machines and hence operating systems.

In the DARPA architecture, there are no application-oriented layers as such, instead the functions associated with these layers have to be written into the user processes. To help the user, however, a number of application processes have been written to provide specific services similar to those provided by the specific application service elements (SASEs) in the ISO application layer. Thus, there is a file transfer protocol (FTP) application process, a virtual terminal (known as Telnet), a remote job entry (RJE) process, a simple mail transfer protocol (SMTP), and so on.

For example, FTP supports the transfer and access of files between a client (user) process and a server (application) process. Typically, a user at a terminal interacts with the client FTP process to access a remote file system that is front ended by the server FTP process. The FTP supports a variety of transfer modes, file store structures and data types, including ASCII, EBCDIC and binary.

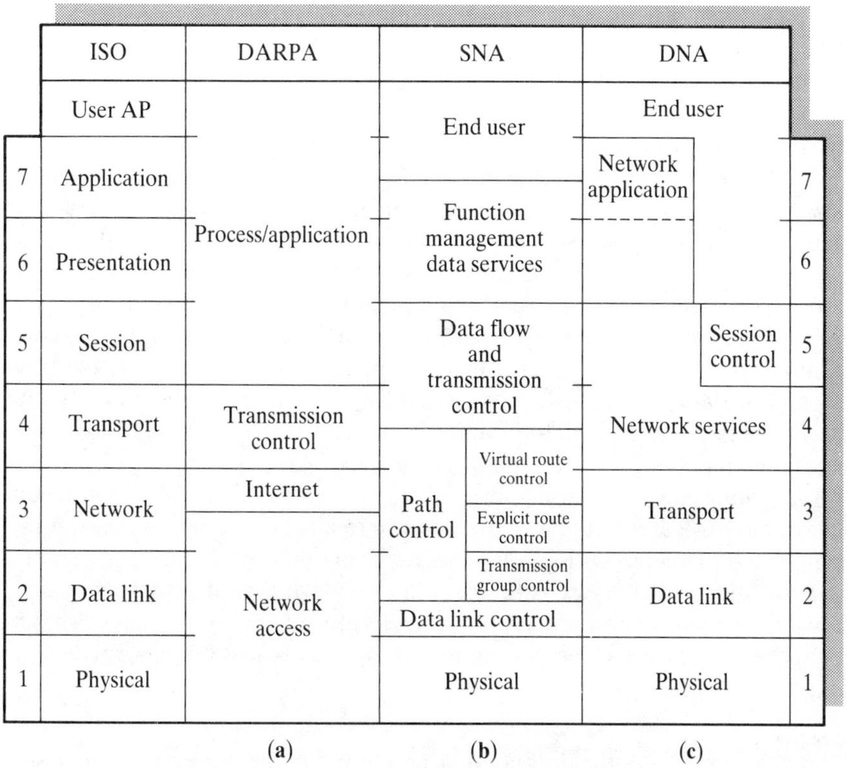

	ISO	DARPA	SNA	DNA	
	User AP		End user	End user	
7	Application	Process/application	Function management data services	Network application	7
6	Presentation				6
5	Session		Data flow and transmission control	Session control	5
4	Transport	Transmission control		Network services	4
3	Network	Internet	Path control — Virtual route control / Explicit route control / Transmission group control	Transport	3
2	Data link	Network access	Data link control	Data link	2
1	Physical		Physical	Physical	1
	(a)		(b)	(c)	

FIGURE C1.1

A comparison of some proprietary protocol architectures.

C1.3 SYSTEMS NETWORK ARCHITECTURE

Systems network architecture (SNA) is the protocol architecture of IBM. The various protocol layers in the SNA relative to the ISO Reference Model can be seen in Figure C1.1(b). The highest layer in the SNA is the **function management data services (FMDS)** layer. As can be seen, it has the functionality of ISO layer 6 but also some of the functions of layer 7. It provides a collection of services to the end user, including presentation services – (transfer) syntax selection and, if necessary, the associated data transformations – and some additional network management services. There are no application entities as such, however, and these are assumed to be provided by end user processes.

In an SNA network, all communications between end users (application processes) are through entities known as **logical units (LUs)**. Unlike OSI, end users do not have a network identifier, instead it is the LUs that have a network address. LUs are also referred to, therefore, as **network addressable units (NAUs)**. Communication between LUs is accomplished by exchanging messages known as **request/response units (RUs)**. Then, as in OSI, headers containing protocol control information are added as RUs pass down through the lower layers. This includes control information relating to the transmission control (session/transport), path control (network) and data link control layers.

As in OSI, no communication can take place (between LUs in the case of SNA) until a session connection has been established between them. Within an SNA, a session connection and a transport connection are one and the same. Thus, the data flow control and transmission control layers collectively provide a similar set of services to the ISO session layer and part of the transport layer. Session connections are established and maintained by the **session control** component of the transmission control layer. The data flow control layer is then responsible for the subsequent data exchange, including interaction management, synchronization and exception reporting.

Unlike the ISO transport layer, the transmission control layer cannot only transfer a message in response to a request from the data flow control layer (that is, an RU) but also from an end user directly, or indeed from within its own layer. All messages to be transferred across the (path control) network carry protocol control information generated by the **connection point manager** component of the transmission control layer. This is then used:

(1) to determine the intended destination of the message – that is, within the layer or a layer above;

(2) to apply flow control and other control functions on the message units (RUs) exchanged between two LUs.

The **path control** and **data link control** layers collectively provide a similar set of services to the ISO network and data link layers. A typical SNA network comprises a mesh topology with a group of one or more physical links connecting each node in the network to an adjacent node. The flow of data units across each physical link is under the control of the data link control layer protocol. In SNA, this is SDLC, which is almost identical to the ISO HDLC protocol.

The provision of a group of links between adjacent nodes is done to achieve enhanced reliability: on receipt of a data unit for transmission, the **transmission group control** sublayer initiates the transmission of the data unit on the first available physical link to the intended destination node, rather than on a fixed link. Clearly, however, although this improves reliability, because of the use of a separate error control procedure on each link, data units may arrive at their destination out of sequence. To allow for this, therefore, the transmission group control protocol employs a sequence numbering scheme to ensure that the order of data units may be re-established by the receiving (destination) node. Also, when only a single physical link is available, improved performance is obtained by the protocol *blocking* a number of smaller data units into a single information frame prior to transmission. It may be concluded from this that the transmission group control sublayer simply enhances the performance of the data link control layer, and hence collectively these are equivalent to the ISO data link layer.

The explicit route control and virtual route control sublayers collectively provide a similar set of services to the ISO network layer. The **explicit route control** sublayer carries out a routing function. In SNA, all routes between any two systems are predetermined and are assigned a **route number**. Also, each node has a routing table that, for each route number, specifies the corresponding transmission control group to be used. Then, on receipt of a data unit, the latter selects a specific physical link, as was outlined earlier.

Finally, the **virtual route control** sublayer provides the transmission control layer with the means of establishing a logical connection – analogously to a virtual circuit/logical channel in a packet-switched network – with a peer transmission control layer. This may then be used to carry message units (LUs) relating to different sessions. The virtual route control protocol then applies flow control on the message units exchanged across this logical link and also fragmentation (and reassembly) of long messages. In OSI, the latter is, of course, a function of the transport layer, and hence the two layers are shown to overlap.

C1.4 DISTRIBUTED NETWORK ARCHITECTURE

Distributed network architecture (DNA) is the protocol architecture of DEC. The various protocol layers in DNA relative to the ISO Reference Model are shown in Figure C1.1(c). The layout shown is intended to demonstrate not only the corresponding ISO layer to which each DNA layer relates, but also the possible communication paths between layers.

The lowest three layers in a DNA collectively provide a similar service to an ISO connectionless (datagram) network. The data link layer in a DNA is known as the **digital data communications message protocol (DDCMP)**. It is responsible for the management and transfer of data messages across the data link connecting adjacent network nodes. Unlike most other proprietary protocol architectures, DDCMP is not based on HDLC, rather it is a character(byte)-oriented protocol. The control characters used are the ASCII control characters but the content of data messages may be either ASCII characters or simply strings of 8-bit bytes.

To allow for this, therefore, each data message has a count field in its header that indicates the numbers of characters/bytes in the message. Also, the error check field is a 16-bit CRC. DDCMP is based on a continuous RQ protocol and supports full-duplex data transfers. It also utilizes piggyback acknowledgements.

The **transport** layer is equivalent to the ISO connectionless network layer. It thus provides a basic datagram service. The DNA transport protocol, however, in addition to performing routing, also performs flow control and some other network management services.

The **network services** layer provides a similar set of services to the ISO class 4 protocol. It thus performs connection management and data transfer services. Connection management is concerned with the establishment (and clearing) of a full-duplex logical channel (equivalent to a combined ISO transport/session connection) between two peer network services layers. Once established, this can be used for both the exchange of messages between two user processes and for the transfer of protocol control and other messages. To achieve this, the established link is comprised of two subchannels:

(1)   a **data subchannel**, which is used exclusively for the exchange of messages (data) between user processes;

(2)   an **other-data subchannel**, which, as its name implies, is used for the transfer of all other messages, including protocol control messages relating to the network services protocol.

The data transfer services associated with the latter control the exchange of data messages between user processes. The protocol includes segmentation and reassembly, error control (using sequence numbers and acknowledgement messages) and flow control. It is thus equivalent to the ISO class 4 transport protocol.

The **session control** sublayer, which is considered part of the network services layer, performs two functions. The first is analogous to the ISO session connection management and the second to the address resolution part of the ISO directory services. In a DNA, as in OSI, user programs (processes) utilize symbolic names when initiating a (session) connection with another user program, and it is the session control sublayer that performs the necessary mapping between the symbolic names used by the user processes and their corresponding physical network addresses. Thus, on receipt of a connection request from a user process, the session control sublayer, after determining the required network address, passes a connect command to the network services layer. The latter then generates a connect (initiate) message and transfers this to the required correspondent network services layer. On receipt of this, the latter passes a connect command to the (peer) session control sublayer which, assuming the required user process is available, returns an accept command to the (peer) network services layer. Alternatively, if the called user process is not currently active, the session control sublayer first initiates its protocol before returning the accept command. The network services protocol then generates and returns a connect confirm message to the initiating layer which, in turn, informs the session control sublayer of the result of the connection attempt. Then, assuming this was successful, user messages may be exchanged across this connection without any further intervention from the session control sublayer. Finally, after all messages have been exchanged, the session control sublayer is used to release the connection.

As can be deduced from Figure C1.1, it is possible for user processes to initiate and carry out a network dialogue by interacting directly with the network services and session control layers. In addition, however, the network application layer offers a similar set of services to the various ISO application entities. For example, the **data access protocol (DAP)** provides a similar set of services to ISO FTAM. In DAP, however, a virtual file structure is not assumed, instead a preliminary exchange of messages takes place between DAPs to ascertain such information as the version of the operating system being used, the type of the file, its organization, record size, and so on.

APPENDIX D

SUMMARY OF STANDARDS ORGANIZATIONS

American National Standards Institute (ANSI) This is a national standards organization comprised of members from computer manufacturers and users in the United States. It is also the US member body of ISO. Its members are involved in the development of standards at all levels in the ISO Reference Model.

British Standards Institute (BSI) This is a national standards organization concerned with the production of standards for use by all forms of manufacturing and consumer industries. It is the British member of ISO and acts as a source for all their documents.

Consultative Committee for International Telegraph and Telephone (CCITT) This is an international standards organization comprised of the Postal, Telegraph and Telephone (PTT) authorities of the member countries. It is concerned primarily with the development and production of standards for interfacing equipment to public telecommunications networks. These include the analogue PSTN, ISDN and PPSDN. It also produces standards for Facsimile, Teletex, Videotex and other value-added services (teleservices).

Electronics Industries Association (EIA) This is a US national standards organization comprised of members from the electronics industry. In the context of data and computer communications, it has produced a range of (physical) interface standards for connecting peripherals to a computer and, more recently, through the contribution of General Motors, has been actively involved in the development of the layer 7 standard for manufacturing message service (MMS). It is a member of ANSI and, through them, ISO.

European Computer Manufacturers Association (ECMA) This is comprised of members from computer manufacturers in Europe including some European divisions of American companies. It produces its own standards and also contributes to CCITT and ISO. Its members are actively involved in the development of standards at all levels of the ISO Reference Model.

Institute of Electrical and Electronic Engineers (IEEE) This is a US professional society that also takes part in the development of standards for use by the computer industry. In the context of computer communications, it has been responsible for the production of standards relating to LANs and, in particular, for those concerned with the physical, MAC and LLC (sub) layers.

International Standards Organization (ISO) This is an international standards organization comprised of designated standards bodies of the participating countries. It is concerned with a wide range of standards, each of which is controlled by a separate technical committee. The technical committee that produces standards for the computer industry is TC97 – Information Processing Systems. This committee has been responsible for the production of the basic ISO Reference Model for OSI and also for the production of the various protocol standards for each layer in the reference model.

National Bureau of Standards (NBS) This is a US national standards organization concerned with the production of standards relating to both ISO and CCITT. It issues standards for equipment purchased by the US federal government in the general area of information processing. These are known as federal information processing standards (FIPS).

APPENDIX E

GLOSSARY OF TERMS AND ABBREVIATIONS

Abstract Syntax Notation One (ASN.1)   An abstract syntax used to define the structure of the protocol data units associated with a particular protocol entity.

American Standards Committee for Information Interchange (ASCII)   In normal usage it is used to refer to the character code defined by this committee for the interchange of information between two communicating devices. The ASCII character set is in widespread use for the transfer of information between a computer and a peripheral device such as a visual display unit or a printer.

Amplitude modulation (AM)   A modulation technique used to allow data to be transmitted across an analogue network, such as a switched telephone network. The amplitude of a single (carrier) frequency is varied (modulated) between two levels – one for binary 0 and the other for binary 1.

Application layer   This corresponds to layer 7 of the ISO Reference Model for open systems interconnection. It comprises a number of application-oriented protocols and forms the user interface to the various distributed information processing services supported.

Association control service element (ACSE)   A protocol entity forming part of the application layer. It provides the generalized (common) function of establishing and clearing a logical association (connection) between two application entities.

Asynchronous transmission   Strictly, this implies that the receiver clock is not synchronized to the transmitted clock when data are being transmitted between two devices connected by a transmission line. More generally, it is used to indicate that data are being transmitted as individual characters. Each character is preceded by a start signal and terminated by one or more stop signals, which are used by the receiver for synchronization purposes.

Automatic repeat request (ARQ)   A technique used for error control over a transmission line. If errors in a transmitted message are detected by the receiving device, it requests the sending device to retransmit the message together with any other messages that may have been affected.

Bandwidth   The difference between the highest and lowest sinusoidal frequency signals that can be transmitted across a transmission line or through a network. It is measured in Hertz (Hz) and also defines the maximum information-carrying capacity of the line or network.

Baseband   A particular operating mode of a transmission line: each binary digit (bit) in a message is converted into one of two voltage (sometimes current) levels – one for binary 1 and the other for binary 0. The voltages are then applied directly to the line. The line signal thus varies with time between these two voltage levels as the data are transmitted.

Basic mode   An ISO international standard protocol defined to control the exchange of data between a master (primary) station and multiple slave (secondary) stations which are connected by means of a multidrop link.

Baud   The number of line signal variations per second. It is also used to indicate the rate at which data are transmitted on a line, although this is strictly correct only when each bit is represented by a single signal level on the transmission line. Hence, the bit rate and the line signal rate are both the same.

Binary synchronous control (BSC)   The name used by IBM for the ISO Basic Mode protocol.

Bit stuffing (zero bit insertion)   A technique used to allow pure binary data to be transmitted on a synchronous transmission line. Each message block (frame) is encapsulated between two flags, which are special bit sequences. Then, if the message data contains a possibly similar sequence, an additional (zero) bit is inserted into the data stream by the sender, and is subsequently removed by the receiving device. The transmission method is then said to be data transparent.

Block sum check   This is used for the detection of errors when data are being transmitted. It is comprised of a set of binary digits (bits), which are the modulo 2 sum of the individual characters/octets in a frame (block) or message.

Bridge   A device used to link two homogeneous local area subnetworks;

that is, two subnetworks utilizing the same physical and medium access control method.

Broadband   A particular mode of operation of a coaxial cable. A single coaxial cable can be used to simultaneously transmit a number of separate data streams by assigning each stream a portion of the total available bandwidth. Data are transmitted by modulating a single frequency signal from the selected frequency band and the data are then received by demodulating the received signal.

Broadcast   A means of transmitting a message to all devices connected to a network. Normally, a special address, the broadcast address, is reserved to enable all the devices to determine that the message is a broadcast message.

Bus   A network topology in widespread use for the interconnection of communities of digital devices distributed over a localized area. The transmission medium is normally a single coaxial cable to which all the devices are attached. Each transmission thus propagates the length of the medium and is therefore received by all other devices connected to the medium.

Community antenna television (CATV)   A facility used in the context of local area data netwoks, since the principles and network components used in CATV networks can also be used to produce a flexible underlying data transmission facility over a local area. CATV networks operate using the broadband mode of working.

Check sum   *See* Block sum check.

Circuit switching   The mode of operation of a telephone network and also some of the newer digital data networks. A communication path is first established through the network between the source (calling) and destination (called) terminals, and this is then used exclusively for the duration of the call or transaction. Both terminals must operate at the same information transfer rate.

Coaxial cable   A type of transmission medium consisting of a centre conductor and a concentric outer conductor. It is used when high data transfer rates (greater than 1 Mbps) are required.

Commitment, concurrency and recovery (CCR)   A protocol entity forming part of the application layer. It provides the means whereby two or more application processes may perform mutually exclusive operations on shared data. It also provides control to ensure that the operations are performed either completely or not at all. It uses the concepts of an atomic action and a two-phase commit protocol.

Common application service element (CASE)   A collection of protocol entities forming part of the application layer that are responsible for providing some common services, such as establishing a logical connection (association) between two application protocol entities.

Continuous RQ A part of a data link protocol concerned with error control. It endeavours to ensure that, if a frame (message) is corrupted during transmission, another copy of the frame is sent. To improve the efficiency of utilization of the data link, frames are transmitted continuously; hence, retransmission requests relating to corrupted frames may be received after a number of other frames have been transmitted.

Cyclic redundancy check (CRC) A method used for the detection of errors when data are being transmitted. A CRC is a numeric value computed from the bits in the message to be transmitted. It is appended to the tail of the message prior to transmission and the receiver then detects the presence of errors in the received message by recomputing a new CRC.

Crosstalk An unwanted signal that is picked up in a conductor due to some external electrical activity.

CSMA/CD An abbreviation for carrier sense, multiple access with collision detection. It is a method used to control access to a shared transmission medium, such as a coaxial cable bus to which a number of stations are connected. A station wishing to transmit a message first senses (listens to) the medium and transmits the message only if the medium is quiet – no carrier present. Then, as the message is being transmitted, the station monitors the actual signal on the transmission medium and, if this is different from the signal being transmitted, a collision is said to have occurred and been detected. The station then ceases transmission and retries again later.

Data circuit-terminating equipment (DCE) The name given to the equipment provided by the network authority (provider) for the attachment of user devices to the network. It takes on different forms for different network types.

Data link layer This corresponds to layer 2 of the ISO Reference Model for open systems interconnection. It is concerned with the reliable transfer of data (no residual transmission errors) across the data link being used.

Data terminal equipment (DTE) A generic name for any user device connected to a data network. It thus includes such devices as visual display units, computers, office workstations, etc.

Datagram A type of service offered on a packet-switched data network (*see also* virtual call). A datagram is a self-contained packet of information that is sent through the network with minimum protocol overheads.

Decibel   A measure of the strength of a signal relative to another signal. The number of decibels is computed as 10 times the log of the ratio of the power in each signal or 20 times the log of the amplitude (voltage or current) of each signal.

Delay distortion   Distortion of a signal caused by the frequency components making up the signal having different propagation velocities across a transmission medium.

Directory service (DS)   A protocol entity forming part of the application layer. It is concerned with the translation of symbolic names (or titles), as used by application processes, into so-called fully qualified network addresses, as used with the open systems interconnection environment.

Extended Binary Coded Decimal Interchange Code (EBCDIC).   The character set used on all IBM computers.

Error rate   The ratio of the average number of bits that will be corrupted to the total number of bits that are transmitted for a data link or system.

Fast select   An optional facility with the X.25 protocol that allows user data to be sent in the call set-up and call clearing packets.

Fibre optic   *See* Optical fibre.

File transfer and manipulation (FTAM)   A protocol entity forming part of the application layer. It enables user application processes to manage and access a (distributed) file system.

Flow control   A technique used to control the rate of flow of frames or messages between two communicating entities.

Frame   The unit of information transferred across a data link. Typically, there are control frames for link management and information frames for the transfer of message data.

Frame check sequence (FCS)   A general term given to the additional bits appended to a transmitted frame or message by the source to enable the receiver to detect possible transmission errors.

Frequency-division multiplexing (FDM)   A technique used to derive a number of separate data channels from a single transmission medium, such as a coaxial cable. Each data channel is assigned a portion of the total available bandwidth.

Frequency-shift keying (FSK)   A modulation technique used to convert binary data into an analogue form comprising two sinusoidal frequencies. It is widely used in modems to allow data to be transmitted across a (analogue) switched telephone network.

Full-duplex A type of information exchange strategy between two communicating devices whereby information (data) may be exchanged in both directions simultaneously. It is also known as two-way simultaneous.

Gateway A device that allows data to be passed from one network to another. Typically, the two networks operate with different protocols, and so the gateway performs the necessary protocol conversion functions.

Half-duplex A type of information exchange strategy between two communicating devices whereby information (data) may be exchanged in both directions alternately. It is also known as two-way alternate.

High-level data link control (HDLC) It is an internationally agreed standard protocol defined to control the exchange of data across either a point-to-point data link or a multidrop data link.

Host This is normally a computer belonging to a user that contains (hosts) the communication hardware and software necessary to connect the computer to a data communication network.

International Alphabet Number 5 (IA5) The standard character code defined by the CCITT and recommended by the ISO. It is almost identical to the ASCII code.

Idle RQ A part of a data link protocol concerned with error control. It endeavours to ensure that, if a frame (message) is corrupted during transmission, another copy is sent. After a frame is sent by the source, it must wait until either an indication of correct (or otherwise) receipt is received from the receiver or for a specified time before sending another frame. It is also known as send (or stop) and wait.

Integrated services digital network (ISDN) The new generation of world-wide telecommunications network that utilizes digital techniques for both transmission and switching. It supports both voice and data communications.

Internet protocol A protocol that provides a link at the network layer between multiple packet-switched networks.

Job transfer and manipulation (JTM) A protocol entity forming part of the application layer. It enables user application processes to transfer and manipulate documents relating to jobs (processing tasks).

Local area network (LAN)   A data communication network used to interconnect a community of digital devices distributed over a localized area of up to, say, 10 km^2. The devices may be office workstations, mini- and microcomputers, intelligent instrumentation equipment, etc.

Logical link control (LLC)   A protocol forming part of the data link layer in LANs. It is concerned with the reliable transfer of data across the data link between two communicating systems.

Manchester encoding   A scheme used to encode clocking (timing) information into a binary data stream prior to transmission. The resulting encoded signal has a transition (positive or negative) in the middle of each bit cell period with the effect that the clocking information (required to receive the signal) is readily extracted from the received signal.

Manufacturing message service (MMS)   A protocol entity forming part of the application layer. It is intended for use specifically in the manufacturing or process control industry. It enables a supervisory computer to control the operation of a distributed community of computer-based devices.

Medium access control (MAC)   Many local area networks utilize a single common transmission medium – a bus or ring, for example – to which all the interconnected devices are attached. A procedure must be followed by each device, therefore, to ensure that transmissions occur in an orderly and fair way. In general, this is known as the medium access control procedure. Two examples are CSMA/CD and (control) token.

Message handling service (MHS)   A protocol entity forming part of the application layer. It provides a generalized facility for exchanging electronic messages between systems. It is also known as X.400.

Microwave   A type of communication based on electromagnetic radiation by means of a transmitting aerial and a receiving antenna or dish. It is used for both terrestrial links and satellite links.

Modem   The name given to the device that converts a binary (digital) data stream into an analogue (continuously varying) form, prior to transmission of the data across an analogue network (MODulator), and reconverts the received signal back into its binary form (DEModulator). Since each access port to the network normally requires a full-duplex (two way simultaneous) capability, the device must perform both the MODulation and DEModulation functions; hence the single name MODEM is used. As an example, a modem is normally required to transmit data across a telephone network.

Multidrop   A network configuration that supports more than two stations on the same transmission medium.

Multiplexer   A device used to enable a number of lower bit rate devices, normally situated in the same location, to share a single higher bit rate transmission line. The data-carrying capacity of the latter must be in excess of the combined bit rates of the low bit rate devices.

Multipoint   *See* Multidrop.

Network layer   This corresponds to layer 3 of the ISO Reference Model for open systems interconnection. It is concerned with the establishment and clearing of logical or physical connections across the network being used.

Network management   A generic term used to embrace all the functions and entities involved in the management of a network. This includes configuration management, fault handling and the gathering of statistics relating to usage of the network.

Noise   The term given to the extraneous electrical signals that may be generated or picked up in a transmission line. Typically, it may be caused by neighbouring electrical apparatus. If the noise signal is large compared with the data-carrying signal, the latter may be corrupted and result in transmission errors.

NRZ/NRZI   Two similar (and related) schemes for encoding a binary data stream. The first has the property that a signal transition occurs whenever a binary 1 is present in the data stream and the second whenever a binary 0 is present. The latter is utilized with certain clocking (timing) schemes.

Optical fibre   A type of transmission medium over which data are transmitted in the form of light waves or pulses. It is characterized by its potentially high bandwidth, and hence data-carrying capacity, and also its high immunity to interference from other electrical sources.

Packet assembler/disassembler (PAD)   A device used with an X.25 packet switching network to allow character-mode terminals to communicate with a packet-mode device, such as a computer.

Packet switching   A mode of operation of a data communication network. Each message to be transmitted through the network is first divided into a number of smaller, self-contained message units known as packets. Each packet contains addressing information. As each packet is received at an intermediate node (exchange) within the network, it is first stored and, depending on the addressing information contained within it, forwarded along an appropriate link to the next node and so on. Packets belonging to the same message are then reassembled at the destination. This mode of operation ensures that long messages do not degrade the response time of the network. Also, the source and destination devices may operate at different data rates.

Parity A mechanism used for the detection of transmission errors when single characters are being transmitted. A single binary digit, known as the parity bit and whose value (1 or 0) is determined by the total number of binary 1s in the character, is transmitted with the character so that the receiver can thus determine the presence of single-bit errors by comparing the received parity bit with the (recomputed) value it should be.

Phase-shift keying (PSK) A modulation technique used to convert binary data into an analogue form comprising a single sinusoidal frequency signal whose phase varies according to the data being transmitted.

Physical layer This corresponds to layer 1 of the ISO Reference Model for open systems interconnection. It is concerned with the electrical and mechanical specification of the physical network termination equipment.

Piggyback A technique used to return acknowledgement information across a full-duplex (two-way simultaneous) data link without the use of special (acknowledgement) messages. The acknowledgement information relating to the flow of messages in one direction is embedded (piggybacked) into a normal data-carrying message flowing in the reverse direction.

Presentation layer This corresponds to layer 6 of the ISO Reference Model for open systems interconnection. It is concerned with the negotiation of a suitable transfer (concrete) syntax for use during an application session and, if this is different from the local syntax, for the translation to and from this syntax.

Protocol A set of rules formulated to control the exchange of data between two communicating parties.

Protocol data unit (PDU) The message units exchanged between two protocol entities.

Protocol entity The code that controls the operation of a protocol layer.

Public-switched data network (PSDN) A communication network that has been set up and is controlled by a public telecommunications authority for the exchange of data.

Public-switched telephone network (PSTN) This is the term used to describe the (analogue) telephone network.

Postal, Telegraph and Telephone (PTT)   The administration authority that controls all the postal and public telecommunications networks and services in a country.

Remote operations service element (ROSE)   A protocol entity forming part of the application layer. It provides a general facility for initiating and controlling operations remotely.

Ring   A network topology in widespread use for the interconnection of communities of digital devices distributed over a localized area, such as a factory or block of offices. Each device is connected to its nearest neighbour until all the devices are connected in the form of a closed loop or ring. Data are transmitted in one direction only and, as each message circulates around the ring, it is read by each device connected in the ring. After circulating around the ring, the source device removes the message from the ring.

RS-232C/RS-422/RS-423   Standards laid down by the American Electrical Industries Association for interfacing a digital device to a PTT-supplied modem. RS-232C is also used as an interface standard for connecting a peripheral device, such as a visual display unit or a printer, to a computer.

Send and wait   *See* Idle RQ.

Service access point (SAP)   The subaddress used to uniquely identify a particular link between two protocol layers in a specific system.

Session layer   This corresponds to layer 5 of the ISO Reference Model for open systems interconnection. It is concerned with the establishment of a logical connection between two application entities and with controlling the dialogue (message exchange) between them.

Signal-to-noise ratio   The ratio between the power in a signal and the (unwanted) power associated with the line or system noise. It is normally expressed in decibels.

Simplex   A type of information exchange strategy between two communicating devices whereby information (data) may only be passed in one direction.

Slotted ring   A type of local area (data) network. All the devices are connected in the form of a (physical) ring and an additional device known as a monitor is used to ensure that the ring contains a fixed number of message slots (binary digits) that circulate around the ring in one direction only. A device sends a message by placing it in an empty slot as it passes. This is then read by all other devices on the ring and subsequently removed by the originating device.

Specific application service element (SASE)   A collection of protocol entities forming part of the application layer responsible for providing various specific application services, such as file transfer, job transfer, etc.

Star A type of network topology in which there is a central node that performs all switching (and hence routing) functions.

Statistical multiplexer (stat. mux) A device used to enable a number of lower bit rate devices, normally situated in the same location, to share a single, higher bit rate transmission line. The devices usually have human operators, and hence data are transmitted on the shared line on a statistical basis rather than, as is the case with a basic multiplexer, on a preallocated basis. It thus endeavours to exploit the fact that each device operates at a much lower mean rate than its maximum rate.

Synchronous transmission A technique used to transmit data between two devices connected by a transmission line. The data are normally transmitted in the form of blocks, each comprising a string of binary digits. With synchronous transmission, the transmitter and receiver clocks are in synchronism and a number of techniques are used to ensure this.

Teletex An international telecommunications service that provides the means for messages, comprising text and selected graphical characters, to be prepared, sent and received.

Time-division multiplexing (TDM) A technique used to share the bandwidth (channel capacity) of a shared transmission facility to allow a number of communications to be in progress either concurrently or one at a time.

Token bus A type of local area (data) network. Access to the shared transmission medium, which is implemented in the form of a bus to which all the communicating devices are connected, is controlled by a single control (permission) token. Only the current owner of the token is allowed to transmit a message on the medium. All the devices wishing to transmit messages are connected in the form of a logical ring and, after a device receives the token and transmits any waiting messages, it passes the token on to the next device on the ring.

Token ring A type of local area (data) network. All the devices are connected in the form of a (physical) ring and messages are transmitted by allowing them to circulate around the ring. A device can only transmit a message on the ring when it is in possession of a control (permission) token. A single token is passed from one device to another around the ring.

Transmission medium The communication path linking two communicating devices. Some examples are twisted pair wire, coaxial cable, optical fibre cable and a microwave (radio) beam.

Transport layer This corresponds to layer 4 of the ISO Reference Model for open systems interconnection. It is concerned with providing a network-independent, reliable, message interchange service to the application-oriented layers (layers 5 through 7).

Twisted pair A type of transmission medium consisting of two insulated wires twisted together to improve its immunity to interference from other (stray) electrical signals that may otherwise corrupt the signal being transmitted.

Videotex A telecommunications service that allows users to deposit and access information to and from a central database facility. Access is through a special terminal comprising a TV set equipped with a special decoder.

Virtual call (circuit) A type of service offered on a packet-switched data network (*see also* datagram). Using this service, prior to sending any packets of information relating to a particular call (message transfer), a virtual circuit is established through the network from source to destination. All information-carrying packets relating to this call then follow the same route and the network ensures that the packets are delivered in the same order as they were entered.

Virtual terminal A protocol entity forming part of the application layer. It enables an application process to have a dialogue with a remote terminal in a standardized way, independent of the make of the terminal.

V.24/V.35 Standards layed down by the CCITT for interfacing a digital device to a PTT-supplied modem. V.24 is also used as an interface standard for connecting a peripheral device, such as a visual display unit or a printer, to a computer.

Wide area network (WAN) A general term used to describe any form of network – private or public – that covers a wide geographical area.

X.25 An internationally agreed standard protocol defined for the interface of a data terminal device, such as a computer, to a packet-switched data network.

X.3/X.28/X.29 A set of internationally agreed standard protocols defined to allow a character-oriented device, such as a visual display terminal, to be connected to a packet-switched data network.

Zero bit insertion *See* Bit stuffing.

REFERENCES AND FURTHER READING

Chapter 2

Bertine, H. U. (1980), 'Physical Level Protocols', *IEEE Transactions on Communications*, **28** (**4**), pp. 433–444.

Bleazard, G. B. (1982), *Handbook of Data Communications*, NCC Publications.

Chou, W. (1983), *Computer Communications*, Vol. I: *Principles*, Prentice-Hall.

Davies, D. W. and Barber, D. L. A. (1973), *Communication Networks for Computers*, Wiley.

Freeman, R. (1981), *Telecommunication Transmission Handbook*, Wiley.

Stallings, W. (1985), *Data and Computer Communications*, Macmillan.

Chapter 3

Bleazard, G. B. (1982), *Handbook of Data Communications*, NCC Publications.

Davies, D. W. and Barber, D. L. A. (1973), *Communication Networks for Computers*, Wiley.

Intel Corporation (1978), *The Intel 8251A/S2657 Programmable Communications Interface*.

McNamara, J. E. (1982), *Technical Aspects of Data Communication*, Digital Press.

Peterson, W. W. (1981), *Error Correcting Codes*, MIT Press.

Chapter 4

Bleazard, G. B. (1982), *Handbook of Data Communications*, NCC Publications.

Chou, W. (1983), *Computer Communications*, Vol. I: *Principles*, Prentice-Hall.

Davies, D. W., Barber, D. L. A., Price, W. C. and Solmonides, C.M. (1979), *Computer Networks and their Protocols*, Wiley.

Schwartz, M. (1987), *Telecommunication Networks*: *Protocols*, *Modeling and Analysis*, Addison-Wesley.

Stallings, W. (1985), *Data and Computer Communications*, Macmillan.

Tanenbaum, A. (1981), *Computer Networks*, Prentice-Hall.

Chapter 5

Bleazard, G. B. (1982), *Handbook of Data Communications*, NCC Publications.

Davies, D. W., Barber, D. L. A., Price, W. C. and Solmonides, C. M. (1979), *Computer Networks and their Protocols*, Wiley.

Intel Corporation (1978), *Using the 8273 SDLC/HDLC Protocol Controller*.

ISO TC97/SC6/N1501 (1977), *HDLC – Classes of Procedure*.

ISO 1745 (1981), *Information Processing – Basic Mode Control Procedures for Data Communication Systems*.

Schwartz, M. (1987), *Telecommunication Networks*: *Protocols*, *Modeling and Analysis*, Addison-Wesley.

Stallings, W. (1985), *Data and Computer Communications*, Macmillan.

Tanenbaum, A. (1981), *Computer Networks*, Prentice-Hall.

Chapter 6

ISO 8072/3 (1983), *Information Processing Systems – Transport Service/Protocol*.

ISO 7498 (1984), *Information Processing Systems – Open Systems Interconnection – Basic Reference Model*.

ISO 9074 (1986), *Estelle: A Formal Description Technique*.

Martin, J. (1981), *Computer Networks and Distributed Processing*, Prentice-Hall.

Pouzin, L. and Zimmerman, H. (1978), *A Tutorial on Protocols*, Proceedings of the IEEE.

Schwartz, M. (1987), *Telecommunication Networks*: *Protocols*, *Modeling and Analysis*, Addison-Wesley.

Sloman, M. and Kramer, J. (1987), *Distributed Systems and Computer Networks*, Prentice-Hall.

Stallings, W. (1985), *Data and Computer Communications*, Macmillan.

Tanenbaum, A. (1981), *Computer Networks*, Prentice-Hall.

Chapter 7

Bleazard, G. B. (1982), *Handbook of Data Communications*, NCC Publications.

CCITT (1981), *Character Terminal Access to Public Packet-Switched Data Networks – X3, X28, X29*.

CCITT (1984), *Integrated Services Digital Networks – I Series Recommendations*.

Davies, D. W., Barber, D. L. A., Price, W. C. and Solmonides, C. M. (1979), *Computer Networks and their Protocols*, Wiley.

ISO TC97/SC5/N2743 (1981), *Network Service Using X25 and X21*.

Martin, J. (1981), *Computer Networks and Distributed Processing*, Prentice-Hall.

Meijer, A. and Peeters, P. (1982), *Computer Network Architectures*, Computer Science Press.

Schwartz, M. (1987), *Telecommunication Networks*: *Protocols, Modeling and Analysis*, Addison-Wesley.

Stallings, W. (1985), *Data and Computer Communications*, Macmillan.

Chapter 8

Cooper, E. (1986), *Broadband Network Technology*, Sytek–Prentice-Hall.

Hopper, A., Temple, S. and Williamson, R. (1986), *Local Area Network Design*, Addison-Wesley.

IEEE (1985), *CSMA/CD Access Method – IEEE 802.3*.

IEEE (1985), *Token Bus Access Method – IEEE 802.4*.

IEEE (1985), *Token Ring Access Method – IEEE 802.5*.

IEEE (1985), *Logical Link Control – IEEE 802.2*.

Schwartz, M. (1987), *Telecommunication Networks*: *Protocols, Modeling and Analysis*, Addison-Wesley.

Stallings, W. (1987), *Local Networks – An Introduction*, Macmillan.

Chapter 9

Alber, A. F. (1985), *Videotex/Teletex – Principles and Practices*, McGraw Hill.

EIA RS-511 (1986), *MMS: Service and Protocol Definition Draft 5*.

ISO 8326/7 (1985), *OSI: Session Service/Protocol Specification*.

ISO 8822/3 (1985), *OSI: Presentation Service/Protocol Specification*.

ISO 8824/5 (1985), *OSI: ASN.1/Encoding Rules*.

ISO 8571/1-4 (1985), *OSI: FTAM Service/Protocol Specification*.

ISO 8831/2 (1985), *OSI: JTM Service/Protocol Specification*.

ISO 8649(2)/50(2) (1986), *OSI: ACSE Service/Protocol Specification*.

ISO 8649(3)/50(3) (1986), *OSI: CCR Service/Protocol Specification*.

ISO 9040/1 (1986), *OSI: VT Service/Protocol Specification*.

Sloman, M. and Kramer, J. (1987), *Distributed Systems and Computer Networks*, Prentice-Hall.

Stallings, W. (1985), *Data and Computer Communications*, Macmillan.

Tanenbaum, A. (1981), *Computer Networks*, Prentice-Hall.

Chapter 10

Chambers, F. B., Duce, D. A. and Jones, G. P. (eds.) (1984), *Distributed Computing*, Academic Press.

General Motors (1987), *MAP/TOP Network Management Requirements Specification – Draft for Comment*, GM Technical Centre.

IEEE (1986), *LAN Systems Management – Draft IEEE 802.1 Part B*.

Motorola (1986), *Motorola MAP Design Seminar and Software Product Description*.

Sloman, M. and Kramer, J. (1987), *Distributed Systems and Computer Networks*, Prentice-Hall.

Appendix A

Peebles, P. Z. (1987), *Digital Communication Systems*, Prentice-Hall.

Peterson, W. W. (1961), *Error Correcting Codes*, MIT Press.

Viterbi, A. J. (1971), 'Convolutional Codes and their Performance in Communication Systems', *IEEE Transactions on Communications*, **19(5)**.

Appendix B

Davies, D. W., Barber, D. L. A., Price, W. C. and Solmonides, C. M. (1979), *Computer Networks and their Protocols*, Wiley.

NBS (1983), *Data Encryption Standard – FIPS publication 46*.

Tanenbaum, A. (1981), *Computer Networks*, Prentice-Hall.

Appendix C

Cerf, V. and Cain, E. (1983), 'The DOD Architecture Model', *Computer Networks*, October.

Loveland, R. (1979), 'Putting DECNET into Perspective', *Datamation*, March.

Meijer, A. and Peeters, P. (1982), *Computer Network Architectures*, Pitman.

Stallings, W. (1985), *Data and Computer Communications*, Macmillan.

Appendix D

IEEE material can be obtained from: IEEE Press, 345 East 47th Street, New York, NY 10017, U.S.A.

ISO and CCITT material can be obtained from: International Telecommunications Union, Place des Nations, 1211 Geneva, Switzerland.

INDEX

67060   67060

TK   Halsall, Fred.
5105 Data communications,
,H35   computer networks,
1988   and OSI

ACRONYM

DATE DUE

JAN 10 1995
JAN 0 8 1995
APR 1 3 1995
APR 2 3 2003
JAN 2 3

JTM	Job transfer a...
LAN	Local area net...
LAPB	Link access p...
LED	Light-emitting...
LLC	Logical link co...
MHS	Message hand...
MMS	Manufacturing...
MUX	Multiplexer
NAK	Negative ackn...
NBS	National Bure...
NMS	Network man...
NRM	(Unbalanced)...
NRZ	Non-return to zero
NRZI	Non-return to zero inverted
OSI	Open systems interconnection
PAD	Packet assembler–disassembler
PBX	Private branch exchange
PDN	Public data network
PDU	Protocol data unit